Beyond
Praetorianism:
The Latin American Military in Transition

Beyond
Praetorianism:
The Latin American Military in Transition

Edited by

Richard L. Millett
and
Michael Gold-Biss

 North·South Center Press
UNIVERSITY OF MIAMI

The mission of the North-South Center is to promote better relations and serve as a catalyst for change among the United States, Canada, and the nations of Latin America and the Caribbean by advancing knowledge and understanding of the major political, social, economic, and cultural issues affecting the nations and peoples of the Western Hemisphere.

To order or to return books, contact Lynne Rienner Publishers, Inc. , 1800 30th Street, Suite 314, Boulder, CO 80301-1026, 303-444-6684, fax 303-444-0824.

Library of Congress Cataloging-in-Publication Data

Millett, Richard,   1938-
    Beyond praetorianism : the Latin American military in transition /
Richard L. Millet, Michael Gold-Biss
        p.   cm.
    Includes bibliographical references and index.
    ISBN 1-57454-000-9 (pbk. : alk. paper)
    1. Latin America—Armed Forces. 2. Civil-military relations—Latin
America. 3. National security—Latin America. 4. Latin America—
Politics and government—1980- I. Gold-Biss, Michael, 1963- II. Title.
UA602.3.M55   1995
355'.0098—dc20   95-41548
                                                                        CIP

Printed in the United States of America/EB-NC

00 99 98   5 4 3 2

Contents

Foreword

Ambler H. Moss, Jr.

T his book is the product of several years of collaborative study by a broad range of scholars. Their viewpoints are certainly diverse, but they share an important quality — they know their subjects profoundly. The North-South Center is pleased to have played a supporting role in this project, which was initiated by Adjunct Senior Research Associate Richard L. Millett. He has made a lifetime study of the military in Latin America and is as respected by the military establishments themselves as he is by their critics.

Studies such as this are central to the Center's mission of producing policy-relevant research. It is our hope and expectation that this book will be of value to students and professors, government planners, legislators, and the increasingly sophisticated and well-informed citizenry of the Americas.

Since any of us can remember, if we have worked in the inter-American field, the military enters immediately into any equation of the region, whether broad topics or nations are under discussion. The role of the Latin American military has been controversial and not just in Latin America. During the entire Cold War period, it has generated burning controversies within U.S. domestic politics and in debates and discussions over U.S. foreign policy.

During the Cold War, roughly from 1948 until 1989, there were three ways the United States looked at Latin America. From the right (and largely including the foreign policy establishment), Latin America was viewed as an element in the East-West struggle, i.e., Washington vs. Moscow and after 1959, its Havana surrogate. As recently as 1986 (ironically, only three years before the Berlin Wall fell), President Ronald Reagan was still issuing dire warnings about communist takeovers in Latin America that could result in hordes of desperate peoples seeking to take refuge in the United States. Obviously, under such scenarios, many Latin American military establishments (but not all, nor always) were able to enjoy privileged client status with Washington.

During this same period, a second current of U.S. policymaking viewed Latin America more in a North-South context, emphasizing development and economic and social issues. This tended to be the perspective of much of academia and of many Latin Americanists within the foreign policy establishment. Even though the Alliance for Progress is identifiable as a Cold Warrior's reaction to Fidel Castro, the developmental or North-South character of the policy's implementation prevailed. Such a perspective did not pose a direct threat to Latin American military establishments, however. The East-West axis was always there, and the military could find a role within essentially statist economic policies.

The left of the U.S. political spectrum, emphasizing social justice and equity, always identified the Latin American military as a major contributor to, if not the principal cause of, the region's problems. Except for the application of a strident human rights policy in the early part of the Jimmy Carter administration, and not uniformly toward all countries, this viewpoint seemed to be a short-lived phenomenon in the application of U.S. policy. Yet it gave hope and stimulus to democratization and to a changed role for the military once the Cold War was ended. In some cases, it also saved lives. Former Argentine President Raúl Alfonsín once remarked to me that had it not been for Carter's human rights policy, he probably would have been dead.

In December 1994, in Miami, the Summit of the Americas brought together 34 freely elected heads of state and government — the entire Western Hemisphere with the sole exception of Cuba. Such an occurrence was something that few, if any, Latin Americanists ever thought they would see in their lifetimes. This is not to say that they see this condition of the hemisphere either as permanent (as Richard Millett rightly points out) or as proof that all the countries are full-blown democracies by any reasonable measurement. It is, nonetheless, extremely encouraging. Economic issues, such as free trade and the expansion of investment, logically dominated the Summit agenda. Another mark of its success was its ability to schedule a meeting of hemispheric defense ministers for late July 1995. Again, such a meeting reflects the profound changes in the hemisphere and in the nature of military establishments and their relationship to civilian authority.

Those of us old enough to remember the last inter-American Summit, held by the Organization of American States (OAS) in Punta del Este in 1967, are struck by the immense contrast with the Miami Summit. Punta del Este, of course, was more typical of inter-American meetings. Of the governments represented there, ten out of 26 were headed by non-democratically elected leaders. Two countries that seemed to have deeply rooted democracies, Chile and Uruguay, would fall victim to military dictatorships in the years following that Summit. It is not surprising that such a Summit, held in such a different political and economic context, would be destined to have no permanent impact.

At Punta del Este, some of the attendees fit the stereotype of a uniformed head of state. The most obvious fact at Miami was that they are gone. Nevertheless — and this is the value of the study — military establishments remain in Latin America (except in Panama where, in emulation of Costa Rica, the military was abolished). Their role is changing, but they are still influential and, in many countries, have not fully redefined their role.

Each country's situation is different, but there seem to be a number of identifiable common threads, or factors, that explain the changes.

First, it is impossible to exaggerate the importance of the end of the Cold War. The ability to act as the client of Washington or of elements within it came to an end. For over four decades, the military in many Latin American countries knew that powerful U.S. policy objectives, such as promotion of human rights, of democracy, or even of U.S. economic interests, could nearly always be displaced by a Cold War interest — that is, anticommunism. No government is totally predictable, however, and Latin American military leaders occasionally gauged Washington incorrectly, with disastrous results. The Argentine military rulers were obviously delighted at the policy switch from the Carter to the Reagan era on human rights and happy to help organize and train the Nicaraguan "contras" for the United States. How could Washington, they reasoned, not be supportive or at least neutral when they invaded the Falkland/Malvinas Islands? Similarly, the Panamanian dictator Manuel Antonio Noriega had spent a lifetime working with

U.S. intelligence agencies and, most recently (by the mid-1980s), working covertly with Oliver North in "contra" operations. How could Washington turn against its valuable friend and asset over the issue of drugs? (And even then, of course, all the faces of "Washington" did not turn against Noriega in unison.)

Second, the 1990s saw a vastly changed role of the state itself in Latin America, largely because of the disastrous experience of the "lost decade" of the 1980s. New economic doctrines effected a reversal of state-oriented developmental policies. Privatization, the shrinking of the state, the adoption of market economies, a search for private foreign investment, and the opening of freer trade became the order of the day in a short period of time. During the earlier period, military governments in some countries had borne the onus of failed economic policies, dampening their appetite ever to try again to run national economies. In other countries, economic rationalization has led to shrunken defense budgets, a vivid example being Argentina, and to governments getting out of businesses related to defense production.

Third, the inescapable fact of a globalized economy — any remaining nonbelievers should read Robert Reich's *The Work of Nations* — has made a great impact on Latin America. Economic integration was, in fact, the centerpiece of the 1967 Summit, but no one was prepared to take it seriously. Substantial movement toward integration was already a fact before the Free Trade Area of the Americas (FTAA) became the centerpiece of the Miami Summit. By then, there were already 24 free trade agreements criss-crossing the Western Hemisphere, of which the North American Free Trade Agreement (NAFTA) was only one.

It is inevitable that the FTAA will affect Latin American security policies by creating a greater harmony of interests among Western Hemisphere countries. It is arguable, although far less clear, that it will reinforce democracy internally within countries. The *Declaration of Principles* signed at the Miami Summit binds together the principles of free markets and democracy, among others. The linkage was not specific, however. The Summit documents that commit countries to the creation of the FTAA do not, as, for instance, did the Treaty of Rome in 1957, stipulate that the FTAA is an economic club open only to democratic members. Had that been the case, a better name might have been the Economic Community of the Americas. In that sense, it was an opportunity missed, although, realistically, the Americas were probably not yet prepared for such a step.

A fourth factor is, however, that there are signs of greater political integration (or harmonization), even if this follows at a great distance behind economic integration. The Santiago Commitment of 1991 in support of democracy would have been unthinkable in the 1980s. As Ambassador Hernán Patiño Mayer illustrates, the OAS working group that he headed on regional security went far beyond the old Cold War relationships in breaking new ground for hemispheric security policy. During April 1995, three civil-military conferences were held in preparation for the July defense ministerial. These were organized, respectively, by the U.S. Atlantic Command, the National Defense University, and the U.S. Southern Command; among the several co-sponsors and participating organizations, the North-South Center was pleased to be involved. At all three, high-level military officers, civilian officials, and academic experts developed security themes in an atmosphere of extraordinary harmony and shared perspectives.

What all of this means must be carefully sorted out, as this book does successfully. One thing is clear, as Richard Millett states quite categorically, "Security issues will never again be the exclusive preserve of a military caste." It also means a convergence of viewpoints along the range of security issues (not always understood previously as first-rank security issues), such as illegal drug trafficking, international crime, migration, and protection of the environment according to international legal accords. The participation of Latin American countries in international peacekeeping commitments also reflects the internationalization of their foreign policy roles in helping to deal with the "new world disorder" that follows the Cold War era.

A fifth factor not to be overlooked is the realization by the United States that it needs Latin America as an economic partner. The congressional battles over the approval of NAFTA, in November 1993, and over the accords of the Uruguay Round of the General Agreement on Tariffs and Trade (GATT), in November-December 1994, show that there is still resistance in this country to the concept of global economic interdependence. Yet the partisans of that concept won the battles. Since President George Bush's announcement of the Enterprise for the Americas Initiative in June 1990 (which included the FTAA concept), subscribed to by President Bill Clinton even while he was a candidate, U.S. policy has been consistent. The trade figures alone are compelling. U.S. exports to Latin America increased from a level of around $30 billion in 1986 to about $90 billion in 1994 and, according to the

Department of Commerce, will be a larger market for U.S. goods and services than Europe by the year 2000.

There is no way the United States can afford to lose such a market or to fail to take advantage of it. That is why, at the first significant post-Summit event, the trade ministerial in Denver in June 1995, Washington sent in its top-level trade team — White House Senior Advisor Mack McLarty, U.S. Trade Representative Mickey Kantor, Secretary of Commerce Ron Brown, Secretary of Labor Robert Reich, backed up by other high officials. The spillover effect of such sustained attention by the United States, acting in accord with its modernized set of national objectives, will be felt in all areas of inter-American relations. It has already broadened the dialogue when economic issues are understood to be integral to national security strategy.

All of these factors help establish a new role for Latin American military establishments. This study will frustrate those looking for a nice, simple, consistent paradigm, however. It is important to analyze the enormous difference the military establishments play in each country's situation. Moreover, as the study demonstrates, new sources of tension arise to replace the old ones that have disappeared. As our own military has experienced, the fight against crime and drug trafficking exposes military establishments to sources of corruption and to human rights abuses. The modernization of the administration of justice, necessary to development, creates friction with military establishments conveniently avoided in the past.

The title of the book correctly uses the word "transition," and that is a chief virtue of this study. It is a sophisticated look at a process in midstream.

Introduction

Michael Gold-Biss and Richard L. Millett

This study examines the nature and roles of Latin America's armed forces in a post-Cold War world. Using both topical and national approaches, it focuses on recent changes in, current status of, and future prospects for the military institutions that for so long have played a dominant role in this region. In most nations, a return to at least formal structures of a democratic system preceded the collapse of the Soviet Union and the end of the Cold War. The end of that East-West confrontation reaffirmed this reality and produced fundamental alterations in both the threats faced by the military and the relations of the armed forces with external powers. The experiences of the 1982 Falklands/Malvinas conflict and, even more fundamentally, the Gulf War also clearly indicated the heightened costs and greatly diminished potential benefits of conflicts over territorial disputes. Unfortunately, the temptation to resolve such issues by force persists, as demonstrated by the clash between Peru and Ecuador. Yet this case has also demonstrated the inter-American community's determination to contain and, where possible, quickly resolve these conflicts.

Newer issues — those related to narcotrafficking and other aspects of international crime, defense of the environment, peacekeeping, and coping with growing resources for demilitarization — have come to the forefront of the agendas for both military and civilian institutions in Latin America. At the same time, continuing issues of civilian-military relations — the interactions of military, police, and judicial systems; the armed forces' role in national development efforts; and the controlling of insurgencies and civil disorders — impact on the current status and future orientations of these institutions. These altered agendas, combined with massive changes in both international and domestic realities, mean that traditional responses to these problems are increasingly irrelevant.

Diminished threats from insurgencies, governmental inability to control the flow of information, the necessity of operating within a global economic system, and a loss of ability by weaker states to manipulate external actors — these realities of the post-Cold War world pressure military institutions to become supportive of efforts at peace negotiation, to accept significant reductions in strength and budgets, to reduce their roles in the political process, and even to reexamine their traditional immunities and autonomy. This volume examines all these factors and offers possible scenarios for regional developments. In particular, the following areas are explored:

1. The implications of the end of the Cold War for inter-American military relations and for military ties with the rest of the world;

2. The impact of these changes on national security doctrines and on traditional concepts of national sovereignty;

3. The current status of, and future prospects for, military intervention in the political process, as well as for relations with the judicial systems and the police;

4. The impact of newer missions such as those related to environmental issues, narcotrafficking, and peacekeeping;

5. The process of demilitarization, including the impact of negotiated ends to insurgent conflicts; and

6. Scenarios for the evolution of Latin American military establishments in the coming decade and factors that will be most likely to shape this evolution.

Against the background of democratic transitions throughout the continent and the end of the Cold War, Ambassador Hernán Patiño Mayer of Argentina examines "The Future of Cooperative Hemispheric Security in the Americas" (Chapter 1). Building on his experience as president of the Working Group and Special Commission on Cooperation for Hemispheric Security (1991-1993) of the Organization of American States (OAS), Ambassador Patiño Mayer expresses his conviction that the Americas have reached the point where it is now feasible to speak of a "wider multilateral approach to the subject of security" than that which previously conditioned inter-American relations, especially during the Cold War. The disappearance of the East-West confrontation has allowed the Americas to focus on a "cooperative" approach to hemispheric security that gradually is replacing the confrontational history of the last five decades. Premised on the common challenges faced by the region's states and their willingness to work in a concerted fashion to resolve them, Ambassador Patiño Mayer concludes that efforts by the OAS, with the assistance of the United Nations (UN), can serve as the context for promoting international peace and security, for cooperating to strengthen institutions and structures of democratic practice, and for resolving conflicts peacefully. Ambassador Patiño Mayer sets the context for discussion of the evolving nature of civilian-military relations in the Americas by providing a global and hemispheric framework in which to locate and develop this difficult relationship. Reminding observers and practitioners alike that the military is a permanent fixture in the social, political, and economic realms of the region, he argues that "one of the basic duties of political leadership is to achieve the definitive integration of the armed forces into democratic systems, allocating responsibilities and missions that strictly are circumscribed to the role traditionally assigned to the armed forces, the main objective of which is the maintenance of an adequate capacity to defend the national territory and fulfill international commitments in terms of peacekeeping or peacemaking."

While the role of the hemisphere's armed forces has been changed dramatically by the transition to civilian rule, it also has been impacted by the emergence of new regional issues, including combatting drug trafficking and, in the future, safeguarding the democratic transition processes. These broader issues and specific case studies are developed in the other contributions to this volume.

Jack Child considers "Peacekeeping, Confidence-Building" (Chapter 2) and other security enhancement and conflict-resolution mechanisms increasingly applied in the Latin American context by the OAS, the UN, and regional governments as part of an overall heightened emphasis on interregional cooperation and conflict avoidance. Peacekeeping and confidence-building measures (CBMs) provide two increasingly important roles for Latin America's militaries. The recent inter-American meeting on CBMs held in Santiago, Chile, demonstrated a growing high-level appreciation of their importance. In Latin America, CBMs were used successfully in the Central American peace process, where such measures included proposals for creating demilitarized zones and joint boundary commissions as well as strengthening direct intergovernmental communication. This experience was applied subsequently in South America, especially among the Southern Cone countries, not — as had been the case in Central America — to resolve actual ongoing tensions but rather to preempt potential conflict. In addition to their involvement in CBMs, Latin American militaries have assumed more prominent roles in UN peacekeeping and peace-observing operations. These roles, Child concludes, "can make interstate conflict in Latin America less likely and thus permit a more realistic assessment of genuine military needs" in the future.

While Latin American militaries are "adapt[ing] to new realities — [though] not new missions," many of the region's democracies — according to Max G. Manwaring in "Guerrillas, Narcotics, and Terrorism: Old Menaces in a New World" (Chapter 3) — continue to confront serious challenges of governability that, if unresolved, present high risks to fragile democratic governments. Manwaring considers the national security and stability dialogue from the perspective of internal challenges to Latin American governments, challenges that the armed forces play important roles in confronting. Using the activities of *Sendero Luminoso* in Peru and the "narco-insurgent nexus" in the Andean countries as prominent examples of such challenges, he notes that the Peruvian government possessed no concerted strategy for confronting the Sendero challenge until 1992 and that drug control efforts in the Andean countries — including interdiction; income replacement, crop eradication, and substitution; and U.S. extradition or sanctions — have "generally been perceived to be ineffective." Since U.S. drug interdiction programs and recent "ad hoc crisis actions" to counteract narcotrafficking have met with minimal success, Manwaring recommends a new approach focusing *inter alia* on multilateral action and a "holistic and long-term commitment of resources and will."

The redefinition of Latin American military missions in the contexts of the region's recent democratic transitions and the altered global environment of the 1990s is considered further by Carina Perelli and Juan Rial in their chapter, entitled "Changing Military World Views: The Armed Forces of South America in the 1990s" (Chapter 4). The future of the region's armed forces is challenged by diminished budgetary resources, substantial social and economic development needs, and expensive technological changes in military equipment. It is at least equally challenged by the absence of a cohesive and compelling mission for the armed forces as well as by regional integration initiatives that further diminish the prospects for interstate military conflict. Among possible future scenarios for Latin America's militaries, Perelli and Rial include gradual marginalization as a prominent force in society. They also note, as do many of the volume's other contributors, that the multifaceted challenges confronting the region's militaries and the future of civilian-military relations have not been addressed adequately by Latin American governments.

The final chapter in the section on "Themes and Issues" focuses on "The Regional Security System (RSS)" in the Eastern Caribbean (Chapter 5). The RSS, as Gary Brana-Shute indicates, emerged in the context of the Cold War and U.S. concern with the politico-ideological orientations of Caribbean states. While formed to combat communist influence, the activities of the RSS have incorporated a broad array of internal and external security activities, including disaster relief, immigration control, smuggling prevention, and narcotics interdiction and eradication. The United States, since the 1983 invasion of Grenada, has conducted joint military exercises with the RSS and has supplied RSS member states militarily. Brana-Shute identifies several different forms of military activity in which RSS forces increasingly will be involved, including participating in regional and international peace-keeping, preparing for disaster relief, combatting narcotrafficking, and counteracting internal subversion and insurgency.

The "Case Studies" section of the book begins with an examination of the unique role occupied by Mexico's armed forces in Latin America. As discussed by Stephen J. Wager in "The Mexican Military: The Dilemma of Functioning in a One-Party System" (Chapter 6), that military's role, for much of the present century, has been premised on subservience to civilian leadership and noninvolvement in national politics. Mexican politics, following the 1917 revolution, was demilitarized gradually and the armed forces subordinated to the civilian presidency. Hence, "Mexico's military remains the only armed force in Latin America that has not intervened directly in politics since World War II." Its role and activities have focused on the preservation of internal security and stability, including civic action functions and drug eradication efforts. These roles have enhanced the institution's status within society. Yet the military's close association with the Partido Revolucionario Institucional's (PRI) monopolization of political power at times makes it vulnerable to criticism. Further, Wager notes that the following question remains unanswered: Does the military's loyalty "rest first with the Constitution or with the PRI-dominated government"? The strains imposed by recent events in Chiapas and by declining support for the PRI may go a long way toward answering that question.

With the collapse of Soviet communism, Cuba's armed forces lost their primary external patron and supplier. As Richard L. Millett notes in "From Triumph to Survival: Cuba's Armed Forces in an Era of Transition" (Chapter 7), the end of the Cold War compelled the Cuban military to shift its mission from supporting revolutionary forces abroad to focusing on domestic, economic, and security requirements. In the absence of external threats, the future mission of Cuba's Revolutionary Armed Forces (FAR) — with their unique heritage rooted in the 1959 revolution — is uncertain. The FAR's effectiveness will be challenged by Cuba's fiscal constraints and pressing economic needs as well as by shifts in the country's foreign policy, especially in the area of relations with the United States. Millett concludes that while open military opposition to the Castro regime is unlikely, the Cuban military "is condemned to a prolonged struggle for institutional survival."

Luis Humberto Guzmán's chapter, "Nicaragua's Armed Forces: An Assessment of Their Political Power" (Chapter 8), examines the historical relationship between the Sandinista Popular Army (EPS) and the exercise of political power in Nicaragua. Guzmán notes that while "the party and the armed forces appeared as a single fused body" immediately following the 1979 revolution, "the development of specialization limited the identity of each of these institutions" over time. During the transition period from the Sandinista to the Chamorro government, the military was granted significant autonomous status and authority in several areas, including national territorial defense, without adequate civilian oversight. The military also has increased its presence in both the formal and informal sectors of the economy. Despite this apparent power, the armed forces in Nicaragua confront serious challenges, including the loss of their primary external patron (the Soviet Union), a crisis in discipline, and a questioning of their future utility, given their inception in a Cold War era that no longer provides a relevant mission. Noting that "the Sandinista armed forces cannot continue to exist in their present form," Guzmán suggests that the forces be reformed to undertake the three central missions of territorial control, combatting narcotics trafficking, and civil defense.

Bonnie Tenneriello, in "Unfinished Business: Military Reform and Peace Processes in El Salvador and Guatemala" (Chapter 9), analyzes contemporary and long-term challenges in the democratic transitions of two Central American countries, both of which experienced prolonged civil crisis. However, these countries' civil wars differed considerably. In El Salvador, for instance, the relatively equal power of insurgent and government forces and greater international, especially U.S., involvement facilitated pressures for national reconciliation and serious investigation of human rights abuses. El Salvador's earlier reconciliation process contains important lessons for Guatemala. In accordance with the "National Stability" theory developed under General Gramajo, influential Guatemalan military "modernizers" have downplayed the "national security" approach of former military hardliners and emphasized "the importance of economic integration and internal stability" for the country's future. However, a number of problematic areas in Guatemala's reconciliation process remain, including accounting for human rights abuses, purging the country's armed forces and dismantling its repressive apparatus, and institutionalizing a civilian police force and a functioning judiciary. Given these many challenges, Tenneriello argues that the United States should actively encourage Guatemala's move toward the demilitarization and democratization of society by providing economic assistance, trading privileges, and favorable loans, as well as working through the OAS. She concludes that, even though Guatemala is unlikely to develop the same safeguards on the democratic process as has El Salvador, ultimately "internal and external conditions favor the creation of human rights guarantees and assertion of civilian authority over the military" throughout Latin America.

Tricia Juhn, in "Life After Wartime? Civil-Military Relations in the Salvadoran Reconstruction" (Chapter 10), focuses specifically on the challenges El Salvador confronts in sustaining efforts to limit military involvement in national politics and establish civilian control of the armed forces in accordance with the 1992 accords that ended the country's civil war. She concludes that while the accords constituted a critical initial step, Salvadorans' failure to define "clear, positive visions of civil-military relations in their postwar society" could endanger the permanence of the present reform process.

Brazil's military, according to Max G. Manwaring in "Brazilian Security in the New World Disorder: Implications for Civil-Military Relations" (Chapter 11), will, in the future, become an evermore important actor in the country's political and economic policy processes. Brazil's future stability and power — as well as its quest for *grandeza* or greatness — depend on extending the reach of the country's armed forces and further developing its defense industry. However, future stability and power also depend on progress in the areas of economic development and nation-building, two critical components of the country's national security equation. "Underdevelopment and the resultant poverty have been defined as Brazil's most overwhelming threats." Manwaring concludes that Brazil — while in transition and confronting numerous challenges — will emerge as a major international actor.

Deborah L. Norden, in "The Transformation of Argentine Security" (Chapter 12), examines changing concepts of national security and the military's role in society in Argentina during the post-1982 period of civilian leadership. Like other Latin American militaries, Argentina's armed forces, prior to the country's democratic transition, possessed "a very broad, integrated approach to the definition of the nation," incorporating — in addition to external defense — economic development and prevailing political and ideological orientations within the country. Raúl Alfonsín came to power in 1982, determined to prevent a resumption of military involvement in national politics. He reduced the military budget and oversaw the passing of a National Defense Law that juridically defined, and hence limited, the military's role in society and politics. His regime also sponsored investigation of human rights abuses committed under the previous military regime and focused on diplomatic, as opposed to military, approaches to regional defense issues. Carlos Menem's policy focus on "economic and security goals [pursued] simultaneously through internationalism" further downplayed the conceptions and role of the military in defining and achieving national objectives for Argentina.

The national security doctrine of the Peruvian armed forces — as defined and elaborated by the Centro de Altos Estudios Militares (CAEM) in the 1950s — has emphasized "the direct relationship between national security and national development and poverty alleviation." The Alberto Fujimori administration, however, according to Dirk Kruijt in "Peru: The State Under Siege" (Chapter 13), during the years of civil war with the Shining Path, consistently prioritized "bullets instead of development." Its failure to devise "a coherent antipoverty policy" exacerbated the country's economic situation, increasing popular dissatisfaction with the government and contributing to a vast informalization of society and economics, which further diminished governmental control.

This project is the outcome of a close collaboration between the co-editors, stretching over a period of more than six years. Our objective was, and continues to be, offering innovative perspectives on Latin American security in the post-Cold War world. From the beginning, we sought to encourage interdisciplinary approaches, taking advantage of differing areas of specialization, research methodologies, and interpretations, bringing together experienced as well as young scholars from throughout the Americas and Europe. Although we would have wished to incorporate even more views into this volume, we are pleased that the diversity of voices speaking on the military and security in the Americas is representative of the expanding nature of the field. It has been rewarding to work with our authors, who have generously given their time and experience to enrich our understanding of the evolving nature of the military and society in Latin America.

During our years of collaboration, we have jointly convened panels at meetings of the Latin American Studies Association (LASA), where most of the contributors to this volume met to present their work, exchange critiques and comments, and provide much-needed mutual support. To coordinate our busy schedules has not been easy, but with good humor and persistence all obstacles have been overcome. This work was not supported by any grants from our respective academic institutions. Southern Illinois University at Edwardsville, the North-South Center of the University of Miami, and St. Cloud State University, however, did provide the academic locales and bases that allowed us to develop our collaboration. The people whom we have to thank include, of course, our authors, whose patience finally has come to fruition. On a personal level, Denice Millett and Erika G. Alin provided love and encouragement to Richard and Michael at levels that continue to go above and beyond the call of duty of any partner and friend. This book is dedicated to them and their continued forbearance and support.

I

The Future of Cooperative Hemispheric Security in the Americas

Hernán Patiño Mayer

A genuine and effective inter-American hemispheric security system must be constructed upon a community of states that has as its premise the acknowledgment of shared responsibilities, interests, and values and expresses the decision to assume, preserve, and protect them from situations of risk or threat. A hemispheric security system cannot be created independent of a solid regional political system that, by means of a credible and efficient institutional framework, guarantees not only the appropriate operation of the system but also, and most important, the attainment of the political, social, and economic objectives of the region. Aiming at a wider multilateral approach to the subject of security, the countries of the hemisphere are striving to augment and accelerate the processes of hemispheric cooperation and integration. The process of democratization experienced by most of Latin America, the end of the global conflict due to the Cold War, and, though it may appear paradoxical, the socioeconomic crisis that besets all the nations in the hemisphere, including the United States, have reignited the ever-postponed expectation of moving toward genuine unity, progress, and peaceful

1

cooperation in the Americas. On the other hand, the 1994 border conflict between Peru and Ecuador, for example, has not only cost lives and wasted economic resources but has also detracted from the prestige of the region, affected the process of subregional integration, and, to some extent, tarnished the accomplishments of the Miami Summit.

Mutual distrust and crises that ensue endanger political stability and impede or seriously delay regional integration, thereby making it more difficult for the hemisphere — and each of its nations — to join the developed world. The challenge posed by the recent war between Peru and Ecuador suggests that a coherent hemispheric security system would serve as a fitting and efficacious tool for achieving the political goals the nations of the Organization of American States (OAS) have set and that such a system must be developed while there is still time to do so.

This combination of developments, along with other related events, has contributed to the reemergence of the OAS as the forum for the political discussion of hemispheric economic integration and security cooperation. If the authoritarian regimes of the recent past had persisted, if the ideological conflict of the East-West confrontation had continued to divide the hemisphere's people, and if the structural crisis of the global and regional economies had not shaken even the most developed nations of the continent, the OAS would probably have continued to languish in the same fashion as most other regional multilateral forums. Indeed, the renewed prominence of the OAS parallels the increasing importance of the United Nations as a preferred venue for the political resolution of long-standing and emerging conflicts.

Evolution of the Hemispheric Security System

The notion of collective security — treating aggression against one nation as an attack on all states — has been present in regional political instruments and organizations since the inception of the inter-American system after World War II. The great difficulty this concept has encountered, however, is the lack of a commonly held and equally shared perspective regarding the values to be protected and the risks to be prevented by the member states. On the whole, the alleged lack of efficiency, or rather the selective efficiency of this idea, is due to the fact that the mechanisms at the system's disposal were used in the context of, and as a function of, the U.S. perception of security within the framework of a global conflict. In effect, the

United States incorporated collective inter-American security into the framework and imperatives of the Cold War. As a consequence, essential values for the rest of the regional community, such as the consolidation of democracy, respect for human rights, and social and economic development, were defined, weighed, and often overshadowed by and subordinated to the evolution and the needs posed by the East-West confrontation. Due in part to this historical process, the hemispheric security system has been reduced to little more than a symbolic manifestation. It is important to emphasize that the hypothesis that served as the system's foundation is undergoing total revision in response to the uncertainties of the emerging world order that is replacing the geopolitical and ideological confrontation of the superpowers.

Principles of the Hemispheric Security System

In accordance with this theoretical construct for the inter-American hemispheric security system, the implementation of such a new system would require progress on agreement regarding the following assumptions:

1. The existence of shared responsibilities, values, and interests among the participant nations. It is imperative to note that nations, like individuals, have responsibilities that in some cases go beyond their own interests.

2. The existence of a common will to assume such responsibilities, protect values and interests, and prevent as well as respond to threats that might affect them.

3. The decision to institutionalize mechanisms aiming at collective initiatives for the prevention of threats as well as for the protection of the values and interests that make up the regional heritage of cooperation.

Identification and Existence of Shared Values

Attempting to reform the inter-American security system is a daring venture that has undergone historical frustrations no one can guarantee will not be repeated. The Americas maintain the fiction of a security system that is just as obsolete as it is inefficient. In their current form, the hemisphere's legal instruments and institutions are manifestly inadequate for responding effectively to current and potential future challenges. The Inter-American Reciprocal Assistance Treaty, for example, ceased being inter-American a long time ago and has proved to have little to do with reciprocal assistance either. In fact, 40 percent of the American states, the most notable being Canada, have not even signed it.

Inter-American institutes, such as the Inter-American Defense Board and the Inter-American Defense College, suffer from similar limitations and are totally underused. If its connection to the OAS were defined, the College, for example, would offer the possibility of becoming an Inter-American Defense University, devoted to training civilian and military officials in security matters. Interforce conferences operate in conjunction with these bodies in the absence of clear coordination between them and a precise definition of their relationship with the policy-making bodies of the inter-American system or, in some cases, with national policy bodies. The "military diplomacy" upon which these conferences are currently based must be reviewed in order to align it with the hemisphere's new institutional reality.

Despite such problems, conditions have never been better for a thorough review of all these untidy components of the so-called continental security system. If this project is not to be subject to purely emotional or willful formulations and processes, we must identify the values, interests, and responsibilities that the nations of the hemisphere share and from whose defense, protection, and execution no state in the region can feel alienated. A purely academic reading of the current hemispheric reality might lead to the conclusion (perhaps a hasty one) that the combined presence in the hemisphere of the world's only superpower and a majority of developing countries would make impossible, or at least utopian, not only the establishment of a system such as the one described but also the existence of shared values and interests. While this asymmetry presents serious difficulties, these can be overcome by combining, on the one hand, a consensual definition of interests and values and, on the other, a system in which institutions are capable of acting efficiently and equitably in the pursuit of system objectives.

The hemispheric superpower will backtrack in its traditional tendency to act hegemonically only if multilateral initiatives demonstrate their efficiency to confront threats and respond to challenges. Such a state of affairs will have to be achieved without concessions to special national circumstances and within an equitable framework of shared interests and values. The maintenance of peace, the protection and promotion of human rights, the consolidation of democratic regimes, the socioeconomic development of the region, the generation of evermore efficient mechanisms for hemispheric integration, and the true strengthening of regional organizations are clear examples of accepted, shared, and mutually reinforcing values. The obsolete Cold War system based on distrust must be replaced by a new system that is capable of consolidating the future of the region. The key point in this process is the reestablishment of mutual confidence that was so severely shaken by decades of mutual suspicion and countless contradictions. Politically, the nations of the region cannot afford to resign themselves to an unsatisfactory present; indeed, the complacency of such a situation must be overcome. Competition must make way for cooperation, and isolation must become integration.

The disappearance of the threat of global military confrontation, progress in terms of cooperation, and the enhancement of confidence at the subregional level seem to be creating a better environment for constructive consideration of the issue of security in the hemisphere. This provides an opportunity, unique at least for the current generation, to design a regional system based on a set of common values and interests that will guarantee stability and increase the capabilities of each of its members. At a time when uncertainty seems to be the outstanding feature on the international scene, the Americas offer exceptional conditions for a redefinition of relations under terms that should be more efficient, participatory, and equitable.

Mutual Distrust

For almost two centuries of inter-American history, mistrust appears to have been the only product that was effectively capitalized, the only real hemispheric "savings." Even today, some armed forces continue to define threat in terms of potential aggression by neighbors against their territorial integrity. This mistrust, which is a self-fulfilling prophecy, has resulted in disagreements' accumulating over successive generations; at the same time, it has created new prejudices and resentments. Put bluntly, while the United States has failed to trust in the capabilities of the countries of the region to govern themselves within a framework of democratic values and institutions and manage their socioeconomic development, the rest of the region has come to perceive the United States as the main source of its frustrations as well as a quasi-magical actor responsible for its recovery. The time has come to put an end to these mutual reproaches and unreasonable expectations. The past cannot be changed. However, it is possible for the countries of the region to assume national and collective responsibilities, thereby attempting a new modality for a successful hemispheric relationship. It would be as fruitless to ignore the feeling of mistrust that serves as a basis for the architecture of the current inter-American system, yet it would also be an unwarranted assumption to maintain that the region's actors are unable to overcome their apprehensions. Change is both desirable and possible.

Cooperative Security: Definition and Objectives

A more constructive approach to issues of collective security, characterized by strategies that incorporate the implementation of preventive measures to inhibit the capability and the potential for aggression, would greatly contribute to inter-American harmony and unity. The objective, of course, is not the utopian eradication of war, total disarmament, or the elimination of armed forces but the use of collective measures to minimize the possibility and the scope of threats of aggression. The ultimate goal should be the elimination of any possibility of conflict between states in the hemisphere, not simply for the sake of peace but also as a contribution to the systemic development of the integration process. Cooperative security goes beyond the traditional concept of offensive-defensive alliances, underscoring its preventive rather than its reactive character. The same thing that is happening in health care is happening in security; nowadays, more attention and resources are being devoted to preventive medicine than to restorative medicine.

Cooperative security, which has only been explored at a global level, can be expanded and refined at the regional level, especially in the case of the American hemisphere. The Americas, with the exception of a few unfortunate, sporadic events, do not share the historic tradition of intraregional wars that characterize other areas in the world. This essential factor allows for the possibility of cooperating in the area of security with a much greater depth and scope than are possible in other regions. One of the principal objectives for the establishment and implementation of cooperative security in the region should be the elimination of the traditional hypothesis that intrahemispheric conflict is an inherent characteristic of inter-American relations. Indeed, the historical record would indicate that international war is truly the exception in the Western Hemisphere, which is not to say that conflict is absent from the region's international politics.

Among those elements that can contribute to developing a cooperative security system are the following:

1. A defensive, not offensive, configuration of national armed forces;

2. Confidence-building measures such as information, public education, access and monitoring, transparency, a record of the transfer of conventional weapons and defense budgets, greater exchange among armed forces, and joint technological developments;

3. The establishment of multilateral forums for the discussion and prevention of situations that could develop into future conflicts; and

4. Coordinated participation in an organized international response for the prevention or deterrence of aggression, which does not imply the promotion or establishment of multinational intervention forces in the hemisphere.

This list is perhaps somewhat uni-dimensional, for it approaches the issue of security solely from the military perspective. In this regard, it is important to emphasize that the concept of security goes beyond what is strictly military to encompass areas such as the viability of democratic systems, socioeconomic development, environmental protection, migration, and other situations that could affect the security of a nation, none of which would require a military response. These considerations are related to security, but due to their very nature, they must be addressed by means of political initiatives rather than coercion in order to protect and promote the well-being of the citizenry. This does not imply, however, that security issues that may require a military response have disappeared. One of the greatest difficulties faced by the hemisphere's leaders when addressing this question is the recognition that the concept of security is both broad and complex in scope, but that under any definition, there is a clear necessity for the continued existence of the military institution.

Civil-Military Relations and Hemispheric Security

In summary, notwithstanding the recognition that the military sphere is only one area in the wide spectrum of security considerations, the military cannot be overlooked or omitted from the establishment of a cooperative security system. For this reason, the relationship between political power and the armed forces is an essential element if cooperative security is to be successful. Although many analysts may contend that the determination of the nature of this relationship is an internal affair, the lack of a precise definition — especially in terms of the subordination of the military to civilian political leaders — has manifested itself repeatedly in the political instability of a great part of the hemisphere as well as in conflicts among states in the region, affecting essential values of the inter-American system such as democracy and peace. Thus, one of the basic duties of political leadership is to achieve the definitive integration of the armed forces into democratic systems, allocating responsibilities and missions that are strictly circumscribed to the role traditionally assigned to the armed forces, the main objective of which is the maintenance of an adequate capacity to defend the national territory and fulfill international commitments in terms of peacekeeping or peacemaking. This means that the countries of the region must set aside institutional formalities and redefine the role of political leadership, which in the past felt little inclined to assume leadership of the military fully. The lack of definition of roles has become clearer in practice than in theory, since most constitutions in the hemisphere establish the subordination of the armed forces to political authority.

The deficiencies of civilian leadership were aggravated by the fact that in the process of transition to democracy, the definition of the role of the armed forces was not provided by most democratic leaders. After having had long and dramatic confrontations with the armed forces, these leaders have now turned their attention to ways in which to settle and overcome their past disputes.

Through cooperation, it is possible for countries in the Western Hemisphere to advance significantly while updating the role of military institutions within the institutional framework of democracy and the continent's vocation for peace. Although such confidence-building measures alone do not resolve conflicts, they help reframe mistaken perceptions and create a favorable climate for political and diplomatic resolution of differences.

The Role of the OAS in Hemispheric Security

When considering the future role of the OAS in hemispheric security, it is appropriate to be cautious of the prophetic definition of capacities and functions. This, of course, is true for all politics since roles are defined through practice, and political space is conquered only as a result of success and effectiveness. The progressive expansion and consolidation of democracy in the hemisphere as well as the profound transformations in the international sphere have provided a favorable framework for the consideration of a hemispheric security system within a modern, integral perspective of security and disarmament. Within this framework, the use of multilateral political mechanisms for the definition of the hemispheric tradition of cooperation will doubtlessly contribute to balancing the traditional power asymmetries in the hemisphere. A growing articulation of responsibilities, values, and regional interests in the multilateral area will allow the bases of a new hemispheric security system to be laid in a consensual fashion. For this to be feasible, however, it will be necessary to strengthen the OAS and its ability to act and assert itself effectively in the multilateral context. Once the distortions imposed by the Cold War are overcome, the regional security subsystems should become capable and effective in response to the security demands of the states of the region and those of participation and coordination with the global system. With the absence of a global threat, the opportunities for regional cooperation should be more visible and viable.

To achieve this end, it is necessary to solve the problem of leadership and competition in the OAS. In this regard, Chapter VIII of the United Nations Charter is a starting point. It defines in a clear and broad manner the role of regional organizations in the establishment and maintenance of international peace and security. Thus, at this stage of the redefinition of hemispheric security, the OAS is the adequate forum to promote the following actions:

1. Define, together with the United Nations, its role in the promotion of international peace and security.
2. Promote the improvement of cooperation mechanisms oriented toward the strengthening of the institutions and structures of the most vulnerable states in the region.
3. Reaffirm the commitment to the peaceful solution of controversies and, if it be the case, revise the existing regional instruments for such eventualities.
4. Promote the exchange of information in areas linked to defense and security so as to strengthen confidence and improve information and communication channels.
5. Stop the proliferation of weapons of mass destruction and promote the transparent, public transfer of conventional weapons.
6. Create a center for the prevention, management, and settlement of controversies and disputes without inhibiting existing ad hoc mechanisms that have proved their effectiveness.

7. Provide political support for holding future meetings of the Inter-American Conference of Defense Ministers to continue the process begun in 1995 at Williamsburg, Virginia.

To conclude, for many years the Americas have suffered the consequences of an anarchic vision of security based on a strategy that held that states, to guarantee their survival, should focus exclusively on increasing their military and economic capabilities. This vision promoted mistrust and fear and placed obstacles on the path to cooperation and integration. Circumstances have changed, however. As the Chiefs of State noted in their final communiqué issued at the 1994 Miami Summit, "The broadening and consolidation of democracy in the Americas offers the opportunity to apply the traditions of peace and cooperation that have prevailed among the countries of the Western Hemisphere. Our goal is to strengthen the mutual trust that will help bring about the social and economic integration of our nations."

The OAS cannot postpone addressing the task of strengthening democratic governance in the Americas. A year ago, no one could have imagined Peru and Ecuador at war over a territorial dispute, nor could anyone have foreseen the effects of the financial crisis in Mexico. This, without a doubt, is an enormous undertaking. The strengthening of democratic institutions, sustainable development, the protection of human rights, arms control and limitation, and the preservation of the environment are indispensable elements for the establishment of democratic societies living with security and in peace. Judging by the evidence of the far-reaching consequences of recent events in the hemisphere, those of us who have made up our minds not to renounce the future must demand that those who are reluctant accept their share of responsibility and commit resources as well as rhetoric to the task of developing cooperative hemispheric security.

II

Peacekeeping, Confidence-Building

Jack Child

"Ciudadano el soldado,	"Citizen soldier,
deponga de la guerra	put aside the livery
la librea . . . ."	of war . . . ."

Andrés Bello, *La agricultura de la zona tórrida,* 1826

Introduction[1]

I n his often-cited ode exalting the civil virtues, written as Spanish America was finishing its struggle for independence, the Venezuelan-Chilean poet and diplomat Andrés Bello asked the soldiers of his day to put down their instruments of war and take up roles more appropriate to the post-war period.

This chapter examines two roles the Latin American military might consider (and indeed already has) as appropriate in meeting the challenges of the post-Cold War era. Although neither role is new and neither would ever be primary, both have the potential to make an important contribution to the delicate process of moving beyond praetorianism and the doctrines of counterinsurgency, hemispheric defense, and national security that have characterized many of the Latin American militaries during the past three decades. The two roles examined in this chapter are especially significant because of the way in which they affect the militaries' involvement in their nations' relationships with neighboring states, international organizations, and the outside world. They can also have an impact on the size and budget of the military institutions affected.

The two roles to be examined are 1) peacekeeping, the use of the military in third-party interposition roles under the mandate of the United Nations or another international organization, and 2) confidence-building, the process of seeking measures that would make conflict with potential adversaries less likely.

Basic Concepts

B efore exploring the nature of these two roles in greater detail, it is important to reiterate that neither would ever be fundamental for the Latin American militaries. In all probability, their basic, stated role will continue to be that of military institutions throughout history: defense of national sovereignty. Nevertheless, they also carry out another basic mission — one that usually remains unstated — that of institutional self-preservation and the protection of special privileges, size, budget share, and political influence. One of the present controversies regarding peacekeeping and confidence-building is the concern among many senior military officers that these two new roles might indeed affect their ability to defend national sovereignty and perhaps, more significantly, diminish the size and influence of their institutions. As a result, discussion of these roles must proceed carefully, and with joint civilian and military participation, so as to avoid the perception that these talks are thinly disguised attacks on the military.

Peacekeeping[2] (and the associated terms, peace observing and peace verifying) involves the prevention and termination of hostilities through the peaceful presence of a neutral third party. The peacekeeping contingent (which can include military and civilian personnel) does not seek to enforce peace or impose solutions to the conflict by sheer power. Instead, it attempts to create the conditions that would lead to dialogue and the eventual resolution of conflict. In short, its mission is to create space and time in which to allow the combatants to cool off and permit the diplomats to do their work. Thus, peacekeeping is not the settlement of a dispute by an overwhelming supranational force intent on imposing an outside solution to a conflict, nor does it stem from collective security sanctions in which an alliance's military response is triggered by an act of aggression.

As used here, peacekeeping is carefully distinguished from peace enforcement, which is defined as the employment of major military units, under the UN or another international organization's aegis, to impose peace by overpowering one or more of the parties involved in the conflict. Peace enforcement is provided for under Chapter VII of the United Nations Charter when a situation arises that is a "threat to the peace, breach of the peace, or act of aggression." Article 42 of the Charter authorizes the Security Council to take necessary military action to restore or maintain peace and security, while Article 43 provides for UN member states to make military forces available for UN use, under the control of the UN Security Council, acting with the advice of the Military Staff Committee. In practice, the only application of this provision to date occurred in 1950 during the Korean War, when the temporary boycott of the Security Council by the Soviet Union permitted the remaining members to vote to approve such a force. Throughout the rest of the Cold War, the reality of a veto by one or more of the five Security Council powers blocked the possibility of peace enforcement under Chapter VII. More recently, the UN came close to peace enforcement during the 1991 Gulf War but stopped short, choosing instead to permit a coalition of member states to act on the UN's behalf to force Iraq out of Kuwait. With the demise of the Soviet Union, and perhaps reflecting the lessons of the Gulf War, a number of diplomats[3] have proposed that the UN take a more aggressive stance on issues of peace and security, which would include invoking Articles 42 and 43 of the Charter and perhaps even having standby military forces available for immediate use by the Security Council. Although not considered further in this chapter, this peace enforcement role is one in which some larger Latin American military establishments might become involved sometime in the future.

Confidence-building measures (CBMs) are techniques designed to lower tensions and make it less likely that a conflict would break out through a misunderstanding, mistake, or misreading of the actions of a potential adversary. CBMs emerged from attempts by the Cold War superpowers and their military alliances (the North Atlantic Treaty Organization [NATO] and the Warsaw Pact) to avoid nuclear war by accident or miscalculation. However, CBMs have also been employed at other levels of conflict situations and in different regions of the world (including Latin America), though they might not have been termed CBMs. Typical CBMs might include notifying neighboring nations when maneuvers of a certain size are planned near sensitive border areas; establishing direct communication links ("hot lines") between neighboring governments and military establishments; exchanging information on the size, deployment, budgets, and weaponry of the military; exchanging personnel in planning and training activities; demilitarizing border areas; establishing joint patrols along these demilitarized areas; and increasing contacts (and thus encouraging military transnationalism) through international military activities such as peacekeeping missions and multinational defense colleges.

These basic concepts are also related to peacemaking — diplomatic techniques to resolve conflict through negotiation and related approaches — and peacebuilding — the development effort that attempts to reduce conflict by attacking its basic economic and social causes. The nature of the relationship of these various concepts can perhaps best be illustrated by means of Figures 1 and 2.[4]

Figure 1
A Conflict Resolution Spectrum

Peace Enforcement
Imposition of a temporary end of conflict by major force.
Examples: UN in Korean War, IAPF in the Dominican Republic, 1965 (14,000 troops)

Peacekeeping
Third-party neutral interposition by a substantial contingent.
Example: UNFICYP in Cyprus (6,400 troops)

Peace Verification
Third-party neutral presence by a significant contingent, possibly unarmed, to verify and monitor compliance with a treaty.
Example: ONUCA in Central America (1,100 troops)

Peace Observation
Small "eyes and ears" group sent to a conflict to report back.
Example: two men sent to Belize-Guatemala, 1972

Figure 2
Addressing the Basic Causes of Conflict

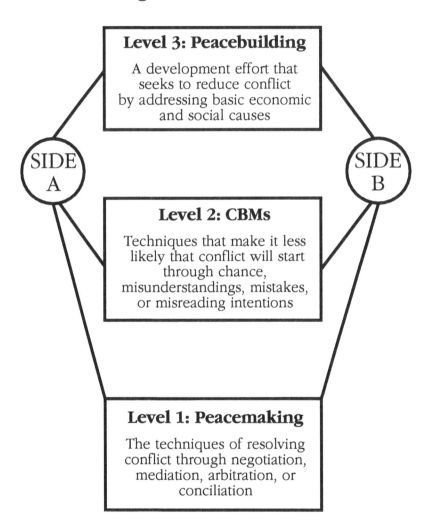

Central America:
Contadora/Esquipulas, ONUCA, ONUSAL
Historical Perspective

The Central American experience from 1983 to the present exemplifies the potential contribution that can be made by peacekeeping and CBMs in a Latin American conflict environment. This experience was particularly important considering that hemisphere peacekeeping had been rather discredited in the eyes of many Latin Americans after the heavy-handed use of the concept to defend U.S. intervention in the Dominican Republic in 1965 and 1966. As many pointed out, the "Inter-American Peace Force" of 1965 consisted of about 90 percent U.S. troops, with the remainder coming mainly from Brazil; logistics and control were firmly in U.S. hands, with the OAS playing essentially a "fig-leaf" role to cover unilateral U.S. intervention.

Because of the special circumstances of Central American conflict in the 1980s and the direct U.S. role in both the Contra war in Nicaragua and counterinsurgency in El Salvador, the United States found it impossible to avail itself of the OAS as it had in 1965. The success of the Central American peace process from 1983 to date has therefore relied on other actors: Central America's Latin American neighbors (the Contadora states of Mexico, Venezuela, Colombia, and Panama), the Esquipulas peace initiative taken by the Central Americans themselves, and the United Nations, through its first two peacekeeping missions ever undertaken in the Western Hemisphere: ONUCA (UN Observer Group in Central America, 1989-1991) and ONUSAL (UN Observer Mission in El Salvador, 1991-1994).

CBMs were a key element in the Central American peace process, as will be detailed below. Although CBMs have always existed in some form or another in the hemisphere's conflict situations, the Central American peace process marked the first time in a Latin American conflict when CBM terminology and techniques were explicitly used. This was no accident; it reflected the key role played by the UN and by certain outside actors (e.g., Canada and the International Peace Academy) in bringing these ideas to the peace process.

The significance of peacekeeping and CBMs in the Central American peace process was twofold. Not only did these two approaches contribute to the solution of the conflict; they also served as examples of the value of these two approaches to other Latin American conflict situations and were indications of how the hemisphere's military institutions might apply these notions as new roles in the changing environment of the post-Cold War. This process also provided regional military establishments with practical peace-keeping experience. Further, one Latin American nation (Venezuela) provided ONUCA with a battalion of infantry at the key moment of Contra demobilization in mid-1990; Argentina provided patrol boats to monitor the Gulf of Fonseca, and several other nations of the hemisphere (Brazil, Canada, Ecuador, Colombia, Venezuela, Mexico) provided military observers and other support for ONUCA and ONUSAL.

CBMs in the Central American Peace Process[5]

The presence and importance of CBMs in the Central American peace process can be tracked from the historic Contadora meeting attended by the foreign ministers of Mexico, Panama, Colombia, and Venezuela. This meeting, held on the Panamanian island bearing the same name on January 8-9, 1983, dealt with general statements of concern as well as principles that would lead to a peaceful resolution of Central America's several conflicts. The "Contadora Declaration" itself made an urgent appeal to the countries of Central America to engage in dialogue and negotiation so as to reduce tension and lay the foundations for a permanent atmosphere of peaceful coexistence and mutual respect among states. Because of the very general nature of the meeting, the issue of peace verification using outside observers was not discussed at Contadora. Thus, the CBMs at the first Contadora meeting were not employed at the specific or military level but rather at the more abstract and broader level of appealing for greater trust, communication, and involvement among the various parties to the dispute.

Six months later, meeting at the Mexican resort of Cancún, the presidents of the four Contadora nations met to expand on the work begun by their foreign ministers. The July 17, 1983, Cancún Declaration was more specific than the Contadora Declaration; it included several recommendations that explicitly incorporated CBMs as well as several other approaches to conflict resolution, including international third-party peacekeeping and verification. Security was a major concern of the Cancún Declaration, which focused on effectively controlling the arms race, ending arms trafficking, eliminating foreign military advisors, creating demilitarized zones, prohibiting the use of one state's territory to destabilize another's, and forbidding other forms of interference in the internal affairs of countries in the region. The issue of verification was also given greater specificity in that the Cancún Declaration mentioned the need to establish "appropriate supervisory machinery" in order to verify security commitments.

Confidence-building measures also appear in the Cancún Declaration in the form of recommendations for joint boundary commissions and direct communications between governments as well as for the need to give prior notice of troop movements near borders when the contingents exceed certain limits. The use of the phrase "commitment to promote a climate of detente and confidence" also reflects an increasingly specific appreciation of the utility of confidence-building measures.

The Panama Foreign Ministers Meeting of September 7-9, 1983, produced the "21 Objectives" document, which should be viewed as the foundation on which the subsequent draft treaties were built. The security objectives were the most controversial and were fairly specific. The problem of effective verification remained unsolved by the 21 Objectives document, and the consideration of CBMs was more implicit than explicit.

The years 1984 through 1986 saw the drafting of several "Contadora Acts," none of which succeeded in breaching the gap between the Nicaraguan position and that of the other Central American nations (especially those close to the U.S. position). However, these drafts include CBMs and increasingly show the impact of the advice and suggestions being provided by Canada and other actors. Many of these provisions dealt with verification and were also linked to the need for impartial, third-party, neutral treaty verifiers. The Canadians, reflecting their long experience with UN peacekeeping, strongly recommended that this issue be left in the hands of the United Nations, which could provide a credible political mandate as well as a coherent logistical structure. The various Contadora drafts in these years tended to be incremental and included all (or most) of the verification and confidence-building provisions mentioned in the earlier declarations, draft treaties, and supplementary implementation documents. The CBMs involved communications links (hot lines), provisions for notification of troop movements, ceilings on certain types of weapons and troop units, exchange of information, arms and troop registries, and observation posts and joint patrolling along sensitive borders.

Most of these CBMs and verification provisions were picked up by the drafters of the so-called "Arias (or Esquipulas) Peace Plan" in 1987 when the weakening Contadora process gave way to the Central

Americans' own Esquipulas peace plan. The subsequent process of demobilizing the Contras inside Nicaragua under the Esquipulas peace plan involved frequent applications of a variety of CBMs. In early and mid-1990, the UN peacekeeping presence, ONUCA (with significant military contributions from Canada and Spain and its battalion of Venezuelan paratroop infantry),[6] employed a number of CBMs in its attempts to persuade the Contras to disarm and to keep communications open between the Contras, the Sandinistas, and the incoming Violeta Chamorro administration.

As the Contra demobilization process wound down in mid-1990 and the Chamorro government settled in, the Esquipulas Security Commission continued its work of establishing an inventory of troops and arms and encouraging a broad range of multilateral CBMs. In parallel with the disarmament work of the Security Commission, some progress was being made in developing bilateral confidence-building measures.

The significance of CBMs in Central America in the early 1990s was highlighted at the July 1991 San Salvador presidential summit, when the Hondurans floated their comprehensive disarmament and confidence-building proposal (a "Central American Security Treaty"), which would set ceilings on military inventories and troops. The Honduran proposal had a heavy emphasis on confidence-building measures as a means of diminishing the possibility of interstate conflicts. These confidence-building measures would include a pledge by the Central American nations to forsake the use of force to settle disputes and a commitment from the United States not to support irregular movements in Central America. The proposal also included suggestions of new tasks for the armed forces, such as involvement in the control of drugs and protection of natural resources. Some of the Honduran ideas found an echo in the speeches made at the Ibero-American Summit immediately afterward, including Peruvian President Alberto Fujimori's proposal for a disarmed Latin America.

By 1992, the notion of confidence-building measures was firmly embedded in Central American thinking about disarmament and the lowering of tensions. A number of such measures were included in the Honduran security proposal, and the Esquipulas Security Commission mentioned several others in its various reports to the Central American presidents. For example, in June 1991, plans were announced for the establishment of a formal hot line that would provide secure and immediate telephone links between the presidents of the five Central

American nations plus Panama. Thus, one of the features of the long Contadora/Esquipulas process was the way in which it greatly increased communication between the Central American countries, and especially their presidents, foreign ministers, and senior military officials. This confidence-building measure, along with many others, was an important legacy of the peace process of the 1980s.

In June 1991, the OAS General Assembly, meeting in Santiago, Chile, authorized the creation of a "Working Group on Cooperation for Hemisphere Security." In February 1992, a draft committee document revealed the nontraditional nature of its focus as it defined a "broad security concept" as including such items as cooperation for security, confidence-building mechanisms to strengthen security, democratic stability, human rights, economic security, protection of the environment, critical poverty, nonproliferation and control of unconventional weapons, transparency in arms transfers, nonintervention, and cooperation in the struggle against drugs.[7] The specific references to "confidence-building mechanisms" and "transparency in arms transfers" are clear indications of the significance of CBMs in contemporary Latin American thinking on security issues.

Peacekeeping: ONUCA/ONUSAL

The United Nations Security Council formally created ONUCA when it approved Resolution 644 on November 7, 1989.[8] The 625-person group, consisting of 260 unarmed military observers along with support technicians located in 33 regional bases, would be responsible for halting cross-border infiltration and cutting support for rebels in the region. The countries involved in ONUCA included Venezuela, Canada, Argentina, Brazil, Ecuador, and Colombia.

ONUCA's initial mandate, composition, and operational concept reflected the UN's reluctance to get involved in internal conflicts.[9] This was to be a verification and peace-observing mission, not a full-scale peacekeeping interposition mission, and certainly not peace enforcement; however, as events unfolded, there were brief periods when Contra reluctance to disband threatened to convert ONUCA's role to one of enforcement. The scope of the operation was briefly moved up the conflict-resolution spectrum (see Figure 1) for the period of Contra demobilization, but the United Nations consistently defined ONUCA's mission as one of verification. This limited definition of ONUCA's role was also a reflection of the Latin American resistance to peacekeeping and the UN's preference for smaller observation missions with the lowest possible military profile. The Canadians, who were used to larger peacekeeping missions, frequently called ONUCA a "minimalist" operation, noting that it would have difficulty verifying Esquipulas in the large geographic area assigned to it.[10]

In early 1990, the Contras were showing considerable reluctance to disband. This recalcitrance was due in part to the lack of control on the part of the fragmented Contra leadership as well as to the very real fears among the Contras that if they disbanded and gave up their weapons, they would be at the mercy of the Sandinista military. Although diplomats on all sides pressured the Contras, this hard line was undermined by the reality that 260 unarmed UN observers were not going to be able to force the Contras to do anything. And so, setting aside its historical aversion to peace enforcement, the UN Security Council decided to expand ONUCA's mandate and give it some temporary combat power: a battalion of paratroopers armed with basic weapons. On March 15, the UN Secretary-General addressed the Security Council, requesting that ONUCA be expanded in order to add 116 observers plus an armed infantry battalion of at least four rifle companies (about 800 troops) for the supervision of Contra demobilization. Venezuela, which already was providing observers to ONUCA, had agreed to provide this battalion. Although the Secretary-General's Report did not state that the demobilization would be forced, there was a clear implication that adding armed paratroopers to the unarmed UN military observers would constitute a powerful message to the reluctant Contras.

The demobilization process did not officially end until July 5, when the last elements of the Venezuelan battalion returned home. Exact figures on the number demobilized were somewhat questionable, but approximately 23,000 Contras were processed, and close to 17,000 weapons were recovered and destroyed. With the demobilization of the Contras completed in early July, the ONUCA mandate reverted to the original, rather limited role of concentrating on the borders and watching for violations of the Esquipulas II prohibition on cross-border support of irregular forces.

In November 1990, the Security Council accepted the Secretary-General's recommendation that ONUCA could be cut back somewhat because of its reduced mission. The Council also extended the mission's mandate for six months (twice, until November 1991) and agreed that its main focus would be to maintain a UN presence in the region to serve as a confidence-building measure and deter cross-border support for insurgencies. In effect, ONUCA was becoming a token and "flag-showing" presence waiting for a possible expanded mandate if the situation in El Salvador should lead to an agreement requiring UN verification.

The situation in El Salvador in 1990-1991 was characterized by a continuing civil war and hopes for peace that culminated in intense UN-sponsored talks. These negotiations achieved a cease-fire agreement in the dramatic December 1991 New Year's Eve "Act of New York," which expanded the original ONUSAL — whose mission had been restricted to monitoring human rights — and converted it into a new major UN verification and observation mission. Contra demobilization in Nicaragua provided a useful precedent for the Frente Farabundo Martí para la Liberación Nacional (FMLN) demobilization in El Salvador. With the expanded ONUSAL came the end of the much-diminished ONUCA, whose personnel and assets were quickly moved to El Salvador in January 1992.

ONUSAL differed from ONUCA in one key respect: the police function. A key element in the Salvadoran peace process was that demobilization of the FMLN would be accompanied by demobilization of certain military and police units that had been associated with some of the more brutal human rights violations of the ten-year civil war. A new National Police that would include personnel from both the old police and the FMLN would replace the old security and police forces. These personnel had to be prepared quickly; thus, this training was undertaken by the Police Division of ONUSAL, which included officers from Chile, Mexico, and Guyana as well as several European countries. ONUSAL military observers in the Military Division included officers from Brazil, Canada, Colombia, Ecuador, and Venezuela, while Argentina provided medical officers. The relative activity of the various divisions of ONUSAL can be seen from their authorized strengths. The Human Rights Division included approximately 50 observers, legal advisors, and educators. The Military Division was authorized a staff of 249, with an additional 88 observers deployed for the critical "separation of forces" period in early 1992. The Police Division, by far the largest, was staffed by 631 personnel.

Despite the problems and delays in the original schedule that had been worked out in the December 1991 New York and January 1992 Mexico City agreements, the process was eventually successful, thanks in no small part to ONUSAL's presence. From February until December 15, 1992, the FMLN was concentrated into 15 camps under ONUSAL supervision, where they slowly demobilized and turned in their weapons for disposition by ONUSAL. Simultaneously, key units of the Salvadoran armed forces also demobilized, and officers identified with human rights violations were purged from the military. At the same time, the old Salvadoran National Guard and the Treasury Police were disbanded, and the new Policía Nacional Civil (PNC) was created under a crash training program supervised by the Police Division of ONUSAL.[11] The process was not without its difficulties, however. Elements in the regular Salvadoran police and military, supported by right-wing political elements, resisted the process. In addition, occasional jokes and sarcastic remarks circulated about the Argentine military officers' teaching their Salvadoran counterparts about democracy and about the 113 Mexican police officers' instructing the newly formed Salvadoran National Police in the finer points of corruption.[12]

South America:
CBMs and Historic Border Tensions
Historical Perspective

The South American experience with peacekeeping and confidence-building has been markedly different from that of Central America for the obvious reason that South America did not experience the protracted conflict and peacemaking process that dominated Central America in the 1980s and early 1990s. Thus, no UN peacekeeping presence was established in South America, and no overarching treaty or Contadora/Esquipulas framework existed in which to ground specific CBMs.

Nevertheless, CBMs were of considerable significance in South America during this period, especially when linked to schemes for economic and political integration. The explicit use of CBMs in this connection may well turn out to have as significant long-term effects as in Central America. Of particular interest is the notion that CBMs and shifts in strategic geopolitical thinking can change the role of the military and assist in strengthening the democratic process.[13] The most dramatic shifts have occurred in the Argentine-Brazilian relationship, which has the potential of driving most of the other political, strategic, and economic arrangements in southern South America. However, other equally significant changes, such as in the Argentine-Chilean and the Argentine-British relationships, have been positively affected by CBMs in the past decade.

In other words, CBMs can assist in shifting the strategic paradigm from one based on hostility and conflict-laden geopolitics to one that stresses geo-economics and the geopolitics of cooperation and integration with neighbors.

The Conflict Possibilities

Although often ignored outside of the region, a series of historic strains between pairs of bordering states have always had the potential of flaring up and reaching the conflict stage in South America. Because the military establishments of many of the South American nations have considerably greater potential than their Central American counterparts, any interstate armed conflict could be far more damaging than in Central America (the 1995 Ecuador/Peru conflict clearly had such potential). Furthermore, the military establishments of the nations involved have a vested interest in using these possible conflicts as justifications for their budgets, troop levels, and influence. Their use of classical "war hypotheses" based on geopolitical thinking and historic animosities with neighbors is an enduring feature that has shaped military roles and missions. Thus, CBMs can have considerable potential if they serve to reduce these animosities, diminish the credibility of the "war hypotheses," and make the possibility of conflict less likely.

A thorough examination of these conflict possibilities is beyond the scope of this chapter,[14] but a short list of potential bilateral conflict situations would include Guyana-Venezuela, Venezuela-Colombia, Ecuador-Peru, Peru-Chile, Bolivia-Chile, Chile-Argentina, Argentina-Brazil, and Argentina-United Kingdom. Conflicts that are multilateral would include Argentine-Brazilian competition for influence in the South American "buffer states" (Uruguay, Paraguay, Bolivia), attempts to exercise control over extensive economic or patrimonial maritime zones (such as the Chilean effort to claim a "Mar Presencial"[15]), and issues of sovereignty and resources in the quadrant of Antarctica that is associated with South America (and claimed by Argentina, Chile, and Great Britain, despite the bases of some 18 nations, including the United States).

Impact of Confidence-Building Measures

It is against this backdrop of potential conflict situations that the significance of CBMs in South America must be examined. Although some of these CBMs have been in place for many years, their number increased dramatically in the last decade, and for the first time the language of CBMs was used specifically in connection with international strains in South America. Although it is difficult to document linkages and causality, it appears that the increased use of CBMs in the Central American conflict scenario and the involvement of several South American nations in the Contadora and Esquipulas effort produced a "contagion effect" under which CBM concepts and techniques were transferred from the Central to the South American conflict scenarios. CBMs have had the greatest impact on the so-called "ABC" countries of the Southern Cone (Argentina, Brazil, and Chile) and have been linked to attempts at economic integration in the same area (Mercado Común del Sur, MERCOSUR); there have also been proposals for a collective security agreement that would unify the MERCOSUR countries.[16]

Argentina-Brazil. Within the overall shift from competition to cooperation between Argentina and Brazil, the two major forces in South America, there is a strategic component that is remarkable in light of the fact that the contingency planning of these two nations has always included the "war hypothesis" of armed conflict between them. One basic CBM has been the periodic meetings of senior representatives of their general staffs to discuss matters of common interest and plan for specific measures of military-to-military cooperation such as exchanges of information and joint arms manufacturing. These meetings, which stemmed from the 1985 Iguazú Declaration, began as bilateral meetings. Since then, they have included Paraguay, Uruguay, and Chile as observers, with plans for including these countries as full members. The meetings are now being called a "strategic MERCOSUR" to parallel the economic MERCOSUR.[17] Two of the long-standing areas of dangerous competition — nuclear projects and strains over dams along their riverine borders (sometimes called the "A-Bomb" of atomic rivalry and the "H-Bomb" of incompatible hydroelectric projects) — have basically been resolved by means of cooperative approaches in these two potentially conflictive issue areas between Argentina and Brazil. The degree to which CBM terminology has crept into the resolution of these old problems can be seen in the words spoken by Argentine President Carlos Menem when he signed a decree prohibiting the export of Argentine nuclear and ballistic missile technology to nations that refuse to accept international safeguards: "A lack of transparency [in the past] made us dangerous and untrustworthy."[18] Followers of CBM trends would recognize immediately the significance and origin of the term "transparency" in Menem's words.

Argentina-Chile. The improvement in relations between Argentina and Chile is equally remarkable, given their historic rivalry and the fact that they almost went to war in 1978 over the issue of the Beagle Channel Islands on their far southern frontier. Resolution of that issue by means of papal mediation paved the way for a series of other measures, many of them clearly CBMs between their military establishments. As examples, periodic meetings of the senior naval regional commanders in Puerto Williams, Chile, and Ushuaia, Argentina, (both sites are on the Beagle Channel) can be cited. Likewise, southern air force commanders of Chile and Argentina maintain hot lines and meet periodically to minimize the danger that border incidents might lead to something more serious.[19] High-level discussions between President Menem and his Chilean counterparts over remaining border issues have been accompanied by lower-level military contacts and exchanges of visits aimed at enhancing CBMs.[20]

Argentina-United Kingdom. CBMs in this area are of special interest because of the legacy of the 1982 Falklands/Malvinas war, which could well have been averted had such CBMs existed. Some of the CBMs established by Argentina and the United Kingdom are clearly inspired by those that had been set up between NATO and the Warsaw Pact. Other CBMs may have stemmed from the Central American peace process, in which Argentina played a significant role as part of the Contadora Support Group as well as participation in ONUCA (with both observers and a group of naval patrol vessels in the Gulf of Fonseca). The Anglo-Argentine CBMs are contained in a series of joint declarations signed in 1989, 1990, and 1991[21] and include classic CBMs such as the establishment of direct communication links, exchanges of information, search and rescue procedures, notification of military movements and maneuvers above certain specified levels, and the establishment of certain "rules of behavior."

The Extra-Hemispheric Peacekeeping Experience
Overview

The military establishments of the larger nations of Latin America (with the notable exception of Mexico) have consistently supported most of the major peacekeeping missions of the United Nations. In some cases (e.g., Argentina and Chile), this has been a long-term, historic commitment of from three to six observers in missions that have been supported from the late 1940s to date. In other cases, the support has taken the form of major units (at least a battalion in the range of 500 to 700 personnel), generally deployed for periods of a year. This Latin American support effort has accelerated in the past few years as the United Nations has taken a more activist and interventionist stance in the peacekeeping field, with some key individuals calling for the United Nations to be prepared to engage in peace enforcement as well as peacekeeping.[22] As explained below, at least one army (Argentina's) now formally includes such peacekeeping support as one of its basic missions, while others have assumed de facto peacekeeping roles with an extended commitment into the future. Since it is reasonable to assume that such calls for troop contributions for UN peacekeeping missions will continue and even increase in the future, this role will probably be of growing significance.

Historical Precedents[23]

Over the years, the Latin American support of UN peacekeeping and peace-observing missions has ranked after the principal troop contributors (the Scandinavian countries, Ireland, New Zealand, India, and Canada) and well above that of most of the UN membership. In the United Nations Emergency Force (UNEF I) mission in Egypt and Israel from 1956 to 1967, Brazil provided a battalion for almost ten years (for a total participation of some 5,000 person-years), while Colombia deployed a similar unit for a year. In addition, a Brazilian general commanded UNEF twice during this period. After the 1973 Middle East War, both Panama and Peru provided a battalion to UNEF II for a year.[24] A Peruvian officer also commanded the observer unit in the Golan Heights during this period. Moreover, Colombia provided a battalion and a naval ship during the UN's only previous experience with peace enforcement, the Korean War, and Argentina sent two warships on blockade duty during the Gulf War. Colombia and Uruguay have also provided significant troop units (a battalion of infantry and an engineer unit, respectively) to the Multinational Force and Observers (MFO). The MFO has supplied third-party peace observers in the Sinai desert on the border between Egypt and Israel since 1982. This particular mission was mandated by the Camp David accords; hence, it was not a UN effort.

Recent Involvement in UN Peacekeeping and Peace-Observing Efforts[25]

Latin American involvement in recent operations can be summarized as follow:
UN Truce Supervision Organization (UNTSO, Middle East, 1948 to

date): observers from Argentina (6) and Chile (4).

UN Military Observer Group in India and Pakistan (UNMOGIP, 1949 to date): observers from Chile (3) and Uruguay (1).

UN Observer Mission in Central America (ONUCA, 1990-1992): observers from Brazil (21), Colombia (12), Ecuador (21), and Venezuela (14). Venezuela contributed a battalion (approximately 800 personnel) during Contra demobilization, and Argentina provided four patrol craft and 30 naval personnel for ONUCA's Gulf of Fonseca operation.

UN Iraq-Kuwait Observation Mission (UNIKOM, 1991 to date): observers from Argentina (7), Uruguay (8), and Venezuela (7) as well as a helicopter unit from Chile (50 personnel).

UN Angola Verification Mission (UNAVEM II, 1991 to date): observers from Argentina (7) and Brazil (6).

UN Observer Mission in El Salvador (ONUSAL, 1991-1994): police trainers and observers from Chile, Mexico, and Guyana. Military observers were provided by Brazil, Colombia, Ecuador, and Venezuela; Argentina sent military medical officers.

UN Mission for the Referendum in Western Sahara (MINURSO, 1991 to date): observers from Argentina (15). Peru, Venezuela, and Honduras have also made commitments to provide support.

UN Transitional Authority in Cambodia (UNTAC, 1992 to date): units from Argentina, Chile, and Uruguay. Brazil, Barbados, Costa Rica, Ecuador, Guyana, Jamaica, and Venezuela have also made commitments.

UN Protection Force, Croatia (UNPROFOR, 1992 to date): observers from Colombia and Venezuela. Argentina has sent a battalion plus support units for a total of over 900 personnel.

UN Operation in Somalia (UNOSOM, 1992-1994): military medical personnel from Argentina.

The Argentine Example

As illustrated above, Argentina has been one of the most consistent supporters of UN peacekeeping (as well as the UN/coalition effort in the Gulf War) in the past few years. This involvement is due largely to a deliberate policy by Raúl Alfonsín's and Carlos Menem's administrations to get their nation and its military institutions involved in this type of extrahemispheric UN mission. This effort also reflects the fact that UN peacekeeping is now part of Argentina's formal role statement (Canada takes a similar approach). As stated by the Chief of

Staff of the Argentine Army in a recent interview,[26] the basic mission of the Argentine military institutions, similar to that of most armies, is to defend state sovereignty by providing a credible deterrent against a hypothetical adversary. Nevertheless, they also have several secondary missions, one of which is participation in international peace missions (other secondary missions include assistance in case of natural disasters and support in the struggle against narco-subversion). Argentina also has indicated an interest in working more closely with NATO, especially as NATO redefines its post-Cold War roles.[27] An important link to NATO is Spain. Like Argentina, Spain has made a difficult transition from authoritarian rule to democracy, and its military institutions have also assumed a major role in UN peacekeeping in recent years, most notably in Central America. The contacts between Spanish and Latin American officers have increased through these UN peacekeeping missions, with mutual reinforcement concerning the value of such missions for their militaries.[28]

Motivation and Impact

Assessing the motivation for and the impact of these peacekeeping missions is somewhat speculative. It is possible to assume idealistic motivations such as support for the world organization and altruistic contributions to the achievement of peace. It is also true that individual military personnel usually profit financially from UN service, as do many of their governments, depending on the arrangements made with UN headquarters. The military institutions also benefit by the training and exposure that they derive from such service. From a national perspective, service in UN peacekeeping missions tends to elevate the profile and prestige of the country. Finally, for a military institution like Argentina's, still laden with the baggage of years of military dictatorship, the "Dirty War," and the Falklands/Malvinas defeat, involvement in UN peacekeeping offers the military an opportunity to recover some of the prestige and self-respect lost after many years of negative image in the world and in Argentina.

Service in UN peacekeeping missions also reinforces the ties of military transnationalism by building on the camaraderie of shared experiences with soldiers of many nations. As an example, General Martín Balza, the Chief of Staff of the Argentine Army, remarked that he had been moved by a handwritten condolence note sent to him after two Argentine soldiers were killed on UN duty in

Croatia.[29] The note came from retired British General Jeremy Moore, who had led the British forces in the Falklands/Malvinas campaign in which General Balza had been an artillery commander.

The Backlash:
Opposition to Peacekeeping and CBMs
Overview

It would seem that "motherhood and apple pie" proposals such as peacekeeping and CBMs would generate little opposition, but they have. Thus, success in achieving the goals of these roles for the Latin American military hinges on identifying this opposition and seriously considering the issues opponents raise.

One type of opposition was noted previously in the context of the Central American peace process: the strong suspicion on the part of the Salvadoran military (and the political right wing) that peacekeeping by the United Nations was biased against them and would work against their interests. The fact that ONUSAL's first activities in El Salvador focused on human rights did nothing to allay these actors' negative views. As a result, when ONUSAL began setting up in El Salvador, death threats were made, and warnings were circulated to the effect that Salvadorans should have nothing to do with these foreign interveners who were violating national sovereignty.[30]

Opposition to Peacekeeping Roles

To many Latin American military officers, especially senior officers still clinging to nationalistic geopolitical visions, the notion of sending significant numbers of their officers and troops on peacekeeping missions under a UN flag is troubling because these roles are not seen as part of the "heroic" mission of defending their nation's sovereignty. Indeed, UN peacekeeping missions are frequently perceived to be contrary to this tradition and to lead toward the "denaturing" of the military by making it less aggressive and folding it into some sort of supranational force that will weaken its ability to repel aggressors who threaten national sovereignty. In terms of Argentine General Balza's statement of his army's primary and secondary missions, this secondary mission of peacekeeping has the potential of weakening the military's ability to respond to its primary mission of defending national sovereignty against a hypothetical external threat. In fairness to Latin American officers who feel this way, it should be noted that many senior U.S. officers expressed similar views about the U.S. military's large-scale involvement in UN and humanitarian missions in places such as the former Yugoslavia and Somalia.

To those military officers inclined toward conspiracy theories, peacekeeping (as well as CBMs) is sometimes perceived as part of a neo-Marxist plot to weaken the military and facilitate the victory of the revolutionary left.[31] Many professional military officers dismiss these new roles as well-meaning public relations gestures by uninformed civilian diplomats and politicians who do not really understand the nature of military threats and strategic planning. The theory may be attractive, they would argue, but the reality is that threats and hostile neighbors do in fact exist and that no amount of CBMs can eliminate the possibility of conflict, for which the military establishment must prepare. Peacekeeping and CBMs that are linked to utopian schemes of disarmament, they would add, will eventually weaken the military and the state, lead to instability, and thus ultimately reduce confidence.

In the current context of hemisphere relations, the fact that many suggestions regarding these new roles are coming from U.S. sources is suspect. These ideas are sometimes seen as yet another attempt by the "gringos from the North" to sell the Latin Americans another new concept on how to shape and control their military establishments. Senior Latin American military officers are especially resentful, having endured successive U.S. attempts over the past five decades to persuade them of the value of hemisphere security, civic action, counterinsurgency, counternarcotics campaigns, and U.S.-style civil-military relations.

Opposition to CBMs

CBMs inevitably involve military and intelligence personnel whose training has deeply conditioned them to mistrust potential adversaries and to take "worst case" planning approaches toward these adversaries' capabilities and intentions. At the same time, these individuals have a strongly protective approach toward their own capabilities and limitations, to the point that revealing them is tantamount to treason. In extreme cases, this perceived need for secrecy will keep military and intelligence personnel from effectively communicating with their own civilian leadership. In cases where the military controls the government, indirectly or directly, this sense of secrecy may also be very strong and is likely to keep the general public from knowing much about the capabilities, intentions, and plans of the military. Thus, a basic CBM is effective communication between the nation's own military-intelligence apparatus and its civilians, be they political leaders or common citizens.

In the contemporary Latin American context, CBMs must face the limitation that the military historically has resisted civilian prying into its inner workings. There are relatively few Latin American academics (and even fewer U.S. scholars) with meaningful access to the military, to its discussions of "war hypotheses," or to consideration of geopolitical factors involved in strategic planning. The Latin American military's rigid hierarchical structure and its insistence that the only way to achieve senior rank is through a single military academy make it difficult for civilian academic and political leaders to engage in a meaningful dialogue with their military colleagues. To overcome this limitation, the military's activities must become more "transparent" (to use a CBM term) to its own national civilian leadership, and the civil-military relationship must be made more open and frank through dialogue as well as the development of civilian experts who can work closely with the military. The sending of military officers to civilian universities for graduate degrees and attendance by civilians (representing both government and the private sector) at national defense colleges also contribute to this goal.

In the 1990s, the changing dynamic of civil-military relations in the Western Hemisphere has created another limitation for CBMs: they are seen by many military officers as a thinly disguised way of allowing the civilian political leadership to reduce military budgets and influence by arguing that the Cold War is over, thus reducing the military's need for as many weapons or troops. Unfortunately, much of the rhetoric that has emerged from discussions in the United States and Europe on disarmament and the Cold War "peace dividend" (as well as eloquent speeches at many UN forums) has stressed this link between reduced tensions and the reduction of military budgets, thus reinforcing the militaries' suspicions that this will be used as a rationale to limit their power and perquisites.

Conclusions

Despite these objections to peacekeeping and CBM roles, it seems clear that many of the Latin American military establishments will be considering and implementing these new roles in the years ahead. The 1995 Santiago Conference on CBMs provides clear evidence of the growing importance that regional leaders attach to such missions. For the generally small military establishments of Central America, the most significant influence will be the impact that peacekeeping and CBMs had — and will continue to have — in the Central American peace process. Because of their size and limited capabilities, it is unlikely that these militaries will be asked to participate significantly in UN peacekeeping operations. CBMs, especially those appropriate to their level of forces, political needs, and geographical setting, can be an important tool in making conflict less likely, enhancing integration, and further reducing the level of armaments and troops to their historic pre-1979 numbers.

For the larger military establishments of South America (as well as Mexico, which has generally abstained), UN peacekeeping represents a significant, although secondary, role to play on the world scene. The Argentine example is illustrative here in terms of the way its strong participation in UN peacekeeping in the last few years has been an important instrument of Argentina's foreign policy as well as a potential rehabilitator of a military that lost prestige and morale in a dark period of its history.

The relationship between CBMs and the process of redemocratization is a delicate one. Attempts to link these roles too closely to reductions in military budgets and influence are likely to backfire. However, CBMs can make interstate conflict in Latin America less likely, thus permitting a more realistic assessment of genuine military needs as well as the allocation of a certain amount of military resources to the United Nations for peacekeeping missions.

The role of the United States in this process must be a cautious one. An overeager attempt to push these roles on the Latin American military is also likely to backfire. It would be far wiser to allow the Latin American militaries, working closely with their civilian political leadership, to determine the pace and direction of these new approaches. Fortunately, other nations with more experience than the United States in these fields have indicated an interest in working with the Latin American militaries. Canada and Spain are in the forefront here, and their considerable involvement in the Central American peace process (as well as in UN missions elsewhere) should be used as a vehicle for showing the advantages of greater participation in UN peacekeeping and confidence-building measures with neighbors.

Notes

1. This chapter draws on the author's prior work on peacekeeping and confidence-building in Latin America. The support of the International Peace Academy, the U.S. Institute of Peace, and the Stimson Center is gratefully acknowledged.

2. These definitions are based on those of the International Peace Academy, an independent non-governmental organization associated with the United Nations. See also Jack Child, 1992, *The Central American Peace Process, 1983-1991* (Boulder: Lynne Rienner Publishers), especially Chapter 1.

3. Report by Secretary-General Boutros Boutros-Ghali, June 17, 1992, Document A/47/277. See also the UN's *Disarmament Newsletter* (August/September 1992), 6-7.

4. Child 1992, 6-7.

5. This section draws extensively on the author's *The Central American Peace Process* and on a paper prepared for the Stimson Center at a CBM conference in Santiago, Chile, August 1992.

6. General de Brigada Alvaro R. Barboza Rodríguez, 1991, "El Ejército Venezolano y el Proceso de Paz en Centroamérica," *Military Review* (September-October 1991), 39-45. For a Spanish perspective, see "España inspira confianza," *Revista Española de Defensa* (December 1991), 20-21.

7. OAS, Permanent Council, Grupo de Trabajo sobre Cooperación para la Seguridad Hemisférica, 1992, *Nuevo Concepto de Seguridad*, OAS Document CP/GT/CSH-13/92, (February 12), 3-5.

8. For details on ONUCA, see Report of the Secretary-General, October 11, 1989, Document S/20895 and *The Blue Helmets* (United Nations, 1990), 393-396.

9. Discussions with Mr. Francesc Vendrell, UN Special Assistant to the UN Secretary-General, Ottawa, May 1989.

10. Lisa North, 1990, *Between War and Peace in Central America* (Toronto: CAPA), 190; and Colonel John Joly, 1991, "ONUCA," *Canadian Defence Quarterly* (June), 12-19.

11. *Boston Globe*, July 24, 1992; *InfoPress*, September 3, 1991; *The Washington Post*, December 16, 1992.

12. *U.S. News and World Report*, May 18, 1992, 92.

13. Jack Child, 1990a, "Geopolitical Thinking and Democracy," in Louis W. Goodman, ed., *The Military and Democracy* (Lexington: Lexington Books), 158-160; and Child 1990b, "The Status of South American Geopolitical Thinking" in G. Pope Atkins, ed., *South America into the 1990s* (Boulder: Westview), especially 72-73 and 77-79.

14. See Jack Child, 1985, *Geopolitics and Conflict in South America* (New York: Praeger). See also Raúl Fain Binda, 1989, "La Rémora de los Conflictos Fronterizos," *Uno* (Spain), May.

15. Admiral Jorge Martínez Bush, 1991, "El Mar Presencial: Actualidad, Desafíos y Futuro," *Revista de Marina* (Chile), March, 231-238; Miguel Vergara Villalobos, 1990, "El Factor Naval en la Proyección de Chile en el Océano Pacífico," *Revista de Marina* (Chile), June, 568-585; Jane G. Dalton, 1991, "The Chilean Mar Presencial: A Harmless Concept or a Dangerous Precedent?" LLM Thesis, University of Virginia.

16. Virgilio Beltrán, 1992, "Buscando Nuevos Roles para los Ejércitos de América Latina," International Congress of Military Sociology, Valparaiso, Chile, August 29-31, 37-38.

17. Rut Diamint, 1992, "Medidas de Confianza Mutua," paper presented at the Stimson Center/FLACSO Seminar on CBMs, Santiago, August. See also *Clarín* (Argentina), December 20, 1986; and *Jornal do Brasil*, December 24, 1986.

18. *The Chicago Tribune,* May 3, 1992, 21.

19. Diamint 1992, 11-13. See also Isaac Caro, 1992, "Chile: Medidas de Confianza Mutua," paper presented at the Stimson Center/FLACSO Seminar on CBMs, Santiago, August, 9-12.

20. *Times of the Americas,* August 21, 1991, 3; and *El Mercurio* (Chile), September 2, 1988.

21. The Joint Argentine-U.K. agreements are dated October 19, 1989; February 15, 1990; and September 25, 1991. See Diamint 1992, 5-8.

22. See, for example, the suggestions by Secretary-General Boutros Boutros-Ghali as reported in *The Washington Post,* December 22, 1992.

23. Jack Child, 1980, "Peacekeeping and the Inter-American System," *Military Review,* vol. LX, no. 10, October, 40-54.

24. A joke making the rounds at the time was that Peru was participating in order to learn how to fight in the desert (against Chile during the centennial of the War of the Pacific in 1979), while Panama wanted to learn how to run and defend a canal.

25. Data for this section taken from *The Military Balance* (London, IISS); *The Blue Helmets* (United Nations, 1990); *The Washington Post,* September 22, 1992, A14.

26. *Revista Española de Defensa,* October 1992, 64-65. Also stated by Lieutenant General Martín Balza in a speech to the XIX Conference of American Armies (see *Seguridad Estratégica Regional,* no. 1, 1992, 85-87).

27. Associated Press, 1992, in U.S. Department of Defense, *Early Bird,* October 1, 16.

28. *Revista Española de Defensa,* "España inspira confianza" (December 1991) and "Observadores españoles en la paz de El Salvador" (February 1992a).

29. *Revista Española de Defensa,* October 1992b, 64.

30. *Estudios Centroamericanos,* 1991, "ONUSAL: la reacción de la extrema derecha," no. 512 (June), 579-584.

31. See Child 1992, 161-162.

III

Guerrillas, Narcotics, and Terrorism: Old Menaces in a New World

Max G. Manwaring

It has been suggested that with the end of the Cold War and the resultant "peace dividend," there are only a few limited requirements for armed forces in Latin America. This assumption is based on arguments that international Marxism-Leninism is no longer a threat, local insurgencies are no longer viable, and the so-called drug war is a police rather than a military problem. While the conflict between Peru and Ecuador has forced some reassessment, there is still a general assumption that conflicts between hemisphere nations are also less and less likely. The discussion concerning demilitarization assumes that even if Latin American armed forces are not totally irrelevant, they should be looking for new missions such as peacekeeping or defense of the environment. Latin American military institutions are under pressure either to fold their tents and go away or find something productive to do.[1]

The armed forces of Latin America remain significant and at times dominant institutions in their various societies and cannot be dismissed or changed out of hand. In the context of the emerging "new world disorder," total demilitarization is not a viable option. Principal internal security concerns still need to focus on national security problems that are all too often assumed to be irrelevant in the post-Cold War era.

The most fundamental problem is the military's role in national development. This means addressing root causes of instability under the assumption that lack of development is a threat to national security. Remaining problems include the narcoterrorist-insurgent nexus, including the extreme model of Peru's Sendero Luminoso (Shining Path) insurgents. In addition, the current unstable peace is beset by terrorism, warlordism, proliferating international criminal activities, refugee flows, and border conflicts, all of which have the combined effect of "sundering fragile, but functioning nation-states and gnawing at the well-being of stable nations."[2]

This chapter examines strategic issues and threats that relate to security and civil-military relations in Latin America, describes the threats represented specifically by Sendero Luminoso and the narco-insurgent nexus, and outlines major policy implications for the targeted governments and for the United States. Until these issues and threats are understood and addressed at the strategic level, the consequences of instability will continue to threaten the hemisphere and the world.

The concerns expressed in the stability dialogue considered most likely to dominate national and international politics in the near future reflect an extremely dangerous and volatile world. Indeed, the arguments pertaining to the realities of the post-Cold War world appear to define a most unstable peace.

The first reality of the contemporary international security environment is the change from a bipolar environment dominated by the United States and the Soviet Union to a multipolar world. This new status is defined by the rise of several regional powers and non-state actors — including drug cartels and insurgent and terrorist organizations. Actions of these "new" state and non-state political actors are not easily predictable or necessarily benign.[3]

The second dynamic is that of interdependence. At first glance, national interdependence would appear to be a unifying and co-opting element on the world scene. Yet, opposed nationalisms suggest new and more subtle dangers for the various members of the international community. One of the most salient dangers in this environment involves transnational non-state actors that have become past masters at using competing nationalisms and legal frontiers of traditional nation-states for their own strategic advantage and protection.[4]

The final characteristic that helps define the new world disorder is that of governability. The gravity of this problem is hard to exaggerate. More than one-half of the world's countries have been brought near economic and political collapse by misguided, corrupt, or incompetent leadership. Corruption and incompetence degrade the state and weaken its ability and willingness to deal with real and perceived societal deprivations and injustices. The resultant upheaval can only benefit established or nascent non-state enemies.[5]

These realities challenge the capability of governments to provide meaningful political, economic, and social development and to maintain basic legitimacy. The result of these dynamics operating in the national and international security environment is a vicious downward spiral that manifests itself in a number of disparate activities in which the lowest common denominator is instability. Nonetheless, as important as instability might be in a national or international threat environment, it is only a symptom, not the threat itself. The actual threat stems from a lack of understanding of and a failure to alleviate the various manifestations of political, economic, and social injustices that are the root causes of instability. This is exacerbated by flawed understanding of and failure to deal properly with the insurgencies and narcotrafficking that are the major consequences of instability.[6]

The Most Fundamental Problems: Governance and Instability

B ecause Latin American geopolitical thinking centers on the state as a living organism, problems of governance and national development are of primary importance. As a result, national security and stability are first and foremost a function of internal politics.[7]

The concept of legitimacy is based on the moral right of a government to govern. Popular perceptions of corruption, disenfranchisement, poverty, and lack of upward mobility limit the right — and the ability — of a given regime to conduct the business of the state. Until a populace generally perceives that its government is dealing with these and other basic issues of political, economic, and social injustice fairly and effectively, instability and the threat of subverting or destroying a targeted government are real.

As an example, Peru's retired General Edgardo Mercado Jarrín has described and continues to describe much of Latin America as being in a state of "latent insurgency." Even though most hemisphere nations have elected civilian governments, they also have serious instability problems spawned by lack of development and the resultant chronic poverty, violence, and corruption. This is the essential nature of the threat from Sendero Luminoso, the illegal drug industry, or any other illegal challenger to a regime, and it is there that any response must begin. A campaign that fails to understand that political-moral considerations prevail over military and law enforcement considerations and that responds only to "enemy" military or paramilitary forces is likely to fail.[8]

Sendero's former leader, Dr. Abimael Guzmán, identified the lack of legitimacy of all Peruvian governments since the Spanish conquest as the central strategic problem in the ongoing conflict in Peru.[9] General Mercado Jarrín recognized this aspect of Peruvian violence as early as 1967, and he continues to argue that the key to ultimate success or failure for the narcotraffickers, the insurgents, or the government is the common denominator of legitimacy.[10] This is the prime lesson for vulnerable regimes in the coming decades. Unless national leadership recognizes what is happening at the highest strategic levels and reorients its thinking and actions to deal with the legitimacy issue, the problems of stability and security will resolve themselves: "There won't be any."[11]

The Relationship of Development to Security and Stability

The national security dialogue in Latin America is defining security in terms of stability and national development. More and more, the development task appears to consist of two highly interrelated elements: first, the defense of economic and political sovereignty in an interdependent world that is increasingly aggressive and, second, continued and expanded participation in building a country's agricultural and industrial bases. The reasoning is simple — the formation and execution of political, social, and economic development plans may have a decisive bearing on maintaining a system of representative democracy and on preserving internal as well as external peace.[12]

Thus, "security" must be redefined. In the past, security was a term primarily associated with possible or probable external threats. When applied to internal problems, security tended to refer to military or police force protection against insurgents or terrorists. In the Third World in general and Latin America in particular, large segments of the population have been left to fend for themselves — against each other, against "bandits" and "terrorists," against illegal drug traffickers, and sometimes against their own government and security institutions. If this were not the case, the problem of governability in these countries would be much less severe. The concept of security, therefore, must include activities that will ensure the safety and security of the general populace.[13]

Problems of legitimate governance, development, and security will remain of prime importance in coming decades. Until national leadership recognizes what is occurring at the highest strategic levels and reorients its actions to deal with the legitimacy issue, there will be neither security nor stability.[14]

The Role of the Military in the Internal Security Process

With the exceptions of Costa Rica, Panama, and perhaps Haiti, the various Latin American military institutions are not completely subordinated to civilian power. From colonial times to the present, most of the armed forces of the region, including those of Costa Rica until 1948, have played direct or indirect roles in governance. Constitutionally, they have acted as parallel and autonomous political actors superior to the civil political power. Nevertheless, it is the monopoly on violence — and the willingness to use it — that allows the permanent armed forces to dominate the temporary civil authority. As a consequence, despite the fact that Latin America has moved toward civilian rule, the military institution continues to play a significant role in the internal political process.[15]

The maturation of democratic political reforms, the strengthening of civilian institutions, and military disengagement from the political process are all dependent on economic development and regional stability. This requires the armed forces' playing not simply a nondisruptive role but a constructive role in the development process. Contemporary national well-being demands political, economic, and social solutions to deal with indirect threats as well as political-military efforts to deal with direct security threats.

In this context, the Latin American security dialogue calls for military institutions to adapt to new realities, not new missions. These emerging realities are closely related to problems of internal stability. National security requires more than maintaining readiness against the actions of potential external enemies. Like it or not, national security means wider economic and social development roles for the military institutions over the long term. In the short term, national security necessitates expanded roles against insurgents and narcoterrorists.

Major Threats Associated with Insurgency and the Narco-Insurgent Nexus

Within the context of general world instability, the security and stability dialogues identify two types of what Jacques Maritain calls "prophetic shock minorities" — illegal narcotraffickers and insurgents — working separately or together to attain economic and political power and social legitimacy. That power is achieved by eliminating any possible opponent through intimidation, out-and-out violence, and terror. Regardless of which self-appointed authoritarian group wins out in the end (assuming the narcotraffickers, the insurgents, or their alliance is allowed to win), the legitimation of power is likely to be seen as one variation or another on totalitarianism.[16] Thus, the possible application of the model provided by Peru's Shining Path for the achievement of political power and the narco-insurgent alliance are major threats associated with ignoring the root causes of instability. Within this context, the basic threat is the inability or unwillingness of the state to deal effectively with such transnational non-state actors.

Where the Shining Path Leads

Now that Marxism-Leninism has been discredited in most of the world and old-line Maoist leaders are revising their commitment to the idea of capitalism, a "fourth stage" of communism is emerging. This fourth stage is exemplified by the Sendero Luminoso insurgency movement in Peru. Dr. Abimael Guzmán — also known as President or Comrade Gonzalo — was the leader of this movement until his arrest in 1992. With or without Guzmán's continued leadership, the general concept of the movement provides disillusioned revolutionaries all over the world with a new and more sophisticated model for the conduct and implementation of a successful "people's war." Such a model is threat enough, but again, the Latin American security dialogue identifies the real threat as the inability or unwillingness of government to combat it effectively.

Organization. Guzmán's first concern centered on organization. To achieve his revolutionary vision, it was necessary to establish a dedicated cadre, a political party, a guerrilla army, and a support mechanism. This effort laid the foundation for the subsequent long-term struggle. Organization, not operations, was his key to success.[17]

Objectives. The principal objectives of Sendero are to gain power and to create a "nationalistic," "Indian," and "popular" democracy.[18] Guzmán's view of the new state derives from José Carlos Mariátegui, who was the founder of the Peruvian Communist Party in the 1920s. According to Mariátegui, the original basis for Peruvian socialism is in the pre-Columbian Indian (Quechua) community. That communal system was wrecked by the Spanish conquest and kept down by subsequent colonial and neocolonial elites operating out of Lima.[19]

Shining Path claims to be initiating a new era in which "true people's democracy" will be reestablished.[20]

Although operations have largely been confined to Peru, Sendero's doctrine and logic indicate that the movement aimed eventually to include the entire Indian community of Latin America. New members have to pledge to give their lives "for the triumph of world revolution."[21] Throughout these areas, it is assumed that incumbent government will never respond to popular needs and that Sendero's fourth stage of communism will. Thus, it is regime legitimacy, not military victory, that is the key to control of a state or society.

The Program for Gaining Power. Sendero planned for a protracted struggle, using a long-term, multistage program for gaining power.[22] The first efforts, beginning in 1962, were to establish a dedicated cadre. Guzmán took the time needed to build the strongest possible organizational foundations for the subsequent political and military struggle. During the 1960s and throughout the 1970s, he concentrated on theory and leadership development and on expanding his organization's relationships with relatively isolated peasant communities in the outlying districts around the university. Then, in 1978, Sendero disappeared from public view.

In 1980, as Peru was returning to civilian rule after 12 years of military government, the movement reappeared. Sendero leadership moved from what they called the "strategic equilibrium" to the "offensive" and began to attack the symbols of the bourgeois state. Ballot boxes were burned; the larger cities, including Lima, were blacked out periodically; public buildings and private companies were bombed; dogs and cats were symbolically hanged from lampposts; and attacks on and assassinations of local public figures were initiated.[23] Such actions were designed to "attack the glue that holds society together," to destroy links between the government and the population, and to create a political vacuum that would allow Sendero to become the de facto authority in areas outside of state control.

The third, more violent, stage of the insurgency (i.e., the generalization of violence) began in March 1982 with a major attack on the Ayacucho Department prison and the Robin Hood-like release of its prisoners. This operation was followed by a series of relatively small attacks against civil guard (police) posts, various public works, and a dynamite attack on the presidential palace in Lima. Then, in December 1982, Sendero Luminoso staged a spectacular event. In an attack on Lima's electrical grid, four high-tension towers were destroyed, causing a complete blackout in the capital and six other cities. Minutes after all the lights were out and everyone was in the streets wondering what had happened, Sendero lit a huge hammer and sickle that glowed from a hill overlooking Lima to celebrate Guzmán's forty-eighth birthday.[24]

At that point, the insurgency could no longer be ignored. In January 1983, a state of emergency was declared in five provinces of the Ayacucho Department, and the civilian government turned administrative control of this "emergency zone" over to the armed forces.[25] By mid-1984, the state of emergency had been extended to include 13 provinces in three different southern highland departments.

The fourth stage of the revolutionary program involved the consolidation and expansion of political control. By 1992, this effort essentially had left only the coastal departments and the large cities under central government control.[26] Such rapid territorial expansion would have been impossible without substantial financial support. Lacking outside aid, Sendero relied on the extortion of businesses, including those connected with the illegal drug industry in Peru. More important, however, Shining Path reportedly collected "taxes" from the narcotraffickers in the Upper Huallaga Valley and the other coca producing regions of the country, estimated to be between $30 and $100 million a year.[27]

The last stage of the revolution — besieging the cities and bringing about the total collapse of the state — was not scheduled to take place until the interior support bases were consolidated, the leadership nucleus of the movement was sufficiently large and sufficiently prepared to administer the state, and the major population centers were either strangled economically or psychologically subverted to the point where a relatively small, but direct, military assault could bring about the desired result.[28]

By mid-1992, Peru seemed on the brink of collapse. The pressure eased, however, when Guzmán and numerous senior aides were arrested. Subsequent arrests have disrupted the leadership further and reduced the movement's strength and military capacity. It is worth remembering, however, that Sendero Luminoso has proved to be a patient and resilient organization. While the government has captured Sendero's key leaders and reduced its military capacity, it has not managed to neutralize or eliminate the organization.

Sendero's program for gaining control of the state indicates that it will continue to focus its primary attack on the moral right of Alberto Fujimori's regime — or any other possible rival, including any narcotrafficking organization — to govern Peru.[29] Aside from various "shows of force," there will be no direct confrontations with security forces on any large scale. Sendero will jab and probe, destroy infrastructure, and enforce its will against carefully selected targets, but its primary efforts will continue to focus on the basis of power — the lack of the moral right of an elitist, foreign-dominated, and non-Indian minority regime to govern.

Additionally, the Sendero Luminoso program appears to go beyond the Peruvian state. In that connection, Shining Path is reportedly attempting to radicalize antigovernment factions in Bolivia, Ecuador, Colombia, Argentina, and Chile.[30] At the same time, Sendero Luminoso is considered by some to pose a potential threat in the Indian communities of Guatemala. It is argued that of the major Indianist movements in that country, at least two are oriented toward the Sendero Luminoso model for the achievement of political power.[31] Finally, Sendero appears to be gaining large numbers of diverse adherents in Europe and Turkey who support the "armed struggle" on behalf of the world's poor, migrant workers, and ethnic minorities and against capitalism, right-wing elite-oriented parties, and U.S. influence in the world.[32]

The Response to Sendero's Program. The United States, Peru, and other nations that might ultimately be affected by the destabilizing consequences of Sendero Luminoso's attacks on regime legitimacy have dealt with the problem in piecemeal fashion or even ignored it. The root causes of the conflict, however, continue to act as stimulants to revolutionary violence, and Sendero's organization remains intact and functioning.

From 1980 through 1993, various Peruvian governments dealt with the insurgency on a completely ad hoc basis — without a plan, without intelligence, and in an environment of mutual enmity between the civil governments and the armed forces. After 12 years of suffering, $22 billion in property destroyed, and 25,000 deaths, President Alberto K. Fujimori conceived a political-military strategy based on the concepts of General Mercado Jarrín.[33]

That strategy emphasized that the political war was more important than the military war and that there were additional wars that had to be fought simultaneously — an ideological war, an intelligence war, a bureaucratic war to establish unity of effort, an economic and social war, and a moral war.[34] While this strategy, combined with the fortuitous capture of Guzmán, has significantly reduced Sendero's power, it appears that Peru's leaders do not understand that an organization such as Sendero Luminoso will not be defeated completely by the capture of its leader. This movement will only be eliminated by superior organization and a political-moral strategy designed to neutralize it.

The United States tended to ignore the insurgency problem in Peru, concentrating instead on drug trafficking. From a national security perspective, the punitive eradication and interdiction measures emphasized by the United States in Peru are perceived to be largely cosmetic and not directed at the real power centers of the drug trade. Making criminals of minor employees of the drug industry and coca farmers in relatively inaccessible areas encourages territorial disintegration, provides a steady source of recruits for insurgent organizations, and exacerbates the estrangement between people and government.

The Narco-Insurgent Nexus

Within the past three decades, the nature of insurgencies has changed dramatically throughout the world. One of the most far-reaching transformations began in the 1970s with the growing involvement of insurgent forces with narcotraffickers. Some of these long-term "marriages of convenience" in the Middle East and Asia come quickly to mind — with particular reference to Lebanon and the Golden Triangle.[35] The narco-insurgent connection is not new, and it is not confined to Latin America.

The question, then, is not whether there is an alliance between narcotraffickers and insurgents. The question is whether or not the threats associated with that union warrant real concern and a serious response. Today, there is an emerging consensus among both civilians and military officers that the narco-insurgent nexus is a very sound business merger and is indeed a threat to the security and stability of the Latin American region. However, there is still no agreement on how to respond to this threat.

The State within a State in Latin America. The activities of the narco-insurgent nexus reflect expertise in communications, marketing, transportation, banking, and negotiations with other organizations. It has been noted that the consortium functions in much the same way as virtually any multinational Fortune 500 company. Products are made, sold, and shipped; bankers and financial planners handle the monetary issues, and lawyers deal with the legal problems. Of course, the company has a security division — somewhat more ruthless than that of other major corporations.[36]

In accomplishing its tasks with super efficiency and maximum profit, the general organization has its "capos" (chief executive officers and boards of directors), its councils, its system of justice, its public affairs officers, its negotiators, its project managers, and its enforcers. This organization operates in virtually every country in the Western Hemisphere and Europe. It has at its disposal the latest in high-tech communications equipment and systems and state-of-the-art weaponry. With these advantages, decisions are made quickly that can ignore or supersede laws, regulations, decisions, and actions of the governments of the nation-states in which the organization operates.[37]

As a result, the Latin American national security dialogue does not generally refer to narcotics trafficking in terms of individual "cartels" — at least in the sense of a business organization striving to control the price of commodities such as oil, microchips, automobiles, or even cocaine. Rather, it tends to refer to the whole being greater than the sum of its parts. The security dialogue is concerned about a political-economic-military force that has become a major transnational non-state actor.[38] To be sure, this is a loose and dynamic merger subject to many vicissitudes, but the "marriage of convenience" has lasted and appears to be getting stronger.

As an example, in Colombia, through bribery, corruption, intimidation, and terror, coupled with cosmetic patronage to the poor and direct or indirect manipulation and distortion of the political process, narcoterrorists have gained increasing influence over one of Latin America's best developed democracies. The institutional pillars of regime stability (the bureaucracy, the courts, the police, the army, and even the executive branch) have been infiltrated and suborned. The revelations involving narco-financing of President Ernesto Samper's presidential campaign and the resultant crisis in both internal Colombian politics and in Colombian-U.S. relations are the latest and most dramatic examples of this. Colombia's narcos have achieved a symbiotic relationship with the state, in the process becoming a virtual state within a state. Their power threatens national stability, development, and the future of the democratic system.

Motives for the Alliance. The motives for the narco-insurgent alliance are straightforward. They are 1) accumulation of wealth, 2) control of people, and 3) legitimacy. Together, these elements represent usable power — power to allocate values and resources in a society. Abimael Guzmán has stated, "Except for power, everything else is illusion."[39] Latin America's narcotics trafficking organizations understand that concept.

Billions of dollars in profits coming from the United States and Europe, easy access to high-tech weapons and communications systems, and willing volunteers to serve as hired guns constitute the economic portion of the power equation. This is manifested by the ability of narco-insurgent organizations to buy influence, assassinate opponents, and control local and national political systems.[40]

Examples of establishing control are easily found in the Colombian case. There, members of the drug cartels have run for and been elected to city councils and national legislatures. They argue that they, not the government, are defenders of national sovereignty and individual freedom and that they, not the government, are the providers of economic progress and the real public welfare. Charitable expenditures are made to provide playgrounds, build low-cost housing projects, and do other things for "people" that the government is unable or unwilling to do. As a result, constituencies have been and continue to be developed that are willing to support known drug barons or their representatives for important public offices.[41] If that approach provides results too slowly or fails, however, Colombian narcotraffickers have been known to use their insurgent partners to attack the national judiciary and kill those judges who were impeding organizational progress toward their political objectives.

Objectives. The narco-insurgent nexus seeks the overthrow or control of existing governments.[42] Narco-insurgency is not simply individual or institutional intimidation for financial gain. Nor is it just the use of insurgents as middlemen between coca leaf cultivators and processors. That is simply a business transaction. For narco-insurgents, the protection of coca growers and the corruption of government officials are political moves designed to help achieve the final objective.

The objective is not simply individual or institutional intimidation for some immediate and individualistic criminal gain. Rather, the final objective for the narco-insurgent alliance is the fundamental change or overthrow of governments. In narcoterrorism, there is a merger of efforts in which the narco-insurgent groups constitute an illegal political organization that uses irregular forces and guerrilla tactics along with political, economic, and psychological warfare, propaganda, and terrorism as means to gain its common long-term objective. The governmental change or overthrow effort, therefore, is directed at the political community and its institutions. In this sense, narco-insurgency is not simply criminal action. It is more; it is major political-psychological-moral conflict.[43]

Linkages. The equation that links narcotics trafficking to insurgency turns on a combination of need, organizational infrastructure development, ability, and the availability of sophisticated communications and weaponry.[44] For example, traffickers possess cash and lines of transportation and communication. Insurgent organizations possess followers, discipline, and organization. Traffickers need these to help protect their assets and project their power within and among nation-states. Insurgents are in constant need of logistical and communications support and money. Both groups possess organizational structures that, when combined, can generate an efficient and effective organization that can become a major source of power in itself.[45]

This type of power is generally considered the purview of governments, not non-state actors. However, the narco-insurgent alliance has the economic and military power to equal or better that of many nation-states. This alliance also has other advantages. There are no formal officials who have to be "elected," no national laws or boundaries that must be respected, and no responsibility to anyone outside the organization. The alliance can act as a state, demand to be treated as a state, but, at the same time, escape most of the restrictions imposed on the modern state.

The International Political Agenda. Narco-insurgent organizations also have developed a political agenda for exerting leverage in international as well as national arenas. The narco-insurgent goal of a given national agenda is to promote an "egalitarian social revolution" that will open up opportunities for "everybody" — and give the organization the legitimate basis for controlling some sort of nationalistic "narcocracy." The goals of the international political agenda are to establish acceptance, credibility, and legitimacy among the sovereign states with which the general organization must negotiate.[46]

Examples of means by which this agenda is promulgated include buying, controlling, or intimidating political parties and buying, controlling, or intimidating public, police, and military officials. Since 1985, examples of activities to help develop international legitimacy include strengthening preexisting relations with the Noriega-controlled government of Panama (until 1990); establishing relations with both the Sandinistas and at least one faction of the Contras in Nicaragua (until 1989); making contacts in Honduras that have facilitated shipments of narcotics through that country and Mexico; strengthening relations with the Bahamas, Jamaica, and several other island countries of the Caribbean; developing ties with Cuba, Haiti, Belize, and Suriname; and, with the opening of the European market, developing relations with Argentina, Brazil, Chile, Paraguay, Uruguay, and Venezuela.[47]

The national and international benefits of the alliance can only increase as traditional governments and their external allies, such as the United States, begin to make progress in controlling both narcotraffickers and insurgents. Marriage of convenience or not, this alliance is unlikely to dissolve.

The Governmental Response to the Narco-Insurgent Threat. Drug control measures through the Andean Ridge of South America (the White Triangle) fall into four broad categories. They are generally perceived to be ineffective. The first primarily involves training and equipping police and military forces specifically for narcotics interdiction missions. This has involved the creation of elite units for what has generally been considered a punitive role, in that it pertains almost exclusively to relatively unimportant small farmers and laborers rather than more significant elements within the illegal drug industry. The second category includes income replacement, crop eradication, and crop substitution measures. In these cases, interdiction and eradication have been stressed, while viable crop substitution efforts have not progressed much over the years. The third type of counterdrug effort is "North Americanization" of the problem. This involves such measures as kidnapping and extradition to the United States of traffickers who might not be convicted in the courts of their own country. The fourth category is sanctions. The strongest pressures in this regard include withholding economic and military aid for not complying with a U.S.-prescribed counterdrug program.[48] These efforts have been known to inflame already strong nationalistic and anti-"North American" emotions to the discredit of a given Latin American government and the United States.[49]

Additionally, South American governments have what they think are reasonable economic, political, and security concerns about the possible impact of successful U.S. counterdrug programs. Their argument is that the drug war being conducted in the White Triangle is a "North American" problem that the United States would rather fight outside its own political borders and that it is a degradation of the national sovereignty of the nation-states within which it is being conducted. This "North American" war also conflicts with more important internal issues such as the need to reduce unemployment, to maintain economic and political stability, and to fight nascent or long-standing insurgencies.[50]

In these circumstances, it should be no surprise to find that the Andean Ridge countries of Latin America have had dismal records in administering U.S.-supported antidrug programs over the past several years. As an example, in 1985, President Hernán Siles Suazo promulgated a decree to eradicate 4,000 hectares of coca leaf in response to U.S. threats to cut off aid to Bolivia if he did not cooperate in the eradication effort. The program was underfinanced, poorly conceived, riddled with corruption, and timidly implemented; it remains basically uncompleted. In time-honored Hispanic political tradition, the Bolivians would "obey, but not comply." As a consequence, the business of coca production goes on as usual behind a facade of not-too-effective measures.[51] Similarly, in 1994, U.S.-initiated and supported spraying efforts in Colombia eradicated 4,900 hectares of coca leaf. At the same time, Colombian farmers were adding 9,117 hectares of new coca to those already under cultivation. Opium and cannabis cultivation were also outstripping efforts at eradication, making the drug eradication program in Colombia essentially irrelevant.[52]

One observer has pointed out that the only thing that the counterdrug effort in the White Triangle has accomplished has been to force the narcotraffickers to change their means of transport, their routes, and their residences from time to time.[53] As a result, "the illegal drug trafficking industry continues to be strong, ruthless, rich and adaptable; (and narcoterrorists) continue to exploit weaknesses of governments beset by economic-political instability and social unrest."[54]

Conclusions. The narco-insurgent alliance represents a complex threat that requires a change in perspective: first, from unilateral responses to multilateral and unified responses; second, from primarily blunt military and police tools of action to people-oriented instruments of action; third, from traditional, plodding, decision-making bureaucracies to modern, super-fast, decision-making organizations; and fourth, from ad hoc, crisis-action efforts to holistic, long-term commitments of resources and will.

The first step in developing an appropriate response to the problems outlined above is to recognize the implications of world disequilibrium and popular sovereignty and begin to deal with the relationship of instability to legitimate governance. The second step is to realize that a populace-oriented model appears to be the best way of addressing the problems. Every policy, program, and action — military, police, political, economic, opinion-making — must contribute directly to the maintenance and enhancement of the ability and willingness of the nation-state to control its territory and societal organizations in a culturally acceptable manner and to generate the economic, social, and political development that people want and need.

In this context, military and law enforcement operational and tactical factors relating to a specific aspect of narco-insurgency must become subordinate to the general sociopolitical struggle. If that effort is not based on a realistic analysis of the societal situation in question, no number of arrests made, no number of narcotraffickers killed, no number of cocaine-producing labs destroyed, no number of kilos of cocaine interdicted, and no number of hectares of coca leaf eradicated could possibly help.

The challenge, then, is to come to terms with two facts: 1) contemporary conflict — at whatever level — is essentially a sociopolitical conflict, and 2) it is time to rethink ways, means, and measures of effectiveness for countering the very politically and economically oriented transnational narco-insurgent phenomenon.

Implications

In pessimistic national security terms, the post-Cold War era provides new challenges to old realities: what to do about problems of governance and instability, the threat of insurgency, and the transnational challenge of the narco-insurgent alliance.

Policy implications for targeted governments are sobering. If governments cannot, or do not, respond to the legitimate problems of their peoples by attacking and eventually alleviating the root causes of dissatisfaction and instability, no amount of police or military effort will help. On the other hand, once an insurgent or illegal drug industry organization (or an alliance) is established and well financed, trained, and disciplined, it will not be completely defeated by reforms designed to eliminate the cause. The organization will only be defeated by a superior organization and political-moral strategy designed to neutralize or eliminate it. Again, however, the sum of the parts of a desired military-police effort equals not only a certain capability to develop and exert deadly force but also to coordinate that capability with political, economic, psychological, and moral objectives.

Such a coordinated capability implies at least two fundamental nontraditional education and training requirements. First, there is a need to attune military and police minds to cope with the many ways that political and psychological considerations affect the use of force. Second, there is a requirement to attune military, police, and civilian minds to understand that battlefield victories only have meaning to the extent that they contribute to the legitimate strengthening of the state.

If governments and their security organizations do not or cannot understand and implement a political-moral war instead of a strictly military-police effort, the scenarios of anarchy, or the dictatorship of a revolutionary government based on the Sendero Luminoso ideology, or some sort of narcocracy are all real possibilities. These are the realities of the new world disorder. If the military institutions of Latin America are to adapt to these new realities, there is an additional alternative: a form of praetorianism.

Because of the traditional foundations of military power and influence in the various Latin American republics, the armed forces as institutions will continue to play major roles in national and international politics. Thus, whether one likes it or not, or whether one is prepared for it or not, solutions to national and international issues — such as governance, development, and the various forms of instability — will require the involvement and cooperation of the military institutions. The national security and stability dialogue in Latin America, however, tends to reject the suggestion that the only solution to chronic contemporary disorder is an authoritarian military solution. The problems are too great to be dealt with effectively by a single institution.[55]

Historically, praetorianism has been a relatively simple thing. An example would be the action of a small military contingent in the imperial capital of Rome. As the sole resident military force in Rome, the Praetorian Guard manipulated the prestige and legitimacy of the Senate to impose its own candidate as head of state. Thus, the Guard exercised definitive power in the imperial Roman political process. Nonetheless, that exercise of power was narrowly focused and based on the legitimacy of the Senate.

A modern praetorian government may develop when civilian institutions become dysfunctional and lose legitimacy and the military institution steps into the void to play a direct or indirect role in the political process. Such a regime, however, would not be able to deal with the myriad issues confronting governance without wide popular and institutional support. Thus, a modern praetorian government requires a plebiscite or elections to establish its own legitimacy for broad political, economic, social, and security actions. The result would be a military government with a propensity to enforce social harmony rather than defend individual rights and the democratic process.

By increasing corruption and undermining the credibility of elected civilian governments, the narco-insurgency alliance contributes to a loss of faith in the democratic system and to the danger of a revised praetorianism. These are the realities of power in Latin America. Policymakers and students of international affairs will continue to ignore them at their peril.

The policy implications for the United States and the Western community regarding the transnational narco-insurgent alliance are far-reaching. Probably the most important — from a U.S. policy perspective — is that fragile democracies are at risk. Equally important — from the perspective of policy and practicability — is that the various threats posed by insurgents and narcotraffickers are not being countered at the strategic level. Finally, even though many actual or potential conflicts are not now taking place in locations considered to be of vital interest to the United States or another Western country, there are enough to cause concern. In the context of multipolarity, interdependence, and the destabilizing problems associated with the issue of governance, it is only a matter of time before one vitally important political actor or another will be mortally threatened. By then, it will probably be too late to exert decisive influence on the situation.

The United States has three choices. First, policymakers can continue to ignore the threats associated with narco-insurgency. However, it is not likely that the threats will go away. Second, the United States and its allies in the so-called drug war can continue on a business-as-usual basis. This choice is likely to result in the frustration of mutual interests. Third, U.S. policy and decisionmakers may provide constructive support and direction for the change of perspective prescribed above. If this should be the choice — the sooner, the better.

Notes

1. As an example, see Louis W. Goodman, Johanna S.R. Mendelson, and Juan Rial, 1990, *Los Militares y la Democracia* (Montevideo, Uruguay: PEITHO).

2. Leslie H. Gelb, 1994, "Quelling the Teacup Wars," *Foreign Affairs* 73 (November-December): 5.

3. Interviews.

4. Interviews.

5. Interviews.

6. Interviews.

7. Interviews.

8. Interview with General Edgardo Mercado Jarrín (who has held several ministerial-level posts) in Lima, Peru, May 28, 1990; also see General Edgardo Mercado Jarrín, 1986, "El Impacto de la Crisis sobre los Conflictos Geopolíticos," *Defensa Nacional* (Lima: August): 53-83; 1969, "Insurgency in Latin America," *Military Review* (March): 10-20; 1987, "Seguridad y Fuerzas Armadas," *Defensa Nacional*, (Lima: October): 141-153; and 1990, "Subversión: El Desencadenamiento de la Contraofensiva," *Estudios Geopolíticos* (May): 52-60.

9. "El Discurso del Dr. Guzmán," in Rogger Mercado U., 1995, *Los Partidos Políticos en el Peru* (Lima: Ediciones Latinoamericanas), 85-90; and 1986, *Desarollar la guerra popular sirviendo a la Revolución mundial* (Lima: Comité Central del Partido Comunista del Peru), 82-88.

10. Mercado Jarrín 1969.

11. Interview with Ambassador Edwin G. Corr (former U.S. ambassador to Bolivia, El Salvador, and Peru) in Washington, D.C., April 9, 1992.

12. Interviews.

13. Interviews.

14. Interview with Ambassador Edwin G. Corr (former U.S. ambassador to El Salvador, Bolivia, and Peru), Washington, D.C., April 9, 1992.

15. Interviews.

16. Interviews; also see Jacques Maritain, 1963, *Man and the State* (Chicago: University of Chicago Press), 143-144.

17. Interviews.

18. Rogger Mercado U. 1985 and 1986.

19. Mercado U. 1985 and 1986.

20. Mercado U. 1985 and 1986.

21. Quoted in Gustavo Gorriti, 1990, "The War of the Philosopher-King," *New Republic* (June 18): 22.

22. Gorriti 1990.

23. Interviews.

24. Interviews; also see Gordon H. McCormick, 1987, "The Shining Path and Peruvian Terrorism" (Santa Monica, Calif.: Rand P-7297), 11.

25. Interviews.

26. Interviews.

27. Interviews.

28. Mercado U. 1985 and 1986.

29. Interviews.

30. Interviews; also see Simon Strong, 1992a, "Where the Shining Path Leads," *The New York Times Magazine,* May 24, 35; also see Simon Strong, 1992b, *Shining Path: Terror and Revolution in Peru* (New York: Random House), 224-259.

31. Interviews.

32. Strong 1992a, 13-17.

33. Interviews.

34. Interviews.

35. Mark S. Steinitz, 1985, "Insurgents, Terrorists, and the Drug Trade," *Washington Quarterly* (Fall): 147.

36. Interviews.

37. Interviews; and interviews with journalists Jaime de Althaus, José Gonzales, Raúl Gonzales, Gustavo Gorriti, and Alejandro Guerrero in Lima, Peru, May 24-28, 1990; interviews with General Alberto Arciniega (Ministry of Defense), General Oscar Noel Brush (former minister of the Interior), General Edgardo Mercado Jarrín and Dr. José Barsallo Burga (also a former minister of the Interior) in Lima, Peru, May 28-30, 1990.

38. Interviews.

39. "El Documento Oficial de Sendero," in Rogger Mercado U. 1985, 110.

40. Interviews.

41. Interviews.

42. Peter A. Lupsha, 1989, "Towards an Etiology of Drug Trafficking and Insurgent Relations: The Phenomenon of Narco-Terrorism," *International Journal of Comparative and Applied Criminal Justice* (Fall): 63.

43. Interviews.

44. Peter A. Lupsha, 1987, "The Role of Drugs and Drug Trafficking in the Invisible Wars," in Richard Ward and Harold Smith, eds., *International Terrorism: Operational Issues* (Chicago: University of Chicago Press), 181.

45. Interviews; and Alvin Toffler, 1990, *Powershift* (New York: Bantam Books), 159-183.

46. Interviews.

47. Interviews; and Douglas W. Payne, 1989, "The Drug 'Super State' in Latin America," *Freedom at Risk* (March-April): 7-10; Mark Rosenberg, 1988, "Narcos and Politicos: The Politics of Drug Trafficking in Honduras," *Journal of Interamerican Studies and World Affairs* (Summer/Fall): 143-165.

48. Interviews.

49. The Colombian response to the 1996 U.S. decertification provides a classic example of this.

50. Interviews.

51. Interviews.

52. United States Department of State, Bureau for International Narcotics and Law Enforcement Affairs, 1995, *International Narcotics Control Strategy Report: March, 1995* (Washington, D.C.: Department of State), xxxii and 88.

53. Interviews; also see Bruce M. Bagley, 1988a, "The New Hundred Years War? U.S. National Security and the War on Drugs in Latin America," *Journal of Interamerican Studies and World Affairs* (Spring): 161-181; 1988b, "U.S. Foreign Policy and the War on Drugs: Analysis of a Policy Failure," *Journal of Interamerican Studies and World Affairs* (Summer-Fall): 189-212; and 1988c, "Winning Battles, Losing the War: U.S. Anti-Drug Policies in Latin America," *Hemisphere* (Fall): 31.

54. Ambassador Melvyn Levitsky, Assistant Secretary of State for International Narcotics Matters, 1993, *Review of U.S. Efforts to Combat the International Narcotics Trade*, Statement before the Subcommittee on International Security, International Organizations and Human Rights of the House Foreign Affairs Committee, Washington, D.C., May 11.

55. Interviews.

IV

Changing Military World Views: The Armed Forces of South America in the 1990s

Carina Perelli and Juan Rial

Beyond Military Rule

The recent transitions to democracy that have taken place in Latin America usually have featured the armed forces of the respective countries as main actors. Only Panama and Haiti, where the military institutions were virtually destroyed by external intervention, are clear exceptions to this rule. Given that the regimes that were replaced had been dictatorial, these military forces, by commission or omission, played an important part in the process of democratic change.[1] In most cases, the military institutions negotiated the change with a variety of political organizations, usually political parties, and these culminated in an election and the installation of the new regime. As a point of comparison, in the Mediterranean, the Spanish military forces also participated in the transition process, but not as a main actor representing the withdrawing authoritarian regime. In a few exceptional cases, there was no negotiation but, rather, a retreat of the armed forces from the political scene in order to rebuild an institution that had been severely damaged by political failures and professional defeats. This is what happened in Argentina in the 1980s, which was a process that paralleled the situation in Greece in the 1970s.

In Latin America, there were no cases of transition to democracy promoted by the armed forces without prior negotiation with other political and social actors, as happened in Portugal. The "Happy Revolution" did not lead to a socialist regime but instead, after a short lapse, to progress on the road to the establishment of a liberal democracy.

Despite the differences in the transition processes in Mediterranean Europe, it should be kept in mind that these took place in a climate that encouraged their development. In effect, the European Community and the European partners of the North Atlantic Treaty Organization (NATO) were very much interested in their taking place, especially at the political, economic, and military levels. The existence of the North Atlantic military alliance provided a major incentive for military establishments to adhere to a democratic model of government.[2] In the countries of the so-called Third World, however, other kinds of difficulties arise. The armed forces do not see such clear advantages in putting an end to their role as political actors. In principle, and this is fundamental, the political systems of the developing world as a whole do not appear sufficiently stable and reliable without active military participation.

In South America, there are examples of diverse forms of change toward democratic institutionalization, but there are also instances of failure. Some cases, such as those of Brazil and Uruguay, involved lengthy negotiations. In Brazil, the "opening up" process, begun at the outset of the 1980s, only reached its culmination when the first direct presidential elections since 1962 took place in 1989.[3] In Uruguay, the military failed to obtain a popular majority to impose a new institutional order in 1980, and this opened the way to a long process of negotiations that culminated in 1984.[4] Chile was also on a long road of change, starting with the approval of a constitutional proposal in 1980, giving the appearance of movement toward civilian rule. This was followed by a monumental change that took place as a result of the 1988 plebiscite, signaling the defeat of General Augusto Pinochet. In 1989 and 1993, Patricio Aylwin and Edward Frei, candidates of a coalition of Christian Democrats and the moderate socialists,[5] won successive presidential elections. The Chilean military still retains considerable autonomy, but under President Frei its political influence has declined.

A negotiated transition also took place in Peru. This changeover involved the convocation of a constitutional assembly, an election, and the legitimation of the Alianza Popular Revolucionaria Americana (APRA) party as a full-fledged member of political society.[6] There were also negotiations between civilian political leaders and the military in Ecuador.[7] In Bolivia, the dictatorship of General Luis García Meza came to an end because of an internal split in the armed forces, which were threatened by a process of disintegration as a result of the prevailing corruption. This process opened the way for a restoration of democracy, facilitated by the links between the members of the political class and the members of the armed forces, which had been renewed following the 1952 revolution.[8] In Paraguay, moreover, the personal dictatorship of General Alfredo Stroessner ended in 1989 as a result of an internal adjustment within the armed forces and the desire for international legitimacy. This transition led to greater liberalization in the country, though the political system cannot yet be characterized as full democracy. Finally, as already indicated, no explicit negotiations were held in Argentina for the transfer of power to civilian leadership in 1982. Instead, a unilateral handing over of the reins of government by the armed forces took place following the military's disastrous defeat in the Falklands/Malvinas conflict.[9]

In Central America, relevant processes in the area of democratization have taken place in all countries. In Guatemala, the armed forces have sought ways to create regimes based on elections contested by political parties. The persistent situation of insurrection in the indigenous zones in the northern part of the country, the weakness and corruption of civilian politicians, and continued military determination to preserve their own immunities have hampered the process of democratization in this country. In Honduras, the role of the military remains substantial, in spite of the fact that the current administration of President Carlos Roberto Reina has made determined efforts to reduce it. In El Salvador, a risky experiment has been attempted: a pacification process that openly incorporates former insurgents into the political system. The military forces of El Salvador have been protagonists in this process, under the pressure of the United States, which urged that this democratization experiment be initiated. In Nicaragua, the change in political regime that took place in 1979 was reversed with the results of the 1990 election. A parallel power structure is the result: a government under the responsibility of a liberal force supported by a military under the control of the revolutionary Sandinistas. In Panama, the U.S. invasion opened a new scenario as the Panamanian Defense Force was disbanded and then recreated as the Public Force, a demilitarized national police under firm civilian control.[10]

The first big challenge faced by Latin America's armed forces after the transition period to democratic political regimes had taken place, having survived without substantial institutional changes, was how to escape the past. The crux of the problem was and remains human rights. This issue, which was promoted during the 1970s through U.S. diplomatic efforts with the intent of placing pressure on the Soviet Union, has had secondary, collateral, and very often not particularly desired or expected consequences in Latin America.

Brazil was able to dodge the human rights problem almost from the outset as the result of a provision by the military regimes that granted them amnesty. The relatively low levels of repression and the maintenance of a strong legitimacy on the part of the armed forces, along with their dominant position, made this amnesty acceptable to Brazilian society.[11] In Uruguay, a lengthy process began in 1985 with the inauguration of the Julio María Sanguinetti administration and ended in April 1989 with a plebiscite that closed the political door on this problem of human rights. However, this process of formal closure displaced the problem into other areas, including the dispute surrounding the building of social memory as a part of the national healing process to overcome the legacy of the dictatorship and repression.[12] In Argentina, the problem has had consequences that have endangered the democratic regime, which lost control of the military forces from 1987 to 1990. The attempt at settling accounts with the armed forces in the style of the judgments at Nuremburg or Tokyo — considering the chiefs of the military forces who had controlled the government between 1976 and 1982 war criminals — did not have the effects sought by the democratic administration that emerged in 1983. Instead, the attempt unleashed intense reactions that ended in 1990 with the last rebellion of the so-called *carapintadas*.[13] President Menem's administration closed the door on this legacy from the past by conceding amnesty to the former *Comandantes*.[14]

In Chile, the same issue of military impunity was conditional on General Pinochet's remaining at the head of the Chilean army. The best insurance for the Chilean military with respect to the past was the constitutional provision that stipulates that the commanders of the armed services could continue in their posts for another eight years, following the December 1989 elections. The issue, however, refuses to go away, as exemplified by the bitter 1995 conflict over the judicial decision to imprison Generals Contreras and Espinoza for their part in the murder of former foreign minister Orlando Letelier. In El Salvador, one of the principal points of the peace agreement refers to the cleansing and attrition of the armed forces. In Nicaragua, accusations of human rights violations directed against the Sandinistas remain a major point of political contention. In Guatemala, moreover, continuing issues of military impunity in the face of massive human rights violations has complicated the peace process and disrupted relations with the United States. In other countries, such as Ecuador and Peru, where civilian transitions took place early in the 1970s, the issue has not been as significant.

A comparison of Latin America's democratic transitions with those that have taken place in other parts of the world demonstrates that there is no single solution to the human rights issue. In Greece in the 1970s, those colonels most involved in human rights abuses went to prison. In Spain, where some leaders urged that it was necessary to forgive but not to forget and others urged forgiving but forgetting only selectively, an amnesty was finally reached. In Portugal in the 1970s, there was immediate punishment for members of the dictatorship's repressive apparatus and later even the hero of the revolution, Otelo Saraiva de Carvalho, went to prison for his extremist rhetoric and actions. However, the human rights issue was not as substantial a problem for these European transitions as it has been for those that have occurred more recently in Latin America.

In almost all the Latin American countries where transitions in political regimes have taken place, the question of the military forces' responsibility for their past actions has arisen. The problem has been especially relevant for the countries of the Southern Cone. The more recent the transition and the more severe the military repression, the greater the intensity surrounding this problem which, in some cases, has complicated the transition itself.

In the cases where the transitions were negotiated, the armed forces did not accept responsibility for the human rights violations committed during the dictatorial periods. They argued that emergency situations of the sort they faced, which had been qualified as war, inevitably led to excesses that should be forgotten as part of the reconciliation implied by the return to democracy.

In every Latin American nation, the problem of dealing with the past complicates progress toward a more democratic future. The dispute between ethics and political realism is resolved differently in various countries according to the degree of real political power the accused have. If they retain significant room to maneuver, it may be necessary to appeal to negotiations implying political realism in order to be able to remove an initial obstacle from the agenda of the military question. This, of course, does not resolve the deeper problem — the attitude of the armed forces regarding human rights — but it may be a first step toward addressing it. Other transitions, like the one that took place in Spain, are a positive example. At the same time, the example of punishment may not be enlightening. The Argentine military obviously was aware of what had happened in Nuremburg and Tokyo but believed that it was justified in its actions in repressing the country's armed movements. Only confidence in civil society can lead the military to move beyond a distrust of the guarantees of individual rights, which the military believes can be used to end regimes that assure its continued political influence and power.

Perceptions and Self-Perceptions of the Armed Forces

A second, closely related problem involves the legitimacy of the military institutions in Latin American countries. Polls that take into account the popularity of various institutions and corporations demonstrate that in Argentina and Uruguay the perception of the armed forces in recent years has been consistently negative. In contrast, in Andean countries, such as Bolivia and Ecuador, where no important outbreaks of violence have occurred, the image of the military is positive. Obviously, in the Southern Cone, the weight of the past is felt. In addition, the statements made during the dictatorial period by the opposition against the armed forces, which they considered a force akin to an armed political party rather than a national institution, are not yet forgotten.

In the case of the democratic transitions in the Mediterranean, the emerging image of the armed forces varied depending on their immediate past. In Portugal, the armed forces made the transition and presented themselves in a "progressive" light. In Spain, by accompanying the passage from Francoism to a democratic administration (despite a few defiant episodes including the "Tejerazo" of February 1982), the military establishment maintained legitimacy in the eyes of the population, even if it failed to arouse enthusiasm. The Greek situation was more difficult; nonetheless, in all cases, the NATO umbrella has made it possible to overcome these obstacles.

In South America two very different situations are found. One is that in Colombia and Peru, where political violence puts the question of the necessity of a professional armed force beyond any doubt. Another very different situation prevails in the countries where political violence does not exist or where it is relatively controllable by interior security forces (police or paramilitary corps). On the other hand, the Central American countries that were at war throughout the 1980s are now experiencing a new situation of controlled violence. In Guatemala, for example, the insurgency drags on. Elsewhere, an uneasy peace is threatened by rising levels of violent crime.

For vast sectors of the public and a large part of the political class in Latin America, a world without wars between nations would seem to make the existence of the armed forces superfluous. Particularly among the middle and upper-middle classes, these professional military corps, whose role is to exercise legal violence, are perceived with a high degree of distrust. However, it would be too risky to believe that a country could do without armed forces. Even Costa Rica has had to create a repressive apparatus, though this force lacks the professional organizational form of an army. In addition, at increasing rates, private security organizations are absorbing police tasks in the countries of the region.

Reestablishing or even rebuilding the public image of the armed forces is a substantial task that must be promoted by political parties, the educated elites, and all those interested in the stabilization of democracy. The alternative implies eliminating the existing military forces. In principle, this does not seem possible since there are no historic examples of armed forces that have "committed suicide." One possibility is to neutralize these institutions, by means of a new force created by a new political regime, a remote scenario in most Latin American countries today. Another possibility replaces existing armed forces with armed gangs loyal to war lords. Neither is realistic nor desirable.

Changing World Contexts

The advent of the 1990s finds the armed forces in each Latin American nation endeavoring to adjust to an institutional system whose rationale and legitimation is based on different criteria from the past. A task that is difficult enough in itself has been made even more complex by the profound changes that have taken place internationally and regionally. These changes mandate the emergence of new global game rules and redefinition of the mission of the military in peripheral countries, such as those of Latin America.

The disappearance of a world conceived in bipolar terms; the defeat of "Marxist socialism" as a genuine alternative; the emergence, in economic and communications terms, of a "global village" superimposed upon an increasingly fragmented political whole; the advent of a "Fortress Europe" bent on internal unification but increasingly entrenched behind borders that are beleaguered by new waves of non-European migration; and the emergence of the United States as the victorious hegemonic power intent on imposing a *pax americana* upon the world, while struggling with internal difficulties that are beginning to be viewed as real security problems — all have shattered the alliances of a world in which conflicts were defined in terms of East and West blocs.

The cataclysm that overtook the Eastern bloc signified much more than an ideological victory for the West. For the first time in the twentieth century, particularly since the end of World War II, the West has no clear, common enemy. With the disappearance of the concept of the West (or, to use a less radical expression, with the advent of the idea that the West has been diminished by its very triumph), the countries of Latin America[15] have lost a political space that had served as the point of reference for their multilateral relations since the First World War. This also signifies the end of a sense of identity that encompassed the armed forces of all the countries involved in the struggle against a common enemy. This idea of a Western "we" was particularly important to the region's armed forces, as it placed them in the same camp as the countries and military institutions from whom they took their lead and partial identity as bulwarks of anticommunism.

The collapse of communism has also led to the enthronement of the United States as the unquestioned global military power, imposing its will either by force (hard power) or by pressure, persuasion, dissuasion, or admiration (soft power). In Latin America, soft-power initiatives have included, at the hemispheric level, the Enterprise for the Americas and the proposed demilitarization of the region as well as pressure on Latin American governments to place issues such as the fight against narcotrafficking, legislation on intellectual property rights, and changes in computer technology policy on their political agendas.

The 1991 Gulf War and its aftermath demonstrated that the United States was prepared to dispatch its legions to impose a *pax americana*. It proved, fairly conclusively, that no Third World army is capable of challenging the technological might that the nations of the advanced world can muster when sufficient political will and consensus exist. The 1982 Falklands/Malvinas War was undoubtedly an important antecedent; yet, the fact that it was limited to a military conflict in a sparsely populated region meant that its global significance was much less clear.

In short, the collapse of the Eastern Bloc and the demise of the Soviet Union signified the end of certainty. In some cases, new specters have emerged to replace communism as the enemy. Some of these specters — such as the rebirth of ethnic nationalism in Europe — only impact Latin America tangentially. Others, such as the growing awareness of the threat of ecological disaster, affect the region directly. In every case, however, the change of direction and the revolution in global power relations call for a repositioning of the actors involved. For Latin America's armed forces, the change is even more complex, given the profound shifts that are taking place in the region.

While the map of Eastern Europe is becoming more and more fragmented, Latin America seems to be bent on realizing its old dreams of integration. The shift in U.S. policy toward the region has already had one result: the establishment of a free trade zone among the United States, Canada, Mexico, and, in the near future, Chile. After often having acted in the international political arena as the champion of the Latin American cause, Mexico's focus of interest has now switched to the North American continent. As Mexico's armed forces attempt to assimilate their nation's integration with a country hitherto defined as their great historical enemy, they will have to come to terms with an existential crisis as serious as that facing many of the region's other militaries.

The North American Free Trade Agreement (NAFTA) is being paralleled by other efforts toward economic integration throughout the region. Argentina, Brazil, Paraguay, and Uruguay signed the Treaty of Asunción to create the Southern Common Market (Mercado Común del Sur, MERCOSUR), which calls for the establishment of a free trade zone leading, in stages, to a so-called "zero tariff." Chile has signed an agreement with Mexico for the progressive reduction of import tariffs and is seeking membership in both NAFTA and MERCOSUR. Mexico has negotiated free trade agreements with several Central American nations. These movements toward regional integration are taking place at a time when Latin America is experiencing important economic recovery after years of stagnation.

Movement toward regional economic integration will contribute to a significant reevaluation of the role of the armed forces and perceived threats to security throughout Latin America. The implementation of integration treaties brings into question old conceptualizations of traditional conflicts among neighboring countries. If these agreements are successful and permanent supranational institutions develop, a debate concerning what types of armed forces and defense policies are called for under such new conditions will become inevitable.

This significant movement toward integration is not the only regional process currently underway that will impact the future role of Latin America's armed forces, however. Accused by neoliberals of having grown fat but not strong, the region's old interventionist and welfare states are under attack from a number of sides. A wave of privatization has already chipped away at many state functions and powers. This movement, furthermore, is being implemented in conjunction with public expenditure cuts and fiscal deficit reductions, unavoidable conditions for renegotiation of the external debt. Structural adjustment processes and the deregulation of economic activity especially impact the subordinate and dependent sectors of formerly preeminent state structures.

As far as security is concerned, a debate on defense policies and law and order — even though often not explicitly articulated — takes place each time budgetary issues are discussed in Latin American countries. A consensus exists on the need for professional forces to maintain law and order and curb growing urban violence, despite the fact that public expenditure cuts often mean security forces are not assigned sufficient resources and that the police forces carrying out this task lack credibility, due to widespread corruption and their lack of professional training and equipment.

In addition, the very existence of the armed forces is often questioned by political and social sectors that view them as a drain on the state coffers of countries hard pressed to find the resources needed to meet other, more urgent needs. Indeed, the meager resources available for national budgets and the multiplicity of demands made on the state mean that, even in countries where such radical criticisms are not leveled against the military, the authorities find themselves forced to divert resources originally earmarked for defense. Military expenditure is usually allocated and cuts in defense budgets are generally made without any discussion of an issue regarded as taboo: the real purpose of Latin America's armed forces.

The military institutions that emerged in the wake of the democratic transition processes were, and to some extent still are, anomalous political actors. Their independence is never called into question, nor is their capacity for generating the violence on which that independence is based. As an independent actor that regards itself historically as the founder of the nation and the ultimate incarnation of the state, the military defines its destiny as indissolubly linked to that of the nation it serves. The armed forces still believe that they have to intervene whenever the nation they serve is under threat (real or perceived).

However, the armed forces constitute a political actor that is unable to secure sufficient legitimacy within the liberal democratic system that Latin American republics use to legitimate their political regimes. This role is not compatible with the professional standards of military organizations in the First World. As a result of this twofold contradiction, the region's militaries occupy an ambiguous place in the political system: they cannot be openly acknowledged as political actors by the other actors involved without violating the principles of the liberal democratic system, nor can they identify themselves as such without introducing a strong cognitive dissonance regarding the accepted definition of the professional role of the military. Notwithstanding, firmly they stand — latent, feared, and often regarded as the sword of Damocles. Therefore, while budget reductions are a fact of life as far as adjustment policies are concerned, they are also used by governments as an indirect means of curbing the military's power. In extreme cases, budget cuts can give rise to an erosion of the armed forces' power through the starvation of resources.

Unexpected support for this policy of curbing the power of the military as an independent actor is coming from the United States, which is promoting demilitarization as part of its policy aimed at stabilizing the region. The identity crisis being experienced by many senior-ranking Latin American military officers stems in large measure from their fear that their traditional ally has turned on its one-time associates and wishes now to convert them into a militarized police force, limiting their activities to the suppression of narcotrafficking, narcoterrorism, and environmental defense.

The issue of environmental defense is particularly sensitive as far as relations between some Latin American countries and the First

World are concerned. Environmental protection is an explosive problem for the military organizations responsible for the defense of national territory and sovereignty. The proposed internationalization of Amazonia as an ecological reserve of humanity, attempts to use the territory of some countries in the region as dumps for First World trash or toxic waste that nobody wants, and pressures to halt the development of nuclear technology in the region are only some of the most publicized issues regarded as serious encroachments on the sovereignty of Latin American states.

The ecological issue is not the only one in which U.S. interference in Latin America is evident, however. The invasion of Panama, the collapse of the Eastern Bloc, and the fragmentation of Yugoslavia and the Soviet empire all appear to herald a new era in which the United States — and First World nations in general[16] — feel that they have a right to intervene openly in the internal politics of countries that, in the First World's view, could create problems for regional or world security. Other less violent forms of interference — such as the pressure brought to bear by embassies for the enactment or repeal of certain laws that affect economic interests[17] or the demand for free access to resources as a non-negotiable counterpart to market access for products — have become an ongoing rather than an occasional feature of international relations.

Not all Latin American nations respond to foreign interference, particularly U.S. interference, in the same way. The response of most countries ranges somewhere between the positions of Argentina and Brazil. The Argentine stance assumes that since Argentina has no other choice but dependence, the country's best bet is to increase its dependence to the point where it actually becomes the spokesperson for the hegemonic power in the region. To some extent, this position could be summed up as follows: only by being truly dependent will Argentina become prosperous and able to enjoy some measure of freedom and hope.[18] Brazil's position calls for both controlled confrontation with the North — in particular the United States — and the attainment of supremacy in the region. To cite an historical analogy, its aim is to restate the *barganha leal*[19] that would allow Brazil to become the region's interlocutor with the developed world.

It is in this context that the issue of the existential crisis[20] among Latin American armed forces should be addressed. This crisis is manifested in a profound reexamination of the hitherto "natural" military identity and ethos, a restatement of the very essence of the professional role by the most lucid analysts, a generalized uneasiness or malaise among the officer corps and even non-commissioned officers, and the abandonment of the military profession by many of its most dynamic and promising members.

Changing Military Missions

If the need for military forces is accepted, the next challenge is to define the roles that should be fulfilled by these forces and the missions that are proper to these institutions. This substantive discussion has not taken place in the countries of Latin America. As has been noted, part of the population, a significant number of the political leaders at the local level, many technobureaucrats of international organizations, and some decisionmakers of the big powers of the First World believe that the armed forces are of little use because classical war no longer exists and they have no desirable role to play in society. Military forces consume significant resources from national budgets and do not produce goods or provide services readily identified as necessary or at least desired. This situation aggravates the delegitimization of the military institutions.

The question of the uselessness of military forces has been posed in tangential ways in many Latin American countries by political groups, the press, and intellectuals. For example, demands for the elimination of compulsory military service, without providing for the creation of a totally professional force,[21] is one of the ways this is done. Another way is the call for profound changes in military education or training. This demand is inappropriate, especially when made without a full knowledge of internal military operations and dogma and without pointing out plausible and appropriate alternative models for a military force.

Many in the region's militaries feel that what lies behind such demands is a desire to neutralize the effectiveness of the military machine and, if possible, destroy it. Of course, many of those who pose these demands have no such purposes in mind. Nonetheless, their lack of knowledge of the peculiarities of the military world leads them to accentuate their positions when they are met with resistance on the part of members of the military establishment.

When there is talk of "reinserting," "reintegrating," or "integrating" the armed forces in society, terms considered "aggressive" by many members of the armed forces, a similar phenomenon also arises. The questioning of the very values of the institution — of Morris Janowitz's "heroic model" and Charles Moskos' "institutional" model — makes discussion between military and nonmilitary actors difficult.[22]

However, the Latin American military forces have not undergone the substantial organizational change that would make them a complex occupational organization, in Moskos's terms. Although members of the military elite admit that a large part of the future armed forces will have the characteristics of an occupational organization, they cannot passively accept forms of discourse that tend to undermine the basis for legitimacy of the military by draining it in terms of organization and missions. By involving the armed forces in nonmilitary activities that range from highway construction to various forms of community support — known in earlier military jargon as civic action and now called "nation building" in the jargon used by the United States — an attempt has been made to gain acceptance for the role of the military as a useful contributor to society. This is a tacit admission of society's criticism regarding the uselessness of the military establishment.

Given that the great majority of Latin Americans believe that classical wars have become obsolete in the region, the military establishment's fundamental problem starts with an apparent lack of a credible mission. Although a half-century has gone by since the last big global conflagration, violence has not decreased but, instead, has taken on new forms. The problem is how to combat violence, and within this framework, the question is whether classical armed forces are a good instrument. The region's military forces approach the 1990s with lacunae in their doctrines as well as in their definition of mission.

For U.S. political decisionmakers (not to imply that the U.S. military holds the same opinion), the country's national security interests in Latin America focus on economic growth and stability. This economic approach to the region is sustained in the vision that drugs and ecological problems are the most important threats. Among the challenges that might require military force, U.S. Department of Defense studies cite terrorism, insurgency, regional and ethnic conflicts, and drug trafficking.[23] For the U.S. military, fighting insurgency means facing low-intensity disturbances; for the Latin American military, on the other hand, it is a question of high-intensity conflicts, inasmuch as these consume practically all available resources and jeopardize the stability and continued existence of affected countries' economic, social, and political systems. Insurgency, for the Latin American military, is not a peripheral conflict; it is often *the* conflict.

Nowadays, however, the principal form assumed by insurrection is armed propaganda and terrorism, whose confrontation requires only an intelligence service and police forces. The contradictions between the interests of Latin America's chief military ally, the United States, and those of its own armed forces are expressed in many different ways. One fundamental difference has been the involvement of the region's armed forces in the drug problem.[24] Also to be taken into account in considering the Latin American military's future missions are the accelerated changes occurring in these societies. Since the 1970s, when Jean François Lyotard,[25] in submitting a report to the government of Quebec, referred to the emergence of a postmodern culture — that is, to the acceleration of the heterogeneity of societies, more evident among the younger generations — the armed forces have had to exist within societies that are difficult to integrate. This produces problems not only in recruitment[26] and in the administration of military obligations but also in the identification of a type of social order that would be feasible for this new society. History is of little help at a time of rapid change and new situations. However, in Latin America, the processes of change are slower; thus, problems and solutions can still be framed within established models.

During the 1990s, the Latin American military establishments face the challenge of designing a mission that is acceptable and credible to the societies and political elites of their countries. This mission should be a military one: the capacity to use violence in response to any adverse contingency, be it external or internal. However, to be accepted, this mission for the military must have more precise guidelines. This issue, which will be the dominant theme of civil-military relations for the coming decade, must be addressed at the political as well as the technical levels.

Material, Human, and Financial Resources

The acceleration of technological change has made it necessary for the military to compete in order to maintain the appearance of having modern forces. One way of maintaining legitimacy for the military is to preserve the technological credibility of the organization. The accelerated rate of change in electronics, transportation equipment, and weapons systems technologies leads to rapid obsolescence of equipment. Latin America's armed forces are faced with a situation in which the military and paramilitary equipment acquired through large investments from the 1970s through the mid-1980s is already obsolete. Expensive equipment — aircraft, ships, and armored vehicles — must be updated in order to improve navigation, weapons and communication systems, and the like. For large countries, modernization is a key issue. For small countries, it is important, though resources are scant.

As the twenty-first century approaches, most military equipment will have a useful life span of less than a decade. In the present period of economic crises and lack of financial resources throughout Latin America, one of the most important challenges becomes the local production of arms and equipment. The possibilities for local production are not very good, however, except for a few of the large and medium-sized countries that can produce certain materiel, such as portable arms and munitions, in limited quantities. Furthermore, experience indicates that domestic factories, even in large countries, cannot survive without exporting their production. In a world where conflicts between states have diminished or ceased, the opportunity for profitable arms sales has also dropped. For example, the end of the Iran-Iraq conflict has led to declines in the military industries of Brazil and Chile. Military industries throughout Latin America thus face a troubling period. U.S. pressures to prevent any attempts to produce high technology weapons of mass destruction have further blocked possibilities for additional development of the region's military industry. Since it is unthinkable for the region's small countries to have their own military industries, the problem of technological obsolescence necessarily implies thinking about how to reequip militaries every few years and at a very high cost that is difficult for such countries to afford.

Furthermore, resource problems confronting Latin American militaries are not restricted to equipment but include personnel problems. The military profession no longer enjoys the prestige it once had. Members of the upper strata of society are rarely present in the officer corps. In turn, at the lower ranks — in civilian terms, "labor" — compulsory military service systems fail to yield good results. Enlisted personnel come from the lower class sectors of the population and very often lack the physical or intellectual preparation appropriate for the current requirements of an armed force.

A predominantly institutional model of military force prevails in all of Latin America. Although Latin American militaries include sectors made up of personnel under contract for fixed terms (or in the case of Uruguay, a force made up entirely of contracted volunteers), the basis for the institution lies not in occupational values but in the traditional values related to honor, military spirit, and esprit de corps. Despite changes in society that make it more difficult to maintain the integration of the military forces along traditional lines, there are few meaningful discussions between military elites and members of the political class regarding the possibility of establishing national services or promoting the best way to recruit and train military personnel.

The only occasion for discussing these problems tends to arise in the context of determining the national budget, when the military question is discussed largely from the political point of view. Normally, such discussions entail an initial stage of talks at the government level between the military command and the ministries of defense and economy followed by discussions at the parliamentary level. Nevertheless, these discussions tend to focus on the overall budget figure; they rarely address the suitability of that figure for defense and military policies and for the programs to carry them out. Of course, at times of crises, there are certain limits that are difficult to exceed. Even if the needs are great, it is difficult to surpass 2 percent of the gross domestic product (GDP) in allocations to the military forces, except in emergency situations and even then only for short lapses. In the near future, the pressures exerted by the techno-politicians of the multilateral agencies such as the World Bank or the Inter-American Development Bank (IDB) could lead to further substantial reductions in military budgets. The adoption of a budget based on plans and programs necessarily obliges the civilian elites to have a knowledge of the subjects under discussion, and this is one of the challenges to be faced in the 1990s.

Civil-Military Relations

Following the transition to democracy, the majority of the political elites attempted to remove the military question from the public agenda. Initially, this would seem to be a very appropriate attitude, but putting it into practice has often translated into trying to forget about the military. Attempts have been made to shut the militaries into an institutional ghetto, to keep them satisfied in their demands for resources by negotiating a budget, and to neutralize them as a political actor. This has been a persistent form of operation on the part of Latin American elites throughout the twentieth century. Control of the military establishment by governments takes on the subjective form that was pointed out some time ago by Samuel Huntington: trustworthy officers are sought for the key posts in the command of the armed forces.[27]

To establish dialogue between political leaders and military officers regarding the aforementioned problems is difficult. A climate of distrust persists between civilian and military elites. The military contends, and not unreasonably, that civilians are not familiar with military problems and do not show much interest in the subject, while civilians argue that the military is seeking to gain influence at the political level. Nevertheless, the crisis of legitimacy that affects some of the armed forces of Latin America, combined with the dangers posed by a rupture in the social order, make it necessary to find some way to improve civil-military relations.

In order to meet the challenges of the end of the century, formulating proposals for change, first of all, requires time for discussion and for the implementation of reforms. Often it is necessary to wait for favorable circumstances. In most Latin American countries, this dialogue was not feasible when regime transitions were taking place, even though at such times it may have been easier to accept major changes, be they in civil-military relations; in recruitment, training, deployment, and professional standards; or in the allocation of resources, taking into account the new organizational guidelines. Nevertheless, opportunities always exist, especially at the beginning of new administrations, provided that urgencies in other areas do not cause the problem to be relegated to an indefinite future for resolution.

Second, the formulation of proposals for change requires a closed and highly informal context for discussion. A context that is too open and public can lead to proposals that are naive, willful, or lacking in true viability. Only after accords are reached should they be presented in the public context for discussion, notably at the parliamentary level, should their implementation require legal action.

Regarding this last point, two kinds of norms should be taken into account: those that refer to the professional organization of the military career[28] and others that imply specific relationships between the military establishment and the rest of the government and the political system. Specific guarantees for both the political system and the military should be detailed and leave no room for doubt. On the other hand, those norms related to more general political problems (which imply definitions regarding the use of military force in circumstances for which it is impossible to have full information in advance) should be ambiguous in their wording. What is most important, however, is to avoid over-legislating. The majority of the norms implemented will be resolutions by the executive branch or by the military institution itself. They should, in fact, be based on effective control, which implies the involvement of a civil elite in military problems and confidence on the part of the civilian and military sectors in their reciprocal tasks.

The military faces the hostility or the neglect of civilians who regard even the present meager military pay as excessive. This hostility is often inversely proportional to the fear that the institution inspires or inspired. Increasingly, Latin American militaries are asked to justify their demands (a roundabout way of asking them to justify their very existence) in the face of more pressing needs in the health, education, housing, and social security sectors.

Despite this, in many parts of Latin America, members of the military still perceive themselves as belonging to a coherent, well-integrated institution with its own doctrines, in sharp contrast to a fragmented society and a state in the process of being dismembered. In other words, they see themselves as members of one of the few stable organizations in the region. For the current generation of middle-ranking and junior officers, non-commissioned officers, and cadets at military academies, this paradoxical situation has become the frame of reference that determines attitudes and molds ordinary behavior.

According to Richard Millett,[29] due to their financial needs and the hostility they face, Latin American militaries often resort to a strategy similar to that of a living organism subjected to hypothermia; they gradually abandon their peripheral functions in order to preserve their nerve centers and those functions and values essential to the body's survival. The institution thus ensures its continued existence, even at the cost of losing certain parts of the organization that have to be sacrificed for the rest to survive.

For such attempts at survival to be successful, however, each branch of the military as well as the options faced must be carefully weighed. Also included in this process must be a sweeping review of the value system that underpins the military's operations. Introspection of this kind, by its very nature, leads to serious self-questioning and existential crises. In an institution composed of different cohorts and generations, this introspection becomes particularly painful due to the different expectations and motivations of the various groups. Coexistence among these military groups is also hindered by the difficulty of negotiating solutions within a formal institution that makes a virtue of verticality.

In addition to the militaries' loss of domestic power and respect, many officers fear that the disappearance of a common enemy may lead to a "balkanization" of military institutions. In a situation of this kind, the collective struggle becomes fragmented, provincialized, and regionalized; the organizations involved lose the common links that once bound them together. Some resort to technocratic arguments in defining the characteristics of this "hypothermic" force. In their view, Latin American military institutions should devote their efforts to raising professional standards — including the ability to handle the latest technologies — so as to equip themselves for the tasks they were designed to perform: the dissuasion of conventional enemies and the maintenance of order. Given the inevitability of cutbacks, this could mean a reduction in the establishment's overall size, but this measure would be offset by the higher quality of its members. This, in turn, would enhance the prospects for inserting retired military personnel into the civilian labor market.

Nevertheless, even allowing for a reduction in the size of the organization, this alternative is expensive in economic, human, and political terms. The combination of a lack of resources and U.S. pressures has forced many militaries to accept unwillingly, and with more than a little resentment, new functions such as combatting narcotrafficking. This particular task is regarded by many militaries as a job for the police. Moreover, most members of the military feel that such activities expose the institution to the inevitable danger of corruption and internal division. In justifying this view, they cite factors such as the enormous resources at the disposal of drug traffickers, the meager salaries paid to military personnel, and the sharp contrast between units engaged in combatting drug trafficking with expensive, U.S.-supplied equipment and others performing traditional tasks with almost no resources. This could lead to the undermining of what the military generally regard as the essence of military values: a long tradition of upholding values such as honor, esprit de corps, obedience, and discipline.

A new era is dawning. In Latin America, the military as a profession is at a crossroads. A series of alternatives are opening up. Some advocate the dissolution of an institution that, like the dinosaur, has fulfilled its purpose. This would leave Latin America's republics at the mercy of the hemispheric hegemonic power. Others have adopted a more dangerous attitude; fearing what might happen if the armed forces were to be abolished, they simply leave them to sort out their own problems while at the same time reducing their budgets. The organization is being allowed to bleed to death but is struggling — desperately and to the end — to avoid this fate. Besides deepening the existential crisis in the institution, this strategy could produce major conflicts. After all, and this cannot be stressed too much, no organization voluntarily commits suicide.

Others support the thesis that the military should evolve into a militarized police force. This alternative combines the drawbacks of both the previous strategies, and, in many cases, it is rejected and resisted even more strongly by many officers. Finally, there is the option of integration, the coordination of forces that would operate in a regional setting, tackling common problems such as the ecological defense of Latin America, the suppression of drug trafficking and narcoterrorism, the control of fishing in ocean regions over which the country exercises sovereignty, and the sharing of equipment and training. This alternative would give the military a dignified role to play, insert it into a regional context, and oblige all the institutions involved to raise their technical-professional standards.

At present, all these possibilities are open. The decision as to which course to follow rests with Latin America's politicians, but it is also contingent upon the existence of an international climate sensitive to the region's problems and supportive of their resolution.

Notes

1. On military regimes and armed forces, see David Collier, ed., 1979, *The New Authoritarianism in Latin America* (Princeton: Princeton University Press); Juan Linz and Alfred Stepan, eds., 1978, *The Breakdown of Democratic Regimes* (Baltimore: Johns Hopkins University Press); Guillermo O'Donnell, 1972, *Modernización y autoritarismo* (Buenos Aires: Paidós) and 1982, *El estado burocrático-autoritario 1966-1973; Triunfos, derrotas y crisis* (Buenos Aires: Universidad de Belgrano); Manuel A. Garretón, 1983, *El proceso político chileno* (Santiago: FLACSO); and Manuel Antonio Garretón, ed., 1984, *Dictaduras y democratización* (Santiago: FLACSO).

2. See Enrique Baloyra, ed., 1987, *Comparing New Democracies; Transition and Consolidation in Mediterranean Europe and the Southern Cone* (Boulder: Westview Press); Fernando Enrique Cardoso, et al., 1985, *Los límites de la democracia*, 2 vols. (Buenos Aires: CLACSO); Guillermo O'Donnell, Philippe Schmitter, and Laurence Whitehead, 1986, *Transitions from Authoritarian Rule: Comparative Perspectives* (Baltimore: Johns Hopkins University Press); and Julián Santamaría, ed., 1982, *Transición a la democracia en el Sur de Europa y América Latina* (Madrid: CIS).

3. Bolivar Lamounier, 1988, "Democratización a través de elecciones," *Opciones* (Santiago) No. 14; Guillermo O'Donnell and Fabio Wanderley Reis, eds., 1988, *A democracia no Brasil-Dilemas e perspetivas* (São Paulo: Vértice).

4. Luis E. González, 1983, "An Unexpected Opening," in *Latin American Research Review* 18: 3; and Juan Rial, 1988, "Transición hacia la democracia y gobernabilidad 1985-1988" in *Pensamiento Iberoamericano* (Madrid: ICI-ECLAC), No. 14.

5. Manuel Antonio Garretón, 1988, "El plebiscito de 1988 y la transición a la democracia," *Cuadernos de difusión* (Santiago: FLACSO) and Carlos Hunneus, 1987, "El efecto boomerang de la Constitución de 1980," *Política y espíritu* (September).

6. Luis Pásara and Jorge Parodi, 1988, *Democracia, sociedad y gobierno en el Perú* (Lima: Cedys); Henry Pease García, 1981, "Del reformismo militar a la democracia tutelada" in *América Latina 80: Democracia y movimiento popular* (Lima: Desco).

7. Nelson Argones, 1981, *El juego de poder; De Rodríguez Lara a Febres Cordero* (Quito: CEN) and Catherine Conaghan, 1985, "Democracy by Attrition: Parties, Civil Society and Political Order in Ecuador," (Quito: mimeo).

8. James Malloy and Eduardo Gamarra, 1987, "The Transition to Democracy in Bolivia," in James Malloy and Mitchell Selligson, eds., *Authoritarians and Democrats: The Politics of Regime Transition in Latin America* (Pittsburgh: University of Pittsburgh Press). Also see René A. Mayorga, 1986, "Democratización y modernización del estado: El caso de Bolivia," *CLACSO/UNDP/RCA*, 86/001.

9. José Nun and Juan C. Portantiero, eds., 1988, *Ensayos sobre la transición democrática en Argentina* (Buenos Aires: Punto Sur).

10. See Edelberto Torres Rivas, ed., 1987, *La democracia posible* (San José: Educa); and 1988, "Centroamérica: Democracia de baja intensidad," *Pensamiento Iberoamericano*, 14. On the U.S. effort in Nicaragua, see Max G. Manwaring and Court

Prisk, 1988, *El Salvador at War: An Oral History* (Washington, D.C.: National Defense University Press).

11. *Brasil nunca mais* (São Paulo, 1988). An English version is also available, translated by Joan Dassin.

12. Juan Rial, et al., *El referendum uruguayo* (San José: CAPEL) and Carina Perelli and Juan Rial, 1986, *De mitos y memorias políticas. La represión, el miedo y después* (Montevideo: EBO).

13. The "carapintadas" are a military faction that opposed President Alfonsín's efforts to reduce military budgets and hold officers accountable for human rights abuses and other crimes. Their name (painted faces or carapintadas) comes from the camouflage makeup they wore during the coup attempts. There were three against Alfonsín beginning in 1987 and one in 1990 against President Menem. Menem offered initial pardons to the carapintadas in October 1989, then extended this at the end of 1990 to most remaining officers. But those who participated in the December 1990 uprising against him were jailed until 1992.

14. The 1989 and 1990 pardons conceded by President Menem put an end to the investigations of most of the officers of the armed forces, members of the police force, and the Montonero leaders for human rights violations and political crimes. Amnesty was also granted to the military, which under the command of Lieutenant Colonel Rico had revolted and called for recognition of the military action implemented as of 1976. The next step was the release of the Military Junta members who were brought to trial beginning in January 1984, including former presidents Lieutenant General Jorge R. Videla, the notorious Admiral Emilio Massera, and the historical leader of the Montoneros, Mario Firmenich.

15. This region was defined by the European political scientist and ambassador Alain Rouquié as "the Far West" in the same sense one talks about the "Far East." See Alain Rouquié, 1987, *Amerique Latine: Introduction a l'Extreme Occident* (Paris: Du Seuil).

16. To give but one example, Spanish Foreign Minister Francisco Fernández Ordóñez was reported by the Spanish newspaper *Tribuna* on September 30, 1991, as stating, "Fortunately, the idea of noninterference in the internal affairs of other countries is being discarded."

17. This is the case of legislation on pharmaceutical patents and computer technology, to mention only two of the most sensitive current issues.

18. Rather frivolously, the Argentine Minister of Foreign Affairs stated in 1991 that his country's policy vis-à-vis the United States should be "of a carnal nature" and, if necessary, "abject."

19. Term coined by Golbery do Couto e Silva (1967), in his book *Geopolítica do Brasil* (Rio de Janeiro: Jose Olympio), to characterize the constant negotiating between the United States and Brazil involving haggling over positions.

20. This term was coined by the Brazilian Admiral Fernando Ferreira Vidigal.

21. At present, totally professional forces exist only in the Dominican Republic (created after the disbanding of the Guard in 1965) and Uruguay. On Uruguay, see Carina Perelli and Juan Rial, 1992, "Uruguay: Una fuerza militar de profesionales," *Peitho, Documentos de Trabajo #88* (Montevideo: Peitho).

22. Morris Janowitz, 1960, *The Professional Soldier: A Social and Political Portrait* (New York: Free Press) and Charles Moskos, 1978, "From Institution to Occupation: Trends in Military Organization," in *Armed Forces and Society* 4.

23. See U. S. Department of Defense, 1991, "Primer for Inter-American Cooperation" (Preliminary Draft), July.

24. On the ambivalent meaning of cocaine production and trafficking, very different positions can be found in the books by Fabio Castillo, 1987, *Los jinetes de la cocaína* (Bogotá: Documentos Periodísticos), who condemns and urges strong actions against drug traffickers, and by Mario Arango, 1988, *Impacto del narcotráfico en Antioquía* (Medellín: published by the author), who favors legalizing drugs. On the relationship with Colombian guerrillas, see Alfredo Molano, 1987, *Selva Adentro* (Bogotá: published by the author).

25. Jean François Lyotard, 1984, *La condición postmoderna; Informe sobre el saber* (Madrid: Cátedra).

26. See Juan Rial, 1992, "The Recruitment of the Officers Corps and the Problems of Stability of Democracy. A View from South America," Report to the United States Institute of Peace (Montevideo).

27. Samuel Huntington, 1957, *The Soldier and the State* (Cambridge: Harvard University Press).

28. As an example of study on the subject, see Juan Rial, 1992, *Estructura legal de las Fuerzas Armadas del Uruguay; Un análisis político* (Montevideo: Ciesu-PEITHO).

29. Verbal statement made during a meeting in Washington, D.C., in 1991.

V

The Regional Security System (RSS)

Gary Brana-Shute

T he RSS does not pretend to have the capacity to deter
or defeat any large-scale foreign aggression. . . .
Should such an attack take place, a substantial
outside support would be essential. . . . The RSS can be
likened to an insurance policy. . . .[1]

Historical Overview

T he independent states of the Eastern Caribbean, known collectively as the Organization of Eastern Caribbean States (OECS), are
all former British colonies, and until gaining independence, their
security and defense needs were the responsibility of the United
Kingdom.[2] With independence, each assumed responsibility for its own
security and defense requirements. However, these local, island-specific
political transformations coincided with two larger regional and international currents that led to a modification of country-specific and U.S.
policy definitions of Caribbean defense and security arrangements.[3]

The perceived political and economic instability produced by the
gradual withdrawal of Britain from the region was interpreted by U.S.
policymakers under Presidents Jimmy Carter and Ronald Reagan as a
strategic vacuum in the Caribbean area. The Cold War was in full force,
and concern over Soviet- and Cuban-led destabilization and, in the
case of Grenada, outright military involvement was inflamed further by
both extraregional and internal Caribbean political-military move-

ments. There were civil wars in Nicaragua and El Salvador. Jamaica lurched to the left in the opening years of the 1970s. The New Jewel Movement coup in Grenada in 1979 was the first in the English-speaking Caribbean and would lead to U.S. military action. Allegations of Soviet combat troops in Cuba in 1979, although not a surprise, were a concern. The general unreliability and vulnerability of the Duvalier regime in Haiti continued, and uncertainty arose over the degree of democratic consolidation in the Dominican Republic. The destruction of the Cubana Airlines flight out of Barbados and the strafing of Bahamian fishing vessels by Cuban warplanes in the late 1970s smacked of terrorism. Two mercenary attempts to overthrow the government of Barbados, three military coup attempts in Dominica, a dissident riot in Union Island of St. Vincent and the Grenadines, the continuing flirtation of Guyana's President Forbes Burnham with Cuban and Soviet diplomatic envoys, and the 1980 military coup in Suriname were all evidence of discontent and vulnerability.[4]

When asked what it would require to overthrow an Eastern Caribbean mini-state, Prime Minister Eugenia Charles of Dominica coolly replied to President Reagan, "Ten men in a leaky old boat." Not as exaggerated as it initially sounded, this warning prompted U.S. policymakers to staunch what they perceived to be a growing Marxist menace throughout the region. The Department of State and the Pentagon formulated a strategic defense policy that placed regional issues within an East-West global framework.[5] An ultimate result was the creation of the Regional Security System (RSS), the organization formed to provide for security and defense of the Eastern Caribbean and Barbados member states.[6] The RSS is governed by a Memorandum of Understanding (MOU) signed in October 1982 by the prime ministers of Antigua and Barbuda, Barbados, Dominica, St. Vincent and the Grenadines, and by St. Lucia in November 1982. Since the signing of the original document, Grenada and St. Kitts and Nevis have also become signatories. Requests for defense or intervention assistance are made to, and must be approved by, the RSS Council of Ministers, which consists of the prime ministers of each of the seven member states and the RSS coordinator. If the request is agreed to without dissent, an appropriate response is implemented.

Although the RSS was implemented "as a trip wire to prevent any more Grenadas,"[7] its broader missions include providing for the security and defense of member states against both internal and external threats, a capacity for maritime search and rescue operations, capabilities for disaster relief, increased immigration control, expanded fisheries protection, upgraded smuggling prevention, improved pollution control, and, what is increasingly the major goal, narcotics interdiction and eradication. RSS forces are a mix of regular military personnel from states with a National Defense Force (Barbados and Antigua and Barbuda) and paramilitary police forces (Special Services Units — SSUs) from countries with only a police or constabulary force. A Central Liaison Office, manned by a small, permanent staff of officers from cooperating countries, coordinates RSS activities. RSS headquarters is located near Barbados Defense Force (BDF) headquarters in Bridgetown, Barbados, and is coordinated by the chief of staff of the BDF.[8]

The deployment and operational tasks of the RSS to date have consisted of annual marine, air, and army exercises with RSS signatories and, increasingly, with allied English-speaking countries of the region. RSS units augmented security support in the aftermath of the U.S. invasion of Grenada in 1983.[9] In 1986, RSS units provided a contingent to Grenada to supplement the Grenada Constabulary during the Maurice Bishop murder trials. The RSS also assisted the Trinidad and Tobago Defense Force following the Jamaat al Muslimeen attempted coup in 1990. In this case, 140 lightly armed men held the government of Trinidad and Tobago hostage for five days. Other deployments (for example, Montserrat 1989) emphasized disaster relief following hurricanes.

Since late 1983, the U.S. military has delivered military supplies, including uniforms, vehicles, weapons, and communications equipment, to RSS units and has initiated a modest infantry training program undertaken primarily by Special Operations Forces based at Fort Bragg, North Carolina.[10]

Table 1
RSS Security Forces Overview circa 1988

Country	Defense Force	Police	SSUs	Reserves
Antigua	125	500	—	DF-160
Barbados	300	1,050	—	DF-360
Dominica	—	403	50	P-30
Grenada	—	600	65	—
St. Kitts	—	269	50	P-152
St. Lucia	—	390	56	—
St. Vincent	—	416	50	—

Source: U.S. Department of Defense, 1988.

The annual RSS operating budget of $10 million is shared by participating countries.[11] As the largest and most prosperous member, Barbados covers some 40 percent, while the other countries each contribute 10 percent. Only Dominica and Antigua and Barbuda are regularly in arrears on payments.

Table 2
Security Forces Budget circa 1988

Country	US $ Security	% National Budget	% RSS Budget
Antigua	2.5m	4.8	10
Barbados	10.1m	3.0	40
Dominica	2.9m	4.6	10
Grenada	2.9m	6.3	10
St. Kitts	1.8m	5.0	10
St. Lucia	3.4m	8.0	10
St. Vincent	2.9m	8.0	10

Source: U.S. Department of Defense, 1988.

Exercises and Training

Journalist Bernard Diederich wrote, "The smell of cordite hardly had time to dissipate in Grenada when special forces training teams . . . began landing on the neighboring islands. . . ."[12] The political leader most supportive of the U.S. invasion and subsequent military build-up and expanded deployment of Eastern Caribbean forces was Prime Minister Tom Adams of Barbados, who called for a full-scale, integrated, regional military force with a unified command structure as a logical outcome of the 1982 "Memorandum of Understanding" security pact. He initially proposed a standing force of 1,000 with a budget of some $10 million. Budget and number projections soon grew to a standing regional military of nearly 2,000 and a budget of $100 million. The United States and Great Britain opted for the smaller, less costly, less centrally articulated, militia-like, RSS/SSU system.[13] Adams' unexpected death in 1984 lead to diminution of zeal for a regional defense mechanism and a return to a loosely coordinated RSS based on locally controlled SSUs.[14] None of the leaders of participating states voiced opposition to the defensive arrangement, although the newly elected Prime Minister of St. Vincent, James Mitchell, speculated that economic development was a more effective safeguard against subversion than an armed force.[15]

The initial training program (1983-1984) was conducted by eight- or nine-man U.S. Special Forces Mobile Training Teams (MTTs) on each island. (Jamaica had a twelve-man team.) A headquarters staff in Barbados coordinated the on-island, six-week training regimen that included weapons familiarity, live ammunition firing, and small group tactics. The first group of trainees was finished by January 1984 and produced 40-man SSUs on the islands of Antigua and Barbuda, Dominica, St. Lucia, St. Vincent, and ten from St. Kitts and Nevis. These graduates went to Grenada the next month to serve in the international peacekeeping force and to substitute for U.S. troops who were rotating out of the island.[16]

In late 1985, a new RSS training proposal was implemented by the United States and the United Kingdom and accepted by the RSS countries. The joint U.S./UK team consisted of four U.S. and four British military personnel and was augmented by a British police officer. The military instructors cover all military-related training, while the police officer works with and conducts training with police force-based SSUs. The latter measure was necessary as both U.S. and British law prohibit military personnel from training civilian police forces.[17] Britain has shown some reluctance in providing anything beyond police training and Coast Guard equipment. Consequently, Scotland Yard has taken a more active role in RSS police training activities.

Following the Grenada invasion, the United States instituted a combined military exercise program in the Eastern Caribbean. The U.S. Atlantic Command (ACOM), based in Norfolk, Virginia, has sponsored combined exercises throughout the region, notably the Ocean Venture/Solid Shield/Tradewinds series.[18]

"Operation Exotic Palm," focusing on counterinsurgency, was held in St. Lucia in September 1985. Over 1,300 U.S. personnel joined 266 men from all RSS forces except St. Vincent and the Grenadines. Two UK naval vessels were present, as were observers from Jamaica and Trinidad and Tobago. Two exercises were held in 1986. "Ocean Venture 86" involved landings on Grenada and Vieques (Puerto Rico) and included all RSS forces except Barbados, plus troops from Jamaica, Britain, and the United States. "Upward Key 86" was much smaller and was composed of U.S., St. Kitts and Nevis, and Antigua and Barbuda troops. "Operation Camille" in 1987 — the first to emphasize disaster relief rather than purely military issues — involved all RSS units plus troops from Jamaica, Britain, and the United States. Another exercise later in 1987 was held in Jamaica and was limited to RSS units and their Jamaican hosts. In none of these exercises did those involved exceed 2,000.

The 1989 exercises saw an expansion of participants that continues today. "Tradewinds 89" was held in several phases and at several locations, including Grenada and Puerto Rico. Personnel from RSS units, Britain, the United States, Jamaica, and, for the first time, the Trinidad and Tobago Defence Force participated. "Tradewinds 91," set in Dominica and Puerto Rico, included personnel from all RSS units, Jamaica, Britain, the United States, Trinidad and Tobago, and, for the first time, an army unit from the Guyana Defence Force. The emphasis was on narcotics interdiction, search and rescue missions, humanitarian assistance, and civil action projects. "Tradewinds 92," held in Barbados, emphasized natural disaster relief from RSS forces during a hurricane. "Tradewinds 93" in St. Lucia emphasized the same.

In addition to training and exercises, the U.S. Military Assistance Program (MAP) has provided RSS member nations with hardware. Until 1988 when MAP funds were cut, RSS coast guards received ocean-going patrol boats (65 to 120 feet long) and inshore patrol craft (Boston Whalers). The four SSUs and the two Defence Forces were outfitted with light weaponry and equipment for small-unit tactical operations, such as M-16 rifles and M-60 machineguns.

U.S. funding to the RSS for fiscal year 1992-1993 was nearly $4 million in credits for the purchase of hardware. Dramatic budget reductions Caribbean-wide resulted in the credit allotment to the RSS being slashed to $250,000 for FY 1993-1994.[19]

Despite regular exercises and the inclusion of evermore non-RSS units in RSS activities, the original MOU still does not have full treaty status. Hence, although the Memorandum provides a framework of agreement for the OECS countries and Barbados, it does not empower the MOU with a formal legal status, nor does it permit security treaties to be negotiated and signed with non-OECS countries.

The Netherlands, France, and Canada have close ties to the Caribbean and, with the exception of France, appear willing to increase their role in regional military cooperation.[20] Canada, however, is the only one of these countries with an active training program among RSS countries. Canada is unwilling to become involved directly with the military aspects of the RSS but does provide police and coast guard training, separate from the RSS military force structure. The Royal Canadian Mounted Police contributed $800,000 to equip and train the

Grenada Police Force in 1984 and continues to provide training services at the Regional Police Training Centre in Barbados.[21]

Increasingly, these three countries, along with the United States and the United Kingdom, have focused on the RSS's capacity to deal with the surge of narcotics trafficking through the islands and the impact this has on regional and country-specific security and stability.

Security Issues and Structures in the 1990s

The ninth annual Caribbean Island Nations Security Conference (CINSEC 1993) was hosted by the Trinidad and Tobago Defense Force in March 1993. Participants included militaries from Antigua and Barbuda, the Bahamas, Barbados, the Dominican Republic, Guyana, Jamaica, and Trinidad and Tobago. Police were represented from Dominica, Grenada, St. Kitts and Nevis, St. Lucia, and St. Vincent and the Grenadines. Military and civilian foreign observers came from the United States, Great Britain, France, and the Netherlands.

RSS officers wished clarification of the British government's intention of removing the Royal Navy and Marine Corps from the Caribbean. Prior to 1993, three British officers commanded the coast guards of Antigua and Barbuda, St. Lucia, and St. Vincent and the Grenadines, while British officers were close advisors to the coast guards of Grenada and Dominica. By 1995, only eight uniformed British military, all in Barbados, still were stationed permanently in the Eastern Caribbean. British forces remain in the Eastern Caribbean only in a training and advisory capacity, and none of the officers will be posted directly with the RSS coast guards. The Royal Navy continues to be a donor of goods and services, but it no longer undertakes operations and limits its activities to training regional coast guards from its base in Barbados.

Closer communication and coordination between RSS military and police forces are necessities, as was made evident in the non-RSS countries of Trinidad and Tobago and Jamaica. In Trinidad, during the 1990 coup attempt, all uniformed services participated in the restoration of law and order. The follow-up investigation and preparation for trial were done entirely by police forces. The judicial system came into play to evaluate evidence and make judgments. In this situation, the defense forces, police, and judicial system all were involved intimately in the problem and its resolution. Jamaica, through its Crime Suppression Act, couples the Jamaican Defense

Force with the Royal Jamaican Constabulary to make patrols, maintain law and order, and arrest suspects during times of and in areas of high crime, or as was done recently, deploy for elections in order to assure internal security. In short, closer liaison training between police and militaries, including coast guards, enhances communication in times of stress and strengthens mutual assistance in times of need.

Central to all discussions at CINSEC IX was the issue of expanded systematic training for the RSS and other cooperating countries' coast and defense forces. It generally was recognized that the need for foreign officers (British) commanding coast guard units soon would be past. National officers now command their units and require both replenishment of their equipment and maintenance and upgrading of their skills. The new training challenges included a need for more supervisory, management, and instructional skills in the context of a more formalized, pan-Caribbean, organizational structure. Canadians are active with the coast guards of the RSS, at times providing all the training and education that these units receive. The United States and Britain are involved with coast guards as well, providing vessels, spare parts, and the construction of bases and docks.

For the region, only the coast guards of the Bahamas, Barbados, Belize, and Jamaica provide management training for non-commissioned officers. The coast guards of the Bahamas, Barbados, Belize, Guyana, and Trinidad and Tobago provide a management training module for their junior officers. None of the coast guards have full-time training officers, relying rather on tasking the role as a secondary duty. The coast guards of the small Eastern Caribbean states in the RSS provide only a basic seamanship course for their enlistees.[22] Computers are being set up for databases, management, word processing, and the Regional Maritime Information System (RMIS), an online vessel tracking system operated by the RSS.

Regional collaboration takes place via periodic, ad hoc communication and cooperation among the coast guards of the RSS.[23] RSS maritime units engage in joint search and rescue operations and joint policing of fisheries resources against poachers. Networking and sharing information are undertaken through regular conferences of commanding officers. There is almost no cooperation between RSS coast guards and maritime forces of the other English-speaking states, including even nearby Trinidad and Tobago and the Bahamas. Trinidad and Tobago, interestingly enough, has started to exchange sailors with Venezuela, its nearest neighbor, so as to begin co-familiarization of techniques and procedures and to facilitate language learning.

The need for training and regional cooperation is not lost on land units of the RSS and cooperating states, although training remains more or less uncoordinated. Trinidad and Tobago sent a Mobile Training Team to Barbados and Antigua and Barbuda for a short course, while personnel from the Guyana Defense Force attended one training session in Trinidad and vice versa. Training exchanges have been made between Jamaica and Barbados and the RSS countries and Jamaica. Personnel from Guyana and Trinidad have attended the French-run commando course in Martinique and the jungle warfare course in La Guyane. U.S. army troops maneuvered in Guyana in May 1993.[24] Yet, to quote a speaker at the CINSEC meeting, "The most successful attempt at cooperation in the region to date remains the West Indies Cricket Team."[25] Annual training exercises, listed above, sponsored by the U.S. and British governments, are the only forums that join RSS and regional forces in a coordinated, logistically complex event.

Management and skills training contribute to RSS and broader regional cooperation and effectiveness in a number of ways. A more credible security based on force integration and collective training could be offered to the region as a whole. Cost of training could be reduced significantly through regional training rather than the more expensive bilateral programs now characteristic of most exchange programs. Donor nation contributions could be coordinated more systematically and targeted at regional priorities, rather than addressing sometimes redundant national requests. Local and regional training is more cost-effective for the island nations than the sending of one officer to a foreign school for short-term education and training programs.[26] Further, many skills learned at U.S., British, Canadian, and European academies are not appropriate, or marginally useful, for the needs of junior officers from small island state forces. Rather than relying on foreign service schools, the use of visiting Mobile Training Teams could be encouraged for direct, skills training requirements. Middle-grade and senior-grade officers still require "education," however, at foreign institutions.[27] Courses are required for officer training (which the RSS cannot undertake independently), officer cadets, senior NCOs, sergeants and corporals, and enlisted ranks in management, computer technology, jungle warfare, urban warfare, medical training, signal corps and communications, intelligence, and weapons mainte-nance and use. Additional roles, and hence additional training, for regional defense forces can be categorized under "civic action." Enhanced military participation in vocational and skills training for rural or marginal groups — particularly in Guyana's jungle interior — can be undertaken by the one national institution that possesses the logistical capabilities to insert military personnel as instructors in harsh or inaccessible environments. Similarly, military assets could be used for medical extension work and the engineering, construction, and (re)building of infrastructure. Military-sponsored sports and recreation training can contribute to national physical fitness programs, while culture and language training (in multi-ethnic/lingual states) can contribute to nation-building efforts and civic action programs. In this capacity, the defense forces could broaden their mandate and, rather than limiting themselves to working solely with other government agencies, could work with a variety of NGOs and other grassroots organizations.[28] Finally, assistance during natural catastrophes to which the region is prone — hurricanes, earthquakes, and volcanic eruptions — requires coordination with civilian agencies.

Military Actions and RSS Roles

Are the RSS and its cooperating allies, both regional and nonregional, a credible security force? To a very great degree, yes, although there are complications endemic to all multilateral arrangements, security or otherwise. Definitions and perceptions of security issues and how to respond to them vary from state to state, between big and small, island and continental. This was clear during the U.S. military action in Grenada when the OECS and Barbados stood with the United States while the Bahamas, Belize, Guyana, and Trinidad and Tobago criticized the action for their own political reasons. Thus, consensus during times of crisis may be difficult to achieve. An outside force, such as the United States or, to a much lesser extent, Great Britain, might be able to consolidate mutual interests among the RSS forces more handily than the individual member states themselves.

In fact, no one in the Caribbean believes that the RSS can defend itself against a major outside force of mercenaries, narcoterrorists, or a conventional invasion force. Their strength, as Griffith points out, is "to diffuse local conflagrations and thus avoid superpower interference."[29] This function serves the more important goal of projecting stability and, hence, attracting foreign investment and tourist dollars, thus probably doing more for stability in the end than any number of military forces could. Yet, to be realistic, in a larger arena of more difficult and dangerous issues, the RSS will rely for its effectiveness on winning the support of major foreign powers whose geopolitical interests converge with those of the OECS and their regional allies and thus would be willing to lend support.

Six general categories of military activity will be proposed in which RSS forces could be called upon to participate. The likelihood of involvement more or less increases from number one to number six.

1. *Conventional cross-border attack* from another state, leading to national, subregional or regional conflict. For the member states of the Eastern Caribbean RSS and their regional and international allies this scenario scarcely exists. There are neither serious border disagreements nor, for that matter, serious secessionist movements in twin or multi-island states. For the former, there is the nearly obsolete claim of Guatemala on Belize and the rivalry of Venezuela and Guyana and Guyana and Suriname. In the latter case, of course, a secession movement is a domestic issue first and foremost (for example, Antigua and Barbuda, St. Kitts and Nevis, Trinidad and Tobago, St. Vincent and the Grenadines, and Grenada and Carriacou).

2. *Internal subversion and insurgency.* An international ideological model of insurgency has been replaced by indigenous factors of discontent, usually ethnic, religious, or regional. In fact, there is an increased constancy in poverty and its symptoms — miserable housing, poor sanitation, increasing unemployment, declining economies — that lead to popular cynicism, desperation, unscrupulous political manipulation of genuine West Indian populism, and, perhaps, radicalization. A local insurgency or subversion then would be driven by objective, socioeconomic conditions coupled with frustration with governments that cannot or will not undertake measures to relieve what are perceived to be oppressive conditions. The Jamaat al Muslimeen (Black Muslim) revolt in Trinidad and Tobago in 1990, which resulted in the government being held hostage for five days by 140 lightly armed men, is an example of such a movement. This subversion enjoyed Libyan financing and training and the purchase of arms internationally and also may be housed under category 3 — international terrorism. The Jamaican Defense Force is called out regularly in times or areas of high crime and during elections to maintain internal security. Economic projections suggest that socioeconomic conditions in the Caribbean will decline further through 2000 and that Caribbean people will find themselves in conditions of increased hardship and desperation.

3. *International terrorism.* During the 1980s, Libyan agents were actively involved with left-wing and revolutionary groups in Suriname and the Eastern Caribbean. Attacks against U.S. assets in the Caribbean would make the small, open, weakly guarded states of the region vulnerable to terrorism. Targets of opportunity for terrorists are plentiful and poorly guarded. Fortunately, international support for terrorism is in decline.

4. *Narcotrafficking and penetration by organized crime.* The entire Eastern Caribbean is rife with drug scandals involving high-ranking civilian and police officials. Almost all independent states and remaining colonial possessions are involved.[30] Government corruption and the consequent loss of legitimacy are likely results. Mafia involvement in RSS countries is most evident in St. Lucia where legitimate businesses have been penetrated and serve to front for organized crime assets and capital, but Aruba, St. Maarten, and St. Kitts-Nevis all recently have experienced major problems. In the Netherlands Antilles and Aruba, narcotraffickers and organized crime units have even attacked prisons in order to break out their colleagues. Prison guards are no match for cartel or mafia commandos and their air assault teams.[31]

The Eastern Caribbean, in particular, is penetrated by small boats and aircraft bringing their cargo up the island chain. RSS forces are virtually dependent on U.S. authorities for detection and monitoring intelligence so that they may make seizures and arrests. Hence, the interdiction of narcotics remains a Caribbean issue, not defined in terms of denying access to U.S. markets but, rather, serving as a stabilizing element for OECS governments.[32] The social "fallout" from narcotics hits on levels, including the individual, the family, crime affecting the tourist industry, medical expenses and treatment centers, prisons and rehabilitation systems, corruption at all levels, money laundering and artificial inflation of the economy, cost of living, and a general rejection of the commitment to trades and professions and of the work ethic.

5. *Disaster preparedness,* insofar as the Caribbean is regularly exposed to damaging hurricanes such as, in recent years, Gilbert, Hugo, and Andrew. The human and financial costs have been immense, and RSS forces have maintained law and order and assisted in rebuilding ruined infrastructure. RSS forces have assisted in Montserrat and Jamaica, as well as in their own home countries. Earthquakes and volcanic eruptions are very real threats for the insular Caribbean, particularly the Eastern Caribbean. Disaster-oriented exercises were

held in Barbados in 1992 and included representation from RSS forces and 1,700 civilian volunteers. The 1993 exercise in St. Lucia simulated a hurricane and emphasized communications, damage control, and casualty treatment, as well as maintaining law and order.[33]

6. *Serving as international peacekeepers* through the Organization of American States (OAS) or the United Nations is an attractive role for OECS forces. Basically as police officers, RSS units could be deployed to maintain law and order, support democratization, and strengthen judicial systems. All countries in OECS are democratic — some for nearly four hundred years. RSS forces are not tarred with the reputation of civil rights abuses nor intervention in civilian politics that maligns the reputation of Latin American militaries. In 1994, a contingent of 60 RSS troops (primarily from Barbados) was airlifted to St. Kitts to establish security after narcotics-related prison riots. A Caribbean Common Market (CARICOM) contingent of several hundred from the Bahamas, Barbados, Guyana, Jamaica, Antigua, Trinidad and Tobago, and Suriname participated in the United Nations peacekeeping force in Haiti. Training of this team was provided by the U.S. military, largely in Puerto Rico.

It should be clear to the RSS units and their Jamaican, Trinidadian, and Guyanese allies in particular that peacekeeping situations are relative, with each situation requiring a mix of skills, talents, assets, abilities, and capabilities. Caribbean forces will have to measure their capabilities and interests and match them to the needs of the peacekeeping situation and what they realistically can contribute. Peacekeeping roles in the 1990s, although expanding in numbers of situations and personnel deployed, have not been defined systematically. There are, for instance, terms such as environmental peacekeeping, anti-crime and terrorism peacekeeping, maritime peacekeeping, protective peacekeeping, preventive peacekeeping, peacemaking, peace building, enforcement, and preventive deployments — all currently and interchangeably, it seems, in use.

The U.S. response to these issues is to realize that the problems facing the United States and its allies in the Caribbean are neither ideological nor geopolitical in the sense of the terms used in the 1980s. Demanding new roles for the RSS would be strengthened not so much by arms transfers from the United States but by increased levels of training and education. Sponsoring pan-regional exercises, the provision of regional training programs, the encouragement of regional alliances building on the successes of RSS, and continued financial and logistical support are all worthy investments for the United States. An active U.S. role should, in addition, provide intelligence, planning, and logistics to the small RSS and SSU forces.

The cost of these services is cheap by any regional standard. Moreover, as an insurance policy, the RSS — and other regional forces — are sound. Should the United States be required to enter the region again, having a security structure in place saves time, money, and lives.

Table 3
Naval Units and Their Resources

Country	Personnel	Bases	Vessels	Aircraft
Antigua & Barbuda	28	1	3	—
Bahamas	851	5	30	2
Belize	57	1	8	—
Barbados	201	1	8	—
British Virgin Isl.	10	2	3	—
Cayman Islands	8	1	3	—
Dominica	27	1	3	—
Grenada	30	1	4	—
Guyana	204	1	12	—
Jamaica	233	1	15	—
Montserrat	7	1	2	—
St. Kitts, Nevis	24	1	4	—
St. Lucia	31	1	4	—
St. Vincent, Grenadines	32	1	4	—
Trinidad & Tobago	646	5	25	3
Turks & Caicos Isl.	16	1	3	—
Total	2,412	26	133	5

Source: Caribbean Island Nations Security Conference, Port of Spain, Trinidad, March 30-31, 1993.

Notes

1. Ivelaw L. Griffith, 1992, "The Regional Security System — A Decade of Caribbean Collective Security," *Caribbean Affairs* 5, 3(July/September): 181.

2. Between 1962 and the early 1980s, the English-speaking Caribbean experienced two waves of independence. The first included the so-called "more developed countries": Jamaica and Trinidad and Tobago in 1962, Guyana in 1964, and Barbados in 1966. There followed the Bahamas in 1973, Grenada in 1974, Dominica in 1978, St. Lucia and St. Vincent and the Grenadines in 1979, Antigua and Barbuda in 1980, Belize in 1981, and St. Kitts and Nevis in 1983. British colonies in the region include Bermuda, the British Virgin Islands, Anguilla, Montserrat, and the Cayman Islands.

3. The OECS was formed in 1981 and brought together Antigua and Barbuda, Dominica, Grenada, Montserrat (still a British colony), St. Kitts and Nevis, St. Lucia, and St. Vincent and the Grenadines. Various initiatives supportive of subregional unity were undertaken, including the establishment of a Defense and Security Committee (Griffith 1992, 180). For a discussion of pan-Caribbean security issues, see Ivelaw Griffith, ed., 1991, *Strategy and Security in the Caribbean* (Westport, Conn.: Greenwood Publishing).

4. For a review of politics, economics, and social events in the Eastern Caribbean during the 1980s, see the work of Gary Brana-Shute and Rosemary Brana-Shute in the annual volumes of *Latin America and Caribbean Contemporary Record*, I-IX. There have been several editors, including for volumes I-IV, Jack Hopkins; volumes V and VI, Abraham Lowenthal; and volumes VII to the present, James Malloy and Eduardo Gamarra. The series is published by Holmes and Meier of New York. There were also security issues in the late 1960s and early 1970s, but they were not nearly as dramatic or on the same scale as events of the 1980s: the secessionist move of Anguilla from St. Kitts and Nevis required the presence first of British paratroopers and later Scotland Yard constables in 1969; several small-scale Black Power rebellions in Jamaica in the late 1960s; and the Black Power revolt in Trinidad in 1970, which involved some rebel military units.

5. The literature on this period is varied. For a variety of perspectives, see Michael H. Erisman, ed., 1984, *The Caribbean Challenge: U.S. Policy in a Volatile Region* (Boulder, Colo.: Westview Press); James R. Greene and Brent Scowcroft, eds., 1984, *Western Interests and U.S. Policy Options in the Caribbean Basin* (Boston: Oelgeschlager, Gunn and Hain Publishers); Richard Millett and Marvin Will, eds., 1979, *The Restless Caribbean: Changing Patterns in International Relationships* (New York: Praeger Publishers); Catherine Sunshine, 1985, *The Caribbean: Survival, Struggle and Sovereignty* (Boston: South End Press); Timothy Ashby, 1987, *The Bear in the Back Yard: Moscow's Caribbean Strategy* (Lexington, Ky.: Lexington Books); Alma H. Young and Dion Phillips, eds., 1986, *Militarization in the Non-Hispanic Caribbean* (Boulder, Colo.: Lynne Rienner Publishers); and The Resource Center, 1984, *Focus on the Eastern Caribbean: Bananas, Bucks and Boots* (Albuquerque, N.M.: The Resource Center). Anthony Payne and Paul Sutton's edited work, 1993, *Modern Caribbean Politics* (Baltimore, Md.: Johns Hopkins University Press) is the most current and comprehensive.

6. There was some policy movement before the actual implementation of the RSS in 1982. In response to the Grenada revolution and the publicizing of Soviet forces in Cuba, the Carter administration established a Caribbean Joint Task Force at Key West, Florida, in October 1979. This force was expanded under President Reagan. Eastern Caribbean governments, particularly Antigua and Barbuda, Barbados, St. Kitts and Nevis, and St. Lucia, began a closer cooperation of their coast guard patrols.

7. Gary Brana-Shute and Rosemary Brana-Shute, 1990-1991, "The Organization of Eastern Caribbean States," in James Malloy and Eduardo Gamarra, eds., *Latin America and Caribbean Contemporary Record* 8: B455.

8. RSS forces also include the Coast Guard of Barbados and the Police Marine Wings (coast guard) of Antigua and Barbuda, Dominica, Grenada, St. Kitts and Nevis, St. Lucia, and St. Vincent and the Grenadines. Griffith (1993) provides the best military resource overview in *The Quest for Security in the Caribbean: Problems and Promises in Subordinate States* (Armonk, N.Y.: M.E. Sharpe).

9. The member countries of the RSS and Jamaica issued a formal request for U.S. intervention in Grenada. U.S. forces were supported only nominally during the October 1983 invasion of the island by a token force of soldiers and police from the RSS countries of Barbados, Antigua and Barbuda, Dominica, St. Lucia, and St. Vincent and the Grenadines. Jamaica sent a small detachment and continues to collaborate with RSS activities, although it is not officially a member. The initial deployment amounted to 300 police and soldiers and reached 900 at its high point. The force withdrew late in 1985. The RSS deployment in Grenada was essentially a "coat-tail" exercise. See Mark Adkin, 1989, *Urgent Fury: The Battle for Grenada* (Boston: Lexington Books).

10. For a discussion of national security issues in the English-speaking Caribbean, the sizes of the RSS member states and their forces, the nature of their lethal and non-lethal equipment, and a review of their emergence as a subregional military, see the Area Handbook Series, Sandra W. Meditz and Dennis M. Hanratty, eds., 1989, *Islands of the Commonwealth Caribbean: A Regional Study* (Washington, D.C.: Government Printing Office). Chapters with country-specific military data cover Jamaica, Barbados, Trinidad and Tobago, the Bahamas, the British dependencies, and the OECS. The chapter by Rex A. Hudson, "Strategic and Regional Security Perspectives," is very useful.

11. As will be made clear below, RSS exercises have included a number of countries outside the OECS and the RSS structure and include Jamaica, Trinidad and Tobago, and Guyana. The Jamaican Defense Force includes some 2,500 troops, while the Trinidad and Tobago Defense Force numbers about 2,100. In Guyana, because of ethnic politics in the late 1980s, one has to include paramilitary forces in the overall domestic force structure. Paramilitary units number about 5,000, while the Guyana Defense Force is somewhere in the neighborhood of 5,500. See Andrés Serbin (translated by Sabeth Ramirez), 1990, *Caribbean Politics: Toward Security Through Peace?* (Boulder, Colo.: Lynne Rienner Publishers), 73-74; and George Danns, 1986, "The Role of the Military in the National Security of Guyana," in Young and Phillips, 113-115.

12. Bernard Diederich, 1984, "The End of West Indian Innocence: Arming the Police," *Caribbean Review* 13 (2): 11.

13. Dion Phillips, 1990a, "Barbados and the Militarization of the Eastern Caribbean, 1979-1985," *Latin American Perspectives* 19 (1): 81.

14. Barbados was absolutely essential to the United States for the implementation of the RSS. Dion Phillips (1990b) has chronicled the defense policy of Barbados over

a two-decade period from 1966 to 1988 ("Defense Policy in Barbados, 1966-1988," *Journal of Interamerican Studies and World Affairs* 32 (2): 69-102). Phase 1 (1966-1976): Government views the police as the only security needed. A Coast Guard is established with U.S. assistance in 1974, but unlike Jamaica, Trinidad and Tobago, and Guyana, Barbados does not create a defense force. Phase 2 (1976-1986): The Adams government creates the Barbados Defense Force (BDF), joins the RSS, and takes an active military and political leadership role in the Eastern Caribbean. Phase 3 (1986-present): No substantial change in policy despite talk of reducing the size of the BDF and its budget. Training and participation in exercises continue. The governments of Barbados, following the death of military activist Tom Adams, have shown a general unwillingness to upgrade the Memorandum of Understanding to full and formal treaty status. For a discussion of Jamaica's military policy during the same time, see Humberto Garcia, 1981-1982, "Defense Policy and Planning in the Caribbean: An Assessment of the Case of Jamaica on its 25th Independence Anniversary," *Caribbean Studies* 21 (1-2): 67-123.

15. At the time of its implementation, the RSS brought forth rancorous cries of "militarization of the Caribbean" and, in one headline, the "end of West Indian Innocence." Suffice it to say that the Caribbean has been militarized for quite some time, antedating 1492 for that matter. At the time of its inception in the early 1980s, the strongest military powers in the Eastern Caribbean were the 2,000-strong Grenada Revolutionary Army and their armed Cuban backup and the French Marine units in Martinique and Guadeloupe. The RSS was hardly a "militarizing" presence. See Anthony P. Maingot, 1990, "The U.S. in the Caribbean: Geopolitics and the Bargaining Capacity of Small States," in Anthony Bryan, J. Edward Greene, and Timothy M. Shaw, eds., *Peace, Development, and Security in the Caribbean* (New York: St. Martin's Press), 75.

16. The law governing U.S. foreign assistance bars assistance for police forces. An exception was made for the Eastern Caribbean, where each police force has its own paramilitary SSU that can function as a military unit when needed. Antigua and Barbuda and Barbados (and Jamaica, which cooperates from time to time) have militaries or defense forces, while the rest of the RSS have police or constabulary forces.

17. The British nevertheless collaborate with RSS coast guards through the British Loan Service Officer program. Two- or three-member teams of Royal Navy officers operate with the coast guards of Dominica, St. Lucia, St. Kitts, Grenada, and St. Vincent, while Royal Marine and Army officers are seconded to the Barbados Defense Force. There is some disagreement between the United States and the United Kingdom on the direct seconding of British officers to serve in coast guard units. The United States feels that, with British officers becoming part of the chain of command, there is an inhibiting effect for RSS members to take full control of their forces and, rather, rely on foreign officers to plan and implement programs. The British presence is a turnaround from the late 1970s, when the United Kingdom nearly abrogated its military role in the region. However, British thinking in 1993 is to reduce the total number of loan officers from 19 to about 11 and to consolidate them all in Barbados.

18. For a discussion of U.S. military capabilities in the Caribbean and the political implications of "militarization," see Serbin 1990.

19. This figure includes only hardware. The IMET program, designed to advance training and professionalization, is another budget altogether. The Eastern Caribbean, including Barbados, has been budgeted for $462,000 for fiscal year 1993-1994. The distribution follows: Antigua and Barbuda, $25,000; Barbados, $45,000; Dominica, $68,000; Grenada, $78,000; St. Kitts and Nevis, $60,000; St. Lucia, $101,000; and St.

Vincent and the Grenadines, $85,000. By way of comparison, Jamaica received $450,000; Guyana, $50,000; the Bahamas, $100,000; Trinidad and Tobago, $75,000; Belize, $125,000; and the Dominican Republic, $600,000.

20. The Netherlands and France continue to possess territory in the Eastern Caribbean. French naval and army deployments are stationed on the two French Overseas Departments of Martinique and Guadeloupe (and several smaller dependencies), while Dutch naval forces have access to the Kingdom of the Netherlands members of Saba, St. Eustatius, and St. Maarten. Other Dutch forces are located in Aruba and the Netherlands Antilles, and French regular army and Foreign Legion units are stationed in La Guyane (French Guiana).

21. Phillips 1990a, 82.

22. Seven regional coast guards use a variety of national training institutes to provide some of the management, administrative, and technical training required by their organizations. The Bahamas, Barbados, Guyana, Jamaica, St. Kitts and Nevis, St. Lucia, and Trinidad and Tobago use combinations of universities, community colleges, polytechnical institutes, extramural centers, and technical training institutes as teaching centers. For those coast guards that do not possess any of these facilities, training centers as such do not exist. Students are gathered on an ad hoc basis and lack even basic instructional equipment such as chalkboards, overhead projectors, and flip charts.

23. One impediment to cooperation is the nature of the region's coast guards. Of the 17 English-speaking countries, five have military coast guards of varying strengths and capabilities. The remaining 12 are basically branches of the police force. This civilian-military division presents certain policy and legal issues in the event of using the forces for military action. Further complications arise from the nonstandardization of training, procurement of equipment, and operational procedures. The operation of different types of equipment results in higher acquisition and maintenance costs.

24. It is interesting to note that precisely at the time U.S. troops were in Guyana, the military in neighboring Suriname was putting its civilian government under considerable pressure. Dutch deployment of warships and the coincidental presence of U.S. forces close by caused the rogue Suriname military to back down.

25. Interview, Lt. Col. J. Sandy, Commanding Officer, the Trinidad and Tobago Regiment, CINSEC, Port of Spain, Trinidad, March 30, 1993.

26. Longer-term degree programs that require the Caribbean student to matriculate remain essential. The efforts of the Inter-American Defense College of the Organization of American States at Fort McNair, Washington, D.C., comes to mind. Here the strength of the curriculum, accessibility to resources in the Washington, D.C., metropolitan area (including politicians), and networking with other officers from throughout the region provide an irreplaceable experience that could not be garnered in the Caribbean.

27. MTTs could be employed in a number of physical environments as well. Dominica offers terrain for mountain warfare training, while Guyana could serve as a jungle warfare school. Thematically, both Jamaica and Trinidad and Tobago have experience in internal security operations and counterinsurgency.

28. This suggestion was made by Brigadier Singh of the Guyana Defense Force, CINSEC, Port of Spain, Trinidad, March 31, 1993.

29. Griffith 1993, 190.

30. For a recent summary, see Ivelaw Griffith, 1994, "Security and the Drug Trade," *Caribbean Affairs* 7, 4 (September/October).

31. On several occasions, the Netherlands had to deploy Dutch Marines and Royal State Police to protect prisons in Aruba and Curaçao after threats of attack from cartel traffickers. On one occasion, a Mafia boss was snatched from an Aruba jail and sped by a "go-fast" to Venezuela. [See definition of "go-fast" in note 32.]

32. The interdiction efforts of 31 U.S. agencies has not seen a great decrease in narcotics smuggling to North America. Until a short time ago, some 70 percent of the narcotics entering the United States passed through or over the Caribbean. The trade routes seem to be changing in 1992 and 1993 with more narcotics transhipped along the Pacific coast of Mexico and over mainland Central America and Mexico than before. The Caribbean routes — over water in the western Caribbean, via the Dominican Republic, Haiti, and Jamaica in the central Caribbean, and through Trinidad and island-hopping up the Eastern Caribbean chain — are still tremendously active, however. Methods involve the use of container ships, air drops, and "go-fast" pick-up ships, mother ships and "go-fasts" (stealth boats made of wood or plastic with a low profile), small boats, air transshipping, and connections with mainland gangs with island home-country networks. Four U.S. military commands are involved: Atlantic Command (ACOM), Southern Command (SOUTHCOM), Pacific Command (PACOM), and U.S. Forces Command (FORSCOM). U.S. military forces cannot intercept or arrest anyone in international waters, as they only are empowered to detect and monitor traffic on land, sea, and air. Intelligence is passed on to cooperating countries where their authorities make arrests and seizures. Hence, liaison, integration, and communication are crucial to the multifaceted operation.

33. Valuable lessons were learned by the U.S. Virgin Islands Army National Guard before, during, and after Hurricane Hugo in 1989. They, despite efforts, were underprepared for the storm and were involved simultaneously in maintaining law and order, repairing damage, and assisting casualties, while the guardsmen themselves and their families were victims of the storm as well. The entire island-wide and international communication system was destroyed, and the Guard had to rely on the few cellular telephones they possessed.

VI

The Mexican Military: The Dilemma of Functioning in a One-Party System

Stephen J. Wager

Setting the Scene

Mexico's armed forces have evolved in an atypical fashion, in contrast with those of its counterparts in twentieth-century Latin America.[1] Since World War II, Mexico is the only Latin American nation in which the military has neither been involved in a coup d'état nor governed the country. In fact, the Mexican military has remained fiercely loyal to the legitimate government since the 1930s. Although Mexico has been governed by a virtual one-party system since 1929, top military leaders always have been cautious to voice their support for the "political system" created by the Constitution of 1917 rather than specifically for the single political party that has dominated that system since 1929.

The military's support of elected governments has been a positive force in the political stability Mexico has experienced since the 1920s. Although political opposition has been controlled or co-opted by the government, the simple reality that opposition groups have been allowed to function sets Mexico apart from Fidel Castro's Cuba, the only other Latin American nation that has witnessed an enduring social revolution in the twentieth century. Many might argue that the military in Mexico has a special relationship with the country's monolithic ruling party, the Partido Revolucionario

Institucional (Institutional Revolutionary Party — PRI). The nation's leaders, who belong to the PRI, assiduously have attempted to make the military institution feel an integral part of the ruling system. For that reason, the armed forces long have been perceived as the PRI's enforcement arm.

The military's close association with the less-than-democratic government, though established by the Constitution of 1917, at times has impugned the image of the armed forces. The army can, of course, cite many positive accomplishments. It has safeguarded the Mexican people from both external and internal threats, and its ample contributions in the area of civic action are well documented. Yet the fact remains that it long has been the government's force of last resort. As such, the army has been criticized for its repression against the Mexican people on those infrequent occasions when it has been called upon to restore order. In short, the army has an identity crisis because it has not been able to divorce itself from the political system born of the Mexican Revolution. Nor has the army been capable of distancing itself from the criticism to which that system increasingly is subjected. In a nutshell, this is the dilemma of an armed force that serves a government dominated by a single political party. The well-established rules of the system have left the military with little or no autonomy. As the government goes, so go the armed forces.

Despite these drawbacks, since the 1930s the overall situation of the armed forces in Mexico has been positive. They have been an institutional pillar of the system that delivered Mexico from the destruction of the Mexican Revolution (1910-1920) and turned it into a leading power in Latin America. The armed forces evolved in a manner distinct from their Latin American counterparts because Mexico developed in a unique way. Mexico's extremely violent revolution changed how people perceived the military. In the aftermath of the revolution, the populace expressed an acute sense of antimilitarism. Thoroughly dismayed with the massive bloodletting, they searched diligently for an alternative to the endless string of military dictatorships.

To understand the armed forces better, it is essential to understand the role they have played since 1929 and some of the major factors that contributed to the evolution of their constructive role. The two most critical influences have been the creation of a legitimized "revolutionary political system," embodied by the PRI, and the creation of a unique military ideology that staunchly supports the "revolutionary system."

The Official Party

The demilitarization of Mexican politics was an extended and tedious process. Two factors proved especially important: the formation of a monolithic official political party and the evolution of a unique military ideology. Political demilitarization accurately describes what transpired in Mexico between 1920 and 1940. Prior to 1940, generals played the dominant role in managing day-to-day affairs, some openly and others behind the scenes. When Manuel Avila Camacho became president in December 1940, the government took on a more civilian orientation.[2] By 1940, many revolutionary generals had reached the twilight of their political careers. This transition was completed during the presidency of Miguel Alemán Valdes, who incorporated university-trained civilians into key government positions and rejuvenated the officer corps by promoting younger officers who had been trained to be loyal to government institutions. Alemán, Mexico's first elected civilian president since the revolution, also forced many older generals, who still retained political ambitions, into retirement. Civilian presidents followed Alemán, and since 1952, no military officer has made even a remote attempt to seek the presidency.[3]

The battle to remove the army from its dominant role began in 1920, when General Alvaro Obregón assumed the presidency and immediately sought to move against politically ambitious *caudillos* who were creating havoc throughout the countryside and obstructing the creation of a centralized government. To bring order to the divided revolutionary army, Obregón cut its size by one-half, from 100,000 to 50,000, between 1921 and 1922. He softened the blow for most veterans by setting up special military agricultural colonies that gave ex-soldiers jobs and by agreeing to pay veterans their normal salaries for two years after retirement.[4]

As for the top military leadership, Obregón believed he could buy the loyalty of his generals more easily than he could cultivate it. On more than one occasion, he stated that no general could resist a *cañonazo* or salvo of 50,000 pesos. As a result, corruption became the glue that held military and political alliances together. The president took a different approach with junior officers. He reopened the military college and made sure that aspiring officers were taught that a successful military career depended on a firm commitment to institutional loyalty. To divert the army's attention from political activity, Obregón directed it to engage in a myriad of civic action projects, ranging from road-building and irrigation works to repairing railroads and telegraph lines.[5]

President Obregón's hand-picked successor, General Plutarco Elías Calles, took office in 1924 and continued many of his predecessor's programs aimed at consolidating the control of the central government. Calles ruled officially until 1928 and then unofficially through three puppet presidents until his exile in 1935 by then-President Lázaro Cárdenas. Despite his generally authoritarian policies, Calles made some major contributions toward army professionalism and the stabilization of political power.

Like his predecessor, Calles had to squelch rebellions by disgruntled officers. In defeating these insurrections, he gained the support of the most powerful generals and finally purged the army of its disloyal elements, marking the last time military forces seriously would challenge the authority of the central government.[6] Calles also adopted a wise policy of co-optation that made many generals millionaires, more interested in business transactions than in political careers. His success in curtailing the power of the revolutionary generals facilitated his goal of instilling institutional loyalty among future army leaders. In short, he broke the power of the military *caudillos* and nurtured the emergence of *presidencialismo*, or the predominance of the executive branch in all facets of government.[7] Calles' actions proved to be the first major step in the supplanting of the army by the office of the presidency at the pinnacle of political power.

Calles' greatest contribution to the political stability of Mexico came in the founding of the all-embracing Partido Nacional Revolucionario (PNR).[8] Known as the Partido Revolucionario Institucional (PRI) since 1946, it has facilitated the integration of new and massive social groups into the system. Samuel P. Huntington referred to Calles' accomplishment as "the most striking example of political institution-building by generals."[9] By creating the PNR, he was, in effect, able to institutionalize the revolution.

Calles founded the party on December 1, 1928, his last day in office. He hoped that it would provide a forum within which military and nonmilitary groups could manage diverse interests. The PNR aimed to unify its principal supporters — the army, bureaucrats, peasants, and workers. Jorge Lozoya, a leading authority on civil-military relations in Mexico, has made the astute observation that the PNR was not created to gain power but rather to maintain it. Calles and other leaders opposed active military participation in politics and voted not to create a military sector in the party. Instead, they hoped that bureaucrat, peasant, and worker sectors might offset the army's influence further. Calles believed that major political involvement by the army would inevitably divide that institution and ultimately lead to the collapse of the entire system.[10]

Neither Calles nor his immediate successors could keep the army entirely out of politics. However, the demilitarization of Mexican politics made considerable strides under President Lázaro Cárdenas (1934-1940). In 1937, Cárdenas formally incorporated the military into the official party, which he himself had reformed and renamed Partido de la Revolución Mexicana (PRM). As a new sector in the official party, the army had an obligation to cooperate with the other three sectors. In addition, the number of supporters represented by the party's original sectors outnumbered the members of the army sector by approximately 3.8 million to 55,000.[11] Consequently, the army found itself in a position of being, at most, one-fourth of the political equation. Cárdenas emphasized that point when he said, "[W]e did not put the army in politics. It was already there. In fact, it had been dominating the situation, and we did well to reduce its influence to one out of four."[12]

Noted Mexican sociologist Pablo González Casanova wrote that the military's incorporation into the official party served to increase government control over the military, while simultaneously enforcing a kind of political discipline on the army. He and other analysts generally agree that the military sector proved weak and most likely served Cárdenas' purpose of politically debilitating the army as an institution.[13] However, the political exigencies of the late 1930s demanded military support of and close affiliation with the central government. Internally, the government faced the threat of a burgeoning fascist Sinarquista movement, while externally foreign-owned petroleum companies began pressuring for more concessions. President Cárdenas hoped to incorporate the military into what he called the "union and solidarity pact" in an effort to bolster the power of his government.[14] The military would serve as his trump card, which he could use to coerce support for his policies. The military sector also enabled politically ambitious officers to develop their aspirations within the confines of the official party and not in opposition to it. History would justify Cárdenas' bold maneuver because holding political office never again significantly enhanced an officer's military career.[15]

The demilitarization of politics in Mexico clearly points out how Mexico's military evolved in a style very distinct from its Latin American counterparts. The violence unleashed during the revolution produced a strong anti-praetorian sentiment throughout the population. Even the political elite, composed principally of generals, realized that preservation of the nascent political system depended upon elimination of internecine military conflict. Given the country's bloody history, an antimilitarist approach offered the best hope for the future.[16] Political leaders, most of whom were revolutionary veterans, took responsibility for demilitarizing politics. The result manifested itself in a unique way — stabilized civilian rule in an undemocratic system embraced by a majority of the Mexican people.[17]

In addition, these skilled political and military leaders strongly encouraged the professionalization of new generations of officers as a means of ensuring the military's gradual exit from politics.[18] However, because of the significant role that military leaders played in the creation of this new "revolutionary" political system, the military institution forever would be identified with it and never would be able to divorce itself completely from the system. That situation presents a growing dilemma for the armed forces. Many officers believe that they have been subjected to undue criticism when they are forced to respond to situations created by the government's failure to meet the expectations of some of its citizens. At times, the government, because of the magnitude of a particular disturbance or opposition movement, has called upon the army to quiet or repress the dissenting factions. The outcome in these types of situations has been detrimental to the army's generally paternalistic and popular image.

The Mexican Army's Ideology

While the creation of an official party contributed greatly to the demilitarization of politics, another facet of that process related directly to changes within the military institution itself. A unique military ideology began to develop in the 1920s and crystallized by the 1940s. This rare internal dynamic has served as a signpost for army leaders and also has reinforced the military's exit from politics. The reforms undertaken in the 1920s to professionalize new generations of officers gave rise to this ideology or military culture that indirectly established a set of rules, values, and accepted behavior for all members of the army and provided justification for military actions. At times, it allows the army, as an institution, to distance itself from what might be perceived as the injustices of a specific administration. Because the army defends the constitution and assiduously pursues the goals of the revolution, it also must support the legitimate government, even though it may not always be in accord with specific policies or actions.

This ideology cannot always be defined in concrete terms or concepts and often has been described as abstract or illusory. Since the late 1940s, it has been accepted as an established creed, or what Samuel P. Huntington might call a "professional military ethic," by subsequent generations of army officers and their troops.[19] This creed has manifested itself in the army's mission and daily activities and in speeches and press releases by high-ranking army officers. As a motto, it might be expressed best as *la patria es primero* or "the country comes first." These words, attributed to nineteenth-century revolutionary and President Vicente Guerrero, have provided inspiration to Mexican soldiers for generations.[20]

Although not formally described in any manual or official publication, the principal components of the Mexican army's ideology can be identified as a revolutionary heritage, loyalty, discipline, patriotism, nationalism, and apoliticism. While some of these values, such as discipline, patriotism, and nationalism, are held throughout Latin America, others have a distinct Mexican quality. These principles have qualified, in part, because of their longevity and general acceptance within military circles. They have roots in the late 1920s and 1930s and became well recognized by the end of the Alemán administration (1952).[21]

Mexico's revolutionary heritage is a key element of the military's ideology and is perhaps its most distinguishing characteristic. Such a mystique long has been associated with Mexico. The revolution has come to symbolize social justice, progress, mass involvement, and a distinctly Mexican recipe for democracy. For the army, the revolution is still very much alive, and its members have dedicated themselves to pursuing and achieving its goals.[22] Even more important, the army's revolutionary heritage obligates it to support the Constitution of 1917 and the elected government. In the words of one famous Mexican general, the army "is the support, the sustenance of the state born of the revolution."[23] Officers see themselves as "guardians of the revolution," who constantly work toward the fulfillment of its goals.[24] This devotion to the revolution's democratic ideals is the one feature that truly distinguishes Mexico's army from its Latin American counterparts.

The loyalty frequently alluded to by both political and military leaders can be defined as institutional loyalty. More precisely, that means unwavering support for the constitution and the political institutions begotten by the Mexican Revolution. One historian has traced the importance of loyalty back to the Mexican Revolution. Because of the manner in which the revolution was fought, loyalty held considerably more value among soldiers and their leaders than did discipline and conventional training.[25]

Loyalty also has taken on special importance in traditional Mexican political culture, whose leaders have often hailed the army's institutional loyalty in public speeches and official declarations. A high premium also has been placed on institutional loyalty within army circles. A former Defense Minister, General Marcelino García Barragán, skillfully defined this concept when he said, "...[our] duty is loyalty, discipline, and honor. Loyalty to the constituted government and to the Mexican Revolution made with the blood, effort, and sacrifice of the Mexican people."[26]

Since the late 1930s, loyalty has been implicit in the military's submission to civilian power. Military leaders constantly reaffirm the armed forces' loyalty to the president of the republic and his government. José Luis Piñeyro, an expert on the Mexican armed forces, has noted, "...[since] 1935, the defense ministry has not officially leveled a single criticism against the incumbent president or the ruling party."[27]

As with most military institutions, the Mexican army has become recognized for its discipline. Through experience, the army has shown Mexico's ruling elite that it can be counted on to carry out an order and to follow the directives of the country's political leaders. Discipline has come to signify obedience to the president of the republic, who constitutionally serves as the supreme commander of the armed forces.

Historian Alan Knight offers a useful definition of Mexican patriotism, another key ingredient of the military's ideology. He defines it as "an effective allegiance to the national entity 'Mexico,'" which "involves the defense of Mexican territory, sovereignty, and autonomy."[28] Since the primary mission of any soldier is to be prepared to fight and die in the defense of his country, the Mexican definition of patriotism more often is associated with the army than with any other institution.

The army has incorporated many examples of patriotic service into its ideology and, more than any other institution, has continued to pay homage to the country's patriots. Former President Luis Echeverría Alvarez remarked that patriotism had its highest expression within the armed forces.[29]

Nationalism, an integral part of the Mexican military culture, has evolved from the revolutionary years and represents a firm attachment to everything Mexican and a general independence from foreign influences. After the revolution, military and political leaders made a concerted effort to build an army free of outside influences. Mexico's independent foreign policy, its policies of self-determination and nonintervention, and the rigid defensive posture adopted by the armed forces have helped guide the army down a predominantly nationalist path.[30]

Historical precedents contribute to distrust toward the United States. The army's persistent rejection of any type of formal alliance with the U.S. military has worked to nourish its internal nationalist impulses. Pablo González Casanova has written that the mortar that cements the unity of the Mexican army is a nationalist ideology that has not been destroyed by the inter-American system or institutions.[31] Like the government, the military long has demonstrated a zealous commitment to Mexican nationalism.

Apoliticism, another cardinal feature of the military's ideology, has been considered by many outsiders as the most distinctive characteristic of the Mexican army. Mexico's military remains the only one in Latin America that has not intervened directly in politics since World War II. Apolitical, as it applies to the army, means it has no major influence on political decisionmaking. Because of the PRI's dominant hold on politics and the military's close allegiance to that party, it seems logical to assume that the army is a major political actor. However, this is definitely not the case. The army simply undertakes its missions as outlined in the Constitution of 1917 and its organic law. As José Luis Piñeyro has noted, one of the principal rules of the Mexican political game is that "military leaders do not publicly express their opinions about the economic, political, and social problems of the country."[32]

The constitution subordinates the army to the elected government, and the military has created a tradition of complying with the directives of political leaders. Officers do not make political policy; that responsibility belongs to elected officials. Although the army retains the potential to become a major political actor, since the 1930s it has chosen not to exercise that option. That remarkable tradition becomes more entrenched each year.

The military education system, the army's principal socialization agent, has primary responsibility for implanting the army's ideology in its members. The military academy inculcates cadets with the military values that these future officers will carry with them throughout their careers. Subsequent phases of military training reinforce these values or ideological components.

Due in large part to the influence of this ideology on the institution, the Mexican army has recognized the laws of the Constitution of 1917 as the legitimate source of political power. Moreover, army leaders have opted to respect the decisions of political leaders. Since the 1930s, there have been no open conflicts between military and political leaders because the military has considered itself an institutional pillar of the system that army leaders actually founded. In addition, the army always has adhered to two important political precepts: 1) Military force does not provide an acceptable means of advancing the goals of the revolution, and 2) the maintenance of political power does not depend on the support of the armed forces.[33]

Civil-Military Relations: The Inextricable Link Between the Army and the State

An analysis of civil-military relations in Mexico reveals two critical components, the relationship between the president of the republic and the secretary of defense (SECDEF), who is invariably the senior army general, and the army's compliance with its specific roles. These factors contribute to the well-established and intricate relationship that exists between the army and the state. In the public's eyes, this relationship associates the army directly with the president and indirectly with the PRI.

The President and the SECDEF

Interpersonal relations within the officer corps resemble those practiced at the highest levels of the political system. More specifically, the SECDEF, much like the president in the political arena, exercises very centralized control over the army. Army officers place a heavy reliance on personal relations and discreet alliances. Both the government and the armed forces have a somewhat authoritarian structure with a special emphasis placed on loyalty to one's superiors.[34]

Within the army, all power flows from the top, and the concept of hierarchy holds special significance. The SECDEF wields virtually absolute power, and no critical decisions are made without his approval. At subordinate levels of command, local commanders exercise authority based on the orders from the SECDEF. Commanders follow orders explicitly and express little individual initiative.[35] Major military activities fall under the direct control of the SECDEF, who prefers to delegate only a minimal amount of authority. Officers seeking advancement wisely adhere to the dictates of the high command.[36]

Strong personal relations and unquestioned loyalty play a paramount role in the relationship between the president and his SECDEF. It is often suggested that the president does not always select the most qualified general to be his SECDEF, but rather the one with whom he feels most comfortable.[37] The SECDEF oversees the daily operations of the army and air force as the president's personal representative. However, the president of the republic serves as commander-in-chief of the armed forces by virtue of Article 89 of the constitution.[38]

Interaction between the president and his SECDEF occurs primarily on a political level. Despite the substantial power the Mexican military can exert, it functions foremost as part of a burgeoning bureaucracy whose leaders work hard to promote its interests.[39] In this process, the SECDEF, the military's chief sponsor, relies heavily on the president, the system's principal power broker. Reciprocity is a key ingredient in this relationship. The SECDEF delivers the steadfast loyalty of the army to both the presidency and the government, and the nation's top political leader reciprocates with a wide range of benefits for the military institution.

Despite obvious differences between military and political programs, the army's actions during a particular administration or *sexenio* (six-year term) generally have adopted the overall philosophy of the president in office. For example, during his *sexenio,* Adolfo López Mateos (1958-1964) promoted expanded social security benefits. Not surprisingly, the army enacted the first Law of Social Security for the Armed Forces during his administration. A retired general explained that the army, like the political system, has evolved in *sexenios* since World War II. Moreover, the relationship between the president and his SECDEF proved to be the decisive element in determining what course the military would follow during a particular administration.

Prior to 1946, presidents often spoke on behalf of the army since almost all were former generals. As a show of discipline and loyalty, army leaders deferred to the presidency on key military issues. After World War II, civilian presidents took office, and the SECDEF became the army's principal spokesperson and presented the official military point of view in public.

The SECDEF holds a unique position within the Mexican system. He sets the tempo for the army during a particular *sexenio* in consonance with the desires of the president. He works to gain popular support for the military by sponsoring a wide range of projects that benefit the Mexican people. Within the military, each SECDEF promotes his own special projects and thereby creates his individual legacy.

Since the 1940s, the political status quo generally has been sustained, although political opposition has become much better organized and more vocal in recent years. The system's boundaries have become fairly well established through the years, and that reality has limited the influence the military can exert. During the period 1952-1976, those who served as SECDEF exhibited certain traits that tied them very tightly to both the political system and its leaders. In addition to being handpicked by the president, those SECDEFs came to office with political experience. Elite generals had served as senators, state governors, or presidents of the PRI before being named to the military's top post. One political insider believed that such political experiences helped to convince key political leaders that top military officials were loyal to the system and could be trusted to carry out presidential directives.[40] These officers possessed a clear understanding of how the system could compensate the army for its loyalty and support. Most viewed their office as the ultimate compensation for years of loyal service and expressed their gratitude through unbridled support of the government and the president.

In addition to political experience, age was another critical factor in the selection process. The SECDEFs of this period took office in their sixties, perhaps a deliberate attempt to curb their political aspirations.[41] All had served for more than 40 years and were thoroughly versed on institutional loyalty. Their selection also seems to have been based on a previous relationship with the president, hinting at the unequivocal importance of loyalty in the selection process.

The three SECDEFs who have served since 1976 could not claim political experience as an asset. After World War II, the army hierarchy actively discouraged political aspirations within the officer corps. Consequently, by the 1960s, fewer officers had the opportunity to serve in a high-level political position. In fact, officers demonstrating political aspirations could not hope to reach the highest levels of command. For these recent SECDEFs, their absence from the political arena limited their communication and contact with high-ranking government officials. Moreover, in the 1970s, national political leadership changed from the old-style politician to the blander technocrat, who had never been elected popularly to a political post prior to becoming president. As a result, Mexico's last five presidents have not had extensive interaction with army officers prior to assuming the presidency.[42]

For the "technocrat presidents," interviewing candidates for the SECDEF position has taken on greater importance, with the commitment of loyalty remaining the principal selection criterion. Age and date of rank have also retained importance. The SECDEF post falls to one of the more senior army officers who has celebrated his sixtieth birthday. A new president has to avoid causing undue turbulence at the highest levels of command by not selecting a general too junior in either age or rank. In the case of two recent SECDEFs, Generals Juan Arévalo Gardoqui (1982-1988) and Antonio Riviello Bazán (1988-1994), speculation has it that they were serving in high-visibility positions near the presidential palace in the period following the announcement of the official party's presidential candidate. The candidates had the opportunity to observe those officers, to interact with them, and to assess their loyalty for a few months prior to selecting them.

Despite recent changes in the political careers of presidents and their SECDEFs, the selection of a SECDEF remains the sole prerogative of the president. In turn, the SECDEF pledges the army's loyalty to the president and the nation. Since the revolution, all Mexican presidents have recognized the army as the principal guarantor of the constitution, the government, and the office of the presidency. Army leaders envision their institution as a senior partner in an organization for which the president serves as the chief executive officer.

The Role of the Army

The Mexican army has performed various roles that have proved critical to the maintenance of stability. This stability and its concomitant security have given the nation over 50 years of peace as well as the opportunity for growth and change within a constitutional framework.[43] The Constitution of 1917 and the army's organic law (the military institution's legal code) legally define the military's formal role in society. Those two documents, through the years, have provided the military little autonomy with regard to its principal responsibilities.

In 1926, the first organic law of the armed forces declared that the army's mission was "to defend the integrity and independence of the fatherland, to maintain the rule of the Constitution and its laws, and to conserve internal order."[44] The most recent addition to the organic laws modified that original mission. The task of maintaining the rule of the constitution and its laws has been removed and replaced with assisting the civilian population in times of need, performing civic action works that contribute to the country's progress, and providing disaster relief.[45] Although the army's mission has experienced only a slight modification since the initial organic law, the government had modified the military's mission informally as far back as the 1920s with respect to the performance of civic action.

Mexico's long-standing principles of nonintervention and respect for self-determination, combined with a general disdain for military solutions to international problems, have obviated the need for the armed forces to devote substantial energy to defending the nation from an external threat. As a result, the army has focused on preserving internal order. Political leaders also have encouraged the armed forces to perform roles that benefit the Mexican people and bring credit to the government. Both political and military leaders long have related civic action to the preservation of internal order. The army formally adopted that mission in the 1971 edition of the organic law and later expanded it in the 1986 law. In 1980, a former SECDEF, General Félix Galván López, stated that national security was "the maintenance of social, economic, and political equilibrium guaranteed by the armed forces."[46] Civic action applies directly to the maintenance of the country's economic and social equilibrium by furnishing key services to those in need and alleviating some of the pressure on the government to provide such services. In the post-Cold War era, and especially in light of recent events in Chiapas, leaders definitely perceive the most critical threats to be internal and military civic actions as enhancing internal security. The National Development Plans of the two most recent presidents, Miguel de la Madrid Hurtado (1982-1988) and Carlos Salinas de Gortari (1988-1994), appealed to the army to increase activities that promote the welfare of the people.[47] Through the years, military leaders have come to accept this role willingly because civic action has created a favorable image of the army.

This tradition goes back to the 1920s when the army built roads and irrigation works and repaired railroad and telegraph lines. Such "nation-building" had the added benefit of distracting the military's attention from politics.[48] For many years, these duties focused on the country's more isolated regions and often served as a symbol of the government's far-reaching influence. The specificities of this mission have evolved gradually to meet the needs of a developing society. For example, the army has moved from road construction and eradication of livestock diseases to such activities as participation in illegal drug eradication, security for vital government installations, reforestation, vaccination campaigns, tourist assistance on the highways, and security at the election polls.[49] The net result of these efforts in civic action has been largely positive. At the same time, this role has marked the army as a government institution subordinate to the directives of the president.

Traditionally, drug eradication has been viewed as a civic action function because of its correlation both to internal security and to the overall welfare of the affected population. In recent years, this task has taken on political dimensions as the escalating severity of the problem has had a major impact on U.S.-Mexican relations. While its involvement with this problem dates back to the late 1940s, the army began to intensify its campaign against illegal drugs during the late 1960s. Though the attorney general's office has overall responsibility for the antinarcotics campaign, the manual destruction of poppy and marijuana plants is specifically the army's duty.[50]

Twenty-five percent of the army's active forces participate full-time in this campaign. Not surprisingly, there have been growing allegations of corruption involving military personnel. The Salinas administration, sensing that drugs were becoming a greater threat to internal security, chose to attack the problem head-on, and not even the army has been able to escape public scrutiny, as was customary in the past.[51] Incidents implicating high-ranking army officers in drug trafficking have received broad coverage in the press. The most serious episode occurred in November 1991 and implicated soldiers in the murders of seven federal narcotics agents at a remote landing strip in the eastern coastal state of Veracruz. President Salinas reacted by ordering an investigation by the National Commission on Human Rights. Subsequently, two generals and three other officers were imprisoned for this crime.[52]

Needless to say, these incidents have been an embarrassment to the defense establishment and set the stage for a growing dilemma. The Mexican government has indicated on numerous occasions that it takes narcotics trafficking seriously, and the military plays an integral and expanding role in the government's war on drugs. In performing "police" versus "military" duties, the army finds itself more susceptible to allegations of corruption and human rights violations. Although its efforts in the antidrug campaign are lauded considerably more often than they are vilified, the rumors and accusations of wrongdoing leave the more lasting impression. In that regard, the army's association with the government has detracted from its popular image.[53]

The Mexican army has four sets of defense plans. The first includes plans for defending the nation from a foreign invader, and the second focuses on eliminating threats to internal security. The third and fourth sets provide for disaster relief and drug eradication. Mexico's nonconfrontational foreign policy has all but erased the need for the first class of plans.[54] When not absorbed with civic action, the army directs most of its efforts toward internal security threats. However, it generally does not get directly involved with these threats until they reach crisis proportions. However, when the army does perform this mission, its support of and affiliation with the government become most pronounced. While the performance of that role may subject the army to heavy criticism and allegations of repression, the army has no alternative but to respond to the government's directives. The constitution and the organic law demand loyalty to the institutions of government and to the president of the republic, who also serves as the supreme commander of the armed forces.

Since World War II, the army has reacted to only four major threats to internal security. Those perils included the student movement in 1968, the rural insurgency in the 1970s, the continuing struggle against the drug lords, and the recent insurrection in Chiapas. The army's reaction to the first threat seriously impugned its reputation. The untoward outcome of the "Tlatelolco Massacre" in October 1968 resulted in the deaths of from 25 to 500 people, depending on the source.[55] That incident has caused army leaders to discourage, at all costs, participation in large-scale social protests where soldiers might be called upon to engage in acts of repression against the Mexican people.[56] The army received less criticism for its campaigns against rural guerrillas in the 1970s and the drug lords in the 1980s because those enemies chose violence as the means to their ends. Events in Chiapas have been much more controversial and have subjected the military to national and international criticism and contributed to rifts in the civil-military relationship.

Despite the military's preference for low visibility, the army cannot escape the national limelight easily. Opponents of the government and the PRI are quick to accuse the army of being a political tool of the president. Because of presidential prerogatives, the army has had problems dispelling that label. For example, shortly after taking office, President Salinas decided to flex his military muscles in January 1989 by ordering the army to apprehend the corrupt leader of the national petroleum workers' union, Joaquín Hernández Galicia, nicknamed "La Quina," from his well-fortified compound in the state of Tamaulipas.[57] Later that year, the president sent a few thousand troops to the Cananea copper mine in northern Mexico as a preemptive move against striking mine workers.[58] The "political utilization" of the military always has sent a strong message to the opponents of the system. Many of Salinas' predecessors also were ready to employ the army when it was able to provide critical support for their administrations or ambitions. In such situations, the values and principles encapsulated in the military's ideology have left it virtually no opportunity for autonomous action.

Crisis situations leave the army vulnerable to criticism and have offered the greatest challenges to institutional loyalty. By the 1940s, the army had lost the political capacity to determine its intervention in a crisis. The Mexican Constitution grants the president the power to decide on the army's role in conflict resolution. In other words, the political system compels the army to respond to internal threats.[59] In most cases, army leaders simply follow the orders of their commander-in-chief. While those circumstances do not exonerate the army from acts of repression its members may have performed, they do attenuate the culpability directly affixed to the military.

The Mexican Military Looks to the Future

As the Mexican military moves toward the twenty-first century, tradition will continue to have a major influence on its evolution. Through the years, the military institution steadfastly has opposed significant changes or modifications to its organization and internal workings. The Mexican army has sought support and comfort from the values and principles of its creed. Although the army is beholden to the government, it seeks final approval from the Mexican people. A survey commissioned by the army produced some interesting feedback. Sixty-seven percent of those surveyed had a good opinion of the army, and 68 percent expressed confidence in it. Seventy-three percent of those polled believed that the army was beneficial to the country, 68 percent felt the army was on the side of the people, and 74 percent had a favorable impression of its role in the antidrug campaign.[60] Those findings did not suggest that a need for major change is on the horizon. Of course, they reflected views before the Chiapas uprising.

Since the 1930s, the army has never wavered seriously in its loyalty to the institutions emanating from the Mexican Revolution. By the 1950s, a strong partnership had been molded between the PRI-dominated governments and the military. This alliance has been solidified to a large extent through a process of reciprocity. The government has attended to the needs of the armed forces because at times it relies heavily on military support. As long as PRI officials and candidates maintain a healthy consensus among the Mexican people, the government will have no problem in retaining the army's endorsement. In the past, prominent disputes between the government and the military have been resolved principally through negotiation, which helps to explain both the country's stability and the PRI's ability to maintain power.[61] Whether the current economic crisis will alter that equation remains to be seen.

PRI-controlled governments have determined the path the military has followed since World War II.[62] In retrospect, the rationale for this course of action seems fairly apparent. After 1920, the ethos of the Mexican Revolution legitimized everything within the "revolutionary system" and nothing outside it. The Constitution of 1917 guaranteed the military a permanent and prominent position in this new system, something the army has never jeopardized. Because the PRI eventually became synonymous with the "revolutionary system," strong formal opposition parties never developed in Mexico until the 1980s. Under these conditions, the military has not developed strong ties with any opposition group, and its most powerful bond remains with the state, which has delivered more than 50 years of relative peace and progress.[63]

The army has grown accustomed to taking its cue from the government. The president of the republic sets the standard that state institutions follow. A pertinent example relates to the Salinas administration. Three months after President Salinas took office, an editorial in the army's official magazine spoke of the importance the president had attached to unity. The editorial exhorted members of the army to close ranks and help the commander-in-chief achieve his goal of national unity.[64] The armed forces historically have responded to presidential initiatives. That philosophy suggests little change to the army's missions as the year 2000 approaches. Civic action long has produced favorable results for the nation and has served to enhance the army's image with the Mexican people. Both military and political leaders would be very reluctant to abandon that mission in light of the many benefits it has produced.

The Mexican government has not shown any signs of reducing its efforts in the war on drugs. If anything, the resources devoted to the antidrug campaign have been on the rise. A greater commitment by the government to eradicate this scourge translates into a continuing and perhaps increased army role in that campaign. Although an expanded role in the drug wars may expose the military to greater risks of corruption, army leaders cannot back down from this challenge. To do so would be in direct violation of their hallowed creed, "The country comes first." Finally, the army will continue to perform its most vital mission of internal security by remaining prepared to respond to any serious crisis.

A relatively stable past does not necessarily portend more of the same for the future. The mystique of the revolution has dissipated gradually in the last few years, and the PRI-dominated government faced its first serious political challenge in recent memory during the 1988 presidential elections. The official party candidate confronted strong challenges from both the Left and the Right. Rumors circulated wildly about electoral fraud and how the PRI's candidate, Carlos Salinas de Gortari, actually had lost the election.[65] These rumors later proved to be unfounded, but the election results seemed to illustrate that the era of "easy victories" finally had passed. This was confirmed further in 1994 when, following the assassination of its original candidate, Luis Donaldo Colosio, the PRI actually trailed in the polls for several weeks. While its victory in 1994 was less controversial than the 1988 result, the party failed to win a majority of the vote.

President Salinas responded to these challenges aggressively by modernizing the economy and pushing passage of the North American Free Trade Agreement (NAFTA). However, challenges to the system will not subside. Witness the recent insurgency movement led by the Zapatista National Liberation Army in the problem-filled southern state of Chiapas. Although the army arrested the advance of the insurgents and the government has entered into negotiations with this group, the problems by no means have ended and offer an all-too-vivid illustration of what confronts President Ernesto Zedillo Ponce de León.[66]

Does the loyalty of the military rest first with the constitution or with the PRI-dominated government? The answer to this question would go a long way in clarifying the true character of the military institution in Mexico. The only way to answer this would be to observe the army's response to a victory in presidential elections by an opposition party. Observers then would be able to see if the army could extricate itself from a system its past leaders founded and nurtured. Such a scenario probably will not unfold in the immediate future. As a result, the Mexican army will continue to confront its most perplexing dilemma: having its reputation impugned at times because of its close association with a PRI-dominated system that many have labeled as "undemocratic." Under existing circumstances, the army should prepare itself for the situation expressed in an anonymous Mexican poem — "The people love God and the soldier in moments of danger, not before; when the danger has passed and everything returns to normal, they forget about God . . . and despise the soldier."[67]

Postscript

The 1994 New Year's celebration in Mexico sent shock waves through the Salinas government. One hour into the new year, the Zapatista National Liberation Army, recognized by the Spanish initials EZLN, attacked and temporarily captured four cities in the Los Altos region of Mexico's southernmost state, Chiapas. Although Mexico's political and military leaders denied this uprising had taken them by surprise, there is little doubt that the magnitude of the insurgency caught these leaders totally off guard.

The upstart Zapatistas promptly implored the Mexican people to commit actively to a nationwide movement for "jobs, land, housing, food, health, independence, freedom, democracy, justice, and peace." According to its first proclamation, the EZLN did not aim to destroy the state but rather sought to shift "the balance of forces in favor of popular and democratic movements, thereby isolating and ultimately defeating antidemocratic tendencies within the PRI, the state, and the rest of society."[68] This uprising, a concatenation of endemic economic, political, and social problems in Chiapas and other rural regions in Mexico, has affected the Mexican army in a number of respects. To begin with, the army's response has given impetus to changes in Mexico's long-standing civil-military relationship. More specifically, events in Chiapas forced the military to acknowledge and to respond formally to the nation's transition to democracy.

From the outset of the conflict, the army found itself playing second fiddle to the masked EZLN leader, Subcomandante Marcos. Marcos gained popularity by projecting himself as a modern-day Robin Hood. This led to consternation among army leaders who classified the Zapatistas as traitors. After all, they had declared war on the army, called for nonrecognition of the president, and demanded a new, transitional government.[69]

This conflict had two phases. The first was a military phase that lasted until January 12, 1994, when President Salinas declared a unilateral cease-fire. By that time, the army presence in the region had swelled from 2,000 to 14,000 soldiers, more than enough to cordon off the EZLN stronghold in the Lacandona jungle. The second or political phase commenced after the cessation of hostilities and has been highlighted by the government's appointment of a commissioner for peace and reconciliation and passage by the Mexican Congress of an amnesty decree.[70]

Allegations of widespread human rights violations during the conflict made the army the initial scapegoat for the rebellion. However, as evidence of economic and political repression in the region came more into the public eye, the military received partial exoneration. As the crisis evolved, it became apparent that high-level government officials had been aware of the problems in Chiapas but had underestimated their gravity and opted to ignore them until after the August 1994 presidential elections.[71]

Not since the student movement of 1968 and the accompanying misfortune of Tlatelolco had the army found itself exposed to such a high level of public criticism. The press, both international and local, and numerous nongovernmental organizations subjected the armed forces to severe attacks over alleged human rights violations. In one sense, the conflict in Chiapas represents a watershed for the army. Since the end of the revolution, the army always has been viewed as an *intocable* or untouchable. However, events in Chiapas seem to have brought an abrupt end to this status. What one analyst labeled as an "irregular relationship" between the military and the president appears to have reached a critical juncture, and army leaders have begun to demonstrate serious concern over the impugning of their proud tradition of loyal service to the nation.[72]

Despite having received some valuable support from the army (see, for example, the La Quina and Cananea episodes described above) that allowed him to assert his authority after an inauspicious inauguration, President Salinas remained uncharacteristically silent in his defense of the armed forces. Traditionally, in those few instances when the army has been the subject of public scrutiny, the president of the republic always has spoken out in defense of the military. However, Salinas opted to leave military leaders to fend for themselves.

Consequently, press criticism lodged against the army has been steadily on the rise since 1989.[73]

In 1989, numerous reports circulated throughout Mexico and the United States implicating a former SECDEF in high-level narcotics corruption. President Salinas chose not to offer any disclaimers. He adopted the same approach with respect to the 1991 murder of the federal narcotics agents discussed above. By 1993, the attacks on the military had accelerated. In April 1993, the army's dispute with the Catholic bishop in Chiapas received considerable publicity, most reports siding with the bishop. Some sources suggested a military role in the assassination the following month of a Catholic cardinal in Guadalajara by members of a drug cartel. In December, a truth commission investigating events surrounding the 1968 student move-ment opened old wounds with accusations of army complicity in the student deaths at Tlatelolco. Finally, a high-ranking army officer accused the army of violating the civil rights of its soldiers and officers. Subsequently, a number of journalists chose to sensationalize the story when the officer was jailed, ostensibly for defaming the army's reputation.[74]

As criticism intensified after the Chiapas rebellion, the SECDEF, General Antonio Riviello Bazán, decided to launch a public relations campaign in defense of his institution. This seemed a tacit acknowledg-ment by the military that the transitions to democracy had changed the political modus operandi.[75] The military now finds itself in a highly competitive environment where it must compete with other interest groups for scarce resources. To be successful, the military must formulate new strategies for this period.[76]

These recent developments suggest a distancing by the military from the PRI. In the past, the constitution provided ample legitimation for the close relationship with the PRI. The constitution demands the armed forces' loyalty to presidents who doubled as informal heads of the official party. Given the historically weak political opposition, this relationship was seldom questioned. However, the past decade has seen the rise of viable opposition parties, causing the army to reconsider its close allegiance to the PRI and its leaders to declare strict neutrality in the presidential succession process.[77]

Although the PRI candidate, Ernesto Zedillo, won the August 1994 presidential election by a clear-cut margin, army leaders seem pre-pared to react more cautiously to the dictates of political leaders, especially when such directives might impact negatively on the army's reputation. While this new restraint probably will not affect the way the army performs its missions, it likely will change the military mindset. Comments by an army general illustrate this new trend. He declared that the army would not attack the Zapatistas unless the EZLN attacked first. He further stated that if the president ordered the army to attack, it would do so only if Congress approved the order and if the president decreed a suspension of constitutional guarantees. Comments such as these suggest that the current president will have to make concessions to win back the military's confidence.[78]

As of mid-1996, the situation in Chiapas seems to have reached a stalemate. In the long run, this scenario favors government forces that have surrounded the Zapatistas. Given the PRI's new mandate, the Zapatista movement may be destined for an early burial. Mexico's long-standing predilection for negotiation as a solution to problems does not portend a significant increase in the size of the armed forces in the near future. As the crisis in Chiapas de-escalates, the army will redirect forces back into the antidrug campaign. On a more cautionary note, the disturbing rise in political violence, as evidenced by the assassinations of PRI presidential candidate Luis Donaldo Colosio and PRI president José Francisco Ruiz Massieu and a rash of high-profile kidnappings, requires close monitoring by the Zedillo administration.[79] A continuation of this dangerous trend may force the government to rely more heavily on the military for political security and public tranquillity. The guarantees army leaders attempt to exact in return for their support could provide an early indication as to the future direction of civil-military relations in Mexico.

Notes

1. Mexico's armed forces do not have a single commander. There is a secretary of national defense who commands the army and air force and a secretary of the navy who controls the navy and marine corps. Although exact figures are not available, it is estimated that the armed forces in Mexico number about 130,000. The army makes up about 75 percent of those forces, while the navy and air force represent 19 and 6 percent, respectively. Budgetary allocations correspond roughly with the strength of each service. The army long has been the dominant service in both size and influence. For that reason, this study focuses almost exclusively on the army, and the words *army* and *military* are used interchangeably. For general information about the size, mission, organization, and structure of the Mexican armed forces, see Arturo Sánchez Gutiérrez, 1992, "El estado y los militares en los años ochenta," in Jorge Alonso, Alberto Aziz Nassif, and Jaime Tamayo, eds., *El Nuevo Estado Mexicano, Tomo II, Estado y política* (Guadalajara: Universidad de Guadalajara, Nueva Imagen, CIESAS), 13-42; and Stephen J. Wager, 1984, "Basic Characteristics of the Modern Mexican Military," in David F. Ronfeldt, ed., *The Modern Mexican Military: A Reassessment* (La Jolla, Calif.: Center for U.S.-Mexican Studies), 87-105.

2. This is a principal thesis of Edwin Lieuwen's (1968) *Mexican Militarism: The Political Rise and Fall of the Revolutionary Army 1910-1940* (Albuquerque: University of New Mexico Press).

3. Héctor Aguilar Camín and Lorenzo Meyer, 1990, *A la sombra de la Revolución Mexicana* (Mexico City: Cal y Arena), 213-214; and Felícitas López Portillo, 1991, "Las glorias del desarrollismo: el gobierno de Miguel Alemán," *Secuencia* 19 (January-April): 61-63 and 72-73.

4. Arnaldo Córdova, 1972, *La formación del poder político en México* (Mexico City: Ediciones Era, S.A.), 50-51; and Lieuwen 1968, 57-68.

5. Guillermo Boils, 1975, *Los Militares y la Política en México, 1915-1974* (Mexico City: Ediciones El Caballito), 40; Roger D. Hansen, 1971, *The Politics of Mexican Development* (Baltimore: Johns Hopkins University Press), 158; Virginia Prewitt, 1941, "The Mexican Army," *Foreign Affairs* XIX (April), 613; and Lieuwen 1968, 64-72.

6. Alejandra Lajous, 1985, *Los orígenes del partido único en México*, 3rd ed. (Mexico City: Universidad Autónoma de México), 53-63; and Lieuwen 1968, 75-78.

7. Jorge Alberto Lozoya, 1968, *El Ejército Mexicano*, 3rd ed. (Mexico City: Jornadas 65), 57-58; Aguilar Camín and Meyer 1990, 107-112; Hansen 1971, 61-62; and Lieuwen 1968, 95-109.

8. Daniel C. Levy, 1990, "Mexico: Sustained Civilian Rule Without Democracy," in Larry Diamond, Juan J. Linz, and Seymour Martin Lipset, eds., *Politics in Developing Countries: Comparing Experiences with Democracy* (Boulder, Colo.: Lynne Rienner), 464-465; José Luis Piñeyro, 1985, *Ejército y Sociedad en México: Pasado y Presente* (Puebla: Universidad Autónoma de Puebla), 51-52; Boils 1975, 65-66; and Lajous 1985, 24-25 and 86-87.

9. Samuel P. Huntington, 1969, *Political Order in Changing Societies* (New Haven, Conn.: Yale University Press), 255-256.

10. Huntington 1969, 257 and 318; Lajous 1968, 25-27; and Lozoya 1968, 59-62.

11. Huntington 1969, 318; and Lieuwen 1968, 125.

12. Lieuwen 1968, 125.

13. Frank Brandenburg, 1964, *The Making of Modern Mexico* (Englewood Cliffs, N.J.: Prentice-Hall), 91-94; Pablo González Casanova, 1970, *Democracy in Mexico*, tr. Danielle Salti (London: Oxford University Press), 37-38; Hansen 1971, 94; and Huntington 1969, 317-320.

14. Lieuwen 1968, 123-130; and Lozoya 1968, 65-71.

15. Lozoya 1968, 72-73, writes that 15 of the 36 military representatives at the PRM's constituent assembly went on to hold positions of political importance. Two officers, General Heriberto Jara and Captain Alfonso Corona del Rosal, eventually would serve as presidents of the official party. However, only General Marcelino García Barragán would occupy the post of secretary of national defense (1964-1970). Although Jara and Coronal del Rosal both attained considerable political influence, neither obtained commensurate influence with the army, precisely because of their political status. Lyle N. McAlister, Anthony P. Maingot, and Robert P. Potash, eds., 1970, *The Military in Latin American Sociopolitical Evolution: Four Case Studies* (Washington, D.C.: Center for Research in Social Systems), 37, makes a similar point about the failure of "political" officers to carry out a distinguished "military" career.

16. Phyllis Greene Walker, 1987, "The Modern Mexican Military: Political Influence and Institutional Interests in the 1980s" (M.A. thesis, The American University), 89-91, offers a useful synopsis of this antimilitary bias in Mexican society.

17. Levy 1990, 459-462.

18. Levy 1990, 471-473.

19. See Samuel P. Huntington, 1957, *The Soldier and the State* (Cambridge: The Belknap Press), 62-64, for an explanation of the professional military ethic.

20. This motto tends to be a recurring theme in the editorials of the army's official magazine, *Revista del Ejército* (after 1972 renamed *Revista del Ejército y Fuerza Aérea Mexicanos*), especially in selected August editions commemorating the death of Vicente Guerrero. The secretaries of national defense always have referred to this motto in some of their public speeches. For example, the present defense minister, General Antonio Riviello Bazán, stated that the "armed forces reaffirm their unalterable commitment: 'The Country Comes First,'" in an address to the president of the republic on December 3, 1988, two days after taking office. See Secretaría de la Defensa Nacional, 1989, *Intervenciones y Discursos del Secretario de la Defensa Nacional, General Antonio Riviello Bazán, correspondientes a los meses de diciembre de 1988 a diciembre de 1989.*

21. An independent survey commissioned by the Mexican army solicited comments on the values or concepts that characterized the armed forces. The survey lists eight concepts, and four of those (loyalty, discipline, nationalism, and patriotism) coincide with the components of the army's ideology listed above. See Secretaría de la Defensa Nacional, 1993, *Encuesta sobre el Ejército y la Fuerza Aérea Mexicanos* (Mexico City: Taller Autográfico de la Secretaría de la Defensa Nacional).

22. Robert E. Scott, 1964, *Mexican Government in Transition*, rev. ed. (Urbana: University of Illinois Press), 101; and Levy 1990, 464.

23. Alfonso Corona del Rosal, 1949, *Moral Military Civismo*, 2nd ed. (Mexico City: Talleres Gráfico de la Nación), 220.

24. Robert Wesson, ed., 1986, *The Latin American Military Institution* (New York: Praeger Publishers), 128.

25. Frederick C. Turner, 1967, "México: las causas de la limitación militar," *Aportes* 6 (October): 63.

26. *Revista del Ejército*, January 1966, 7.

27. José Luis Piñeyro, 1989, "The Modernization of the Mexican Armed Forces," in Augusto Varas, ed., *Democracy Under Siege* (New York: Greenwood Press), 126.

28. Alan Knight, 1987, *U.S.-Mexican Relations, 1910-1940*, Monograph Series 28 (La Jolla, Calif.: Center for U.S.-Mexican Studies, University of California, San Diego), 31.

29. Presidencia de la República, 1970, *El Gobierno Mexicano* 1 (December): 30.

30. Adolfo Aguilar Zinser, 1990, "Civil Relations in Mexico," in Louis W. Goodman, Johanna S.R. Mendelson, and Juan Rial, eds., *The Military and Democracy* (Lexington, Ky.: D.C. Heath and Company), 223-225.

31. Pablo González Casanova, 1988, *Los Militares y la Política en América Latina* (Mexico City: Ediciones Océano, S.A.), 69.

32. Piñeyro 1985, 136.

33. Aguilar Zinser 1990, 222.

34. Roderic A. Camp, 1980, *Mexico's Leaders: Their Education and Recruitment* (Tucson: University of Arizona Press), 15-38, provides a useful explanation of these characteristics as they pertain to the political system. Peter H. Smith, 1979, *Labyrinths of Power* (Princeton, N.J.: Princeton University Press), 50-52, offers a good description of the *camarilla*, the Mexican term for political clique or alliance.

35. Wager 1984, 90-91.

36. Boils 1975, 27.

37. Boils 1975, 108; Lieuwen 1968, 114; and McAlister, Maingot, and Potash 1970, 233-234.

38. Secretaría de Gobernación, 1988, *Constitución Política de los Estados Unidos Mexicanos* (Mexico City), 103-104.

39. Interview, May 1991, with former high-level Mexican political official.

40. Interview, May 1991.

41. Archivo General de la Nación, Presidential Archive of Adolfo Ruiz Cortines, file 556.1/105.

42. Luis Echeverría Alvarez (1970-1976), José López Portillo (1976-1982), Miguel de la Madrid Hurtado (1982-1988), and Carlos Salinas de Gortari (1988-1994) fall into this category of "technocrat presidents," not having been elected to political office prior to the presidency.

43. Raúl Benítez Manaut, 1992, "Las Fuerzas Armadas Mexicanas y su relación con el estado, el sistema político y la sociedad," Paper presented at the Consejo Latinamericano de Ciencias Sociales, in Guatemala City, November 11-13, 2-3.

44. *Ley orgánica del ejército y armada nacionales*, March 15, 1926.

45. *Ley Orgánica del Ejército y Fuerza Aerea Mexicanos*, December 8, 1986.

46. Roberto Vizcaíno, 1980, "La Seguridad del País, Fin Primordial del Estado," *Proceso* 22, (September 22): 6.

47. Luis Herrera-Lasso M. and Guadalupe González, 1990, "Balance y Perspectivas en el uso del concepto de la seguridad nacional en el case de Mexico," in Sergio Aguayo Quezada and Bruce Bagley, eds., *En busca de la seguridad perdida* (Mexico City: Siglo Veintiuno Editores), 400-401.

48. Bruno Galindo Trejo, 1970, "Del Civismo en el Ejército," *Revista del Ejército*, (September): 41-43; Boils 1975, 127-129; McAlister, Maingot, and Potash 1970, 209-210; and Prewitt 1941, 613-616.

49. Estado Mayor, Secretaría de la Defensa Nacional, 1989, *I Cuerpo de Ejército, Actividades Desarrolladas Durante el 2/o Semestre de 1989*.

50. See Richard B. Craig, 1978, "La Campaña Permanente, Mexico's Anti-Drug Campaign," *Journal of Interamerican Studies and World Affairs* 20 (May): 107-131; and Sánchez Gutiérrez 1992, 31-33, for an explanation of the army's role in the national antidrug campaign.

51. "Mexican President Vows War on Drugs," *The Chicago Tribune*, October 5, 1989, 8; and "Mexico Will Press Drug War, But Without Any U.S. Troops," *The New York Times*, October 5, 1989, 20.

52. The first incident is addressed in William Branigin, 1989, "Mexican Crackdown on Drugs Steps Lightly Around Military," *The Washington Post*, August 15, 12. The attack on the federal agents is covered in Tim Golden, 1991, "Mexican Army Officers Held in Drug Agents' Deaths," *The New York Times*, December 7, 3; "SDN y PGR: el tiroteo entre soldados y agents federales, por una confusión," *UnoMásUno*, November 13; and Carlos Marín, 1991, "Los judiciales iniciaron el tiroteo contra los soldados," *Proceso*, December 9, 6-10.

53. In a poll conducted by a marketing and research firm in Mexico City, 74 percent of those sampled had a favorable opinion of the army's contributions to the war on drugs, and 70 percent supported a continuing military role in the antidrug campaign even if it produced minor levels of corruption within the military (Secretaría de la Defensa Nacional 1993). However, the impression often put forth in some of the press coverage of the drug wars is not as favorable. See, for example, the May 31, June 7, and July 5, 1993, editions of *Proceso*, in which the lead stories criticize the military's inability to combat the drug lords and allude to growing levels of military corruption.

54. José Luis Piñeyro, 1987, "Presencia política militar nacional en el Distrito Federal: propuestas de análisis," in Pablo González Casanova and Juan Manuel Ramírez Sáenz, eds., *D.F. gobierno y sociedad civil* (Mexico City: Ediciones El Caballito), 69-76.

55. James D. Cockcroft, 1983, *Mexico: Class Formation, Capital Accumulation, and the State* (New York: Monthly Review Press), 240-241; Judith Alder Hellman, 1978, *Mexico in Crisis* (New York: Holmes and Meier Publishers, Inc.), 139-145; Kenneth F. Johnson, 1978, *Mexican Democracy: A Critical View*, rev. ed. (New York: Praeger Publishers), 1-9; Evelyn P. Stevens, 1974, *Protest and Response in Mexico* (Cambridge, Mass.: The M.I.T. Press), 185-240; and Sergio Zermeño, 1985, *México: Una Democracia Utópica*, 5th ed. (Mexico City: Siglo Veintiuno Editores), xvi-23.

56. Benítez Manaut 1992, 7-9. Alan Riding, a long-time correspondent in Mexico City, suggested that political leaders prefer not to use military force to resolve an internal conflict because of the political cost involved. See Alan Riding, 1985, *Distant Neighbors* (New York: Alfred A. Knopf), 92.

57. Herrera-Lasso M. and González G. 1990, 395; and Sánchez Gutiérrez 1992, 35.

58. Lorenzo Meyer, 1989, "Ejército y Cananeas del Futuro," *Excélsior*, September 6, 1.

59. Boils 1975, 101 and 113; and Lozoya 1968, 125-126.

60. Secretaría de la Defensa Nacional 1993.

61. Benítez Manaut 1992, 10.

62. Sánchez Gutiérrez 1992, 42.

63. Herrera Lasso-M. and González G. 1990, 402-403; and Levy 1990, 471-472.

64. *Revista del Ejército y Fuerza Aeréa Mexicanos*, March 1989, 3.

65. Levy 1990, 473-477.

66. See *The New York Times* editions beginning with January 4, 1994, for coverage of this latest insurrection.

67. *Revista del Ejército y Fuerza Aeréa Mexicanos*, May 1992, 3.

68. Neil Harvey, 1994, "Rebellion in Chiapas: Rural Reforms, Campesino Radicalism, and the Limits to Stalinismo," *Transformation of Rural Mexico* 5 (La Jolla, Calif.: Center for U.S.-Mexican Studies, University of California at San Diego), 1-2.

69. Raúl Benítez Manaut, 1994, "El desafío de las guerrillas," *Nueva Sociedad* 130 (March-April): 24-26; Arturo Cano and Daniel Moreno, 1994, "La guerrilla que no existía," *Enfoque*, January 9, 18-20; *Epoca*, January 10, 1994, 8-15; and Andrew Reding, 1994, "Chiapas is Mexico," *World Policy Journal* 11 (Spring): 11-12. Subcomandante Marcos appeared on the popular newsmagazine "60 Minutes" in March 1994, where he was portrayed as a modern-day Robin Hood.

70. Benítez Manaut 1994, 28-30.

71. Interview with Mexican official having close ties to CISN, March 1994; interview with high-ranking Mexican military officer, March 1994; and Raymundo Riva Palacio, 1994, "Entremés Dominical," *El Financiero*, January 23. In his interview on "60 Minutes," Marcos stated that the government had sought to cover up the serious problem in Chiapas in order to ensure safe passage of NAFTA.

72. Carlos Ramírez, 1994a, "Archivo Político," *El Financiero*, February 13.

73. Ramírez 1994a.

74. Roberto Zamarripa, 1993a, "Censura Gobernación declaraciones de Patrocinio; luego rectifica y vuelve a censurar," *Proceso*, October; 1993b, "Informe de la Comisión de la Verdad 68," *La Jornada*, December 17, 1993; Alberto Aguirre and Igancio Ramírez, 1993, "El General Riviello aceptó que en el 68 el Ejército fue utilizado más allá de sus atribuciones," *Proceso*, December 27, 12-14; Manuel Robles and Rodrigo Vera, 1994, "Ocurrencias, contradicciones y mentiras, los recursos del gobierno para cerrar archivos del 68," *Proceso*, January 3, 6-9; Sergio Aguayo Quezada, 1993, "Los misterios del 68," *La Jornada*, December 29; Roberto Zamarripa, 1993c, "Autoritarismo, impunidad y ejercicio irracional del poder dentro del Ejército, ponen en riesgo la seguridad nacional," *Proceso*, December 13, 20-24; Octavio Rodríguez Araujo, 1993, "El caso Gallardo," *La Jornada*, December 23; and Anthony DePalma, 1993, "A Mexican General, in Prison, Says the Army Flouts Rights," *The New York Times*, December 23.

75. "México cree en la lealtad, la practica y la reconoce como valor: Riviello Bazán," *La Jornada*, February 10, 1994; Ramírez 1994a; Carlos Ramírez, 1994b,

"Indicador Político," *El Financiero*, February 18; and Amparo Trejo and Julieta Medina, 1994, "Somos un Ejército para lograr la paz," *Reforma*, February 20.

76. Most of these ideas were developed as a result of discussions with two Mexican academics during a visit to Mexico City in March 1994.

77. Ramírez 1994b.

78. Ignacio Rodríguez Reyna, 1994, "La Hora de los Generales," *El Financiero*, September 27.

79. An editorial in the October 6, 1994, edition of *The New York Times* highlights this growing trend toward political violence.

VII

From Triumph to Survival: Cuba's Armed Forces in an Era of Transition

Richard L. Millett

Introduction

The past dozen years have been a time of profound transition and increasing tension for Cuba's Revolutionary Armed Forces (FAR). At the start of the 1980s, the armed forces had reached a level of power and prestige unprecedented in the history of Latin America. With a total strength of over 150,000 in regular forces, supplemented by additional units attached to the Interior Ministry (MININT) and conscripts assigned to the Youth Labor Army (EJT), it was a modern and formidable force. The Soviet Union had furnished it with large amounts of relatively modern equipment, including MiG-23 aircraft, MI-24 combat helicopters, SA-6 surface-to-air missiles, and T-54/55 and T-62 main battle tanks. While the bulk of these forces were assigned to defense and internal security missions, units and advisors also were stationed in nearly a dozen foreign nations, notably Angola, Ethiopia, Congo, Nicaragua, and Grenada. Estimates of the number of Cuban military personnel serving in such missions ranged up to 70,000. In addition to its regular military involvement, Cuba was providing training and other forms of assistance to insurgent movements in numerous other nations, such as El Salvador, Colombia, and Namibia. At the same time, Cuba itself received major training assistance from the Soviet Union and other East Bloc nations and had Soviet military units stationed in its territory. For Fidel Castro and the FAR, there was a heady sense of being on the winning side of history, as revolutionary socialism seemed to be gaining ground steadily in the Third World.

By 1995, this situation had changed radically. The FAR was beginning a major period of downsizing, its equipment was aging and becoming increasingly difficult to maintain, and its military training and assistance from other nations virtually had disappeared. Morale was declining, a situation highlighted by a rising tide of defections, especially from the air force. The internationalist mission, so central to the FAR's mission in the 1980s, for all practical purposes had ended. According to Defense Minister Raúl Castro Ruz, Fidel's younger brother, the only Cuban military personnel stationed outside the nation were ten military attachés. Far from being on the winning side of history, Cuba found itself increasingly isolated, clinging to an ideology that had been rejected by most of the world and trying to forestall economic collapse. These changes brought into question the nature and missions of the FAR and made its future an open question. The ability of the Cuban government in general and the Defense Ministry (MINFAR) in particular to respond to these growing problems and to adapt the FAR to the new national and international situation will prove fundamental in shaping Cuba's future.

Historical Development of the FAR

The Cuban military differs from its counterparts in the rest of Latin America in several fundamental ways. It does not have its roots in the traditions of the Spanish conquest and, therefore, lacks the traditions of sharp social cleavages between military and civilians or between officers and enlisted personnel. There never has been a serious effort by the FAR to overthrow or, so far as can be told, even to force basic policy changes upon the government. The intricate web of ties between the FAR and the ruling Cuban Communist Party (PCC) acts both to maintain control over and to insure the loyalty of the armed forces. Fidel Castro's role both as leader of the Cuban Revolution and virtual founder of the FAR further strengthens this process. His ties with many senior officers, dating back in many cases to the insurgent struggle against the dictatorship of Fulgencio Batista in the 1950s, not to mention the role of his brother Raúl as defense minister, provide yet another level of control absent in most Latin American military establishments. The relationship between the FAR and the Castro brothers is fundamentally different from that existing between most other military institutions and their commanders. In the traditional case, such figures are products of the military institution, with a high degree of identification with and loyalty to the institution. The Castros, however, are the creators not the product of the institution and expect it to be loyal to them rather than their being loyal to it.

While there are efforts to establish historical links between the FAR and the insurgents who fought for independence from Spain in the late 1800s, today's Cuban military consciously rejects links with the armed forces that existed from the start of the twentieth century until the triumph of Castro's revolution in 1959. Instead, its roots remain firmly planted in the 26th of July insurgent movement that Fidel Castro created and led. As a result, the FAR's military doctrine always has been a mixture of conventional and guerrilla strategies and tactics, an uneasy combination of Soviet training and Castro's own somewhat romanticized military experience.

From early on, the FAR identified world capitalism/imperialism in general and the United States in particular as its natural enemy. The defeat of a U.S.-backed exile invasion at Playa Girón (the Bay of Pigs) in 1961 and the subsequent campaign against internal guerrilla forces, inevitably portrayed as mercenary puppets of the United States, still are portrayed as its greatest triumphs. Indeed, that campaign officially is styled the *Lucha Contra Bandidos* (war against bandits) in order to deny those who fought against the revolution any sense of military legitimacy. This trend continues today, as the regime portrays internal dissidents and even Latin American leaders who dare to criticize the Cuban political situation as "puppets of American imperialism."

If Playa Girón is the FAR's greatest triumph, the humiliation of the 1962 Cuban Missile Crisis is one of its most enduring traumas. It remains a symbol of the possibility of a U.S. invasion, stood for decades as a reminder of the tenuous nature of Soviet commitments to Cuban defense, and provides clear evidence of the limits of Cuban military power. Determination to avoid such humiliations in the future has helped shape Cuban defense doctrine, as well as contributed to the portrayal of the United States as the ultimate threat to national sovereignty. At the same time, the terms under which this crisis was resolved actually reduced the danger of an imminent U.S. attack and allowed the FAR, during the subsequent decade, to develop into a modern, Soviet-style military institution.

The FAR reached a peak strength of approximately 300,000 in the early 1960s. Much of this force, however, was poorly trained and equipped, and maintaining such numbers on active duty posed a huge burden for a struggling economy. As a result, the FAR slowly was reduced during the latter half of the decade, falling below 250,000 by 1970. At the same time, much of the force was employed in agricultural labor, especially during the annual sugar harvests. This, however, proved both costly and inefficient. In the 1970s, reflecting increased Soviet influence, the armed forces underwent a major restructuring. Active forces were reduced sharply, falling to 117,000 by 1975, but equipment and training were upgraded significantly. An active reserve of just under 100,000 was created, and a roughly equal number were assigned to the Youth Labor Army (EJT), a paramilitary force made up of the least educated or reliable conscripts and officers and, for the most part, devoted to agricultural and construction tasks.

All this reflected several basic changes in Cuba's military orientation. By the early 1970s, both the threat of U.S. invasion and the prospects of a series of communist guerrilla victories in Latin America, modeled on the Cuban experience, had receded. Economic failures increased dependency on the Soviet Union which, in turn, increased Soviet influence over the military. The process of U.S. withdrawal from Vietnam, coupled with the era of detente in East-West relations, created a world climate in which Cuba's military role was less than clear. While Fidel Castro still could declare in 1974 that Cuba needed continued growth in its military capacity because, no matter what the state of East-West relations, "our defense can never depend on the good faith of imperialists," the Cuban armed forces seemed condemned to a largely static defensive role.[1]

Throughout the 1960s and 1970s, ties between the state's political and military apparatus were established and strengthened. Their common origins in the insurgent struggle against Batista facilitated this process. So, too, did the overlapping of civil and military assignments and lines of authority in the early years of the revolution. Formal political indoctrination of the military began in 1961, and two years later, party chapters were organized officially within the FAR. The party as an institution, however, never achieved the influence or control over the military that was the pattern in most communist states. Instead, political indoctrination was viewed as a means of supporting discipline and assisting in achieving military goals. While the great majority of officers joined the party or its youth organization, their primary identification remained with the military. Within the party itself, there was a disproportionate degree of military influence at the highest levels. In 1965, 69 percent of the PCC's Central Committee was composed of individuals with military rank. While the percentage of military figures in the Central Committee has declined over time, such figures still occupy over one-quarter of the seats.

This blending of political and military functions reflects both the domination of the Castro brothers and the fact that in Cuba the official party was a product of the revolutionary army. In this regard, its heritage was closer to that of Vietnam or China than it was to the prevailing system in most of Eastern Europe. The result was to produce what Harvard Professor Jorge Dominguez has termed the civic soldier. According to Dominguez, what developed in Cuba during the 1960s was a situation in which one could not, in traditional terms, "speak of either civilian control over the military or military control over the civilians." In stark contrast to the pattern prevailing elsewhere in the hemisphere, Cuba was ruled in large part by military men who govern large segments of both military and civilian life, who are held up as paragons to both soldiers and civilians, who are the bearers of the revolutionary tradition and ideology, who have politicized themselves by absorbing the norms and organization of the Communist Party, and who have educated themselves to become professionals in political, economic, managerial, engineering, and educational as well as military affairs.[2]

While this arrangement kept civil-military conflicts at a level well below that prevailing in most of Latin America, it did not eliminate all tensions. There have been disputes between military commanders and party functionaries, especially when the latter attempted to influence military discipline and conduct. There also were rivalries between the FAR and the Interior Ministry. These grew out of overlaps in jurisdictions, notably in areas of internal security and intelligence, the presence within MININT of combat units, the "Special Troops," an elite unit directly under Fidel Castro's command, and after the reforms of the mid-1970s, the assumption of equivalent military rank by MININT officials. Additionally, problems between the military and civil society were produced by the introduction of compulsory military service under a system that allowed military officials to give preferential assignments, training, and even shortened terms of service to selected individuals. The net effect of such problems, however, has been quite limited. In general, the Cuban model, at least until the end of the 1980s, served the interests of both the military and the party reasonably well.

The 1960s also saw the beginnings of the "internationalist" mission of the FAR. As early as 1963, Cuban units were sent to Algeria to take part in that nation's border conflict with Morocco. In 1966, troops were sent to the Congo (Brazzaville) where they remained, supporting the military regime for nearly 25 years. In the early 1970s, additional forces were introduced into South Yemen and Syria. Yet, compared to the massive interventions in Angola and Ethiopia in the latter half of the 1970s, these were relatively small-scale operations. In these latter cases, Cuban army and air force units played major combat roles, suffering over 2,000 casualties but also achieving significant military successes. In Ethiopia, they helped repel a Somali invasion in the Ogaden region, while in Angola, they defeated attacks by both U.S.-supported insurgents and regular units of South Africa's armed forces. While their efforts were heavily dependent upon Soviet logistical support, operational decisions remained largely in Cuban hands.

The end of the 1970s and the start of the 1980s also witnessed a revival of Cuban-supported insurgencies in the hemisphere. A revolutionary/Marxist regime took power in Grenada, and the Frente Sandinista (FSLN), which had a long history of ties to Cuba, overthrew the Somoza family dictatorship in Nicaragua. Suriname's military dictator asked for and received Cuban military support, and insurgent movements with varying degrees of ties to Cuba appeared to be gaining ground in El Salvador, Guatemala, and Colombia. By the early 1980s, the FAR had become a force to contend with in wide areas of the Third World.

The 1980s: A Decade of Crises

On May 1, 1980, Fidel Castro suddenly announced a major change in Cuban military doctrine and organization. A mass-based territorial militia (MTT), ultimately incorporating nearly 1.5 million people, was to be created, and national defense was to be based upon the concept of a "war of all the people." This meant mass distribution of arms and plans for a prolonged guerrilla-style conflict. It diverted resources from the FAR and created numerous potential problems. These included placing responsibility for the MTT under MININT rather than MINFAR and assigning local defense responsibilities to councils run by the local party head.

These changes were justified later as a response to the aggressive attitude of the Ronald Reagan administration and to subsequent secret Soviet statements that they would not aid Cuba in case of a U.S. invasion. However, since Castro announced the new policy long before Reagan's election, such explanations were obviously inadequate. More likely, the MTT was created for political reasons: to mobilize popular support for the revolution, to revive fears of possible U.S. invasion, and to serve as a check on the power and independence of the FAR.

While the creation of the MTT meant a reduced role for the FAR in domestic defense, other developments in the first half of the 1980s began to erode the FAR's internationalist mission. Most notable was the U.S. invasion of Grenada and the poor performance of the Cuban commander on that island. Cuba's expulsion from Grenada (and the reactive decision of Suriname to expel its Cuban military advisors) represented a humiliating defeat for the Castro brothers and revived concerns about possible attacks on Cuba itself.

Problems in the internationalist mission continued throughout the 1980s. Reports of growing disillusionment with African operations, even among senior officers, began to spread. The war in Angola seemed endless, while in Ethiopia, the Cubans found themselves tied to a brutal regime that dedicated its resources to fighting a popular uprising in Eritrea while its population starved. At the same time, prospects for Marxist guerrilla victories in Central America had receded, and the friendly Sandinista regime in Nicaragua found itself fighting for survival against a U.S.-sponsored insurgency.

Ultimately, Cuba settled for a negotiated peace in Angola, which provided for Namibian independence but also allowed the U.S.-backed insurgents a potential share in government. As Cuban forces began to withdraw from Africa, the regime's position in Latin America suffered further blows, as its only significant supporters in the region, the Sandinistas and the Manuel Noriega regime in Panama, lost power. In Noriega's case, the instrument was a U.S. invasion at the end of 1989; for the Sandinistas, it was an electoral defeat brought about by a collapsing economy and the continuing internal war.

The most significant problems for Cuba and the FAR, however, were taking place not in the Third World but in Eastern Europe. Changes in Soviet leadership in the early 1980s brought to power a government dedicated to internal reforms rather than to international confrontations. This meant reducing subsidies to client states such as Cuba; seeking negotiated rather than military solutions to conflicts in areas such as Angola, Nicaragua, and El Salvador; and valuing accommodation with the United States and the West more than ties with other socialist states. Castro correctly saw the reforms proposed by Mikhail Gorbachev as threatening both his version of communism and his place in the international arena. The results were escalating tensions in Soviet-Cuban relations. All this culminated with the collapse of communist rule in Eastern Europe and the break-up of the Soviet Union. The results were the termination of all military assistance, Russia's announcement of its intention to withdraw its troops from Cuba, and an end to economic assistance that produced a massive, continuing economic crisis.

These tensions had major repercussions within the FAR. Defections by officers, most notably Air Force (DAAFAR) Brigadier General Rafael del Pino, increased. Rivalries between MINFAR and MININT escalated. Reports of discontent and corruption within the military began to spread. All of this culminated in the 1989 arrest, trial, and execution of several senior officers (the most prominent one was Division General Arnaldo Ochoa Sánchez) and the subsequent virtual takeover of MININT by MINFAR.[3]

Arnaldo Ochoa was one of the most prominent and popular officers in the FAR. He commanded troops in Angola and led the Cuban missions to Ethiopia and Nicaragua. Just before his arrest, he was scheduled to take command of Cuba's Western Army, the most powerful of the three armies responsible for national defense. Even the defector, General Rafael del Pino, listed Ochoa, long before his arrest, as one of the two most capable, honest, and popular generals in Cuba.[4] Ochoa and the other officers were accused of corruption and involvement with the narcotics trade. While the evidence against most of the defendants, particularly those assigned to MININT, was strong, that against Ochoa himself was relatively weak. His major crime seems to have been complaining about the treatment accorded Cuban troops returning from Africa.

Ochoa's show trial and execution and the subsequent purging of MININT and its takeover by officers from MINFAR associated with Raúl Castro led to widespread rumors of anti-Castro plots within the military and the security forces. Later announcements of the removal of up to 70 percent of the officers in the Western Army, the force with the closest ties to Ochoa, added further fuel to the rumor mills. However, there is little concrete evidence to support such suspicions. Government actions may have been designed largely to prevent potential problems rather than deal with any actual conspiracies. What seems clear is that discontent was growing, especially among officers who had served abroad or received training in the Soviet Union during the Gorbachev era. There is also some evidence that junior officers were beginning to give greater loyalty to their immediate commanders than to the national leadership. Whatever the truth, Ochoa's execution sent a clear warning to any within the FAR who might be tempted to question regime policies or the leadership of the Castro brothers. With massive economic and political problems looming ahead, the Castros may well have believed such a warning was necessary, no matter what the actual facts of the case. Increased U.S. aggressiveness toward those involved in the narcotics trade, something which a few months later would contribute to the Panama invasion, also may have prompted the purge, as the regime sought to undercut reports of its own involvement in such activities.

Surviving the "Special Period"

The period from 1990 to the present, characterized by Fidel Castro as a "special period in time of peace," has witnessed major changes in the missions and capabilities of the FAR. Perhaps the most basic change has been the end or at least the suspension of the internationalist mission. The last units left Africa in the spring of 1991, and in January 1992, Castro announced his decision to end assistance to insurgent movements as well as military support for existing governments. Internationalism now was defined as maintaining a socialist state in Cuba to provide future hope for the world's poorer nations.

Coupled with the end of international involvement was the virtual cut-off of all foreign training and military assistance and the withdrawal of Russian troops from Cuba.[5] Training of the military in Eastern Europe came to an abrupt halt, and promised deliveries of weapons and supplies never were fulfilled. In fact, Cuba only received eight or ten of a promised 40 MiG-29 aircraft, a quantity so small that problems of maintenance and training may outweigh any military benefits.[6]

The withdrawal of the last Russian troops had a relatively small impact on Cuban defensive capabilities but probably has had a significant psychological impact. The regime reacted to the news of the impending withdrawal first with intense anger, then with unsuccessful efforts to link the troop removal to the United States' leaving Guantánamo, or at least to prolong the process, and finally with resignation, declaring that with the collapse of the Soviet Union, keeping such forces in Cuba no longer made any sense. What was clear throughout this process, however, was the utter incapacity of the regime to influence Russian policy and the military isolation of the nation. No amount of rationalization, political slogans, or claims of self-sufficiency could cover up these unsettling facts.

The economic crisis also began to erode the capabilities and training of the FAR. The cost of maintaining such a large military establishment had long been a drag on the economy, and efforts to cut costs and promote self-sufficiency had begun in the early 1980s.[7] By the start of the 1990s, this effort became increasingly urgent. Between 1989 and 1992, the total value of Cuban exports declined by over 60 percent, and the value of imports fell to only 26 percent of 1989 levels. Fuel supplies were especially hard hit, forcing drastic curtailments in vehicle and aircraft operations. Spare parts for aircraft, ships, vehicles, and other equipment became scarce, increasing equipment downtime and forcing the substitution of inferior parts or the cannibalization of existing equipment. Air Force flight training was reduced sharply, and reports circulated that the navy's "submarine force appears no longer to be operational."[8] In the army, tank training was carried out on homemade simulators. Bicycles and horse-drawn carts were replacing motor vehicles, and there were even efforts to power vehicles with charcoal generators. While official pronouncements continued to maintain that the military was as strong as ever, an increasing body of evidence seemed to contradict such claims.

More difficult to assess is the impact of the "special period" on the FAR's human capabilities and morale. The purge of officers in the Western Army, the increase in military defections, and the greatly increased emphasis in official orders on improving military discipline and political indoctrination all provide evidence of problems. The two MiG pilots who defected in September 1993 indicated that — in the air force, at least — morale was becoming a serious problem. Interviews with other defectors support this thesis of declining morale and growing disillusionment with the leadership and official ideology. Yet, these same interviews give little evidence of any organized opposition movement or of an emerging consensus as to an alternative future for the FAR. The most that can be said is that the military, like the nation at large, is not immune to declining morale, growing cynicism and doubt, and even elements of despair that a massive economic decline, such as the one Cuba is experiencing, causes.

While the FAR's international missions have ended and its combat capacity is declining, its role in the economy actually has increased in recent years. This is a product of several factors. First, the loss of foreign aid and national economic crisis have necessitated massive efforts to promote military self-sufficiency in food production and in maintaining existing equipment. By mid-1990, the high command had decided to attempt self-sufficiency in these areas by 1995.[9] Military units now are assigned increasingly to economic tasks, in many ways returning to pre-1970 practices. Not only do they work in the sugar harvest, they have been mobilized to help plant and harvest other crops, such as grains and tomatoes, and have even been put to work cleaning out the pipes of the Santiago de Cuba water system.

Not all of the FAR's economic activities are devoted to agricultural or civic projects. In recent years, MINFAR has begun its own economic projects, largely related to the tourism industry, hoping to generate increased hard currency revenues. The FAR's own construction company, Unión de Empresas Constructoras, has been involved in building joint-venture hotels and other tourist-oriented facilities. In addition, MINFAR controls Gaviota, a major tourism business that provides internal transport, arranges tours, and even controls residences and restaurants used exclusively by tourists. It is probable that the bulk of hard currency generated by the activities of Empresas Constructoras and Gaviota goes into the military budget.

The military also has entered increasingly into joint economic efforts with civilian sectors. There has been a conscious effort to apply reforms made in military industries to civilian factories: the military has been used to teach civilians management techniques.[10] There also has been an accelerating tendency to devote military resources to producing food for the general population, not just for military units. This was especially evident in the Western Army, which listed such activities as fish and livestock breeding and kelp cultivation among its proudest accomplishments for 1993.[11] The FAR's role in health care also expanded as the capacity of civilian institutions to meet health needs declined. By late 1994, Raúl Castro claimed that 80 percent of those treated at military hospitals were civilians.[12]

In recent years, the FAR has devoted a growing share of its resources to problems of internal security and to what is officially defined as civil defense. The most obvious manifestation of internal security involvement is the virtual takeover of MININT by FAR officers. This, in turn, has produced increased coordination of MININT and MINFAR efforts at internal security, including increased use of reservists in internal security and anti-crime activities.

The prime focus of civil defense issues has been the continued and accelerated construction of a vast network of tunnels throughout the land, designed both to provide shelter and to facilitate communications and troop movements in the event of an invasion. Although diverting increasingly scarce resources into building tunnels as preparation for an invasion that probably will never come strikes most outside observers as ludicrous at best, the MINFAR makes no effort to conceal this program. Instead, it shows the project to international visitors and brags about how much tunnel construction has increased in the past two years.

While the FAR has been involved increasingly in picking tomatoes, cleaning pipes, and digging tunnels, the MTT and other sectors of the government and party have taken growing roles in defense exercises. Official accounts of defense exercises emphasize the participation of the MTT and the role of local Consejos de Defensa, headed by party officials, in organizing such events. Even the minister of higher education has been featured in a *Granma* story on the MTT.[13] The government also has created a defense commission within the new national assembly. The purpose and authority of this commission, which seems to be made up largely of military officers who are also members of the assembly, is still unclear.

In 1993, two massive defense maneuvers were held, with up to one-quarter million active participants and government claims that nearly four million Cubans ultimately would be involved in such exercises. Weapons also were being distributed to workers to deal with rising crime.

The increased emphasis on militia as well as or even in place of regular forces as a fundamental defense tactic has facilitated government plans to reduce the FAR's personnel sharply. While official announcement of this reduction came only in 1993, the process may have begun two years earlier. The period of compulsory military service was reduced in July 1991 from three to two years, with the excuse that this would enable individuals to move more rapidly into the MTT. Current plans envision a 40- to 50-percent reduction in active military personnel that would bring the FAR to a level below that of the mid-1970s.

While the strength of the FAR is declining and its capabilities apparently eroding, the presence of military figures within the government and the ruling party apparatus has remained significant. Military officers now serve as ministers of communication and transportation, as well as heading the MINFAR and MININT. Two hundred forty of the 1,700 delegates to the 1991 Cuban Communist Party Congress were members of the military. Twenty-five members of the Central Committee and six members of the Politburo are also military officers. The Politburo members still come from the generation that fought against Batista, but several younger officers recently have been added to the Central Committee.

As the economic crisis of the special period continues and deepens, the strains on the regime and its armed forces become progressively greater. The result has been a series of ongoing dilemmas that offer few if any good or safe options for the FAR.

Ongoing Dilemmas

Cuba's relations with the rest of the world in general and the United States in particular will have an obvious impact on the missions, capabilities, and morale of the FAR. Anything that reduces the nation's isolation and offers prospects of improving the economy ultimately would benefit the FAR. However, efforts to improve relations with the United States risk undermining the credibility of the threat and contradicting official statements of the intractability of the major potential foe. These contradictions became obvious in the June-July 1993 discussions between Cuban military officials, including Division General Ulises Rosales del Toro, the FAR's chief of staff, and the first deputy vice minister of MINFAR, and the delegation of retired U.S. military and diplomatic officials sent to Cuba by the Center for International Policy. Cuban officials alternated between blaming Washington for everything from the woeful state of their economy to the spread of human and plant infections and expressing appreciation for the Clinton administration's lower level of rhetoric, for prior notification of recent military maneuvers, and for increased contacts with U.S. officials at Guantánamo. Cuban officers also tried to relate their past African experiences to peacekeeping operations and expressed some interest in becoming involved in such activities, but the official Cuban media continue to denounce UN operations in the Persian Gulf and Somalia as "punitive actions by imperialists . . . under the mantle of illegitimate UN Security Council resolutions."[14] Such contradictions cannot be lost on the more perceptive members of the Cuban officer corps: If it is imperialism that is the intractable foe, then how can you hope for anything better from President Clinton? If drugs weaken your major potential enemy, then why seek to cooperate in preventing drug trafficking? If peacekeeping is a cover for imperialism, then why be interested in peacekeeping?

Similar problems and contradictions arise in efforts to improve relations with Latin American and other democratic nations: If Cuba is the last beacon of world, or at least Western Hemisphere, revolutionary ideology, then how can you abandon support for revolutions and praise some of the capitalist governments of the hemisphere? If the United States has become so totally dominant in this unipolar world, then how can you rationally expect governments to break with Washington and support Cuba? Any progress made in reducing Cuba's isolation also has to undermine the credibility of the threat and raise questions about the size and missions of the FAR.

The special period has complicated significantly the FAR's task of defining the threats to national security and preparing to defend against such threats. The basic shift to the War of All the People took place long before the current crisis, but it has remained largely intact despite altered circumstances. If anything, the regime has become even more dependent on militia forces at least to deter, if not actually combat, a U.S. attack.

The potential role of the FAR in national defense has been diminished not only by current doctrine and by growing logistical problems but by lessons drawn from the 1990-1991 Gulf War. The utter incapacity of Iraq's air force, considerably larger than Cuba's, to hinder allied operations and the disastrous experience of Soviet-equipped Iraqi tank formations has led to openly expressed doubts about the role such units could play in defending Cuba. Instead, current doctrine stresses guerrilla tactics, sharpshooters, and special forces, and, if necessary, retreat into Cuba's mountains and rural areas. The clear, if unspoken, assumption in such plans is that any role for air, sea, and armored units will be limited and brief at most. These implications cannot be lost on those assigned to such units. The impact of this situation on officers, particularly fighter pilots and tank commanders, long accustomed to being among the elite within the FAR, is impossible to judge but is potentially very damaging to individual and unit morale.

Cuban defense preparations are hampered by the inability to confront such realities openly and by political inhibitions on many aspects of training. For example, at the Máximo Gómez School, the FAR's premier advanced school, training still concentrates on studying such things as Castro's campaign against Batista, the repulse of the assault at Playa Girón, the French defeat at Dien Bien Phu, and the unsuccessful German siege of Leningrad. Studies concentrate overwhelmingly on socialist bloc successes. Grenada, the Gulf War, the Falklands/Malvinas conflict, or any other battles where Western forces have triumphed are given little if any attention. The relevance of events such as the Leningrad siege or even Playa Girón for contemporary situations is strained at best. What is more, their studies can neither anticipate the irrelevance of much of the FAR's current combat capacity, nor can they deal with any scenario in which foreign intervention comes only after and related to an already raging civil conflict within Cuba. Yet, such scenarios have much more relevance to the actual world situation.

The anticipation of mass-based responses by the MTT and other reserve units confronting a conventional, foreign effort to occupy the island also bears questionable relationship either to the experiences of military history or to the type of assault, should such an unlikely event ever materialize, that U.S. forces actually would undertake. Any serious, informed Cuban officer would have to question the assumptions underlying much of the training, but any open questioning of such assumptions would mean direct criticism of the national leadership and could be expected to prove very negative for one's career prospects. Training exercises involving both militia and units of the FAR have been taking place with increasing frequency, but the extent to which the FAR's professional officers believe these represent useful preparations for a credible threat is questionable.

The FAR's growing involvement in economic tasks also detracts from training and strains morale. The transition from leader of a decorated combat unit in Angola to commander of a tomato-picking or yam-planting battalion has to be difficult and provoke questions about the place and meaning of the military profession in today's Cuba. The increasing involvement of officers in a variety of economic-related tasks, frequently involving assignments to entities with no discernible relation to national defense, tends to erode military skills and produce a new set of interests and loyalties that may conflict with military necessities. There seems little doubt that the military's role in the economy has expanded significantly in recent years. By some accounts, they have even become the leading advocates of economic reforms.[15] Yet such activities both detract from professional military missions and provide increased opportunities for clashes with other branches of government and with the ruling party itself.

Under current circumstances, some level of military discontent is inevitable. Evidence suggests that the Castros understand and have taken steps to limit this. While the military, like the population in general, has seen its standard of living decline and some of its perks and privileges disappear, it has been insulated from the worst effects of the situation. Most retain job security and regular, though steadily depreciating, pay. Efforts at self-sufficiency give the military better access to food than the average Cuban, and uniforms are still available.[16] Medical care remains above the national average, although shortages have forced even the FAR, on occasion, to resort to herbal remedies and techniques such as acupuncture. By early 1994, Raúl Castro announced that the military was manufacturing herbal remedies and that these now made up 70 percent of the medicines used by the armed forces.[17]

Assuming that the current government reacts as have the overwhelming majority of those governments throughout history that have been threatened by similar economic and political pressures, the military will continue to have greater access to pay, food, clothing, and other benefits than will the bulk of the population. Reports recently have surfaced that officers are being given special allotments of consumer goods not available to the general public.[18] The simple logic of regime survival dictates such a course of action. However, this, in turn, creates other problems. If the gap in living conditions between the military and civil society grows too large, the resentment against the FAR is likely to increase, and efforts to identify the armed forces as the defenders of the people will lose even more credibility. In any case, security for those on active duty will have only a limited effect if their families, immediate and extended, face steadily increasing privation.

The government's decision to legalize the acquisition and use of U.S. dollars by Cubans should help raise the living standards of some Cubans but will create another set of problems for the officer corps. As a July 28, 1993, news story from Reuters noted, any "market-oriented change in Cuba has profound social implications and risks cracking the psychological foundation of his [Castro's] revolution," and the dollar reform "diminishes the state's historical role as the sole provider and . . . risks creating two classes in a socialist society, with the privileges not going to the hardest workers or political loyalists, but to those who get the most help from relatives abroad."[19] For Cuban officers, this reform risks eroding what remains of their traditional privileged access to imported appliances and other products. At the same time, those most tied to the regime are least likely to receive funds from abroad. In any case, it could be career damaging and even personally dangerous for a mid- or high-level officer to have such ties with relatives abroad. For the military, the anticipated inflow of dollars could cause special problems if some enlisted personnel begin to enjoy a much higher standard of living than is available to their officers.

Speeding up promotions is another way of containing discontent, especially when, as in Cuba's case, there is increasing evidence of a generation gap within the military.[20] Yet this is especially difficult to do when the armed forces are in a period of major force reduction. Cuba's reductions involve a higher percentage of enlisted personnel than officers, which provides some additional job security for officers but also creates a top-heavy institution where, in the long run, promotions must either come even slower or become increasingly less meaningful.

The question of promotions also encounters the inherent mistrust of the regime toward some of its own mid-level officers, especially those in DAAFAR, who were trained in and perhaps ideologically corrupted by Mikhail Gorbachev's Soviet Union. This "perestroika generation" is more sophisticated and less willing to take regime pronouncements at face value. If it is promoted, confidence in military loyalty may be weakened, but if this generation is discriminated against in promotion, then its disaffection with current conditions will be exacerbated further.

Fidel and Raúl Castro also must deal with the problem of retired officers, especially if their numbers grow rapidly in coming years. There have been highly publicized efforts lately to organize veterans' groups, largely as yet another vehicle of mobilizing regime support. However, such groups will only be attractive if they provide benefits for their members. If they do so, then they will become a new, privileged class, providing another focus for popular discontent. If they do not, then at best they will become increasingly irrelevant; at worst, they may become a forum for complaint or a source of organized opposition.

For a modern military force to be effective, it needs a sense of institutional identity and loyalties, a special sense of pride and place that sets its members apart from the bulk of the population. Efforts to create and promote such attitudes long have been a part of FAR propaganda and political training. Public statements also constantly stress the FAR's identification with the population, its role as the defender of the nation. The problem is the greater the loyalty to the military institution as a whole and to one's own unit in particular, the more this loyalty may conflict with calls for unswerving obedience to the Castro brothers and to the official party and ideology. This is especially true during periods of major economic decline that easily can be blamed on the nature and policies of the national leadership. If such policies negatively impact the capabilities, cohesion, and morale of the institution, then loyalty to the institution produces discontent and even disloyalty to the leadership.

If the testimony of recent defectors is credible, many Cuban officers, especially those from the perestroika generation, actively are concerned about the possible involvement of the FAR in dealing with domestic disturbances. Captain Enio Ravelo Rodríguez, one of two MiG pilots to defect in September 1993, claimed that such concerns were widespread and that should such an occasion arise, "no pilot would be capable of taking any action against the Cuban people."[21] If accurate, his remarks indicate that the political reliability of the FAR has been undermined significantly.

When existing policies are seen as producing negative results for the nation as a whole and the military institution in particular, then efforts at political indoctrination and appeals to nationalist sentiments lose much of their potential influence. They even may become counterproductive, producing cynicism more than loyalty and generating sardonic humor rather than greater efforts. Such attitudes and witticisms, which virtually all observers agree are increasing steadily within Cuba, especially among the young, are virtually impossible for official propaganda to deal with and inevitably lead to further erosion of regime support.

When all else fails, fear remains a potent tool for inculcating discipline or at least inhibiting dissent. Military discipline itself is a key element of control. Respect for one's superiors, near automatic obedience to orders, pride in appearance and unit performance all help keep a military occupied and effective. Traditionally, MINFAR has relied more upon loyalty and pride than upon fear to inculcate discipline and maintain effective control. However, there is mounting evidence that this approach is becoming ineffective and that fear and coercion increasingly are relied upon. As Phyllis Greene Walker has observed, "in the final analysis, the challenge for the regime is to maintain the balance of loyalty over coercion."[22] If current trends continue, this balance will not be maintained, and the potential consequences for the regime are grim at best.

Growing generational gaps — involving disputes over such seemingly mundane issues as haircuts, uniforms, and mustaches — reportedly are afflicting the FAR. MINFAR's response has been to call for even stricter discipline and to increase inspections and unit evaluations. Since negative evaluations can damage or even end a commander's career, older officers, in turn, become less tolerant of any signs of individualism or dissent. Surface conformity becomes more important than unit cohesion, aggravating generational differences and reducing respect for authority.

Fear is instilled in a number of ways. An increasing willingness to use force against those attempting to flee, harsher penalties for even a hint of dissent, and, for officers, the knowledge that unquestioning conformity has replaced international service as the route to promotion all contribute to this. So, too, do efforts to control contacts between the military and civilians and to limit most flying assignments to married pilots, with further preference being given to those with children. The impact of the Ochoa trial and the subsequent purges in MININT and the Western Army, of course, provide the most graphic examples of the fate awaiting those who depart from regime norms.

Not surprisingly, the regime has utilized negative news from Eastern Europe extensively to demonstrate to the FAR what happens to a nation and a military institution should the existing system collapse. Fear of restored influence by the Miami exiles and the United States is also used as a means of control. Paradoxically, some of the exiles' own propaganda, calling for vengeance against Castro supporters and vowing to dismantle all existing security forces, strengthens this government's case.

Finally, there remains the role of the state security apparatus, including a presumed extensive network of informants. The Ochoa case also underscored the regime's determination to treat the failure to report dissent or unauthorized actions within the FAR as the equivalent of participating in such actions and as subject to the same extreme sanctions. Fear that sharing complaints or doubts with any fellow officer may lead to arrest or worse is an effective means of preventing plots from developing within the FAR. However, it also undermines institutional cohesion, replacing ties of shared loyalties with mutual suspicions. Fear as a means of controlling the FAR is the ultimate two-edged sword. Within the military, a growing climate of fear and distrust contributes to the growth of the very ideas and attitudes it is designed to suppress. Increased reliance upon coercion and fear as tactics inevitably raises questions as to the actual strength and confidence of the leadership. A regime that relies on fear usually appears frightened — and therefore weak — itself. Easy to unleash, fear as an instrument of policy is increasingly difficult to control or reverse. The longer a regime relies on such tactics, the greater the chances that they ultimately will produce precisely the attitudes and actions they are intended to prevent.

Conclusions

The crisis currently afflicting the Castro regime has no end in sight. Consequently, the problems and dilemmas that confront the FAR only can be expected to intensify. The armed forces find themselves engaged in a prolonged struggle for institutional and regime survival, two goals that are becoming increasingly incompatible.

If the FAR were a traditional Latin American military institution, such a situation would seem to invite a coup attempt. Yet, as previously noted, the FAR's heritage is distinct, with influences from the former Soviet Union and the peculiar leadership and ideology of Fidel Castro and his revolution shaping its organization, missions, and sense of self-identity. It has no tradition of coup-making or of negotiating as a united, autonomous institution with an existing government. Fidel Castro, the revolution, and the nation always have been intertwined inextricably in its training and in the formulation of its missions. While the ongoing crisis places severe strains on these linkages, the FAR lacks both the internal structures and independent leadership conducive to any effective move against the regime. The conclusion of the 1992 Rand Study, *Cuba Adrift in a Postcommunist World*, that an organized military coup offers an unlikely scenario for the end of the Castros' rule is well founded.[23]

While the FAR is unlikely to take the lead in bringing down the regime, this does not mean that its effective support is by any means ensured. The Castros need several things from their armed forces. First, of course, is at least minimal loyalty, enough to prevent any serious effort to topple the regime. Today, second priority must go to involvement in promoting the economy. This includes everything from increased efforts at auto-sufficiency in food, spare parts, and other supplies to participation in national agricultural tasks, to the current involvement in promoting tourism. However, the military's contributions here always will be limited, and as a whole, it will remain more a drag on than an asset to the economy. For that reason, the military's size and costs must be reduced significantly.

This process, however, undermines the FAR's capability both to deal with potential internal dissent and to repel any external attacks. And, in the real world of today's Cuba rather than that portrayed by official propaganda, control of internal dissent increasingly will pose a more likely threat than any external menace. The government, naturally, has done what it can to prevent serious public disturbances from taking place. In addition to attempts to prevent or inhibit dissent, it has created groups outside the formal security apparatus, such as the "rapid-reaction brigades," organized civilian supporters created to harass and attack any open opposition. Yet, as the economy continues to deteriorate, the possibility that some form of civil disturbance could escalate beyond the ability of such groups and even the police to control increases. Then, the FAR becomes the regime's first line of defense against its own population. However, the military's own traditions and carefully cultivated self-image, combined with its growing internal dilemmas, serve to undermine its reliability in such a situation. While the regime cannot discuss openly even the possibility of such a situation arising, it does continue to claim unbounded confidence in the FAR's total loyalty and reliability. On the other hand, some defectors argue that the armed forces never would turn their weapons on their own population.[24] What actually would happen, of course, is impossible to determine. It would depend on the specific conditions and timing of the incident, the leadership available on the spot, initial actions taken, and a host of other imponderable factors. As Donald Schulz has pointed out, the situation becomes even more unstable and unpredictable should such incidents occur while Cuba is trying to institute a controlled program of limited reform.[25] What is clear is that the longer current trends continue, the less reliable will be the FAR's response should such disturbances break out.

Perhaps the most likely scenario in the event of large-scale internal disturbances would be deep internal splits within the FAR, with some units joining protestors, some trying to avoid involvement, and some FAR and MININT units actively supporting the regime. This would create a major dilemma for the United States, as political pressures to intervene would mount rapidly. Such intervention, however, would alter the nature of the conflict from a domestic clash to a foreign invasion. This, in turn, could lead wavering units to ally themselves firmly with the government in defense of their nation.

Such a crisis may not take place for years, if ever. Meanwhile, the dilemmas confronting the FAR will continue to intensify. The FAR has no good options in confronting the current situation. The skills and equipment it acquired to carry out its missions during the 1970s and 1980s are increasingly irrelevant to the problems of the 1990s. They can shoot down unarmed private aircraft that intrude on their airspace and capture yachts that violate territorial waters, but the bulk of the skills and equipment acquired in the 1970s and 1980s are costly to maintain, increasingly obsolete, and irrelevant to the real threats to regime survival. The FAR is playing an increasingly important role in both encouraging and managing efforts at economic reform, but here, as elsewhere, it is Fidel Castro, not the high command of the FAR, who determines the nature, scope, and pace of change. If many of the FAR's officers are unhappy with existing conditions within their institution and their nation and are worried about where they appear to be going, they, nevertheless, find it most difficult to conceptualize alternate realities that offer significantly enhanced opportunities at acceptable levels of risk or cost. In such a situation, the military is condemned to a prolonged struggle for institutional survival. Over time, such a struggle has an increasingly wearing effect on effectiveness, loyalty, and morale. What lies ahead for the FAR is a long descent to an ill-defined and undesired destination. Within the limits imposed by the political system, the FAR will continue to press for economic reforms but will be much less interested in promoting political change, since its institutional survival continues to be linked to the perpetuation of the current regime. The absence of any better alternatives or independent leadership probably means that this pattern will continue for some time to come.

Notes

1. Quoted in Jorge Dominguez, 1986, "The Civic Soldier in Cuba," in Abraham Lowenthal and J. Samuel Fitch, eds., *Armies and Politics in Latin America*, rev. ed. (New York: Holmes and Meier), 284.

2. Dominguez 1986, 263.

3. This was exemplified with the adoption in December 1994 of a revised defense law that specified ties between the General Staff and MININT and made MININT officers subject to military regulations. See FBIS, 1995, "Speeches to the 20-21 December ANPP Session," *Latin America: Daily Report, Supplement*, January 5, 16-17.

4. General Rafael del Pino, 1987, *General del Pino Speaks* (Miami: The Cuban-American National Foundation), 55-56.

5. Six Russian technical specialists remain under paid contracts to provide training on weapons systems, and there are unconfirmed reports that a few Vietnamese advisors are providing training to the FAR and MTT in guerrilla arms and tactics.

6. The International Institute of Strategic Studies reports that Cuba has eight MiG-29s, two of which are used only for training. Raúl Castro told the Mexican newspaper *El Sol* that ten had been received.

7. A.B. Montes, 1993, *The Military's Response to Cuba's Economic Crisis* (Washington, D.C.: Defense Intelligence Agency), 10.

8. Assessment of the Office of Naval Intelligence cited in Johns Hopkins University School of Advanced International Studies, 1993, *CubaINFO* 5, 8 (June 18): 4.

9. Phyllis Greene Walker, 1994, "The Cuban Armed Forces and Transition," in Donald E. Schulz, ed., *Cuba and the Future* (Westport, Conn.: Greenwood Press), 57-58.

10. Montes 1993, 15.

11. Foreign Broadcast Information Service, 1994a & b, *Latin America: Daily Report*, January 4,17; January 10, 1. Hereafter cited as FBIS.

12. Prensa Latina, 1994, "Interview with Raúl Castro," *Prensa Latina*, September 17.

13. *Granma*, April 17, 1990, 1.

14. FBIS, 1993, February 2, 2.

15. Cathy Booth, 1994, "Fidel's Brother Sets up Shop," *Time*, November 14, 68-69. David Adams, 1995, "Castro's blueprint to build a new Cuba," *St. Petersburg Times*, April 11, 1A.

16. It might be worth noting that while the FAR receives its uniforms, MTT members are expected to supply their own.

17. FBIS, 1994c, February 22, 7.

18. Ricardo Planas, 1995, "Cuba's Search for Stability: Castro's Agenda for 1995 and Beyond," Special Report by Office of Research, Radio Martí, January, 14.

19. Reuters, July 28, 1993.

20. Numerous interviews with and statements by recent defectors refer to a generation gap between the products of the fight against Batista and the revolution's first years and current mid-level officers, especially those who studied in the Soviet Union in the 1980s, as a major and growing cause of friction within the FAR.

21. Larry Rohter, 1993, "Cuban Pilot Says Military Has Woes," *The New York Times*, September 23, 5.

22. Phyllis Greene Walker, 1993, "Political-Military Relations Since 1959," in Enrique A. Baloyra and James A. Morris, eds., *Conflict and Change in Cuba* (Albuquerque, N.M.: University of New Mexico Press), 127.

23. Edward Gonzalez and David Ronfeldt, 1992, *Cuba Adrift in a Postcommunist World* (Santa Monica, Calif.: Rand Corporation), viii and 38-41.

24. See, for example, Christopher Marquis, 1991, "Defector: Uprising in Cuba Inevitable," *Los Angeles Times*, October 26, 17A.

25. Donald E. Schulz, 1993, *The United States and Cuba: From a Strategy of Conflict to Constructive Engagement* (Carlisle, Pa.: Strategic Studies Institute, U.S. Army War College), 33.

VIII

Nicaragua's Armed Forces: An Assessment of Their Political Power

Luis Humberto Guzmán

The history of Nicaragua is characterized by an absence of civilian mechanisms to mediate and resolve conflicts of power. In the face of this political vacuum, violence has emerged as the principal instrument for the settlement of conflicts. As a consequence, there has been a convergence between violence and militarism. It is true that force is the recourse, by default, of militarism. Nevertheless, this does not imply that all violence, that all of the practice of force, is militarism. Nicaragua has lacked throughout its history a professional armed force. There have existed, however, in post-World War II Nicaragua, two permanent armed bodies, with a considerable degree of technical preparedness, but nevertheless, these entities have not been professional or national bodies. Not all organizations of armed individuals constitute armies. Even when these types of bodies are organized on a permanent basis and obey a unified command and authority is transmitted on a hierarchical basis, these elements are not sufficient to make such an organization into an army. This circumstance has stimulated political leaders to develop skills in the manipulation and control of armed groups, but an individual sporting a uniform is not automatically a soldier. In the end, there is a military mind that is not acquired by simply wearing a uniform. In the strictest sense of the word, it is not possible to speak of militarism before a professional armed force has been constituted.[1]

One of the characteristics that has been lacking among the armed bodies existing in Nicaragua — the National Guard (GN) and the Sandinista Popular Army (EPS) — is a national character, since both organizations have displayed factional characters. Their loyalties have been vested in particular individuals or groups, in the case of the GN with the Somoza family and in the case of the EPS with the Sandinista National Liberation Front (FSLN). Their loyalties and commitments have been personal, not national.

Throughout its history, Nicaragua has known politicians with military power, but it has not known military men with political power. Even when those politicians with military power have dominated the political life of the nation, they have not used this power consistently. On the contrary, they have striven to envelop it with a certain degree of civility. Thus, it is possible to contend, as is done here, that Nicaragua has not experienced militarism, since the country has lacked professional armed forces and the political life of the nation has not been militarized; that is, it has not been dominated expressly by the military at the expense of civilian political life.[2] As Amos Perlmutter has observed, a regime is military if the government is administered or overseen by the armed forces.[3] The rigorous and systematic analysis of violence as a political instrument and of militarism as a political regime are still developing subject areas in Nicaraguan social science. The same situation is being experienced throughout the rest of Central America, despite the fact that both subjects have the same importance at the regional level as they do within Nicaragua. Nevertheless, instead of studying these issues, they have been repudiated traditionally, and analysis has been replaced by rhetoric and empty denunciations.[4] At other times, simplistic studies have sought to explain militarism as a consequence of a permanent conspiracy or of economic determinants or as an Iberian legacy.[5]

Since the 1990 elections, the Nicaraguan armed forces have undertaken a process that, based on official declarations, has been directed to their modernization. This process of professionalization is the subject of this chapter. While the history of Nicaragua is certainly important for understanding the contemporary development of the nation's armed forces, the principal focus of this work will be on the period following the July 1979 overthrow of the Somoza dynasty.[6]

Nicaragua's Recent History

The Sandinista National Liberation Front, upon its accession to power, proceeded rapidly to reorganize the state's coercive apparatuses. The Sandinista regime adopted various aspects, institutions, and procedures similar to those found among the one-party states in Eastern Europe. In the political realm, the Sandinista government developed institutions that paralleled the state, and in the political domain, it adopted what can be called the iron triangle: party-state-armed forces. It is important to keep in mind that the embryo of the EPS is found in the guerrilla columns of the Sandinista Front. The major part of the current officer corps of the armed forces comes from the military structures of the Sandinista Front. This explains why, during the first three years of the regime, the armed forces and party were merged as one single body. However, the situation evolved, and a specialization developed in which the party selected some men to serve in the armed forces, while others were destined to be active in the political or economic realms. The important point is that all were the agents of the party serving in different areas of national life. In the area of civilian-military relations, this model is very successful, since it achieves the total subordination of the armed forces to the political elites. Indeed, in the Soviet regime, the subordination of the armed forces to the authority of the party was complete. While the Nicaraguan situation under the Sandinista regime differed from the Soviet experience, it is worthwhile to examine the components of the subordination of the military to civilians as in the communist regimes of the Soviet model.

In this system of civilian-military relations, the cornerstone was the Leninist concept of the vanguard party. The party was conceived as an elite that excels due to its intelligence, its high moral fiber, its authenticity, and its embodiment of the ideals of the working class. Although it is true that the cornerstone of civilian-military relations in the communist models was this concept of a vanguard party, the manifestations of such relations varied widely. Nevertheless, they had three basic features: fusion, symbiosis, and coalition. In Nicaragua, as in Cuba in the initial period following the 1959 revolution, the party and the armed forces appeared as a single fused body. In the course of events, however, the development of specialization began to create divisions.

While both organizations, armed forces and party, came to achieve a particular identity, the principle of the vanguard party was preserved and manifested in the overlap of military and political elites. This meant that leaders of the party also were placed at the head of the military, and the highest-ranking officers of the armed forces were integrated into the leadership of the party. In the case of Nicaragua, the command of the armed forces was exercised, in the early stages, by a collegial body made up of three members of the national leadership of the FSLN (Humberto Ortega, Tomás Borge, and Luis Carrión). The evolution within the armed forces eventually led to the single command by General Humberto Ortega, but the overlap of elites was maintained. By February 1990, 22 members of the armed forces were serving in the assembly of the Sandinista party. This system of elite overlap guaranteed the loyalty of the armed forces to the party, especially because the party was considered the supreme arbiter, the supreme authority to establish values, policies, and ultimately to resolve internal disputes. All conflicts and disagreements, according to that scheme, must be resolved within the party. The vanguard party, then, fulfilled multiple functions, including direction, arbitration, and integration of all issues and disputes among the state and its constituent institutions, including the armed forces.

As a result of the February 1990 elections, this scheme of party-armed forces changed, especially in light of the vulnerability of a party that had made serious mistakes, including a lack of foresight (since it never considered the possibility of losing the elections). This situation forced the armed forces to abandon, at least formally, its positions within the leadership of the party and the Sandinista assembly. All of this implied a fundamental change in values. Now the fundamental thrust of its ideological-political discourse became professionalization. The military also suffered serious reductions in strength and budget, all of this without, as yet, leading to serious instances of insubordination. This lack of apparent dissent demonstrates, on the one hand, an important degree of cohesion. On the other hand, the behavior of the EPS was similar to that of the armies of Eastern Europe faced with the fall of their fundamental system of ideological values and the parties that sustained them.

What, then, is the relationship between the current armed forces and the Sandinista Front? The control exercised by the Front has diminished considerably. The military is not subordinated to the national direction of the FSLN but rather to the personal leadership of

General Joaquín Cuadra and the high command. The presence of a military elite within the party leadership has been reduced considerably, and the presence of the party in the armed forces has become marginal. Party organizations have disappeared from the core of the armed forces, and political indoctrination is confusing and at times contradictory.

The army and the Sandinista Front do, however, have common interests. For the FSLN, the armed forces are a bastion of power, even a monopoly. Neither the government of President Violeta Chamorro nor any other political party has any direct or significant influence over the military. The army, in turn, has utilized the political protection of the FSLN, especially within the parliamentary arena, in order to limit or avoid reductions in its budget and to water down the reform of the military laws. The army protects the legacy of the FSLN and its leaders and remains the only body with the capacity to resolve, in the final analysis, through the use of force, any conflict (it holds a virtual monopoly over the use of force). This relationship appears to have the components of a coalition, in contrast to the symbiosis experienced during the early period following 1979. In effect, the army and the Sandinista Front have a relationship of mutual benefit and face common internal and external threats, despite each having a unique identity. This relationship of mutual protection allows for greater benefits and dilutes the impact of threats.[7]

The Consequences of the Transition

The results of the 1990 elections produced changes within the coercive instruments of the Nicaraguan state (police, intelligence, and armed forces). In the course of the electoral campaign, President Chamorro raised the flag of pacifism. She assured that upon her inauguration the government immediately would eliminate the draft. In light of the electoral results, this was the correct political decision. The majority of Nicaraguan society wished to end forced recruitment of youths who were compelled to participate in the war. The majority of the members of the political council of the National Opposition Union (UNO) assured during the campaign that they would reduce dramatically the size of the armed forces. With these antecedents in mind, President Chamorro faced a difficult dilemma before taking office. Should she keep General Humberto Ortega in his post or cashier him? This problem could not be resolved in the negotiations preceding the taking of office that culminated in the protocol of transition. These were conducted personally and directly by General Ortega, then minister of defense and commander of the armed forces, on the part of the FSLN and on behalf of President Chamorro by her campaign chief and son-in-law, Antonio Lacayo. As a result of these negotiations, the institutional integrity of the armed forces was assured, and guarantees for minor property (such as homes and personal cars) were made to the members of the National Direction of the FSLN and the officer corps of the armed forces.

These negotiations, however, did not resolve successfully the subject of the retirement or continued service of General Ortega at the head of the armed forces. The personal mistrust felt by the president toward the general, along with pressures from the political council of UNO and the Congress of the United States, left this issue pending until the inauguration of the government of President Chamorro, who in spite of tremendous anxiety, confirmed him in his post. During the period of transition, the government of Daniel Ortega made public a law of military organization that, in practice, meant that the armed forces became an autonomous entity without any subordination to civilian power. A military council was created that named the commander of the armed forces, was responsible for promotions, and in general made all the important decisions regarding the armed forces. As a result, the functions of the ministry of defense became insignificant, and the office itself became purely symbolic. President Chamorro has explained that she confirmed General Ortega because she was committed to reducing the military ranks and budget and thus needed an officer with solid authority in that post. It was argued that within the EPS there was no other officer with sufficient authority to assure the cohesion of the armed forces, especially while the institution was subject to a rapid and severe reduction in force and financial resources. It was said that it was best "to deal with a general than with a score of colonels." The most significant changes President Chamorro instituted during the transition and her first two years were the following:

1. Termination of forced conscription;
2. Formal abandonment by the military officers of their party functions within the FSLN;
3. Transfer of the intelligence functions from the government ministry to the control of the EPS;
4. Personal control by General Ortega over the armed forces and intelligence units;
5. Reduction in force to a total of 21,000 men;

6. Reduction in the number of foreign military advisors and departure of all Cuban advisors;

7. Publication of the military budget;[8] and

8. Reforms within the intelligence units.[9]

Strengths and Weaknesses of the EPS

The EPS remained autonomous from genuine civilian control by either the formal commander-in-chief, the president, or the minister of defense for the first four years of the Chamorro administration.[10] Throughout this period, tensions among the military, the Chamorro administration, and the Congress grew steadily, culminating in September 1993 with the president's public call for General Ortega's resignation. After some resistance and prolonged negotiations, an agreement was hammered out that provided for congressional adoption of a reformed military code and General Ortega's resignation in 1995 (with the presumption that he would be replaced by his second-in-command, General Joaquín Cuadra). The new code limited the terms of future military commanders, reduced military legal immunities, and made civilian authority over the armed forces somewhat more explicit. While these 1994 reforms reduced the military's autonomy, they failed to end it, nor did they deal with other sensitive issues such as the military's expanded role in the economy. There are still significant areas where the army exercises considerable autonomy without the necessary civilian oversight. To begin, Articles 92 through 97 of the current constitution of Nicaragua clearly indicate that the army has a dual function in terms of serving the nation and protecting the current constitution. Constitutional reforms adopted by the national assembly in December 1994 but challenged by the Chamorro administration change this wording and place the military clearly under the control of civilian authority.[11] However, even when these reforms come into effect, the nation still will lack adequate enforcement mechanisms, and the ultimate loyalty of the military will remain suspect. As for naming the commanding officer of the armed forces, Decree 291 forces the president to name the highest-ranking officer to this post. When, after prolonged resistance, General Ortega finally retired in 1995, the president had little choice in designating his second-in-command, General Joaquín Cuadra, to succeed him. While General Cuadra's term is now limited by the new military code, the president's ability to dismiss him during that term is limited at best. In effect, the law does not give the president the ability to discharge the commanding officer of the EPS. The same law limits the strategic and tactical determinations to be undertaken by the armed forces in the defense of the national territory. The minister of defense lacks any authority and does not play any role in this area, something that is fundamental to the civilian and democratic control of the armed forces in constitutional democracies. Although the chief of the armed forces formally is not part of the ministerial cabinet, in practice, he participates not only in the so-called security cabinet (including the chief of staff of the president, the minister of government, and the foreign minister), but frequently at the working level in cabinet sessions. The national assembly lacks any formal or specific functions that give it oversight over the armed forces — Article 138 of the Constitution, which defines the functions of the assembly, makes no reference to any such area of competence — and the assembly only has an indirect role through the passage of legislation and the approval of the national budget. Even the 1994 constitutional reforms fail to deal with this issue, adding only a clause that gives the assembly the right to authorize or refuse permission for troops to serve outside Nicaragua.

In terms of civilian presence in any area of the army, the situation is clearly not a favorable one. There are no civilians attending any of the military schools; there are few civilian faculty participating in the education of military officers. There are also no civilian consultants aiding the armed forces, and no real ministry of defense has been created during the first five years of post-Sandinista government. Even though the national police force is responsible for public order, the army also has some functions in this area according to Decree 291. This situation can be explained, in part, by the tendency among Nicaraguans to demand the presence of a "strong man" who will guarantee order so that the economy will function adequately. Civilians also have little to do with promotions in the armed forces, with the president only being able to award the ranks of general, lieutenant general, major general, and brigade general.

Decree 291 allows the EPS to create and administer businesses, and the reformed military code does not address this issue. As a result, the military controls construction companies, furniture factories, and airlines. There are two aspects to these businesses: One is that they are explicitly exempt from the usual competitive bidding imposed on public enterprises, and the other is that until recently, there has been little if any public knowledge of their functioning, including their taxation or supervision by the comptroller general of the republic.

The armed forces also appear to be gathering considerable strength in the informal sector of the economy, especially in taxing business activities in kind. The armed forces, for example, have recognized publicly their activities in the fisheries sector.[12] In the area of legal and judicial processes, the armed forces continue to be subject to their own justice system. The *fuero* still exists and was even expanded by the ability of the armed forces to try any civilian who commits an offense involving the armed forces. Here, again, the constitutional reforms adopted by the assembly end this power, but only slightly limit the military *fuero*. Finally, the armed forces undertake considerable activities in civil defense, including those related to national disasters.

The weaknesses of the military are quite noticeable, despite the above assessment that clearly indicates their considerable autonomy. A fundamental problem faced by the EPS was the loss of its strategic rear-guard, that is, the disappearance of the Soviet Union. Having received weaponry and training, along with important financial and other support from the Soviet bloc, the army now lacks any substantial source of external tactical, strategic, and ideological support. Because of the loss of the ideological and practical significance of communism, the EPS is undergoing a continuing crisis of discipline, values, and organization. This is undoubtedly the result of the EPS' being defined by a civilian-military relations model that no longer fits the new national and international post-Cold War reality devoid of the struggle between capitalism and communism. The technical crisis faced by the military extends beyond the loss of supply sources to the sourcing of replacement parts, thus guaranteeing the premature obsolescence of its weaponry and related equipment. This situation is unlikely to be remedied in the near future; there are no resources available either to purchase parts (which may not even be available, as many military industries in Eastern Europe and Russia have gone out of business) or to replace the existing equipment with new ones obtained from Western Europe or North America. Indeed, the military has been reduced to selling off parts of its weapons inventory in order to raise additional funds.

Changed global and regional political realities, exemplified in Central America by the negotiated end to the civil conflict in El Salvador, have confirmed the current trend away from armed confrontation to peaceful resolution of conflict. In this area, the role of the United States as the source of a new set of ideas premised on regional and local disarmament is a novel development. Along with the government of the United States, since 1991, the World Bank, the International Monetary Fund, and the Inter-American Development Bank have promoted an intense debate over the reduction of military expenditures. Various influential individuals, ranging from the ex-president of the World Bank, Robert S. McNamara, to the director of the International Monetary Fund, Michel Camdessus, have come through Central America advising all parties of the need to reduce military expenditures.[13] Additionally, the bilateral aid that is being provided to the region is framed increasingly by the argument that a government cannot aspire to obtain support for social programs if at the same time it is spending considerable resources on the maintenance of a military establishment.

To a considerable degree, the public is skeptical of the professionalization efforts undertaken by the military, in part because it still is perceived widely as an organization allied with the FSLN. There is also an antimilitarist current among many people that even can be found among some Sandinistas, especially the intellectual sector.[14] This antimilitarism has contributed to the current divisions among the Sandinistas. To this could be added the critique provided by Tomás Borge, who identified the armed forces as a cancer on humanity, even if he later qualified this statement.[15]

The army, for all its power, remains poorly institutionalized, especially in light of the following organizational criteria:
1. An interchangeable command;
2. An area of specialization;
3. A recognized social purpose;
4. A sense of corporate identity and values; and
5. Clearly regulated promotions, retirements, and dismissals.

If these criteria are taken into account, it is apparent that the institutionalization of the army is modest at best. Its greatest strength is organizational; yet within the institution, a clear patriarchal paternalism is evident. The relationship between the chief of the armed forces and the troops is defined in terms of personal loyalty and reciprocal protection. The relations are based less on hierarchy and rank and more on camaraderie, friendships, and personal ties. It is possible for officers of lower rank to have authority over those with higher rank, but with fewer instances evident at the highest levels. At the present time, the armed forces find themselves greatly isolated, lacking international relationships and the technical and professional benefits that these imply. Up to the present time, the outcome of a search for these relationships has been very limited. There are some efforts to approach the inter-American security organizations and the institutions of countries such as Canada.

Missions and Roles of the Armed Forces

One of the greatest weaknesses of the armed forces is the perception among a large segment of the population that there is no reason for their continued existence. This feeling is made more acute when the public becomes aware that the basic functions of public order do not reside within the military but belong to the police. Many people ask themselves why the military absorbs 12 percent of the national budget, competing in size with health and education. The climate of disorder prevalent in the country underlines this critical perception of the military. From this brittle situation, the EPS carefully must present its roles and missions to the public. The following section will consider the conventional roles that the armed forces ascribe to themselves.

Sovereignty is one of the most frequently used concepts by the Sandinistas. In the political lexicon, sovereignty is closely associated with nationalism, as an affirmation or validation of the capacity of the country to make its decisions with absolute independence from any other government. As a part of classical doctrine, sovereignty is an absolute concept, total, indivisible, and unlimited. It has an internal and an external definition. In the internal realm, it signifies that an authority exists that cannot be overcome; no one can place himself above it. In its origins, sovereignty resided in the absolute monarch, and this was later displaced to parliaments as the representatives of the people. Rousseau located sovereignty directly with the people, while others considered the people to be the base on which the state was built. Thus, in the latter interpretation, the concept of sovereignty became circular and diffuse.

In the external area, sovereignty implies that a state makes its decisions with complete independence from other states or other external actors and forces. It is apparent that both of these expressions of sovereignty have been eroded. Constitutional theory seriously has limited the power of the state, aiming to distribute, as opposed to concentrate, power. In addition, the currently popular neoliberal theory perceives the state as a "facilitator," which seriously circumscribes the state's regulating power. At the international level, international organizations, the multiplicity of international non-state actors, and regional integration have all modified the concept of sovereignty. Problems such as energy and environment spill over national borders and exemplify the need to depart from the old autarchic concept of sovereignty. In the economic area, Nicaragua is particularly vulnerable to external forces: The state is especially weak in light of its inability to finance public expenditures through its own income, needing a massive influx of resources from abroad. The armed forces can do little, if anything, when faced with these dilemmas. Indeed, they are perceived as being a further burden on the financial stability of the state. The sovereignty problems faced by Nicaragua are only marginally military; instead, they are essentially economic.

Rather than portraying themselves as defenders of Nicaragua's national sovereignty (a problem of the economic cabinet), the armed forces can portray themselves as the defenders of the territorial integrity of Nicaragua. However, in today's world, threats to dismember the national territory are virtually nonexistent. On the national political scene, even when accounting for the ethnic tensions coming from the Atlantic coast, no organization expresses open desires to secede from the country. This reality frees the EPS from any role in protecting the territorial integrity from internal threats. At the external level, Nicaragua has few boundary disputes. There are limited controversies with Costa Rica over navigation rights on the San Juan River. The only genuine boundary dispute is with Colombia over sovereignty of three uninhabited island reefs. This, however, is an inactive dispute, and neither country is willing to press the issue. Furthermore, considering the difference in forces between the Nicaraguan and Colombian navies, it is apparent that Nicaragua can pursue this dispute only through diplomatic and political means. Thus, the only pending border issue that could involve Nicaragua is not a viable one for the country, if for no other reason than the overwhelming superiority of the opponent's forces.

Nicaragua does not face historical animosities with neighbors, such as those between El Salvador and Honduras or between Guatemala and Belize. This situation strengthens the security of the nation. At the same time, there are no demographic pressures looming on the horizon that could result in an international conflict. In sum, there are no real external threats or problems faced by Nicaragua. An additional consideration is that Nicaragua's armed forces are not an international threat because they lack the offensive weaponry (especially a functional air force), and the country simply does not have the economic resources to sustain a war of aggression. In the final analysis, the threats faced by Nicaragua are those dealing with natural resources and control over the use of its territory.

Nicaragua faces two serious threats involving the use of its sovereign territory. One of these is fishery piracy on the Atlantic coast, and the other is narcotics traffic.[16] At the present time, the country lacks the air and naval units fully to confront these two problem areas. As a result of this assessment, one may speculate that the armed forces could be reorganized to provide them with the personnel and equipment necessary to patrol the Nicaraguan air and waters and enforce sovereignty.

When it comes to the defense of the country's constitution, the EPS is mandated both by the constitution itself and its own regulations to defend it. This, however, is clearly a controversial mission. In the dispute over the legality of the constitutional reforms, the army, with considerable success, has adopted a strictly neutral position, but there is no guarantee that such would always be the case. Under present circumstances, though, it is counterproductive even to consider resolving political issues through the use of force, especially at the domestic level. Even from the Sandinista camp, criticism has been made of suggestions to defend democracy and the functioning of the government through the use of force, and the argument has been offered that problems in this area must be resolved by the correct functioning of the institutions themselves.[17] The historical experience of Latin America and Nicaragua demonstrate that coercive institutions, despite their frequent intervention in politics, tend to exacerbate problems rather than resolve them. In conclusion, the strongest argument for the reevaluation of missions for the armed forces falls almost exclusively within the realm of the defense of territorial sovereignty to protect natural resources, combat narcotics trafficking, and act decisively in the case of national disasters.

A Proposal for a Policy for the Resolution and Administration of Conflicts

During the 1980s, the armed conflicts in Central America were largely internal struggles, conducted within a single country and caused principally by endogenous factors. The last international conflict was the so-called Soccer War between El Salvador and

Honduras in 1967, which lasted for 100 hours and during which hostilities were suspended because both combatants ran out of ammunition. Recent Central American history demonstrates an absence of wars between the constituent republics, and the only one that did take place during the last 25 years demonstrates the material weaknesses of the Central American nations to sustain a war for a period that exceeds five days of combat. The prolonged internal struggles only have been sustained by large external resources. The seven-year struggle in Nicaragua between the Nicaraguan resistance and the Sandinista armed forces probably cost over $1 billion. The Nicaraguan resistance received, through the largesse of the U.S. government, over $321 million, along with large amounts of extra-legally provided resources.[18] There are no reliable sources that would aid in the calculation of the resources provided to the Sandinista armed forces by the East European bloc, Libya, Algeria, and Cuba. Nevertheless, if the organization and operations of an irregular army cost at least $320 million, and even more was spent on the regular armed forces, then a sum hovering around $1 billion was spent on the Nicaraguan conflict.

At the present time in Central America, there are no interstate conflicts that could lead to an international war. Differences between Guatemala and Belize and between El Salvador and Honduras currently are not being pursued actively by the parties involved and thus lack a potential for escalation. Indeed, it is now possible to detect clear instances where these differences are being resolved politically. As indicated before, Nicaragua does not have any serious conflicts with other states that could lead to war. The conflicts that Nicaragua has experienced over the last 25 years are internal, with strong international influences but with clear endogenous origins. It is necessary to establish what types of conflicts these have been, if they have been caused by structural factors or circumstantial developments, what their intensity was, and to what degree they divided society. Contrasting the concept of a divided society[19] with the reality experienced by Nicaragua, one discerns an absence of structural or permanent divisions, as there are no serious linguistic, religious, or regional divisions of substance.

The relevance of conflicts depends not only on their nature but also on their intensity, and this can be determined by the distance that separates the groups in conflict. In the extreme case, the parties involved in such a conflict pursue exclusive objectives.[20] The conflict between Sandinismo and Somocismo was not structural, but it was intense, and the goals pursued by the actors involved were mutually exclusive. The current conflict between the government/Sandinismo and the UNO is not structural, nor, at least based on the public declarations offered so far, is it mutually exclusive.[21] The virulence of the current struggle is more the product of a profound and reciprocal lack of trust, of deeply seated prejudices and individual conflicts than of irreconcilable goals.[22] To this must be added a process of political socialization that stimulates and reinforces the elements of tension, particularly as they are stimulated and promoted by the media, the educational system, and the political style[23] of the Nicaraguan leaders and their organizations.

Nicaragua is largely free of religious, racial, identity, and even ideological conflicts. The divisions between the Atlantic coast and the rest of the nation have been resolved largely by the granting of limited autonomy to that region. The country is, however, subject to conflicts stemming from governmental processes and those originating in social injustice and debt. The social conflict suffered by Nicaragua can be traced to the problem of injustice and marginality that took shape during the Somoza governments. This is a problem that belongs to underdevelopment and the extreme poverty suffered by the majority of the Nicaraguan people. The administration and solution of problems that originate with social injustice and social debt represent a major challenge for any society, especially the political leadership. In any event, it is evident that to respond with repressive instruments does not resolve, but rather, exacerbates these problems. The police and armed forces are simply not capable of resolving social conflicts.

Other principal sources of conflict are the tensions created by the governmental processes in the political system. It is important, first, to recognize that the conflicts between the different branches of government are indicative of, among other things, vitality and independence, with the different branches trying to serve the country following their own criteria and rejecting any subordination that they may consider incompatible with the functions for which they were created. It is, nevertheless, necessary to recognize that among Nicaragua's political class, there exists a political style characterized by demonstrations of physical power, by zero-sum attitudes of winning or losing all, strong intolerance, and a preference for conflict over compromise. This situation is aggravated by a defective constitutional order that favors and even provokes such tensions.

The situation just described forces the reform of the state. The modernization of Nicaragua, especially in the political area, requires the immediate reform of the state, which would have to include the following:

1. A single legislative system;
2. Incorporation of the process of the formation of law in the political constitution;
3. Reduction of the discretion available to state functionaries;
4. The guarantee of the judicial separation of public and private interests; and
5. Protection of the rights of the citizenry before the state.

What to Do with the EPS?

The necessities of a modern state, contrasted with the current Nicaraguan state, attest to the need to reform the armed forces. In their present condition, they remain anchored in the past, pretending to fulfill missions and roles copied from a state and circumstances that have changed drastically. The traditional concept of security, reduced to the military realm, is presently not a defensible one.[24] Former World Bank President Robert S. McNamara openly disqualifies the armed forces as the custodians of internal security, declaring, "When the armed forces appropriate the function of guaranteeing the internal security of a society, in the majority of the cases they are not trying to provide it equally to all citizens. In reality, their efforts many times create a greater instability. With excessive frequency, the security forces do not protect the majority of the population against a minority that has decided to achieve its political and economic objectives."[25]

In present-day Nicaragua, the citizens suffer from physical insecurity.[26] The shortages felt by the citizenry lead to social problems, such as delinquency, which in turn lead to insecurity. These problems, in turn, cannot be resolved by appealing to force. On the contrary, it is necessary to have in place a complex system of incentives that reduce the factors of insecurity for the citizens. The development of these types of programs assumes the existence of, among other things, a sufficient budget that will allow the state to engage in the necessary initiatives. This is precisely what leads to a consideration of reform of the armed forces, where expenditures are viewed as worthless, since they do not contribute to the promotion of security among the citizenry and compete with the allocation of resources to programs that contribute to alleviate poverty, reduce social debts, and, in sum, increase social security.

The budget of the Nicaraguan armed forces has been diminishing since 1989, having fallen from a high of up to 50 percent of public spending during the mid-1980s to the current level of under 12 percent. This is significant, although 12 percent of public spending is still high. While the armed forces exist in their present form, it will be necessary to provide them with resources, and this will not likely be less than the current levels of spending ($60 million per year via the national budget), plus any income generated by the businesses owned by the EPS.

Although it is true that the armed forces do not compete directly with civilian projects in attracting external cooperation, they do so indirectly. One of the characteristics of external assistance is that portions of the assistance destined for civilian objectives are transferred frequently to military objectives. This takes place independently from the wishes of the political actors involved, especially donor countries. Econometric studies of countries as different as Israel and Vietnam demonstrate that at least 40 percent of the assistance destined for civilian objectives is used for military ones, while only 30 percent of military assistance is directed to civilian objectives.[27] This means that the very existence of the armed forces is a factor that influences the determination of public expenditures and the use of foreign aid.

The armed forces are perceived by a large portion of society as a factor of tension and instability. This perception is based on the historical experience of the country. The armed forces have had a partisan function; they have been instruments through which a family, a clan, plotters, a party, or individuals defend their power and parochial interests to the detriment of national interests. This partisanship has been exploited further to preclude the development of political institutions that function and thus allow for the civilian and civilized resolution of conflicts and disputes involving power. From this perspective, the armed forces are considered to be a source of danger and instability for the political process.[28] In Nicaragua, this danger is great since its military leaders have a strong political vocation and inevitably involve themselves in processes that are alien to their military institutional nature. Frequently, the leadership of the army judges, evaluates, and classifies publicly the behavior of the country's political actors. During testimony before the Commission on Defense and Government of the National Assembly, General Humberto Ortega expressed judgments regarding the political attitudes of the vice president of the republic.[29] A year later, in a publication of the EPS, he commented on the activities of the president of the national assembly.[30] General Cuadra, in contrast, has been more circumspect in his public statements.

The Sandinista armed forces were conceived during the Cold War, in a world where there was a global conflict between enemy systems. The disappearance of the Soviet Union, one of the two principal actors in this conflict, created confusion and the loss of identity not only among the armed forces that allied themselves with the socialist camp but also among those that identified themselves with the capitalist world. In 1992, the German minister of defense met with 400 of the highest-ranking officers of the armed forces precisely to confront the difficult problem of finding a reason for being that would legitimate the continued existence of the armed forces after the disappearance of the communist enemy and in the new context where Germany is an active sponsor of a Europe without frontiers.[31] If the German military has problems defining its roles, the issue is obviously much more severe in nations such as Nicaragua.

The aforementioned factors clearly indicate that the Sandinista armed forces cannot continue to exist in their present form. The world in and for which they were created has disappeared, and the conditions in Central America have changed substantially. It would be absurd to think that they can continue to fly flags and pretend to fulfill missions and roles that do not correspond to the current conditions being experienced by Nicaragua. It is necessary to approve and expand the program of reforms in order to transform the current armed forces into an organization that will receive the recognition and backing of all of society, that does not diminish political stability, and is efficient in carrying out the missions assigned to them. This process requires substantial and substantive international cooperation in order to fund reforms of the armed forces. As noted above, between 1982 and 1987, the war in Nicaragua cost at least $1 billion, while the cost of reform is infinitely less than that, at around $200 million.

The reform of the armed forces supposes the cashiering of 12,000 soldiers and officers, nearly two-thirds of the total number currently in service. The funds would be used to pay for retirements, professional retraining, the creation of new organizations for civilian training and empowerment, and credit for the development of investment projects for the military who retire. It is also necessary to envision the transfer of sectors of the armed forces to other state institutions with exclusively civilian objectives. Businesses owned by the military must be privatized and reformed to benefit their workers. The 7,000 remaining service personnel must go through a process of professional development so that they can fulfill the following missions: 1) guarantee territorial control, 2) combat narcotics trafficking, and 3) provide for civil defense.

This armed body must be created as an institution that serves the nation, whose members are obedient, professional, non-partisan, and do not debate basic civilian policy decisions. Its behavior must be framed by the three missions indicated above and any others provided by the constitutional system. This armed body must receive training adequate for its missions and roles that corresponds to a new national force. The system of earnings, promotions, and retirement must be established clearly by law, and the relations of the armed forces must be governed by criteria of rank and hierarchy. The ranks within the armed forces must correspond to their actual size and function. The two highest ranks must be conferred by the national assembly as a result of a two-thirds' majority vote, as proposed by the president of the republic. A similar procedure must be used to name the chief of staff and commander of the armed forces. The training and education of the armed forces must include civilian professors and instructors. The educational process also must emphasize the principles of due obedience, non-partisanship, and professionalism.

All military expenditures must be authorized by a yearly budget law. This presupposes creation of legal mechanisms to verify military expenditures. It also implies that the armed forces cannot own businesses or engage in financial activities. The businesses currently owned by the EPS would be privatized. The existence of military industries, the active involvement in financial activities, and the direct receipt of monies by the armed forces have the double negative effect of removing the institution from civilian control and exposing the armed forces to corruption. The activities of the armed forces must be subject to the same rules and regulations that apply to other state institutions, such as public bids for services and uniform reporting and auditing procedures.

The intelligence branches must be reorganized. The current organizations of intelligence in Nicaragua are a creation inspired by the models of Cuban and East European intelligence.[32] Their style of operation has lacked all legal regulation; no civilian official is a member of their command, nor have they been subject to civilian oversight. The operations of these entities far exceed the current needs of Nicaragua. Almost all members of the security apparatus were educated and trained under principles prevailing at the time in Cuba and Eastern Europe. These circumstances appear to indicate that the processes of reform needed in this area must be profound and substantive. In the first place, their activities must be subject to law, must be by their very nature civilian, and must be subject to governmental supervision through parliamentary and judicial procedures.[33] The general objectives of the intelligence community must be specified in the law establishing it and must be framed by constitutional principles, including personal responsibility for actions undertaken by individuals who break the law.

Recent reforms of the military code and of the constitution are a beginning in this process but are by no means a final answer to the issues of civil-military relations and democratic consolidation in Nicaragua. Along with the reform of the armed forces and the intelligence bodies, it is necessary to establish a law of civil service that creates an obligation for all Nicaraguans, regardless of gender, to serve in public institutions, including the military, for up to 18 months. Compensations could include scholarships. The nation also needs a transformation of the processes of political socialization, including the norms and criteria that govern the conduct of political affairs. Today, political socialization in Nicaragua actually encourages conflict, even if structural faultlines do not exist in society. Nicaraguan society must reform profoundly those mechanisms that artificially create a climate of tension and conflict. This supposes, among other things, changes and reforms in the system of values, which currently encourages individuals to engage in confrontation and struggle rather than negotiation or compromise. One of the reasons for the success and progress of many developed nations is their ability and capacity to establish a climate of cooperation.[34] In brief, it is necessary to make the peaceful and constructive elements of the Nicaraguan culture prevail over those that are negative and destructive. The development of a culture of peace is a subject that has been taken on happily by important parts of Nicaraguan society and is supported by the development of movements around the world that are concerned with the promotion of a culture of peace and the adoption of mechanisms that favor coexistence over confrontation.[35]

Notes

1. Ignacio Sotelo, 1977, "Modelos de explicación del militarismo latinoamericano: Una interpretación histórica," *Revista de Sociología* (Madrid) 7, 80. In his article, "Teorias de las intervenciones militares en América Latina," Napoleon Chow (1973) cites several authors who consider the National Guard with a professional army and consider that the Guard dominated the political life of the time. *Estudios Sociales Centroamericanos* (San Jose) 3, 138.

2. Gianfranco Pasquino, 1981, "Militarismo," in N. Bobbio and N. Mateuccin, eds., *Diccionario de Política* (Mexico City: Editorial Porrua), 1000.

3. Amos Perlmutter, 1980, "The Comparative Analysis of Military Regimes: Formations, Aspirations, and Achievements," *World Politics* 33, 1: 96.

4. A similar assessment can be found in Edelberto Torres-Rivas' (1989) prologue in Gabriel Aguilera Peralta's *El Fusil y el Olivo* (San José: EDUCA), 11-14.

5. An excellent exception to this reductionism can be found in Alain Rouquié's (1984) work who, in regard to Nicaragua, correctly determines that the National Guard was a praetorian body. *El Estado Militar en América Latina* (Buenos Aires: Emece Editores SA), 11-23.

6. The classic study of the National Guard is still Richard Millett, 1977, *Guardians of the Dynasty* (Maryknoll, N.Y.: Orbis).

7. Amos Perlmutter and William LeoGrande, 1982, "The Party in Uniform: Toward a Theory of Civil-Military Relations in Political Systems," *American Political Science Review* 76, 4: 788-789.

8. Many observers received the information provided by the ministry of finance with skepticism since they doubted the veracity of the data on the military budget. They found, when looking at the lifestyles of many officers, indications that they were not compatible with the declared income. The highest salary in the armed forces, according to the ministry of finance, is $200 per month, along with subsidies for housing, transportation, fuel, and other items, which would amount to an income of $1000 per month.

9. According to General Ortega, these reforms took the form of a reduction in the size of these units and a limitation of the activities undertaken in this area, including the inability to conduct searches and arrests directly. See the transcripts of the declarations made by General Ortega during his testimony before the Commission of Defense and Government of the National Assembly on June 5, 1991.

10. The framework used in this section to evaluate the EPS is taken from Alfred Stepan, 1988, *Rethinking Military Politics; Brazil and the Southern Cone* (Princeton, N.J.: Princeton University Press), 93-102.

11. Foreign Broadcast Information Service (FBIS), 1994, "Nicaragua: Text of Constitution, Proposed Reforms," *Latin America: Daily Report, Supplement*, November 10, 7-8.

12. These activities were confirmed publicly by Lieutenant Colonel Ricardo Wheelock, chief of public relations of the EPS, in a letter sent to the newspaper *La Prensa* and published on October 13, 1991.

13. See several articles on the subject in *Finanzas y Desarrollo* 28, 3 (September 1991); 28, 4 (December 1991); and 29, 1 (March 1992).

14. One of these critiques of militarism can be found in the publication *Pensamiento Propio (Our Own Thoughts)*. See issue 88 (March 1992).

15. See comments of Borge in the March 25, 1992, issue of *Barricada*.

16. At the request of the government of Nicaragua, the Norwegian government in April 1991 sponsored a technical mission, made up of a Norwegian expert, an officer of the Nicaraguan navy, and an expert of INPESCA (the Institute of Fisheries), to assess the capacity of the Nicaraguan government to control access to its territorial waters. Among the conclusions of the mission are the threat of fisheries piracy and the alleged activities of narcotics traffickers.

17. Trish O'Kane and Raul Marin, 1992, "Reverso de la Medalla" and "La Tentación del Caudillismo," *Pensamiento Propio* 88 (March).

18. A detailed calculation of the financial assistance provided by the U.S. Congress to the Nicaraguan resistance can be found in Nina M. Serafino, 1989, *Contra Aid: Summary and Chronology of Major Congressional Action, 1981-1989* (Washington, D.C.: Congressional Research Service), 17.

19. See Arend Lijphart, 1988, *Democracia en las Sociedades Plurales* (Mexico), 4.

20. See Eric Nordlinger, 1972, *Conflict Regulation in Divided Societies* (Cambridge: Harvard University Center for International Studies), 8.

21. The political platforms offered by the FSLN and UNO in 1990 included important similarities in most fundamental areas.

22. Nordlinger 1972, 8.

23. See Arnd Morkel, 1966, "Uber den Politschen Stil," *Politisches Vierteljahresschrift* 7: 1119-1137; and Johan P. Olsen, 1983, *Organized Democracy: Political Institutions in a Welfare State* (Oslo: Universitetsforlaget [U.S. publisher, Columbia University Press]), 199-207.

24. An extensive discussion on the modern and democratic concept of security can be found in Juan Somavía and José Miguel Insulza, eds., 1990, *Seguridad Democrática Regional* (Santiago: Editorial Nueva Sociedad), 7-10.

25. Robert S. McNamara, 1991, "La reducción del gasto militar en el Tercer Mundo," in *Finanzas y Desarrollo* (September): 26-28.

26. The International Foundation for the Global Economic Challenge (FIDEG) undertook a poll in Managua during December 1991 and found that one of the shortages most felt by residents of the capital was physical security. There is a high level of insecurity that is manifested in the most diverse forms and circumstances. Citizens do not feel secure due to the lack of public lighting and the danger of traffic, and they express this insecurity as pedestrians, bicyclists, or bus passengers.

27. See Saadet Deger and Sen Somnath, 1992, "Military Expenditure and Economic Development," *Proceedings of the World Bank Annual Conference on Development Economics 1991* (Washington, D.C.: World Bank), 163-173.

28. Saadet Deger, 1992, "World Military Expenditure," *SIPRI Yearbook 1991: World Armaments and Disarmament* (Stockholm: Stockholm International Peace Research Institute), 163.

29. Transcript of the testimony of General Humberto Ortega before the commission of defense and government of the national assembly, June 5, 1991.

30. See the military balance sheet of the first half of 1992, *El Nuevo Diario* (Managua), May 27, 1992.

31. See *Welt am Sontag* (Hamburg), May 17, 1992.

32. During June 1992, the *La Prensa* (Managua) newspaper published a series of reports confirming the strong involvement of the German Democratic Republic and Cuba in the organization and functioning of the intelligence organizations created during the Sandinista government. The reports revealed a high degree of impunity with which these bodies operated and the absolute lack of laws that controlled and regulated their activities.

33. On intelligence oversight, see Alfred B. Prados and Richard A. Best Jr., 1990, *Intelligence Oversight in Selected Democracies* (Washington, D.C.: Congressional Research Service, Library of Congress).

34. A detailed description of this process in various Western countries can be found in Ronald Inglehart, 1977, *The Silent Revolution: Changing Values and Political Styles among Western Republics* (Princeton, N.J.: Princeton University Press).

35. Elise Boulding, 1992, "The Concept of Peace Culture," *Peace and Conflict Issues after the Cold War* (Paris: UNESCO).

IX

Unfinished Business: Military Reform and Peace Processes in El Salvador and Guatemala

Bonnie Tenneriello
with Geoff Thale and Richard L. Millett

"Nicaragua has won! El Salvador will win! And Guatemala will follow!" Those who chanted this during demonstrations in the 1980s had revolutionary triumph in mind, but it has turned out to be the sequence to negotiated peace. Of course, a peaceful transition is much more ambiguous and slower than a military victory. If Nicaragua's contra war ended first, its politics have quickly become war by other means. El Salvador is still in the midst of its transition, and the March 1994 elections represent only an important first test. Guatemala's road to peace and democracy also continues to be at least as slow and bumpy as those of its neighbors.

Thorny issues of military power and accountability for human rights abuses have been at the core of both El Salvador's and Guatemala's peace processes. The January 1992 accord that ended El Salvador's civil war mandated military purging, reduction, and restructuring, along with reform of the police, judiciary, and intelligence apparatus, in order to establish human rights guarantees. These steps were to be taken simultaneously with the demobilization and disarmament of the Farabundo Martí National Liberation Front (FMLN) guerrillas. In addition, both sides accepted an international "Truth Commission" to investigate abuses each had committed. These reforms were designed to be the basis for building democracy in El Salvador.

Guatemalans watched this process next door, some with hope and others with fear. The future of democracy in Guatemala depends on whether the army will accept the kinds of institutional reforms that its Salvadoran counterpart did. The obstacles are many. The Guatemalan National Revolutionary Unity (URNG) is much weaker than the FMLN, threatening neither the government's hold on power nor business profits the way the FMLN did. The armed forces are far less dependent on external assistance and thus less sensitive to international pressure. In Guatemala, both grassroots groups and an emergent modernizing business class are just beginning to play a political role, while both of these constituencies played crucial roles in ending the Salvadoran war.

Nevertheless, encouraging trends have developed in Guatemala. These were thrown into relief by the May-June 1993 constitutional crisis. Civil society showed unexpected strength when confronting President Jorge Serrano's power grab, and business, labor, the press, and grassroots groups all united in favor of the democratic process. The crisis also revealed greater divisions within the military and a greater sensitivity to external pressure than most outside the institution had realized. Despite these advantages, Ramiro de León Carpio — the former human rights ombudsman who was catapulted to the presidency — faced a difficult balancing act between high popular expectations and the continuing reality of military power. Ultimately, like his predecessors, he became dependent on military support and failed to confront the basic issues of military impunity and autonomy. Whether his successor, Alvaro Arzu, will be more successful remains to be seen.

A key variable for the long-term success of both the Salvadoran and Guatemalan processes will be international involvement. Observers in Washington are struck by how willing Central American actors across the spectrum are to engage with U.S. policy, after decades of distrust and resentment over past U.S. interventions. Ironically, just as the opportunities for a constructive U.S. role are growing, money and attention from Washington are fading fast. This is short-sighted, for if these fragile accords disintegrate under the pressures of poverty, military hegemony, and political polarization, the bill will be much higher.

Two Distinct Conflicts

El Salvador's and Guatemala's civil wars share roots in deep social and economic inequality, but in many ways they were and are different wars. The "Guatemalan solution" came to signify scorched-earth counterinsurgency, as the army used any and all means to contain a guerrilla threat that reached near-insurrectionary levels in the early 1980s.[1] In the process, military and paramilitary death squads decimated civilian political dissent through massacres, assassinations, "disappearances," and forced exile. The communities that were destroyed in Guatemala were primarily indigenous and viewed by elites as second-class citizens. "Don't be an Indian" is a reprimand common among the *ladino* elite. Tragically, the soldiers on the front line who committed the massacres were also largely indigenous, usually pressed into service and themselves brutalized.

The Salvadoran conflict, in contrast, was less destructive of civil society. While the army and paramilitary groups slaughtered civilians and engaged in political assassinations, unions, human rights groups, and the religious community still were able to express opposition views throughout the course of the war, and the FMLN maintained strong links with segments of the civilian population. This reflected the stronger organizational heritage of Salvadoran civil society where the cultural and racial divide between the city and rural villages (mostly non-indigenous or *ladino*) was not so great as in Guatemala.

Of course, the FMLN also committed abuses. However, in contrast with Guatemala, the Salvadoran insurgents' military strength also provided a check on unbridled military repression, with a "política de respuesta" that guaranteed that the army would suffer the consequences of an attack on civilian FMLN supporters. The military's dependence on U.S. assistance also enhanced U.S. congressional pressures to curb human rights abuses. Finally, both the military and the FMLN came under increasing pressure from a wide variety of international bodies to respect international humanitarian law, with its key distinction between civilian and military targets.

In the final analysis, despite some $6 billion in U.S. aid, the Salvadoran army was too corrupt and inefficient to win the war,[2] and the FMLN possessed enough military skill to sustain a stalemate. This equilibrium imprinted a special character to the peace process, enabling the FMLN to win greater concessions than are likely to come out of Guatemala's peace process. This also reflects the fact that in El Salvador the United States remained a major player throughout the war, and U.S. congressional human rights concerns were always factored in. In contrast, the Guatemalan army's ruthless and efficient strategy was carried out without direct U.S. aid, and so the U.S. Congress had little means to express human rights concerns. (Arms sales from the United

States continued,[3] and the Guatemalan military received substantial help from Israel and Taiwan, but these actions were much harder for Congress to grapple with.)

If the wars were different, it is logical that the peace processes have also been different. In its similarities and differences, the Salvadoran transition can shed light on what lies ahead for Guatemala and its armed forces.

El Salvador's Road to Peace

In a Washington conference early in 1993, Representative Mario Valiente of the governing National Republican Alliance Party (ARENA) gave a nod of approval to Joaquín Villalobos, the most brilliant of the FMLN's military strategists: "A year ago, when Mr. Villalobos returned to El Salvador, if I saw him walking my way, I would turn away. I was not ready to shake his hand or even talk to him. But a year has gone by, and now I can. I feel comfortable when I shake his hand, and I think he does too when he shakes mine."[4] This sort of camaraderie between erstwhile enemies brought a kind of euphoria to the country in the first year after the accords were signed. Yet that euphoria dissipated rapidly, as the battlefield shifted to the political arena with the advent of elections in March 1994.

Military stalemate and the country's exhaustion with the war brought the FMLN and the Salvadoran government to the table. Neither side could afford to sustain the conflict politically, and neither could win militarily. The private sector, and even ARENA founder (and death squad leader) Roberto D'Aubuisson, came to realize this. ARENA saw that it could guarantee its political future far better by signing peace accords than by sustaining the war. Ironically, it was the politically astute D'Aubuisson who kept the far right in line during the negotiating process and helped prevent a bloody response from the death squads. The FMLN also saw that it would have to move from the military to the political battlefield if it were to remain relevant. Its military actions were growing less and less popular in a country battered by warfare, and its internal political support could not be sustained indefinitely while war persisted. The FMLN's November 1989 offensive demonstrated unexpected military prowess, but it also showed that a revolutionary insurrection would not happen.

This internal shift toward peace was reinforced by growing pressure from the international community. After the November 1989 massacre of six Jesuit priests and two women, the U.S. Congress — led by the powerful Representative Joseph Moakley — put the Salvadoran armed forces on notice that its days of unlimited subsidy were over. When the George Bush administration came to support the peace process, it had access to ARENA and the armed forces. The FMLN, for its part, was learning that even if it came to power, it could not count on subsidies from the Soviet Union as Cuba had received. Its political representatives were also under growing pressure from Latin American leaders to negotiate an end to the conflict.[5] Moreover, while the insurgents' arms supply seemed sufficient, logistical arrangements were made more difficult by the defeat of the Sandinista Front in Nicaragua's 1990 elections. The changing international context made it possible for the United Nations to play an active role in the Salvadoran peace talks, not simply observing but actively mediating, proposing compromises, and refereeing disputes.

The formula that ended the Salvadoran war traded FMLN demobilization and disarmament for the purging of the military and restructuring of the armed forces, security forces, intelligence apparatus, judiciary, electoral system, and other institutions. All of this took place with unprecedented supervision from the United Nations Mission for El Salvador (ONUSAL). Its activities reached their height during the 1994 elections, when ONUSAL deployed over 700 observers in regional offices across the country.[6]

The emphasis in the peace accords was on creating democratic structures, not on deep socioeconomic reforms. With the exception of programs to reintegrate ex-combatants into civilian life and to distribute small plots of land to core FMLN supporters in rural areas, the rebels left their social and economic goals to be pursued in the arena of electoral politics. Implementation of the accords has, in many ways, been as much a tug-of-war as their negotiation, due in part to lack of political will and in part to the accords' lack of specificity. Reluctance to complete important reforms was evident throughout 1992, as the government dragged its heels on vital matters such as the formation of a new National Civilian Police[7] and a new civilian State Office of Intelligence, and the FMLN, in turn, delayed its planned demobilization of combatants.[8]

Once it completed demobilization on December 15, 1992, the FMLN lost its main leverage in pushing for government compliance with institutional reforms. International pressure had to fill this vacuum, during a pre-electoral period when both Left and Right were jockeying for advantage.

Reforms to correct a corrupt, ineffective, and politicized judiciary were slow to come, in part because they were not specified fully in the text of the accords, in part because the powerful and conservative Supreme Court clung to power, and in part because the problems were entrenched and endemic to the judicial system.[9] Police reform was given special importance during the negotiations, as a means to guarantee safety for demobilized FMLN combatants and, more broadly, to create human rights safeguards. This also reflected the fact that the existing police were integrated with and controlled by the armed forces. Abandoning earlier demands for a share of power within the army, the FMLN instead accepted participation in a new National Civilian Police (PNC), alongside former members of the military-controlled National Police (PN). The PNC membership formula that was finally accepted was 20 percent former FMLN, 20 percent former PN, and 60 percent civilian. The PNC began gradual deployment in 1993, but it was way behind schedule and underfunded. The government's attempt in 1992 to move former members of the National Guard and Treasury Police — both military units — into the PN and the PNC was thwarted by ONUSAL's declaration that such a move violated the accords, but the episode furthered distrust. In September 1992, both forces were finally dissolved, although some of the personnel simply were incorporated into the military. Over the next two years, the PNC was deployed fully and the old PN finally demobilized. However, the new force experienced repeated attempts to politicize its leadership and undermine its independence. It also faced the strains of confronting a rapidly mounting escalation of organized criminal activities. In the fall of 1995, an evaluation conducted by ONUSAL called for major changes in the PNC, saying that corrective measures were "necessary" to avoid the risk of losing its status as an institution at the service of the community, reverting instead to a closed power structure with growing signs of authoritarianism.[10]

Reductions in the armed forces and changes in military mandate, doctrine, and training proceeded as planned, but the purging of officers mandated by the accords came only after protracted U.S. and UN pressures. Military commanders openly attacked the credibility of the three-member Ad Hoc Commission that had been appointed to review the records of officers and make binding recommendations for dismissals. Though the "cleansing" was initially to have been completed by October 15, 1992, it was postponed repeatedly, and it was not until July 1, 1993, that the last of the officers in question were removed from their posts.[11] This compliance came only after open pressure from the UN and the United States, including the suspension of U.S. military assistance.[12]

The FMLN also seriously undermined the accords by secretly warehousing heavy weaponry after all of its arms were to be handed over and destroyed. The explosion of a massive arsenal belonging to the Popular Forces of Liberation (FPL) faction in Managua, Nicaragua, on May 23, 1993, exposed the extent of force they had retained. Subsequently, the FMLN was forced to identify for ONUSAL five additional weapons depots in Nicaragua. In addition to the arms, forged documents and plans for a kidnapping ring were found. Though few observers believed the FMLN capable of or interested in reviving the war, these discoveries represented a clear violation of the accords and did grave damage to the FMLN's credibility.

Accountability for human rights abuses was acknowledged in the peace accords as an essential counterpart to institutional reforms and purges, and a Truth Commission of three international jurists was established "to seek, find, and make public the truth about acts of violence committed by both sides."[13] As the Commission's Research Director, Carlos Chipoco, noted, "This is the first time in the history of international armed conflicts that the two warring sides were courageous and honest enough to agree to an investigation of their own behavior and to enable that investigation to be carried out by an independent international agency. In other country cases, . . . the winners investigated the vanquished."[14]

In its March 1993 report, the Commission assigned responsibility for most of the well-known cases of abuse, which, given the tradition of official denials of human rights abuses, was an unprecedented vindication of the victims and condemnation of the perpetrators. The Commission's findings, however, were limited by time, resources, and uneven cooperation. The Salvadoran government provided "less than full support to the Commission," according to Americas Watch, and the Defense Ministry gave only partial answers on a number of cases.[15] The Commission reported that FMLN responses were also "in some cases, partial" although the FMLN attributed this to the irregular nature of the war and lack of records.[16]

Given these limitations and the stringent evidentiary standards that the Commission set for itself, its findings were remarkably thorough and well documented. Nevertheless, the Commission findings could not be comprehensive. The coverage of FMLN abuses was criticized by Left and Right as uneven, since the People's Revolutionary Army (ERP) faction — which acknowledged responsibility for atrocities it had committed — took most of the blame, while other organizations' abuses were not investigated in as much detail.[17] At least as troubling, right-wing death squads that orchestrated political violence were, for the most part, untouched. The Commission report acknowledged that these groups, "often operated by the military and supported by powerful businessmen, landowners, and some powerful politicians, have long acted in El Salvador and remain a potential menace."[18]

Among its recommendations, the Commission urged that all military officers named in the report be removed from the armed forces and all civilian officials named be removed from public office. It further recommended that all military officers, FMLN members, and civilians named in the report be prohibited from exercising public office for ten years. The death squad problem was deemed "so serious that the Commission calls for a special investigation of death squads in order to reveal and then put an end to such activity." The Commission also urged a number of reforms to the "highly deficient" justice system, including constitutional reforms to allow the replacement of the Supreme Court and its President, Dr. Mauricio Gutiérrez Castro, whom the Commission cited for "unprofessional conduct." These recommendations largely expand on goals established within the peace accords, and in some cases, they have served as a prod to implementation. In particular, the naming of military personnel involved in abuses gave impetus to demands for compliance with the recommendations of the Ad Hoc Commission, and the government agreed to carry out military purges two weeks after the report was released.

Since most measures depended on compliance from the ARENA-dominated executive, legislature, and judiciary — particularly unlikely in a pre-election year — many never achieved full compliance. The Truth Commission report did effectively abort the potential presidential candidacy of Gutiérrez Castro, but he and the Supreme Court accused the Commission of "obvious partiality" and categorically rejected its recommendations on the judiciary.[19] Neither did the legislature move to dismiss the Court nor challenge its power. No investigation was launched of the death squad apparatus — long thought to contain leading ARENA figures.

On March 20, 1992, two days after the Truth Commission report was published, ARENA and its conservative allies passed a sweeping amnesty law in the National Assembly. While opposition political leaders had said that an amnesty could be acceptable in principle, they said that the passage of this one, before any of the Commission's recommendations had been fulfilled, was premature, and they objected to its breadth.[20] The day after the amnesty took effect, two military officers convicted for the Jesuit massacre — in the most highly publicized human rights trial in El Salvador's history — were freed.[21]

These hurdles to the peace process are not described in order to convey a sense of futility, for the fact that the framework of the accords has held is of far greater importance than any shortcomings in compliance. These problems, however, illustrate the urgency of continued international engagement with El Salvador's peace process.

The March 1994 elections were a first test for El Salvador's new political order, and much had to be done to lay the groundwork for the incorporation of the left into the political process. One major problem was the slowness of the Supreme Electoral Tribunal in registering voters and cleaning up old voter rolls. Noting an estimated 700,000 unregistered Salvadorans in mid-1993, the United Nations warned that failure to process growing numbers of applications could "produce an irremediable delegitimization of the electoral process."[22] Eventually, with UN assistance, the majority of these voters were enrolled, but problems with the registry continued through the elections.

The elections, while not fraudulent or dishonest, were poorly organized; significant numbers of voters did not find their names on polling lists and were unable to vote. Turnout was a disappointing 65 percent. The former rebels replaced the Christian Democrats as the nation's second-largest political force, winning one-quarter of the seats in the National Assembly and forcing ARENA's presidential candidate, Armando Calderón Sol, into a run-off election, which he won by a two-to-one margin.

El Salvador still faces daunting challenges. ARENA's domination of the political process has resulted in resistance to change in the police and, especially, in the judiciary. Military and police reforms, clearly defined in the peace accords and subject to international scrutiny, were more successful, but death squad structures were not fully dismantled nor their members brought to justice.[23] Political violence has diminished greatly but has not disappeared. As ONUSAL noted in its July 1993 report, "It is a certainty that there have been homicides which denote a criminal organization and which have used methods and procedures analogous to those used in the past by the death squads."[24]

In addition, the peace accords barely dealt with the poverty and inequality that gave rise to El Salvador's civil war and continue to undermine the fabric of Salvadoran society. The proliferation of weapons caused by the war, combined with high levels of unemployment among ex-combatants from both sides, have greatly increased violent crime and given even greater urgency to socioeconomic development. All the promises of assistance to ex-combatants, both military and guerrilla, also have failed to be fulfilled. This has led to demonstrations and protests that, at times, have turned violent.

ONUSAL's mandate ended, and the mission officially departed on April 30, 1995. A small 30-person mission (MINUSAL) remained another six months, but then it, too, departed, removing a major buffer and arbiter of conflicts. Salvadorans themselves are the ultimate guarantors of their transition; however, both government and opponents will look to the international community for support during the difficult months to come.

Guatemala's Challenges

If El Salvador's reforms offer the minimum guarantees necessary for a democratic process, they are still more than Guatemala is likely to see. It is often noted that the Guatemalan military is far more independent from the United States, far less threatened by insurgency than was the Salvadoran army, and thus has less of an incentive to compromise. Nevertheless, the fatalism that has surrounded analysis of Guatemala gave way to a new sense of dynamism and hope when a May 1993 bid for absolute power by then-President Jorge Serrano failed, leading to Serrano's ouster and the ascent of former Human Rights Ombudsman Ramiro de León Carpio. In the wake of Serrano's attempted *autogolpe* ("self-coup"), civil society seemed to gain strength, and new modernizing currents appeared in the business community and the military. Progress toward peace continued under de León Carpio, and despite numerous disruptions, accords were reached on human rights and on indigenous rights and identity. Negotiations accelerated in January 1996 when Alvaro Arzu became president. Arzu took a direct role in the negotiating process, setting September 15, 1996, as a target date for signing a comprehensive peace agreement. The URNG agreed to a ceasefire and an end to the collection of "war taxes," giving further impetus to the peace process.

While numerous obstacles — many connected with negotiations over the military's future role — remain, the situation in the spring of 1996 was hopeful.

There are many reasons for the long delay in ending Guatemala's civil conflict. Civil society has been weak compared to El Salvador, where popular and religious groups played an important part in creating a consensus for peace. Alongside El Salvador's military battles was a lively public discourse that repression never extinguished. This kind of discourse is reviving in Guatemala with a new generation of popular leaders. Their movements are only beginning to recover their numbers in a still insecure climate. Furthermore, political parties of the left were decimated in Guatemala and only began to revive with the 1995 elections. Political parties across the spectrum have become discredited by the rampant corruption and inefficiency of government during the last eight years of civilian rule. Finally, the private sector historically has not represented a constituency for peace in the same manner as the Salvadoran business community. The war simply has not hurt the Guatemalan elite as much, and full democratic representation for the indigenous majority — who now toil for less than subsistence wages — would imply deep social reform.

Nevertheless, some of these conditions are changing. The crisis that brought de León Carpio to the presidency provided a kind of biopsy of Guatemalan society and the way in which different groups perceive their own interests, with some interesting results. The private sector demonstrated that it had no need for a de facto antidemocratic government. Threatened with sanctions from the United States, the European Union, and elsewhere, business groups played a pivotal role in negotiating an end to the constitutional crisis. Even before the international threats, all the major private sector organizations publicly opposed Serrano, and for the first time these groups made common cause with labor and popular organizations.

The army, which has never been as close to the business elite as its Salvadoran counterpart, proved responsive to the concerns of the private sector and international actors. Divided between a new pragmatic generation of officers (the "institutional" perspective, according to Guatemalan political scientist Héctor Rosada Granados) and the more traditionally minded older generation (the "counterinsurgent" perspective), the military neither actively supported nor firmly opposed the self-coup. The pragmatic line of thought — that backing Serrano would destroy progress toward political modernization and cost the army all the credibility it had regained in the years after its holocaust — ultimately prevailed, forcing Serrano into exile.

Thus, while conventional wisdom holds that the Guatemalan military is impervious to international pressure, shrugging off criticism and sanctions, its behavior during the *autogolpe* showed a different reality. Even if some within the armed forces were willing to shed Guatemalan blood, suffer international isolation, and install a military government, they were unable to influence the high command. Ramiro de León Carpio, a critic of the military as human rights ombudsman, in the end was probably acceptable to the military as president because he was the only available candidate with broad enough respect to stabilize the country and reestablish legitimate government.

An important factor in military and private sector calculations seems to have been the strength and breadth of opposition in civil society to de facto rule. In recent years, constituencies long silenced by terror have begun to reclaim their voices. Despite constant threats, harassment, and selective killings, popular groups have mobilized enough numbers to be a significant political force among student associations, human rights groups, labor unions, Mayan groups, landless peasants, displaced people, widows, and others affected by war. After winning the 1992 Nobel Peace Prize, indigenous activist Rigoberta Menchú emerged as an important leader, although only a few years earlier one hesitated to mention her name in a public place or over tapped phone lines. Impunity for human rights abuse is squarely in the center of public debate, with such cases as the military murder of anthropologist Myrna Mack serving as rallying points.

The press has reflected these political shifts, with increasingly pluralistic coverage in recent years. Though still subject to threats, harassment, occasional violence, and significant self-censorship, the media have begun to address openly the issues of human rights, the security forces, and socioeconomic inequality. Journalists played a crucial role in galvanizing public opinion during the *Serranazo* and openly defied the would-be dictator despite police cordons around publishing offices. In at least one press protest, free copies of banned newspapers were handed out to the public.

Ironically, Serrano deserves some credit for allowing these trends to emerge. His authoritarian style and the apparent corruption and inefficacy of his government were political liabilities, and at least partly to counter these weaknesses and sustain his legitimacy as president,

Serrano gave priority to peace talks with the URNG. David Holiday of Americas Watch notes that as the talks continued, the level of political violence diminished, perhaps because abuses could be political liabilities to each side in the negotiations. (Holiday observed a similar dynamic during El Salvador's negotiations.) Threats, violent attacks, and killings continued to target the press and human rights and popular groups; the climate of insecurity should not be understated. Yet at the same time, the government's initiation of various prosecutions of military officers confirmed that impunity for human rights abuse was a legitimate concern — even when the net results from the trials were unsatisfactory.

Serrano's self-coup was a desperate attempt to salvage political viability for his government as his one good card — the peace talks — disintegrated. Bishop Rodolfo Quezada Toruño had just announced that he was withdrawing as conciliator, as both sides dug in their heels and the talks remained stalled on human rights issues. Facing corruption charges and street protests, Serrano assumed that dissolving Congress would be as popular in Guatemala as it had been in Peru when President Alberto Fujimori took the same step. Serrano's failure demonstrated that despite the myriad problems of civilian rule — rampant corruption, drug trafficking, street crime — most citizens no longer saw authoritarian government as an acceptable solution.

When he took office, de León faced formidable tasks in restoring credibility to government and arrived without a political party base or even the benefit of a formal election. As Héctor Rosada, later named the government's chief peace negotiator, observed soon after the crisis:

> A new president has taken office almost without meaning to . . . . Assuming presidential authority, not political power, confronts the new president with the challenge of having to be commander-in-chief of an army that he had condemned for violating human rights. . . . The new president will have to act as an expression of national unity, in a society which is poor, divided, confrontational, and violent, one which lacks a national vision of the crisis and, consequently, a national strategy for confronting it.[25]

With only two-and-a-half years to govern, de León was given little time to translate his strong popular mandate into concrete reforms in the military, police, judiciary, and elsewhere, all of which would be needed to guarantee full political participation and human rights.

Under Serrano, Guatemalan Bishop Monsignor Rodolfo Quezada Toruño had acted as "conciliator" in the talks, while the UN was consigned to observer status. De León's initial proposal was to establish two tracks, with talks to establish a ceasefire held in Mexico under the mediation of the United Nations and the Organization of American States (OAS) and a "Permanent Peace Forum" established in Guatemala with diverse social sectors to debate national problems, with Monsignor Quezada Toruño acting as conciliator. A higher profile for the UN would allow the international community to play a more active role in encouraging both sides to negotiate seriously and would help lay the groundwork for future UN assistance to carry out the accords. When Monsignor Quezada Toruño withdrew as mediator, the UN was well positioned to replace him in that role.

The failed *autogolpe* elevated to the military high command officers who had been associated with a pragmatic tendency, one that acknowledges Guatemala's place in the international community, understands the pitfalls of military rule, sees massive repression as an unstable method of government, and understands the economic roots of insurgency. This line of thinking is a positive and significant impetus toward modernization within the military. However, many of these "institutionalists" themselves have been associated with human rights abuses, and despite their ascent, it has been difficult to convince the armed forces of the need for accountability for past human rights violations or deep institutional reforms and downsizing.[26]

Military modernizers first asserted themselves in the March 1982 coup that ousted the hand-picked successor to dictator Romeo Lucas García. The young officers who seized power had begun to question the wisdom of direct military rule and the utility of scorched-earth counterinsurgency, recognizing the grievances that led *campesinos* to support the guerrillas. Under General Efraín Rios Montt, the army launched a two-track counterinsurgency effort of "beans and bullets." Villages destroyed by the army were then rebuilt by the army, and the traumatized survivors were brought back in to live on army handouts under strict army surveillance. "Model villages" (including a few notorious reeducation centers in Alta Verapaz) sprang up, later to metamorphose into "development poles." Male residents of the highlands were pressed into "civil defense patrols," serving as informants and sometimes as foils for the army in combat.[27]

Rios Montt was himself ousted in August 1983, and his successor, General Oscar Humberto Mejía Víctores, presided over the drafting of a new constitution and the return to civilian rule. Under his watch, development poles and civil patrols flourished. After civilian President Vinicio Cerezo took office in January 1986, a new contribution to counterinsurgency thought came from General Héctor Alejandro Gramajo, who became Cerezo's Minister of Defense. Gramajo developed the theory of "national stability" to replace old notions of "national security." However, two abortive coup attempts demonstrated the degree of dissent within the military, and mounting political violence narrowed the political space available to popular groups and the press. The counterinsurgent purpose of the national stability model was never consistent with full political expression, and the politics it advocated often seemed less than democratic.

Modernizers who now occupy key places in the high command are cut from this cloth. Politically minded, they understand Guatemala's place in the world and the importance of economic integration and internal stability. The end of the Cold War, the consequent evaporation of East-West tensions, and the reorientation of U.S. hemispheric security policy provide more fertile ground for their ideas than existed under Cerezo. The ideological ground has fallen out from under hardline advocates of a "national security" approach. When it comes to issues of human rights accountability and military reform, however, some of the steps needed to insure democracy are still very difficult pills for the military institution to swallow and difficult for civilians to impose.

An accounting of responsibility for human rights abuse will be needed to lay the groundwork for institutional reform and national reconciliation, just as in El Salvador and elsewhere in the hemisphere. Yet Guatemala's abuses likely will be harder to reconstruct than anywhere else in Latin America, given the scale of the killing, the difficult terrain, and the totality of terror in the early 1980s. During the worst years, no non-governmental human rights groups could function, so the kinds of data gathered by Chilean, Argentine, and Salvadoran activists do not exist in Guatemala. The eradication of entire villages and the subsequent militarization of the highlands also did much to destroy memory. It will take considerable time, staff, and resources to come to terms with Guatemala's trauma.

Purging of the armed forces may also be more difficult in Guatemala than in El Salvador. While many individuals have been retired or removed from command positions, the military seems determined to prevent any external agency from judging its members. When one officer actually was convicted of involvement in the murder of a U.S. citizen, Michael Devine, he quickly "escaped" from military custody and fled the country.[28] It remains a massive challenge to establish individual responsibility, which is a prerequisite for truly effective purging. The Guatemalan army's relative independence may make things harder as well. Even in El Salvador, it took months of concerted pressure from the United States and the UN to force the military to comply with the "cleansing" mechanism that had been accepted in negotiations, and international leverage is weaker in Guatemala. Additionally, it is possible that U.S. defense and intelligence agencies have less information to offer on Guatemala, since ties were weaker than with El Salvador. However, revelations of CIA contacts with officers allegedly involved in the murders of Michael Devine and Guatemalan insurgent leader Efraín Bamaca Velasquez have produced the release of a significant body of material regarding U.S. contacts with the Guatemalan military that could prove helpful in allocating responsibility in a few specific cases. Yet impunity remains entrenched in both civil and military society. The frustrations that have marked the efforts of the United Nations Mission for the Verification of Human Rights and of Compliance with the Commitments of the Comprehensive Agreement on Human Rights in Guatemala (MINUGUA) since its establishment in September 1984 illustrate just how difficult the task of dealing with this will be. MINUGUA's presence has not led to any significant decrease in human rights violations, nor have its activities resulted in any arrests of individuals associated with the military or with the insurgent groups. In its October 1995 report, MINUGUA noted, "Due process is disregarded in high-profile cases in which members of the army or persons linked to it are implicated" and concluded, "The persistence of impunity is the fault of the Government."[29]

Dismantling the repressive apparatus will be another difficult task. Though some units — such as the Presidential General Staff (*Estado Mayor Presidencial*) — have become notorious for abuse,[30] much of the "bureaucracy of death"[31] remains obscure. Military intelligence thoroughly permeates the countryside, leaving an invisible web of civilian and plainclothes informants and assassins. Military control of the police is less clear. Rather than simply run the police (as the Salvadoran and Honduran armed forces did), the Guatemalan military accepted titular civilian police chiefs but placed military officers in operational positions at the middle and upper levels of the bureaucracy. Informal links between the military and police occur at all levels, from the rural village to Guatemala City headquarters.[32] A crucial first step in the right direction was taken in August 1993, when the notorious Department of Presidential Security of the Presidential Guard was disbanded, but much more remains to be cleaned up.

The role of the military in domestic intelligence is an especially difficult issue. In 1994 President de León Carpio prepared and sent to Congress a bill to restructure the intelligence services and institute some form of civilian control over them. The bill, however, has been criticized widely for failing to end military involvement in domestic intelligence and for lacking any clear lines of civilian authority over military intelligence activities.[33] The issue remains a major obstacle to effective demilitarization.

Demilitarizing the country will be a long-term project. Civil patrols have killed civilians under army orders, killed to settle personal feuds, spied, and attacked neighbors who refused to patrol. Though increasingly relaxed in many parts of the country, patrol duty has remained obligatory in many areas, particularly in zones of conflict. The military has begun to curb the patrols and has agreed that they will be abolished as soon as a peace accord is signed, but the bitter and violent divisions that they created within communities will not heal overnight. Neither will the thousands of guns that were handed out evaporate, even after the patrols are abolished. This will take time and the kinds of employment opportunities and basic government services that Guatemalans have never seen.

Constructing a civilian police force and a functioning judiciary in isolated mountain and jungle villages will be one of the hardest tasks of all. Many of these towns have only the most tenuous relationship with civilian government, and many do not speak the government's language — Spanish. The passage of a modern criminal procedure code in 1993 established the framework for an effective judiciary, but overcoming the physical and cultural divides will require very substantial resources, sensitivity, and leadership.[34]

Finally, the army will have to come to terms with civilian oversight of its budget and practices. This will mean breaking with a military culture that has been particularly insular and establishing respect for civilian leadership. The corruption and inefficacy of the Serrano and Cerezo administrations, as well as the demonstrated venality of the Congress, have done little to encourage movement in this direction.

The URNG, like the military, will have to adapt to new circumstances and make concessions. If the insurgents insist on resolving all the abuses within the Guatemalan military before they disarm, they may lose an opportunity to demilitarize the country. In El Salvador, the FMLN calculated that it could negotiate demilitarization and human rights guarantees and then struggle for further change through the political system. It would be unrealistic for the URNG to hold out for more.

The URNG, like the military, also faces internal problems. It will be difficult to persuade mid-level commanders and their troops to lay down arms, when personal risk will be involved (no matter how many guarantees are negotiated). URNG factions have different approaches toward war and politics, some more politically minded and some more militaristic, and finding unity will be a challenge. Unless the commanders can show some achievements from 33 years of war, their future in the political arena will not be bright. Those responsible for abuses of civilians should be held accountable and barred from duty in any future security forces, but accountability will be difficult to establish — for all the reasons that apply to the military.

In 1996, conditions for negotiations and reform are as good as they are likely to get. Civil society groups are asserting their political strength; pragmatists seem to be ascendant in the military, and the new civilian president possesses both integrity and a strong popular mandate. These advantages are fragile, though, and civil-military relations are potentially volatile. International pressures on human rights probably have contributed to the military's decision to support a rapid conclusion of the peace process, but they also have fueled the fears and resentment of hard-line elements within the institution.

The situation is complicated further by the military's rapid changes in leadership. From 1990 through the first quarter of 1996, seven different generals have served as Minister of Defense. This rapid turnover reflects an increase in civilian control, but it also produces institutional instability and contributes to divisions within the officer corps. The autonomy and impunity of local commanders remain major issues as does the continued impunity of officers involved in human rights violations or criminal activities. With agreement on the future of the military institution constituting the last major obstacle to a peace accord, this situation is fraught with potential danger. For the moment, the armed forces' leaders apparently believe that such an accord is in their interests, and prospects for resolving these issues — at least, on paper — seem relatively bright. In the murky and conflictive world of Guatemalan military politics, however, there is no certainty that this will endure.

Lessons for the United States

Washington has offered a fascinating vantage point on Latin America over the last few years, and it is remarkable to see how quickly the end of the Cold War has begun to change attitudes both in Central America and in the United States. The history of U.S. intervention in the region left a residue of bitterness and distrust, but new channels of communication are now opening. In 1991, the U.S. ambassador and the commander of the United States Military Group for the first time ventured out to visit an FMLN stronghold, and now FMLN leaders are regular visitors to the Pentagon and U.S. State Department. Former FMLN leaders have even urged an expanded U.S. military presence in El Salvador as a means of curbing abuses by the armed forces. After years of apologizing for Guatemala's human rights abuses, the reports of the State Department and U.S. Embassy in Guatemala now bear some relation to reality, and, as a result, embattled Guatemalan human rights groups now talk to a U.S. Embassy they would have shunned a few years ago. Even the URNG now perceives the United States as desiring a peaceful resolution of the conflict and the establishment of curbs on the military's power.

These shifts in attitude have occurred as U.S. policy toward the region has been redefined in economic rather than military terms, leading to new conceptions of U.S. interests. Abusive militaries are seen as a hindrance to stability and economic growth, rather than a bulwark against leftist takeovers. There are still inconsistencies in U.S. policies, but the discourse has changed fundamentally. In addition, unilateral action has been, to some extent, supplanted by multilateral diplomacy, as evidenced by the United States' willingness to work within the framework of UN and OAS oversight in El Salvador and Nicaragua.

Sadly, the opportunity to help Central Americans consolidate democracy may be lost. After Washington spent some $7 billion on the region during the 1980s, U.S. aid and attention are now near the vanishing point. When the Ronald Reagan administration saw the isthmus as a priority Cold War battlefront, its support for the Nicaraguan Contras and the Salvadoran military brought constant and vigorous congressional debates. Now Central America — indeed, all of Latin America — has dropped so far from the radar screen that the region must line up with Africa and the rest of the developing world for crumbs that fall from the shrinking foreign aid pie.

U.S. Military Policy

Though far less a central component of policy to Central America than it was under the Reagan administration, U.S. military policy still matters. U.S. relations with the Salvadoran and Guatemalan armed forces must be consistent with the U.S. expressed desire to support demilitarization and democracy. The United States should stop encouraging "nation-building" as a legitimate military enterprise through joint civic action projects like road construction and health brigades. In El Salvador, this kind of activity flies in the face of accords to downsize the military and restrict its mission to "defend[ing] the sovereignty of the State and the integrity of its territory."[35] Why not help combatants enter civilian life, instead of encouraging army units to take on new tasks? In Guatemala, such exercises reinforce the sense of military competence and civilian incapacity and associate the United States with an abusive force.

The United States should exercise caution in military training, even in the name of human rights. Energetically designing schemes to promote democracy abroad, the Clinton administration has revived and advanced an idea developed in the Bush State Department: human rights training and the promotion of civilian-military dialogue. Proponents assert, with reason, that improved communication between the military and civilians is vital to building democracy, and certainly encouraging such dialogue is a worthy objective. However, the history of human rights abuses committed by Latin American officers after training by the United States refutes any notion that democratic values are transmitted easily. Attitudinal changes matter, but only structural controls and mechanisms of accountability will guarantee respect for human rights. Human rights training should not be used simply to "sweeten" military training and make it palatable to congressional critics.

Another component of training, now receiving new emphasis, holds more promise: the promotion of civilian authority over the military, including the training of civilians in defense management and oversight. This type of program may have a positive role to play in a transition like El Salvador's, and Guatemalan President Arzu might make good use of it. However, only if clear benchmarks for success are laid out and evaluations conducted will we know how much impact these programs have. They must be broadly inclusive of representatives from non-governmental groups and legislators across the political spectrum, as well as of the executive branch, if they are to have a truly democratizing effect.

Narcotics trafficking is Central America's newest security threat, and Guatemala is the country most affected by money laundering and cocaine transshipments. While there have been some large arrests, high-level military involvement continues. For example, though Guatemalan Lieutenant Colonel Carlos Ochoa Ruiz was arrested for shipping cocaine for the Cali cartel and discharged from the military, U.S. Drug Enforcement Agency (DEA) requests for his extradition to face charges in the United States were denied, and Guatemalan courts freed him. There is no easy solution to this problem, but anti-drug efforts must not send a signal of complacency on human rights.

Democratization Aid

Democratization aid should be used carefully and watched closely. Such aid may reinforce positive institutional changes and encourage dialogue. However, if it is given before there is a clear commitment to reform within the counterpart institutions, it may legitimize the status quo and simply be wasted. This is the lesson of years of aid to the Salvadoran judiciary. These programs should also reach out to non-governmental groups across the spectrum. There have been steps in this direction, but Washington has much work to do if it is to overcome its well-deserved reputation for political partiality. Here, the United States should recognize its limitations — for some groups, it may be neither advisable nor appropriate to accept U.S. money.

Public Diplomacy Counts and Multilateralism Can Work

Although Central America has dropped way down on the U.S. policy agenda, for El Salvador and Guatemala — as well as the rest of the region — the United States is still the single most important bilateral relationship. What the United States says and does in international forums matters enormously. Within the OAS and the UN, the United States can encourage an active posture in support of democracy (as it did during the 1993 Guatemala crisis). The United States can help keep both bodies strongly engaged in the implementation of the Salvador accords and the creation of strong democratic guarantees for Guatemala. Attention should be paid not only at the level of the UN Security Council and OAS Permanent Council but also within the UN Human Rights Commission and the Inter-American Human Rights Commission.

Conclusions

With all the unfinished business in El Salvador and Guatemala, lasting peace is not guaranteed in either country. Decisive political support for institutional reform in El Salvador will be needed to create a level playing field for elections and afterwards to continue democratization and reconciliation. In Guatemala, the new president needs U.S. support. The best way to help him (and democrats in the country) is to link support to improvements in human rights, democratic reforms, and good-faith negotiations. These years are a turning point for both countries; the United States is already far too intertwined with their histories to play a passive role.

Now that East-West tensions are gone, and economics is increasingly at the center of international relations, government by repression has outlived its usefulness. In El Salvador and Guatemala, as elsewhere in the hemisphere, conditions favor the creation of human rights guarantees and assertion of civilian authority over the military. This will be a long and difficult process, and democracy will be neither stable nor meaningful until the social and economic gulfs that divide these countries are bridged.

Notes

1. Some 50,000 to 75,000 people were killed in the early 1980s, primarily from a highlands indigenous population of 3 million. By the army's estimate, 440 villages were destroyed. See Washington Office on Latin America, *Security and Development Conditions in the Guatemalan Highlands* (1985) and *Who Pays the Price? The Cost of War in the Guatemalan Highlands* (1988).

2. See Benjamin C. Schwarz, 1991, *American Counterinsurgency Doctrine and El Salvador: The Frustrations of Reform and the Illusions of Nation Building*, prepared for the Under-Secretary of Defense for Policy and published by RAND. Schwarz arrived at the $6 billion figure by combining direct aid ($4.5 billion, including $1 billion in military aid), unsubsidized military credits (over $850 million), and an estimated Central Intelligence Agency (CIA) investment of $500 million (see p. 2).

3. See Allan Nairn, 1986, "The Guatemala Connection," *The Progressive* (May).

4. Mario Valiente and Joaquín Villalobos were both speakers at a conference, "El Salvador: Sustaining Peace, Nourishing Democracy," sponsored by the Woodrow Wilson International Center for Scholars and the Washington Office on Latin America on April 2, 1993.

5. See Tom Gibb and Frank Smyth, 1990, *El Salvador: Is Peace Possible? A Report on the Prospects for Negotiations and U.S. Policy* (Washington, D.C.: Washington Office on Latin America).

6. For a discussion of ONUSAL's mandate and performance and the challenges of implementing the peace accords, see David Holiday and William Stanley, 1993, "Building the Peace: Preliminary Lessons from El Salvador," *Journal of International Affairs* (Winter); and Americas Watch, 1992, *Peace and Human Rights: Successes and Shortcomings of the United Nations Observer Mission in El Salvador* (September 2).

7. Washington Office on Latin America, 1992, *El Salvador Peace Plan Update #1: Setbacks in Crucial Police Reform*, May 7; and "Informe del Secretario General sobre las actividades de la ONUSAL desde la entrada en vigor el 1 de febrero de 1992, de la cesación del fuego entre el Gobierno de El Salvador y el FMLN," May 26, 1992, in United Nations, 1995, *Las Naciones Unidas y El Salvador* (New York: United Nations), 251-260; U.S. General Accounting Office, *Aid to El Salvador: Slow Progress in Developing a National Civilian Police* (Washington, D.C.: U.S. General Accounting Office, September).

8. For background on compliance, see Hemisphere Initiatives, 1992, *Endgame* (Cambridge, Mass.: Hemisphere Initiatives, December 3) and 1993a, *Justice Impugned: The Salvadoran Peace Accords and the Problem of Impunity* (Cambridge, Mass.: Hemisphere Initiatives, June). See also periodic reports from the United Nations Secretary-General on the work of the United Nations Observer Mission in El Salvador.

9. See Holiday and Stanley 1993, 423-424; and Hemisphere Initiatives 1993a, 9. For a thorough discussion of the state of the Salvadoran justice system and implementation of reforms, see Lawyers Committee for Human Rights, 1993, *El*

Salvador's Negotiated Revolution: Prospects for Legal Reform (New York: Lawyers Committee for Human Rights, June).

10. "Informe del Secretario General sobre las actividades de la ONUSAL, October 31, 1994," in United Nations 1995, 623.

11. Under this last timetable, those named were to be removed from duty by June 30, 1993, and retired by December 31, 1993.

12. See United Nations Security Council, January 9, 1993, "Letter Dated 7 January from the Secretary-General Addressed to the President of the Security Council"; see also letter to President Alfredo Cristiani from Representatives Joseph Moakley, Lee Hamilton, Robert Torricelli, and 142 other members of the U.S. Congress, May 24, 1993.

13. Americas Watch, 1993, "From Madness to Hope: The Twelve-Year War in El Salvador," *Accountability and Human Rights: The Report of the United Nations Commission on the Truth for El Salvador* (New York: Americas Watch, August 10).

14. Chipoco was speaking at the conference, "El Salvador: Sustaining Peace, Nourishing Democracy," cited above.

15. Americas Watch 1993, 11-12.

16. See Americas Watch 1993 for discussion of attempts to influence the Commission's report, including the visit of a government delegation to the United Nations in early 1993 that requested the report's publication be delayed for five years or at least until after the March 1994 elections and all names be omitted. Two "reliable sources" cited by Americas Watch said that the FMLN also had asked the Commission not to name names, though the FMLN vehemently denied this (see p. 13).

17. See Americas Watch 1993, 25-27, for further discussion of shortcomings in reporting on FMLN abuses. The FMLN leadership jointly assumed responsibility for the crimes attributed to the insurgency by the Truth Commission. It agreed to accept collectively the Commission's recommendation that those associated with abuses be barred from public office for ten years — but only if the government and ARENA party also agreed to abide with the recommendations.

18. See Americas Watch 1993, summary.

19. Foreign Broadcast Information Service LAT-93-058, March 29, 1993, 8.

20. For a detailed discussion of the March 1993 Amnesty Decree and previous amnesties, see Lawyers Committee for Human Rights 1993, 74-82.

21. The release of Colonel Guillermo Alfredo Benavides and Lieutenant Yusshy Mendoza had been recommended by the Truth Commission, given the problematic and partial nature of the trial in the case.

22. "Incorporación de actividades de observación electoral a ONUSAL," Informe de la Misión Preparatoria (May 6, 1993), 12-3, cited in Hemisphere Initiatives, 1993b, *El Salvador Elections 1994: The Voter Registration Tangle* (Cambridge, Mass.: Hemisphere Initiatives, July). For background on electoral issues, see both of those reports and Southwest Voter Research Institute, 1993, *Delegation Report: The April 1993 Elections Monitoring Delegation to El Salvador* (Albuquerque, N.M.: Southwest Voter Research Institute and the Free and Fair Elections Project of the National Agenda for Peace in El Salvador and the Center for Democracy in the Americas, May).

23. In July 1995, the PNC captured 14 suspected death squad members, including three PNC agents: *Central America Report* (Guatemala), August 11, 1995, 11.

24. *Informe del Director de la División de Derechos Humanos de la Misión de Observadores de las Naciones Unidas en El Salvador hasta el 30 de abril de 1993*, unofficial translation from Spanish, (United Nations, July 2, 1993), 7.

25. Hector Rosada Granados, 1993, "Perspectivas para la sociedad Guatemalteca en el proceso de retorno a la institucionalidad," unpublished ms. June 18.

26. For an interesting discussion of counterinsurgency in Guatemala, see Ken Anderson and Jean-Marie Simon, 1987, "Permanent Counterinsurgency in Guatemala," *Telos* (Fall), 9-46.

27. See WOLA 1985 and 1988, cited above.

28. Statement of Col. Allen C. Cornell, USA (ret), to the Senate Select Committee on Intelligence, Hearing on Guatemala, April 5, 1995.

29. United Nations, General Assembly, 1995, "Third Report of the Director of the United Nations Mission for the Verification of Human Rights and Compliance with the Commitments of the Comprehensive Agreement on Human Rights in Guatemala," October 12, 37.

30. See Americas Watch, 1993, *Clandestine Detention in Guatemala*, March; United Nations Economic and Social Council, 1992, *Report by the Independent Expert, Mr. Christian Tomuschat, on the Situation of Human Rights in Guatemala, prepared in accordance with paragraph 13 of Commission Resolution 1992/78*, December 18.

31. The phrase is taken from Allan Nairn and Jean-Marie Simon, 1986, "The Bureaucracy of Death," *The New Republic*, June 30. The article is an unusually detailed look at Guatemala's repressive apparatus.

32. See WOLA, 1992, *Habits of Repression: Military Accountability for Human Rights Abuse under the Serrano Government in Guatemala*, December.

33. Rachel Garst, 1995, *Military Intelligence and Human Rights in Guatemala: The Archivo and the Case for Intelligence Reform*, (Washington, D.C.: Washington Office on Latin America, March 30).

34. See WOLA 1992 for a discussion of judicial reform in Guatemala It is worth noting that the 1996 "Accuerdo Sobre Aspectos Socioeconómicos y Situación Agraria" negotiated between Guatemala's government and the URNG contains a lengthy section dealing with the need for establishing an effective judicial system in rural areas.

35. See Chapter I, Section 1, Paragraph A. of the January 16, 1992, accords signed in Mexico City.

X

Life After Wartime?
Civil-Military Relations in the
Salvadoran Reconstruction

Tricia Juhn

The hurly-burly of pluralist democracy is very different from the controlled military-oligarchy dominance of the Latin American past. Recognition that the military is one of the strongest formal institutions in societies that are in dire need of political and social coherence poses challenges to Latin American civilian leaders that are very different from those confronted by their developed-nation counterparts. In short, if new roles are not learned that permit civil-military trust and cooperation, the future of Latin American politics will continue to be chaotic. Under such circumstances, the military might not hold formal power but would keep titular civilian leaders on short leashes, limiting the continued development of their nations.[1]

Introduction[2]

After ten years of civil war in El Salvador failed to produce a clear-cut winner, a consensus began to emerge that armed conflict should be abandoned in favor of a negotiated political solution. In January 1989, the George Bush administration launched a White House initiative to restore bipartisan consensus on Central America,[3] signaling the decline of U.S. political and material support for the Salvadoran government's counterinsurgency campaign against the Farabundo Martí Front for National Liberation (FMLN).

Two months later, the National Republican Alliance (ARENA) candidate Alfredo Cristiani won the presidential elections,[4] replacing the Christian Democratic (PDC) administration of José Napoleón Duarte (1984-1989), whose contributions to the peace process were lost amid charges of corruption, incompetence, and inefficiency.[5] Cristiani's electoral victory heralded a clear change of direction and tone, although not in the way many predicted. Initially viewed as a "scion of the oligarchy who [led] a political party that once relied on death squads, Cristiani's willingness to declare and defend his democratic beliefs won him respect even from the guerrillas."[6]

On November 13, 1989, the FMLN launched its largest coordinated attack on the capital city. The insurgents insisted that their military objective was to bring the government and the armed forces (ESAF) back to serious negotiating after inconclusive October talks in Moravia, Costa Rica. The following weeks saw air strikes on civilian neighborhoods, the FMLN takeover of the Sheraton Hotel, and the November 16 murders of six Jesuits and two of their employees.[7] The offensive ended when the guerrillas withdrew from San Salvador on December 7.[8]

Subsequently, negotiating teams from the government of El Salvador and the FMLN spent 22 months in United Nations-sponsored peace talks. These culminated in the December 31, 1991, New York Agreement, and the ensuing ceasefire, signed January 16, 1992, in Mexico City (the Chapultepec Agreements).

A key aspect of the agreements revolved around the disposition of the armed forces in postwar El Salvador. The demands of counterinsurgency had swollen the ranks of the army from 11,000 soldiers in 1979 to 57,000 in 1989.[9] When the war ended, it became impossible to ignore evidence linking the military to violations of its own citizens' human rights. In the midst of a worldwide swing toward electoral politics, an army the size of El Salvador's became at once untenable and unfashionable, in light of the virtual disappearance of East-West tensions. Although progress toward an improved political system — that is, democracy — hinged on demilitarization, Salvadoran civil society was ill prepared to offer material or social inducements toward this end. As such, the accords were more an attempt to create the conditions for military extrication from politics than evidence of a decisive endgame.

The progress, since the peace accords, toward redefining the nature and role of the Salvadoran armed forces beyond praetorianism is examined below.[10] Signed by both the government and the rebels, the agreements reflected the intention of both parties to diminish the military's political influence and autonomy by sharply curtailing its force structure and mission. This was principally to be accomplished in the following ways: 1) by cutting force structure in half, 2) by removing from command those officers linked to the most egregious violations of human rights, and 3) by relieving the Ministry of Defense of authority over civilian law enforcement, delegating those duties to a new civilian police force.

While such measures constitute important progress, they are by themselves an inadequate foundation for civil-military reform in El Salvador. The progress of El Salvador toward sustainable democracy requires an explicit, articulate strategy for redefining civil-military relations in the context of peacetime and postwar reconstruction. Discussions of the nature and direction of Salvadoran politics have concentrated disproportionately on what the armed forces will no longer do, as opposed to what they should do. This is a recipe that virtually guarantees difficulties over the next few years.

In El Salvador, the armed forces held direct power from 1932 to 1979 and de facto power thereafter.[11] Despite this, the institution of the armed forces is virtually a black hole. What little is known seems to be based on a combination of myth fueled by ideology. To one extreme are those who view Latin American militaries as a monolith, collectively responsible for the excesses of the region's bureaucratic-authoritarian regimes. To the other extreme lie apologists who justify the abuse of citizens by citing national security doctrines. Reticence toward exploring the Salvadoran military has as much to do with problems of access as with lack of interest. Interest in the substantial *apertura* surrounding Salvadoran politics has not been accompanied by a similar trend regarding the military.[12]

Garrison

The army, air force, and navy were created to defend El Salvador's national territory from external incursions, generally anticipated from Guatemala and Honduras. In response to a burgeoning economy based on the export of coffee and indigo, the National Police was created in 1867. In 1912, the National Guard was established to keep order on behalf of the coffee barons. The Treasury Police was founded in 1933 to control contraband, the traffic of which deprived the government of its tax base. In practice, police duties were subsumed by and overlapped with those of the military and intelligence apparatus beginning in 1945. A 1961 decree (Number 275, Article 5) placed all of these corps under the authority of the Ministry of Defense.[13]

The armed forces were called upon to serve four basic functions for the oligarchy. First, they protected the oligarchy's crops and property from sabotage and theft. Second, they served as bodyguards from potential kidnappers or assassins. Third, they sanctioned individuals and groups, such as union activists or peasant associations, that were perceived as threats to the interests of the hegemonic social group. Fourth, until the 1979 coup, the military governed El Salvador through official parties, the Revolutionary Party of Democratic Unification (PRUD) and then the Party of National Conciliation.[14] The military regime institutionalized itself within a constitutional framework and used it to manipulate uncertainty in the democratic process (such as Napoleón Duarte's 1972 presidential bid). Thus, the military could be at once "elected, constitutional, and undemocratic."[15]

With the army in firm control of the state apparatus, the oligarchy could concentrate on running business. This relationship was simultaneously symbiotic and asymmetrical. It was symbiotic because both groups benefited from the arrangement: Members of the oligarchy were protected from crime, violence, and labor mobilization. In return, individual members of the armed forces earned a living and served a social purpose, expressed as the mission of the military institution.[16]

In El Salvador's case, the economic and social benefits derived from being a member of the armed forces were not incidental and could not be taken for granted as "normal" remuneration for professional services rendered. The armed forces provided a very important outlet for individual economic improvement and social esteem in a society where opportunity for economic and social mobility was constricted, not just by the severe limits of the political economy but also, as largely determined before birth, by race and ethnicity, a major determinant in the distribution of individual motivation and opportunity for achievement.

The military-oligarchy alliance was asymmetrical because "the oligarchy looked down on their military partners, who in turn felt great social resentment toward those who bankrolled them."[17] The implication was that the military was useful for its willingness to employ brute force and to handle the daily grind of governance, but its value to the world at large and the community in particular ended there. This alliance supported a model of hegemonic domination by a small group of coffee exporters.

Civil War

The 1979 victory of the Nicaraguan Sandinistas over dictator Anastasio Somoza Debayle prompted the Salvadoran military to reevaluate its role, focusing the perception of threat on an internal communist insurgency. The armed forces subsequently adopted a strategy of counterinsurgency similar to those of the Southern Cone armies during the 1970s.

The Salvadoran army of 1979, however, was not equipped properly or trained to conduct such a war.[18] Looking for more troops, equipment, training, and funding, the military turned to the United States. Eager to avoid another leftist takeover in Central America, the United States responded by sending $68.1 million in direct economic assistance in fiscal year (FY) 1980, of which $6.2 million was earmarked for security assistance. In comparison, U.S. aid in FY 1979 had totaled only $9.6 million, with no security assistance. Over the same period of time, the number of troops in the Salvadoran army nearly doubled, from 10,000 to 17,000.[19] During the course of the war, the ESAF received more than $1 billion in U.S. aid.[20]

The conjunctural opportunity for the transformation of the traditional military-oligarchy alliance arose from the military's access to the lucrative spoils of war, its demonstrated improvement in command and combat,[21] and the militarizing effect of the war on state and society.[22] This, in turn, effected a change in the oligarchy's behavior in the political arena. In the early 1980s, this group, nearly universally recognized as "bent on the preservation of privilege,"[23] organized itself into a political party to join the electoral game in El Salvador. Known as the National Republican Alliance (ARENA), this party managed to escape its initial image as an instrument of the militarized right and emerge as the major political instrument of the business community. Following major defeats in 1984 and 1985, ARENA mounted an impressive 1989 presidential campaign from which its candidate, Alfredo Cristiani, emerged the victor.

ARENA's participation in the electoral process signaled the oligarchy's preference for open-ended political contest over an almost certain power-sharing, and likely subservient, arrangement with the armed forces. As Dr. Arturo Valenzuela observed in the Chilean case, it was not "the expression of some ideological preference, but merely the pragmatic choice of conservatives who perceived representational institutions to be in their best interests once military solutions to domestic conflicts became inviable."[24]

While there is not space here to discuss the motives and behavior of all El Salvador's political actors, it is instructive to focus on the relationship between the military leadership and ARENA, which during the peace process served as ruling party, government negotiator, and the organized representation of conservative interests. During the peace process, ARENA maneuvered to reestablish authority over a military formerly "constrained by the political culture of the dominant internal . . . class, whose self-interested liberalism constitutes a restraint on the organicist tendencies of the men in uniform."[25] Although the ARENA government and the military sat on the same side of the negotiating table, facing off against the FMLN, the logic of military extrication pitted one against the other.

An open democratic forum became ARENA's best opportunity to curtail military autonomy, creating in effect an alliance between the oligarchy and civil society to return the army — one of considerable combat capability and political autonomy — to the barracks. The unanticipated moderate tone of the Cristiani government and its tenacity at the negotiating table supported this argument; ultimately, the creator and financier of the armed forces helped provide the political space for military extrication from the civilian political arena. Still unknown is whether ARENA's attempts to negotiate the military back to the barracks signifies support for inclusionary representational politics or is a strategy to reassess the elite's traditionally privileged access to power and resources.[26]

Life After Wartime

Defining a new role for the military in society taxed the resolve and resourcefulness of all parties — the government, the army, and the FMLN. As in other cases of authoritarian breakdown, military extrication from politics was delicately negotiated rather than swiftly wrought.[27] Each of the three parties stockpiled small victories, relieved at the resolution of every issue that did not, miraculously, force a direct confrontation. The process thus far has been terse, beholden only to its own logic, and open-ended. In general, each side's representatives resolved the most contentious issues for the short term, that is, sufficiently so as to allow all parties to sign the peace accords — no small accomplishment under the circumstances. However, the implementation of these short-term solutions has created other, equally difficult problems of state policy.

Cuts in Force Structure

The peace accords called for a reduction in force from about 53,000 troops in 1992 to about 26,000 — a significant step toward the demilitarization of the state.[28] In 1992, U.S. military assistance fell by over one-half, with the Salvadoran government taking similar measures to reduce the military budget.[29]

Halving the military, however, created two sets of problems of equal gravity: first, what 26,000 ex-soldiers,[30] who had probably joined the "military as vehicle for upwardly mobile men who would otherwise have little opportunity . . . in civil society,"[31] would now do for a living. Technically barred from joining the new civilian police, a large pool of men with very specialized skills was released into the severely constrained Salvadoran economy. Many have blamed demilitarization for a rise in violent crime hitherto unknown in El Salvador. The second set of problems, elaborated on below, was to define the mission and the prerogatives of the remaining ESAF.

Retiring the High Command

Despite the clear intention of the peace accords' authors, President Cristiani had great difficulty "purging" key members of the *Tandona*, a clique of officers from the thirty-sixth graduating class of the military academy widely believed to have controlled the army during the war.[32] Arguably, the president was able to do so only because of international pressure generated by the release of the UN Truth Commission report and the opportunity created by the Salvadoran Congress's approval of a general amnesty shortly thereafter.[33]

The Truth Commission report called for the removal of 103 military officers, including the members of the high command, and named then-Minister of Defense General Emilio Ponce and six other military officers in the planning of the 1989 Jesuit massacre. On March 20, 1993, shortly following the release of the report, the legislative assembly (where ARENA held a majority of seats) pushed through a general amnesty for people implicated in human rights abuses. On July 1, 1993, having promised the UN Secretary-General that he would, in fact, make major changes to the army high command, President Cristiani swore in Colonel Humberto Corado Figueroa to replace the retiring Ponce. Also retired at that time were the vice minister of defense, the assistant army chief of staff, and the latter's deputy.[34]

Although the amnesty was assailed widely by opposition politicians as a violation of the spirit of the peace accords,[35] its enactment nonetheless allowed democratic gains to be made in other ways. First, it defused an open confrontation between the military high command, the FMLN leadership, and civilian leaders, which surely would have hindered the peace process considerably. Second, it likely diminished any institutional or individual tension among officers, both among the accused and among those officers who did not partake in the excessive use of force. Third, the amnesty did not prevent public revelations of those officers and civilians linked to death squad activity and human rights abuses, although disclosure is not the same as justice. At its most benign, the amnesty was presented as a halfway point between impunity for the accused and intransigence on the part of the accusers. Detractors of the amnesty pointed out that it was a sign of weakness on the part of the new government that attempted to restore legitimacy to the military institution by whitewashing the truth of its past.

Prerogatives

Neither the purges nor the amnesty, however, substitute for clear policies that establish rules for and consequences of professional conduct for future generations of officers and soldiers. The absence of such policies is even more troubling since the accords do not spell out procedures for installing civilian oversight over the armed forces, a situation that reflected a lack of civilian expertise in military affairs — common in societies where the political classes abdicated discussions of and decisions about war to the armed forces. The net effect of this kind of segregation was to preclude meaningful civilian leadership, reflected, for instance, in a civilian minister of defense, debate and disclosure regarding military budget outlays, and civilian input into military policy.

One arena of impending conflict between civilian and military leaders is the ESAF's administrative control over a number of public institutions. During the civil war, rebel forces regularly destroyed infrastructure, so the army took over several public services whose functioning was viewed as critical to the survival of the state. Although the security threat has diminished considerably, military officers still direct the state phone company, National Administration of Telecommunications (ANTEL); the water works, National Administration of Aqueducts and Water (ANDA); and the port authority, (CEPA),[36] notable omissions in the otherwise energetic pursuit of privatization by the Cristiani government.

National Defense vs. Public Security

Mandated by the peace accords, the separation of army and police duties through the creation of a new civilian police academy (ANSP) and civilian police force (PNC)[37] signaled an important structural-functional change in Salvadoran civil-military relations. The de jure differentiation of national defense issues from public security[38] issues in El Salvador marked a radical departure from business as usual, whereby enforcing the law and upholding public order were traditionally the purview of the military.

The peace accords included a wide range of social reforms, divided into higher and lower priority programs. Included in the high priority category of reforms were the establishment of the new civilian police force and academy, technical assistance to judicial and democratic institutions, a land transfer program, and a National Reconstruction Plan to reintegrate ex-guerrillas into civil society and remedy extreme poverty. In the lower priority category of reforms were three other components of the National Reconstruction Plan, which called for aid to the social and productive sectors, rebuilding infrastructure, and investing in the environment.[39]

The details and timing of the land transfers and the National Reconstruction Plan were not defined precisely during the negotiation but were to be worked out by the parties as the postwar period wore on. Regarding the demilitarization of law enforcement, however, the agreement is explicit. Chapter one of the Chapultepec Accords redefined the missions of the armed forces to preclude law enforcement and routine duties of public security by stating that public security will be the responsibility of the PNC, while the armed forces will be charged with national defense, the object of which is to guarantee sovereignty and territorial integrity in the face of an external military threat.[40]

The accords called for the dissolution of the National Guard and the Treasury Police, which was accomplished in 1992. In accordance with the terms of Chapultepec, the new civilian police academy and the civilian police force were established by the legislative assembly on June 25, 1992. The full deployment of 5,940 new police officers across the 14 departments of El Salvador was largely completed by the end of October 1994,[41] at which time the PNC was subsumed under the authority of the Ministry of the Interior. During the transition period (February 1992-October 1994), the old PN operated directly under the presidency, supervised by the police division of the ONUSAL.[42]

In 1993, over the objections of international observers, President Cristiani deployed about 3,000 members of the armed forces to supplement the national police in high crime areas. Three months later, 7,600 National Police were still on the payroll, despite the deployment of nearly 1,300 new civilian police officers.[43] The remaining National Police were to be phased out gradually as PNC officers were deployed around the country. Progress on this score stalled in February 1994, when Cristiani announced that the demobilization of the PN would be suspended, owing to the rising crime rate and the March elections. When the crime rate continued to climb, the Salvadoran government began to utilize the military more and more in police roles. They patrolled the highway between the capital and the airport, intervened in labor disputes, and, in February 1995, were ordered by the president to undertake anticrime patrols throughout the nation.[44] While police forces were no longer under military control, the army itself was functioning more and more as a national police force.

Need for New Missions

The rhetoric surrounding demilitarization and democratization has not afforded much room for frank discussion of the army's new role in this process, almost as if shrinking the size of the military were tantamount to improving it. This, of course, is hardly the case. With troops and resources on the wane, a rising crime rate straining to the breaking point the capacity of a novice, undertrained and underfunded civilian police corps, and the low probability of foreign invasion, it is an opportune moment to install clear, concise definitions for the postwar ESAF.

Other than policing, alternative occupations of peacetime armies are not readily available options for the ESAF.[45] For example, the military involvement in antinarcotics initiatives carries with it a whole separate set of implications, most of which distract from the demilitarization of public security as outlined in the peace accords. Research across Latin America reveals that "militarization of the drug war . . . poses major risks for the violation of citizens' legal rights and due process . . . promote(s) conflict among state institutions, and . . . has subjected the institution to the pervasive corruption that has affected every other agency charged with fighting drugs."[46]

Civic action programs — in developed countries, a standard method of building good relationships between soldiers and citizens — are politically sensitive in El Salvador. To critics, military participation in civic projects (for example, "Fuertes Caminos," a 1993 roads projects held jointly with the U.S. military) is too reminiscent of the government's "hearts and minds" campaigns carried out as part of its rural wartime strategy and contradicts the goals of the peace accords by enhancing military involvement in civilian development initiatives.[47] It also siphons money that would be spent more efficiently in direct assistance to civilian development programs.

Predictably, the army has not acquiesced quietly to its new, more circumscribed status. One report by a U.S. observer attributed the substantial budget shortfalls in setting up the ANSP and the PNC (estimated at $182 million as of November 1993) partly "to the fact that El Salvador has never had a real police force before, and partly to the acquisitive behavior of the armed forces."[48] For example, just prior to the signing of the peace accords, the Ministry of Defense transferred the Military School into what would have been the site of the new police academy, putting about 300 students onto a 114-acre facility. Before turning over the old police technical school in Santa Tecla, the army stripped it of everything, down to the light bulbs.[49] While there is little evidence that this kind of behavior is anything more than the army's desire to defend its diminishing resources, it invites criticism and contributes to the obstructionist image of the armed forces.

Additional events have caused the United Nations and other international actors to call into question the intentions of the armed forces and the autonomy of the incumbent government. In October 1992, ONUSAL discovered that 11 of the 18 candidates presented as former members of the National Police were actually members of the Army, Treasury, or National Guard, in violation of the peace accords.[50]

Furthermore, the government was accused of creating obstacles when the author of the UN report on the progress of human rights in El Salvador, Pedro Nikken, was denied a visa to enter the country. Nikken reported an increase in political violence, delays in the timetable of the accords, and "worrisome symptoms of military influence in the area of police work." He also thought the judicial system unable to bear the burden of increased law enforcement activities resulting from the deployment of the PNC.[51]

Despite these problems, Salvadorans and international participants in the peace process have reason to be satisfied. With substantial assistance from ONUSAL, the country has witnessed the withdrawal of FMLN and army personnel from combat positions, the demobilization of the guerrillas, the reduction of the armed forces, and the dissolution of two of three police forces.

Conclusions

The triumph of the peace accords was to negotiate an end to the war by defusing the most immediate and most explosive of the country's issues to the satisfaction of all parties — for example, by removing the controversial High Command from office but retiring its members with full honors. It provided a point of departure for a new nation, with new forms of participation, contestation, and governance. Now the challenge for Salvadorans is to articulate clear, positive visions of civil-military relations in their postwar society.

Neither vanquished nor disgraced in battle, the armed forces share a corporate identity forged through more than a decade of military and political warfare. This reality will be critical in shaping the future of civil-military relations. Progress toward democracy is contingent on negotiating complex, dynamic relationships between civilian leaders and military officers, predicated on clearly defined societal functions, mutual professional integrity, and deference to the rule of law. If civilian and military leaders cannot forge new roles for the armed forces, soldiers may interpret electoral politics as a threat to their social and economic status. At the same time, for leaders to move beyond a rhetorical adherence to democratic civilian rule, the armed forces must perceive the policies that govern it as explicit and efficacious and civilian control as intrinsic to military legitimacy and integrity.[52] All these things require a sharp reversal of the attitudes — by civil society as well as military — that permitted the historical dominance of praetorianism.

Short of total demilitarization, "belief in [a democracy's] legitimacy . . . even by a majority of the electorate is insufficient for stability. Belief in that legitimacy on the part of those who have direct control of armed forces is particularly important."[53] The lack of civilian experts trained and educated in military matters must be redressed, as it imperils the possibility of substantive civilian authority in the form of a civilian minister of defense, transparency in budget process, and input into military policy. Until clear, competent civilian leadership emerges in the security arena, the armed forces will resist putting their institution into the hands of civilians.

Continued progress in civil-military relations requires better knowledge than currently exists. Fuller understanding of the ESAF as an institution, within its own national context and as part of the inter-American security system, could best be accomplished if it were possible to examine allocations of resources, including budget line items, equipment transfers, and personnel deployment.

Equally vital to enhancing postwar civil-military relations is the task of articulating clear responses to the basic issues. Clear doctrine concerning military roles and missions and command and control direct the debate toward delicate and urgent matters of governance. Answers to such inquiries are all the more pressing since the end result of postauthoritarian processes is never a foregone conclusion; a return to violence and arbitrary justice is as conceivable as a movement toward authentically expanded participation and contestation. Negotiating the issues raised here may qualify as the most foreboding aspect of the peace process and one that Salvadorans ignore, quite literally, at their own peril.

Notes

1. Louis W. Goodman, Johanna Mendelson, and Juan Rial, eds., 1989, *The Military and Democracy: The Future of Civil-Military Relations in Latin America* (Lexington: D.C. Heath), Introduction.

2. I am grateful to Doug Kincaid, Louis W. Goodman, Damian Fernández, and Enrique Baloyra for comments and suggestions. Shortcomings of this analysis are entirely my own.

3. Robert Pear, 1990, "Congress Skeptical As Ever on Salvador Aid," *The New York Times*, January 14.

4. Cristiani's margin of victory was 54 to 36 percent.

5. This is regrettable because much of the groundwork for reconciliation was laid by the Christian Democratic Party (PDC). Weathering murder (e.g., the 1980 murder of Attorney General Mario Zamora), factionalism (among Duarte, Fidel Chávez Mena, and Adolfo Rey Prendes), corruption, the army, the death squads, the left, the right, and the U.S. Embassy, the PDC fought tenaciously to create space for competitive politics in El Salvador. It is hoped that future treatments of the regime consider that it held office when "governing the country resemble[d] a fool's game [and] the performance of any government [was] likely to be considered unsatisfactory." Enrique Baloyra-Herp, 1987, "The Seven Plagues of El Salvador," *Current History*, 413-434; and Enrique Baloyra-Herp, 1982, *El Salvador in Transition* (Chapel Hill: University of North Carolina Press), 99.

6. James LeMoyne, 1992, "Out of the Jungle: El Salvador's Guerrillas," *The New York Times Magazine*, February 9, 29.

7. The victims were University of Central America Rector Ignacio Ellacuría, S.J.; Director of the Human Rights Institute Segundo Montes, S.J.; Director of the Institute of Public Opinion Ignacio Martín-Baro, S.J.; Professors Armando López and Juan Ramón Moreno; Fe y Alegría Director Joaquín López y López; their cook, Julia Elba Ramos, and her daughter Lisette. Enrique Baloyra-Herp, 1991, "Persistent Conflict in El Salvador," *Current History* (March): 124.

8. *Latin American Weekly Report* 48 (1989), December 7, 1-2.

9. A.J. Bacevich, James D. Hallums, Richard H. White, and Thomas F. Young, 1988, *American Military Policy in Small Wars: The Case of El Salvador* (Washington, D.C.: International Defense Publications), 24.

10. See Amos Perlmutter and Valerie Plave Bennett, eds., 1980, *The Political Influence of the Military* (New Haven, Conn.: Yale University Press), 179-184; and Nicolás Mariscal, 1978, "Militares y Reformismo en El Salvador," *ECA* 23 (February): 12.

11. For discussions of the military as government and as political party, see Baloyra 1982; Dermot Keogh, 1985, "The Myth of the Liberal Coup," *Millennium*, February 5; Richard Millett, 1984, "Praetorians or Patriots: The Central American Military," in Robert S. Leiken, ed., *Central America: Anatomy of Conflict* (New York: Pergamon Press); and Alain Rouquié, 1986, "Demilitarization and the Institutionaliza-

tion of Military Dominated Polities in Latin America," in Abraham F. Lowenthal and J. Samuel Fitch, eds., *Armies & Politics in Latin America* (New York: Holmes and Meier).

12. Knut Walter and Philip J. Williams, 1993, "The Military and Democratization in El Salvador," *Journal of Interamerican Studies and World Affairs* 35, 1 (January): 40.

13. Guillermo Galván Bonilla, 1994, "Transición y seguridad pública en El Salvador: La nueva Policía Nacional Civil (PNC)," prepared for the research project "Civil-Military Relations and Police Forces: Problems of Democratization in Latin America" sponsored by the Latin American and Caribbean Center, Florida International University (preliminary draft), 6; and Shirley Christian, 1983, "El Salvador's Divided Military," *Atlantic Monthly* (June): 51-52.

14. Baloyra 1982, 34-35. See also note 10.

15. Rouquié 1986, 453-454.

16. The spirit and letter of the missions of the Salvadoran armed forces have been the subject of heated debate. See, among others, Christopher Dickey, 1984, "Obedezco pero no cumplo," in Leiken, *Central America: Anatomy of Conflict*, 33-48.

17. Christian 1983, 53.

18. Max G. Manwaring and Court Prisk, 1988, *El Salvador at War: An Oral History* (Washington, D.C.: National Defense University Press), 60.

19. Bacevich et al. 1988, 5.

20. Ana Arana, 1989, "El Salvador's New President Avoiding Hardline Policies," *The Miami Herald*, July 29, 20A.

21. Millett 1984, in Lowenthal and Fitch, 210-211.

22. Walter and Williams 1993, 40.

23. Baloyra 1982, 309.

24. Arturo Valenzuela, 1990, "Chile," in Larry Diamond, Juan Linz, and Seymour Martin Lipset, eds., *Democracy in Developing Countries: Latin America* (Boulder, Col.: Lynne Rienner Publishers), 165.

25. Rouquié 1986, 448.

26. See Enrique Baloyra-Herp, 1983, "Reactionary Despotism in Central America," *Journal of Latin American Studies* 2, 15 (November): 308.

27. See Rouquié 1986, in Lowenthal and Fitch, *Armies and Politics in Latin America.*

28. On February 1, 1993, President Cristiani and General Víctor Suanzes, then head of ONUSAL, certified that the reduction of the armed forces was complete (FBIS-LAT-93-021), 8.

29. "Efforts to Satisfy National Civilian Police Equipment Needs" (GAO/NSIAD93-100-BR, December 1992, 5).

30. The demobilized guerrilla troops are not counted in this number.

31. Millett 1984 in Lowenthal and Fitch.

32. On the *tanda* system of allegiances, see Millett 1984 and Dickey 1984.

33. "De la locura a la esperanza (From Madness to Hope)," by U.S. lawyer Thomas Burgenthal, former Colombian President Belisario Betancur, and former Venezuelan Foreign Minister Reinaldo Figueredo Planchart. Prepared for the UN Truth Commission, New York, 1992-1993.

34. They were, respectively, Generals Orlando Zepeda, Gilberto Rubio, and Mauricio Vargas ("Army High Command Out But Not Down," *Central America Report*, July 9, 1993, 198-199).

35. "Amnesty in Salvadoran Case Denounced as Against Spirit of Peace Pact," *The New York Times*, March 22, 1993, A2.

36. Walter and Williams 1993, 55-68.

37. The progress of the PNC is well documented. See, among others, William Stanley, 1993, *Risking Failure* (Cambridge, Mass.: Hemisphere Initiatives) and numerous reports by the U.S. General Accounting Office, the Washington Office on Latin America, and Americas Watch.

38. According to A. Douglas Kincaid and Eduardo Gamarra, national defense is "defending the sovereignty of the national state and territory against external threats," and public security is "enforcing the law under the free exercise of political, civil, and human rights." In democratic systems, the military and the police, respectively, are charged with these functions. Kincaid and Gamarra, 1994, "Police and Military Relations: The Challenge of Public Security and Democracy in Latin America," prepared for the XVIII International Congress of the Latin American Studies Association, Atlanta, March 10-12.

39. "El Salvador: Implementation of Post-War Programs Slower than Expected," (GAO/NSIAD-94-10, January 1994), 5.

40. Galván Bonilla 1994, 31.

41. Jack Spence, George Vickers, and David Dye, 1995, *The Salvadoran Peace Accords and Democratization* (Cambridge, Mass.: Hemisphere Initiatives, March), 6.

42. *Los Observadores de las Naciones Unidas para El Salvador* consist of Spain, Brazil, Canada, Ecuador, India, Ireland, Sweden, and Venezuela ("Boinas azules españoles para la paz en El Salvador," *Revista Española de Defensa* 48, February 1992, 6-13).

43. GAO 1994, 8.

44. Spence, Vickers, and Dye 1995, 9.

45. James Brooke, 1991, "Latin Armies Are Looking for Work," *The New York Times*, March 24, E2.

46. Kincaid and Gamarra 1994, 5-7.

47. Margaret Palek with George Vickers and Jack Spence, 1993, *Justice Impugned: The Salvadoran Peace Accords and the Problem of Impunity* (Cambridge, Mass.: Hemisphere Initiatives), 33-42.

48. Stanley 1993, 12.

49. Stanley 1993, 6.

50. Stanley 1993, 7-8.

51. "El Salvador: ONU, Severo informe sobre derechos humanos," *Inforpress Centroamericana*, February 24, 1994, 5.

52. Augusto Varas, 1989, "Civil-Military Relations in a Democratic Framework," in Goodman, Mendelson, and Rial, 209.

53. Juan Linz, 1978, *Crisis, Breakdown, and Reequilibrium* (Baltimore: Johns Hopkins University Press), 17.

XI

Brazilian Security in the New World Disorder: Implications for Civil-Military Relations

Max G. Manwaring

Brazilians always have suspected they are special. They began to observe this phenomenon as early as 1640, when they expelled the Dutch from the Pernambuco region without any help from Portugal. The suspicion was confirmed during the period from 1807 through 1821, when the Portuguese empire was ruled from Rio de Janeiro. Brazilians also have noted that they have been spared much of the turbulence and disintegration that often has characterized the history of their neighbors, and, in spite of various centrifugal forces, the country has held together to remain larger than the continental United States.[1]

Moreover, Brazil has made a relatively peaceful, pragmatic, and successful transition from being a producer of agricultural and mineral products to having the world's eighth-largest industrial economy, with as solid an infrastructure as many so-called developed countries possess. Its $500 billion economy is twice that of all of Eastern Europe combined. Brazil continues to build additional infrastructure steadily at a growth rate in gross domestic product (GDP) of about 4 percent a year.[2]

This is not to say that Brazil has no problems but that Brazilians are justified in the generally good feelings they have about themselves and their country. It is not uncommon to hear, "The future belongs to Brazil" or, in a more nationalistic tone, "Nobody can hold Brazil back." A lighter approach to the subject is that "God is a Brazilian." But, if not, and if Brazil from time to time appears to be teetering on the edge of an abyss — not to worry: "Brazil is bigger than the abyss!"

Thus, the theme of this chapter and the guiding end-point of national security policy is what Brazilians call *grandeza* — greatness. To develop this theme, it is necessary to 1) examine the major components of the security equation — the development of the nation and the development of power; 2) define the perceived threat; and 3) outline the implications for the role of the military and for resultant civil-military relations in Brazil. Such an exercise will illustrate two points. First, Brazilian national security policy relates to types of conflict that are both causes and consequences of internal and external political, economic, social, and military disequilibrium. Second, the resulting requirements prescribe an extremely broad role for the armed forces over the long term.

The Brazilian Security Equation

In the past, security was a term primarily associated with possible or probable traditional threats concerning strategic access or denial from other nation-states. When applied to internal problems, security tended to refer to military or police protection against terrorists, insurgents, or drug traffickers. The current national security dialogue in Brazil focuses on enhancing popular perceptions of relative well-being.

The Brazilian security dialogue has been attempting to define well-being in terms of stability and national development since the early 1960s. More and more, that task appears to consist of two highly interrelated elements: first, the defense of economic and political sovereignty in an interdependent world that is increasingly aggressive and, second, continued and expanded participation in building a country's agricultural and industrial infrastructure. The reasoning is straightforward — the formation and implementation of political, economic, and social development plans have a decisive bearing on preserving internal and external peace.[3]

Thus, the two major themes that are most relevant to the Brazilian security environment focus on 1) a nontraditional definition of security that requires the development of the nation and 2) the relatively nonconventional development of power. These two themes constitute a circular system and support each other. Clearly, however, the first is not as well developed and operationalized as the second.

The Development of the Nation

The contemporary security dialogue centers on the problems and consequences of modern governance. The gravity of the governability issue is hard to exaggerate. Widespread crime, food riots, looting, protests, and strikes are in the news virtually every day. Nevertheless, while keeping the short-term law and order requirement in mind, the security dialogue stresses more and more that these social problems are spawned by lack of Brazilian development and the resultant chronic poverty, violence, and corruption. As a consequence, success in establishing national security no longer will be defined exclusively in terms of killing or jailing dissidents or establishing strong, dictatorial control over civilian populations. Rather, internal security is being defined more and more as stability, and stability is dependent on both the political and the economic development of the nation.[4]

The Need for a Holistic Effort. The Brazilian dialogue points out that the task of generating stability requires the legitimization and strengthening of the national political system as well as the modernization and professionalization of the national economy and the security forces in order to cope with "conflict as a whole." That task means preparing for multidimensional conflict on a number of fronts, ranging from physical combat with an enemy to the building and protection of infrastructure, to the initiation of an all-out, long-term reform program that would alleviate long-standing political, economic, and social grievances.

The stability and progress that can be generated by the above actions — under an umbrella of legitimacy — probably are described best as political-economic-social-professional development. The Brazilian dialogue emphasizes that balanced development is a fundamental requirement for any successful campaign to achieve stability and, thus, internal and external security. That requirement equates with a holistic nation-building effort. The fulfillment of this imperative would consist of all those activities necessary to strengthen popular support for government through substantive, coordinated improvement in the civil and military bureaucracies, the economy, and the society.[5]

Redefining Nation-Building. The major implication of this aspect of a long-term, multidimensional approach to development is that nation-building involves much more than simply building things, providing medical and dental attention, or teaching technical proficiency — and then going away.

Nation-building is the development of people who can and will fight corruption and inefficiency; who can and will build roads, schools, and health care facilities; who can and will strengthen their own national, regional, and local institutions; and who can and will create and maintain the necessary linkages among and between institutions within Brazilian society. Such would be the beginnings of stability with real development.

Contemporary civilian and military positivists in Brazil argue that experience demonstrates that the motivation of individuals in these tasks will not come through the natural course of events. In most instances, motivation is developed through a long-term, holistic program based on the vast body of social science knowledge currently available.[6]

The Architecture for Brazilian Development. An example of this social science knowledge is found in Brazilian national security doctrine. That doctrine provides the basic architecture and the rationale for governmental allocation of values and resources for national well-being. It is a result of research done over the years at the Superior War College (ESG) and synthesized principally by General Golbery da Couto e Silva, General Carlos de Meira Mattos, and others.[7] As a result, the various civilian and military regimes that have governed Brazil since the end of World War II have been provided with a conceptual framework to teach and implement policies and programs designed to achieve the progress and power of the country — *grandeza.*

In the aftermath of the international economic recession of the late 1970s and the return to civilian government in 1984-1985, however, the armed forces made a strategic withdrawal into the background of Brazilian politics. The military now argues that there is no intention of exercising guardianship over the government or society. The national security concept is simply a logical, coherent, far-reaching architecture that defines what the goals of a catholic and democratic state should be and how to attain them. Nevertheless, implicit and explicit requirements prescribe a broad and long-term role for the armed forces.[8]

Implications. The sphere of institutional military concern and activity relating to Brazilian national development has been defined to include broad political, economic, social, and traditional security matters on the national and the international scene. The most salient of these security concerns include protecting Brazilian citizens and national interests along thousands of miles of relatively undefined frontiers bordering on 11 other nations, establishing Brazilian sovereignty and control over the Amazon Basin, and protecting sea lanes and the emerging sea industry in the South Atlantic. Such concerns are necessarily amorphous and not easily operationalized. They are also politically sensitive. As a consequence, a more basic concern for elite unity and institutional preservation appears to be evolving that stresses the development of the national power element of Brazilian security doctrine.

Lessons learned from such diverse sources as Brazil's own experience with the French fleet in the 1963 "Lobster War," Argentina's "Dirty War" of the 1970s and its disastrous conflict with the British over the Falklands/Malvinas in 1982, the Iraqi defeat by the Western Alliance in the Gulf War, and the ongoing Peruvian conflict with narco-insurgent forces all reinforce Brazilian perceptions that there is a close and obvious connection between win/loss outcomes of internal and external conflicts and the level of national development.

The Development of Power

Development in the simplest terms consists of security and economic growth. Continued development of Brazil's agricultural and industrial bases generates the economic growth that results in internal and external stability and security. The notion of power in these terms is more than a quantitative and qualitative evaluation of existing armed forces. It consists of three basic, interrelated elements: 1) actual military strength, 2) the ability to project force over long distances (that is, reach), and 3) the ability to sustain force over time in an adverse environment (sustainability) in order to exert the country's wishes in support of its interests.[9] In turn, the quantitative and qualitative enhancements of these elements of power support the development of the nation.[10]

Military Strength. Conflict, regardless of the level of intensity, must be fought with people. Territory, airspace, and critical land and sea transportation lanes must be controlled physically. As a rule, the larger the armed forces of a given state, the better that state's fighting capability in relation to that of another or to an internal challenger. Training, morale, discipline, equipment, and leadership are important qualifiers; however, in the end, the ratio of attackers to defenders tends to be the most important qualifier of all.

Shortly after taking governmental power in 1964, General Humberto Castelo Branco made it clear that one of the purely military tasks of the revolution would be to reorganize, modernize, and strengthen the armed forces so that they would be capable of effectively assisting the state in controlling all Brazilian national territory and in taking its rightful place at the highest levels of international security affairs.[11] As a consequence, and despite the fact that as an institution the military is considered to have lost more than it gained during the 20 years it exercised political power, the strength of the Brazilian armed forces has risen from 190,000 in 1965 to 336,800 in 1994. This increase puts Brazil on relatively the same numerical level as Italy (322,300).[12]

A 1983 law — which may never be implemented because of the chronic shortage of funds — authorizes significant changes in peacetime strength. As an example, the army is authorized to go to a 20-division force of 592,668 officers and men over a ten-year period.[13] That would put Brazil on a numerical level slightly higher than France (453,000), Iran (528,000), and Pakistan (580,000). Nonetheless, present estimates are that the army will remain under 400,000.[14] The same law provides for a 7,000-man increase for the navy but actually would have generated a 100 percent increase in fleet units. The air force would have gone from 42,800 to 62,800. Because the army, the navy, and the air force have been unable to implement these plans fully, they are in the process of "doing what can be done with what has been given": They are expanding and modernizing a force that they hope someday will compare favorably with most of the major powers of the world.[15]

Reach. The size and even the quality of an armed force may have little significance in the context of world or internal affairs. There are other factors, such as reach or projection of power, that affect the ability of an armed force to play a significant role outside its normal place of activity. The most readily identifiable means of accomplishing the tasks associated with the projection and sustaining of power over long distances are airlift and sealift. Again, the greater the capacity, the greater the relative advantage. Conversely, the smaller the capacity, the lesser the advantage.

In terms of military air and sealift, Brazil ranks low in comparison with a sample of other regional powers and considerably below such countries as Britain and France.[16] The ability to project force in the internal and international security arenas is not confined strictly to military assets, however. Although not part of the regular military structure, long-range civilian transport aircraft and the merchant marine represent an extremely valuable capability that could and would be used in any exigency. The British demonstrated this capability very well during the Falklands/Malvinas War, and that lesson reinforced policies the Brazilians already were beginning to implement.[17]

Brazil has undertaken the development of a world-class international airline (VARIG) and merchant marine to help in its general economic growth and as a part of the strategy of enhancing international and national economic and military power. As a result, the merchant fleet has increased steadily since 1974 and now counts itself among the world's top 15.[18] In terms of major civilian transport aircraft, Brazil, with 176, is clearly ahead of India (93), Nigeria (72), Egypt (43), Iran (44), and Poland (42). Brazil ranks between Germany (200) and Italy (132), but it still has a long way to go to catch Britain (618) or France (355). In terms of this portion of the reach factor, it appears that Brazil is beginning to compete with nations commonly thought to be viable powers in the contemporary multipolar world.[19]

Sustainability. Sustaining even a small force over long distances is complex and difficult. Elements that might indicate the ability to sustain and increase military, as well as economic and political, power over time would include several indicators. In the interest of manageability, only three will be examined here: 1) Brazil's defense industry, 2) its nuclear development program, and 3) the issue of national will.

Brazil's Defense Industry. Relentless pressures from external debts have made exports the country's lifeblood. These dynamics have produced a reaction that linked civilian manufacturers with the military-foreign policy elites and led them to pursue a pragmatic expansion of arms production. By the 1980s, this expansion had become a major key to economic growth and self-sufficiency and was an important part of the Brazilian national security strategy.[20] Brazil's defense industry, however, has fallen on hard times since the Persian Gulf War led to the loss of its major external buyer — Iraq. Moreover, the government has not protected the industry with compensating domestic purchases. The industry has been left to struggle through a major economic downturn without much support.[21]

Currently, Brazil produces about 75 percent of its own arms requirements — compared to only 5 percent in the 1960s — and exports more than 20 different weapons systems, including short- and mid-range missiles, to approximately 30 countries. Although not as dynamic as it was in the 1980s when it generated up to $1 billion a year in badly needed foreign exchange, Brazil's defense industry is still by far the largest and most advanced in Latin America and one of the most advanced in the developing world.[22] Brazil is still the seventh-largest exporter of armaments to the developing world, after the United States, Russia, Britain, France, Germany, and China.[23] In national security terms, the defense industry also contributes to self-sufficiency and continues to develop technology that, in turn, helps other parts of the economy.

The Nuclear Development Program. Given Brazilian strategic thinking, a large and independent nuclear power production capability is a necessity for the country. The nuclear development program would be the crowning point in the realization of Brazil's *grandeza.*

Brazilian leaders have been content to continue research and nuclear power development together with the decision to establish a vast, independent industry designed to produce badly needed energy for domestic consumption. This program is a manifestation of geopolitical thinking that has more than economic and social ramifications, however. With a nuclear power production capability and the theoretical ability to manufacture nuclear explosive devices, coupled with improving strategic and tactical delivery system capabilities, the implications are clear.[24]

For example, if the nuclear plant at Angra dos Reis (Angra I) were only producing at 30 percent of capacity, it has been estimated that Brazil could produce five 20-kiloton weapons per year. Moreover, the production from Angra I and Angra II, plus that from Angra III when it is completed, would give Brazil a capability three times greater than that of such celebrated nuclear powers as India and Pakistan.[25]

The question of why the political decision has not yet been made to create a nuclear weapons capability for a larger and more formidable military establishment is answered, in part, by the fact that Brazil has not had the money to complete an ambitious nuclear development program that goes well beyond Angra III. Additionally, the United States put a great deal of pressure on Brazil to stop its nuclear development program.[26] Nevertheless, a well-established nuclear industry is a necessary capstone for a country involved in world-class competition. Its development continues slowly and quietly.[27]

The Issue of National Will. An examination of power in terms of strength, reach, and material sustainability is instructive in itself. In addition, the concept of national will has become an increasingly important variable in the calculation of world power. A.F.K. Organski and J. Kugler have asserted that will, per se, is not the vital difference that allows a given state to prevail over its possible enemies. Rather, it is the capacity of a government to penetrate a society effectively and extract resources from it. This ability implies legitimate and strong governmental institutions. Revenue data provide good, strong indicators that can measure that capability. Moreover, these types of data indicate a level of capability to administer, coordinate, and sustain various types of goals across the conflict spectrum in the contemporary world.[28]

Ray Cline argues that will, when combined with strategic purpose, is the most critical factor in calculating a nation's potential for protecting and enhancing its well-being. The key "contributory strands in the fabric of national will" are the level or degree of feeling people have of belonging to a nation, the effective strength of national leadership, and the relevance of national purpose to national interests as perceived by citizens. Again, as with Organski and Kugler, these indicators imply legitimate and competent governmental institutions.[29]

In either case, it is not will, per se, but political competence and legitimate governance that are key to national development and security in the modern world. The better a government can perform in extracting resources from society, without using undue coercion, the more successful it can be in governing. The better the control, the better the capability to fulfill tasks imposed by the internal and international security environments and to generate the will to sustain a political, economic, informational, and military fight. This type of development is an integral part of any viable security equation. In this context, Brazil falls to the bottom of a list of countries with which it might be compared — including India and Nigeria.[30] The determination of wealthy Brazilians to avoid paying taxes, combined with chaotic divisions of fiscal authority between national and state governments severely constrains the federal government's ability to fund programs.

Summary

The ultimate economic, political, social, and military development of Brazil is the legitimizing basis for national security policy. Armed forces strength, reach, and sustainability are important elements in a general stability/security equation. Each has its own general functions to perform, which interact with political will elements to provide for the development of the nation and the development of projectable power.

Brazilians, like many others, have emphasized economic development and military security under the assumption that social and political development would follow automatically. This has not happened. Economic development has created a disruptive political reform dynamic of its own. In Brazil, the development of political competence based on a foundation of moral legitimacy is a rising challenge that soon must be met.[31]

In political competency and legitimacy terms, Brazil remains significantly behind those countries, such as France, that have a greater ability to administer, coordinate, and sustain political, economic, psychological, and military conflict. This is a major national development problem that has yet to be addressed politically since civilians resumed control of the government in 1985. Thus, it is only as Brazil further develops these and other fundamental capabilities that it will begin to assume its logical place among the powers of the world.

Brazilians are the world's experts at achieving an accommodation. *Dar un jetto* (the aptitude to manage, to engineer something to one's advantage) is as much a Brazilian institution as Carnival or the samba. Make no mistake — there will be a way to resolve the political problems that stand in the way of *grandeza*. Certainly, there will be variations on the themes from time to time, but — if history and the mitigating political role of the military are any indicators — Brazilian security policy will continue to be quiet, cautious, and relatively consistent. It generally will be directed toward the development of the country and the enhancement of the armed forces' capability to protect internal and external interests.[32] Consequently, Brazil may be expected to maintain a relatively low profile in international politics until *grandeza* is, in fact, achieved. That will have been the greatest *jetto* of all.

The Perceived Threat and New Missions for the Military

Brazil's national security dialogue focuses on national development. That problem relates specifically to the root causes of instability. In that context, the consequences of instability manifested by terrorists, nascent insurgents, illegal drug traffickers, conventional power vacuums, and possible external enemies may create challenges or concerns but not threats.[33] It is underdevelopment and the resultant poverty that are perceived as Brazil's most overwhelming threats.[34] At the most fundamental level, however, the real threat would be defined as the possible inability of the state to develop the economic means to maintain internal order and progress and to exert effective influence in international security affairs.[35]

As compelling as the specific causes and consequences of instability may be, they must be understood and dealt with on three general levels. The consequences of instability can be categorized as third-level threats to national security. Root causes must be recognized as second-level threats. The inability or unwillingness of governments to develop and implement long-term, morally acceptable means to sustain internal stability and development and to defend national interests must be understood as a first-level (most fundamental) threat. To the extent that any given national security strategy incorporates all three levels, its chances for success are enhanced.

For example, once an illegal internal or transnational challenger, such as a narcotics cartel, becomes firmly established, first-level reform and development efforts aimed at second-level root causes may be insufficient to neutralize the organization that is generating a third-level threat. The illegal challenger will be defeated only by superior organization and a political-moral-military strategy designed to neutralize or eliminate it. The sum of the parts of a desired countereffort to deal with a third-level threat equals not only the capability to coordinate national and international political, economic, and moral objectives on the first and second levels but also to exert effectively deadly force at the third level.[36]

Those who advocate new missions for the Brazilian armed forces, such as undertaking an internal humanitarian role, supporting the police in law enforcement functions, taking on a major drug enforcement role, accepting international peacekeeping missions, increasing forces in frontier areas, or filling the power vacuum in the Amazon or the South Atlantic, miss the point on two levels. First, these are not new missions. The armed forces have provided such functions in the past and continue to do so.[37] Second, these missions only address symptoms of internal or international instability. In these terms, the nation must look beyond short-term, cosmetic efforts to deal with symptoms and address the causes of instability. Thus, the attempt is to lead the nation in its long-term development and defense by means of enhancing armed forces strength, reach, and sustainability. The policy objective is for the Brazilian military to help the state grow out of its problems and continue the movement toward *grandeza*.[38]

Conventional wisdom advocating the requirement to find new missions for the military institution misses another point at another level. The security dialogue argues that the contemporary requirement is to adapt to new realities. The new realities direct attention to two critical internal and external facts. First, internally, there is a requirement to be able to exert effective deadly force against drug or criminal organizations or any internal or transnational actor with a cause it is willing to pursue with violence. Second, externally, there is a requirement to be able to protect vital national interests in an increasingly disorderly world. In these national security terms, the armed forces are not irrelevant.

Implications for Civil-Military Relations

The general implications of these new realities are interesting. First, it would appear that the Brazilian military institution will, in fact, continue to define threats and concerns in terms of security and development. The armed forces also will determine the means and the level of effort, if any, to deal with any given security or development problem.

Second, concentration on this reality means increased involvement in internal security matters, increased cooperation in regional and selected international security matters, and appropriate budgets to accommodate these needs. In this connection, the military is likely to become even more deeply involved in the political-economic decision-making processes than it is now.

Third, the modern world is much too complicated to allow a strictly military solution to provide any kind of real response to the nation's fundamental security and development problems. Brazil's armed forces may be expected to resuscitate a dialogue designed to help civilians understand the issues of geopolitics and national security and to help the military elite appreciate the nationalism and the competence of civilian political elites. The desired end-state of such an exercise would be to generate the pragmatic political reconciliation necessary for transition to a stable, prosperous, and democratic community.

Fourth, if a civilian government deviates too significantly from the armed forces' doctrinal blueprint for security, development, and stability, the military continues to believe it has the obligation to provide the necessary corrective measures. Such concerns and obligations hold whether or not there is internal or external opposition.[39]

It may be recalled that the main feature of the development of military involvement in Brazilian politics is the *poder moderador*. This moderating power was inherited from the monarchy and incorporated into the various subsequent constitutions of the republic. Legally, however, the military institution has become more than an arbiter or moderator in the political process. It is also a guarantor of public order and democratic institutions.[40] Such reflections on the basic law of Brazil are not simply the private statements of a given general or admiral suggesting personal biases. One of the fundamental characteristics of the moderating power is that it has been derived from the constitution, through the elaboration of the judiciary, the executive, the legislature, and — in Brazil's case — military commanders with usable power at their disposal.

The transition to civilian rule in Brazil has not been managed by equals. The military regime took the initiative with the *abertura* (political opening) in the early 1980s and has remained in a position to influence the course of political change significantly over the succeeding years. In that connection, some political actors have been excluded, radical changes have been blocked, and a slow and orderly transition has taken place. Thus, the Brazilian military institution escaped the humiliation, isolation, and sanctions the Argentine armed forces have had to face in their return to the barracks. The Brazilian military simply resumed its former position behind the proverbial throne and has remained an integral part of the system.

The final implication of Brazil's new realities is clear. Despite the election and installation of civilian governments since 1985, the military institution is not folding its tents and quietly going away. Rather, the Brazilian military institution is in the process of redefining and adapting its corporate will in order to survive and prosper in contemporary and future environments. Its ability to react appropriately to changing internal and external political, economic, psychological, and security circumstances is an important key to survival and success. As a consequence, the armed forces likely will continue to provide a controlling elite, acting as the agent of national modernization and development.[41]

Conclusion

As always, Brazil is in transition. There have been and there will be times when it might be difficult to determine where the transition is taking the country. Yet, the astute Brazilian always will know that it is part of the *jetto* that will allow the evolution to reach *grandeza*.

The length of time that it will take to achieve that advantage is dependent on several factors. First, there are actions on the international level that Brazil may or may not be able to influence. Examples would include such things as increases in the price of oil, whether or not a given market might be closed to Brazilian products, and wars from which the country might profit or not.

External debt, inflation, and privatization problems must be resolved in a manner that will encourage investment and allow Brazil to continue to develop. This means that a political as much as an economic solution to the problem is required.

In the past, priority has been given to basic issues of economic development. Other areas that could contribute to national growth and security — social development and political and administrative reform come to mind immediately — are not as well advanced in Brazilian thinking and policy actions. The country must develop a will to penetrate the entire society so that the government can manage, coordinate, and sustain political, economic, and social goals effectively. The degree to which this objective is achieved at home will determine the level of influence Brazil can exert abroad. This achievement, coupled with creating a viable democracy, will define more than anything else Brazil's progress toward *grandeza*.

These and other obstacles to attaining *grandeza* are not likely to be overcome soon. However, beyond the cynicism of "Brazil is the country of the future — and always will be," there is a quiet confidence within the country that things will go Brazil's way. They always have. Thus, when Brazil emerges into the ranks of the key players in the international arena, it will probably be in one of two ways. First, if events catapult that country into a situation where it must play a major role, it will appear in style — as a Brazilian should. On the other hand, if international events allow, Brazilians would prefer to arrive on the scene without anyone having realized that they weren't there all along.

In the meantime, the principle that security policy is to be used as a tool for development will continue to prevail privately if not publicly. If Brazil should falter along the way to its destiny, remember — Brazil is greater than the abyss.

Notes

1. João Pandia Calogeras, 1939, *A History of Brazil*, trans. Percy Alvin Marten (Chapel Hill, N.C.: The University of North Carolina Press), 189-191.

2. "A Survey of Latin America," *The Economist*, November 13, 1993, 19. Also see *The World Factbook, 1992*, (Washington, D.C.: CIA), 39.

3. Golbery da Couto de Silva, 1957, *Aspectos Geopolíticos do Brasil*(Rio: Biblioteca do Exercito), 66. This argument is restated in José Sarney, 1986, "A President's Story," *Foreign Affairs* (Fall): 116; and in "Para SAE, guerra social ameaca a segurança," *Folha de São Paulo*, November 16, 1992, 1-5. It also has been implied that economic power can, to a considerable extent, become a substitute for military power in the world of the future. See Carlos de Meira Mattos, 1964, "O Pensamento Revolucionario Brasileiro," *Journal do Brasil*, November 15, Caderno Especial, 6.

4. These and subsequent assertions are, in fact, consensus statements based on a series of interviews with senior Brazilian civilian and military officials. The intent is to allow anonymity. The interviews were conducted by Max G. Manwaring from July 1986 through May 1993. In subsequent notes, these consensus statements are cited as Interviews.

5. Golbery da Couto de Silva 1957, 16 and 66. Also see Golbery da Couto de Silva, 1955, *Planejamento Estrategico* (Rio: Biblioteca do Exercito), 22-25.

6. Golbery da Couto de Silva 1957 and Interviews.

7. In addition to Golbery 1957 and Meira Mattos 1964, see Vice-Almirante Armando Amorim Ferreira Vidigal, 1989, "Uma Nova Concepçao Estrategico par o Brasil — Um Debate Necesario," *Revista Maritima Brasileira* (July-September): 49-71; Vidigal, 1990, "Reflexoes Adicionais sobre 'Uma Nova Concepçao Estrategico para o Brasil—Um Debate Necessario,'" *Revista Maritima Brasileira* (July-September): 49-61; Capitão de Mar e Guerra Lucimar Luciano da Oliveira, 1989, "Novos Aspectos Geopoliticos do Brasil," *Revista Maritima Brasileira* (January-March): 35-51; da Oliveira, 1988, "Proposta de um Novo Conceito de Geopolitica," *Revista Maritima Brasileira* (July-September): 87-104; and Juacy da Silva, 1987, "Doutrina e Metodos da ESG: Uma Visão Global," *Revista da Escola Superior de Guerra* 8: 91-120.

8. Interview with Minister of the Army, General Leonidas Pires Gonsalves, in Washington, D.C., January 1987. Also see Capitão de Mar e Guerra Rayder Alencar da Silveira, 1990, "O Papel do Militares no Sociedad Moderna," *Revista Maritima Brasileira* (July-September): 139-146; and Almirante-de-Esquadra Mario Jorge da Fonseca Hermes, 1989, "O Estagio de Desenvolvimento Nacional e as Forças Armadas Profissionàis," *Revista Maritima Brasileira* (July-September): 31-47.

9. Interestingly, Klaus Knorr's "putative" military capability concept is very similar. See Klaus Knorr, 1977, "On the International Uses of Military Force in the Contemporary World," *Orbis* (Spring): 92-110.

10. Golbery da Couto de Silva 1957 and 1955.

11. President Humberto Castelo Branco, speech to the Brazilian Army General Staff in Rio de Janeiro, August 25, 1964.

12. International Institute for Strategic Studies, 1970, *The Military Balance, 1970-1971* (London: IISS), 74; and 1995, *The Military Balance, 1994-1995* (London: IISS), 55 and 208.

13. The substance of the law was reported in *O Estado de São Paulo*, December 2, 1983, 7.

14. IISS, 1995, 46, 128, 159.

15. Rene Luria, 1989, "The Brazilian Armed Forces: Budgets and Ambitions Diverge," *International Defense Review* (July): 933-937.

16. IISS 1995.

17. See Decio Mauro Rodrigues da Cunha, 1974, "A Expansão da Marinha Mercante" (mimeographed), March 20, 19-35; Ten Cel Theo Espindola Basto, 1984, "Malvinas, Uma Guerra Para Reflexão," *A Defesa Nacional* 712 (March-April): 75-108; Cel Luis Paulo Macedo Carvalho, 1984, "Intereses e Responsabilidades do Brasil no Atlantico Sul," *A Defesa Nacional* 711 (January-February): 75-80; Nelson Vieira Ferreira de Mello, 1983, "O Conflicto das Malvinas e Seus Ensinamentos," *A Defesa Nacional* 706 (March-April): 31-34; and Vice-Almirante Joãn Carlos Goncalves Caminha, 1988, "A Guerra das Malvinas: Conjecturas e Consideracoes Estrategicas," *Revista Maritima Brasileira* (October-December): 47-60.

18. This ranking does not include countries that provide "flags of convenience." UN, 1993, *Statistical Yearbook, 1990/1991* (New York: United Nations), 681-685; Vice Admiral J.C. Goncalves Caminha, 1985, "The South Atlantic: A Brazilian View," *Naval Forces* (March): 57; and Klaus Wolff-Casado Revuelta, 1985, "The Brazilian Defense Industry," *Military Technology* (October): 93. Also see UN, 1993, "Merchant Vessels under Construction," (UN) *Monthly Bulletin of Statistics* (April): 238-241.

19. UN 1993, *Statistical Yearbook*.

20. Interview with Vice Admiral Alfredo Karam, Minister of the Navy, reported in *Jane's Defense Weekly*, June 29, 1985, 1277. Also see Capitão de Mar e Guerra Fernando M. Baptista da Costa, 1990, "Industria Belica Brasileira: Sus Problemas e Perspectivas Futuras," *Revista Maritima Brasileira* (July-September): 95-108; and Vice Almirante Armando Amorim Ferreira Vidigal, 1988, "A Importancia da Industria Belica para a Seguranca Nacional," *Revista Maritima Brasileira* (October-December): 25-44.

21. Mario Roberto Vaz Carneiro, 1993, "Brazil's defense industry faces up to its problems," *International Defense Review* (April): 323-326; Dean Martins, 1994, "Brazil - The Armed Forces of a Regional Superpower," *Jane's Intelligence Review Yearbook, 1994/1995* (London: Jane's), 144-145.

22. "Market Overview - Brazil," 1994, *Latin America and Australasia* (Alexandria, Va.: Jane's Information Group, October), 8.

23. Interviews; Patrice Franko-Jones, 1992, *The Brazilian Defense Industry* (Boulder, Colo.: Westview Press); and *SIPRI Yearbook, 1992: World Armament and Disarmament* (London: Oxford University Press), 272.

24. On several occasions over the past years, the various military and civilian governments have affirmed the exclusively peaceful nature of the nuclear development program. Nevertheless, a nuclear explosive device developed for peaceful purposes can be as destructive as one designed for the military. A country exploding such a device would de facto become a nuclear power. Moreover, it has been reported

that military versions of the Sonda I, II, and III mid-range rockets have been sold to various Third World countries; see *Manchete*, May 13, 1989, 120-122. A theoretical capability to produce nuclear weapons, coupled with the real capability of delivering them, places Brazil in an interesting position regarding its nuclear status. Somewhat different views of the Brazilian nuclear program are found in David J. Myers, 1984, "Brazil: Reluctant Pursuit of the Nuclear Option," *Orbis* (Winter): 881-911; and Max G. Manwaring, 1984, "Nuclear Power in Brazil," *Parameters* (Winter): 40-46.

25. These estimates are based on conservative and old data and, therefore, should not be overstating the case in any way. See SSI, 1979, *The Evolving Strategic Environment* (Carlisle Barracks, Penna.: Strategic Studies Institute, U.S. Army War College), 17; and IAEA, 1980, *Power Reactors in Member States* (Vienna, Austria: International Atomic Energy Agency), 24. Moreover, four-to-five years ago, military and civilian officials, such as Admiral Pinheiro de Silva, president of the Navy's Special Projects Coordinating Board; Claudio Rodrigues, superintendent of the Nuclear and Energy Research Institute; and Rex Nazareth, president of the National Nuclear Energy Commission, publicly affirmed Brazil's independent nuclear capability. See *O Globo*, March 2, 1988, 8; *O Globo*, April 9, 1989, 9; *O Globo*, April 16, 1989, 32; and *O Globo*, April 23, 1989, 31. The comparison with India was made in the Woerner interview.

26. See note 25.

27. Interviews; and Manwaring 1984.

28. A.F.K. Organski and Jaeck Kugler, 1978, "Davids and Goliaths: Predicting the Outcomes of International Wars," *Comparative Political Studies* (July): 141-181.

29. Ray S. Cline, 1994, *The Power of Nations in the 1990s: A Strategic Assessment* (New York: University Press of America), 97-112.

30. The sources used to obtain the data that resulted in Total Government Revenues Per Capita for this variable come from *World Tables, 1992* (Baltimore, Md.: Johns Hopkins University Press for the World Bank), 84-667; and *World Economic Outlook 1992* (London: The Economist Intelligence Unit), 30-317.

31. An expanded examination of legitimacy can be found in Max G. Manwaring, 1993, "The Umbrella of Legitimacy," in *Gray Area Phenomena: Confronting the New World Disorder,* ed. Max G. Manwaring (Boulder, Colo.: Westview Press), 77-91.

32. As an example, see Daniel Zirker, 1995, "The Brazilian Military and the Amazon Region: National Security vs. the Environment," paper presented at a North-South Center-sponsored conference on "Security in the Post-Summit Americas," National Defense University, Washington, D.C., March 30.

33. Interviews.

34. *Folha*; and "Militares defendem protecão a soberania," *Correio Braziliense,* August 23, 1992.

35. Interviews.

36. See Robert Thompson, 1970, *Revolutionary War in World Strategy, 1945-1969* (New York: Taplinger), 8.

37. Interviews; and Max G. Manwaring, 1968, *The Military in Brazilian Politics* (Ann Arbor: University of Michigan, microfilm).

38. Interviews.

39. Interviews.

40. Since 1824, the various Brazilian constitutions have established the armed forces as 1) national and permanent institutions, 2) defenders of the *Patria,* 3) guarantors of the constitutional powers, and 4) guarantors of law and order. Most recently, on July 23, 1991, Complementary Law 69 was approved, granting — among other things — the armed forces the status of guardians of law and order.

41. Interviews. Also see Wendy Hunter, 1993, *The Brazilian Military after the Cold War. In Search of a Mission,* paper prepared for the Fourth Annual Workshop on Latin American Security Issues, May 25, Santa Fe, New Mexico; and Jorge Zaverucha, 1993, "The Degree of Military Political Autonomy during the Spanish, Argentine, and Brazilian Transitions," *Journal of Latin American Studies* (May): 283-299.

XII

The Transformation of
Argentine Security

Deborah L. Norden

I n the decade following the Falklands/Malvinas War, the role of the
Argentine military changed dramatically. In 1982, the armed forces
directly controlled the Argentine government, as they had for
regular periods since 1930 and consistently since 1976. At the same
time, military concerns appeared to dominate both relations with
Argentina's neighbors and relations between the military government
and the civilian population.

Today, military concerns and solutions appear to be subordinated
to a more encompassing approach to national welfare, practically
reversing the infamously militarized national security model. After a
second round of free presidential elections in 1989 (a novelty in
Argentina), the civilian regime appeared increasingly secure, no longer
quite so vulnerable to military intervention. Beyond that, diplomacy
and alliances had become the primary means of achieving security.
Military force had become largely a supplement (one element contributing to Argentine security) and, in fact, even a tool to strengthen the
all-important international alliances.

This chapter explores the evolution of military missions in
Argentina during this period of radical change. After discussing
what appear to have been the Argentine military's primary concerns
in the years prior to the 1983 transition to democracy, the focus will
be on efforts to transform the armed forces during the
postauthoritarian period, from the demilitarization efforts of the
Raúl Alfonsín administration to President Carlos Menem's attempts

during his first term to restructure the armed forces and redefine military roles.

The transformation of the military's role was possible because of a unique set of circumstances that converged to antiquate earlier approaches to security and mandated some kind of new alternative. The first of these circumstances, the war against Great Britain over the Falkland/Malvinas Islands, served to underline the weaknesses in Argentine military strategy and the international character of almost any war in the contemporary era. The second circumstance, less unique to Argentina, was the wave of democratization that swept away authoritarian and communist regimes throughout Latin America and Eastern Europe. For Argentina, the latest transition to democracy occurred in 1983, following on the heels of the Falklands War, culminating in a new national constitution in 1994.

Finally, perhaps the most consequential transformations arose at the greatest distance. After a series of events marked by the collapse of the Berlin Wall (November 1989) and the final dissolution of the Soviet Union (December 1991), the Cold War dissipated, along with the entire bipolar world system. Throughout the world, military roles had been designed around an international order that no longer existed. In Argentina, as in other Latin American countries, these momentous changes posed a critical challenge to the civilian government. With both domestic and international politics so completely reconfigured, what should be done with the armed forces? Within this new international order, how could national interests best be pursued?

Pre-1983 Military Orientations

In the years before 1983, the Argentine military's concerns were largely those of an unstable regional player. On the one hand, the armed forces played an active role in national politics, guarding and fighting against both actual and perceived potential threats to an essentially conservative political order. On the other hand, long-standing border disputes plagued Argentina's relations with its western and eastern neighbors, Chile and Brazil, and Argentine claims to sovereignty over the British-controlled Falkland/Malvinas Islands increased in fervor. Despite these tensions, the bipolar world granted a certain sense of security to the Argentine military. Argentina's consistently anticommunist stance practically guaranteed the support of the United States in the event of renewed leftist insurgency, despite some historical ambivalence about excessive allegiance to the North

American power. During the initial Reagan years, however, shared anticommunism provided the basis for a relatively comfortable relationship with the United States.

Geopolitics and the National Security Doctrine

In the decades preceding the Falklands/Malvinas War, a geopolitical conceptualization of omnipresent threat and nation-state competition dominated Argentina's approach to defense. According to Jack Child, "proponents of the organic vision of the nation-state tend to take a pessimistic and Darwinian view of international relations, in which the strong states grow stronger and the weak submit or perish."[1] Neighbors were perceived not as potential allies but rather as potential enemies. Within countries, geopolitics led to distrust of any uninhabited or undeveloped spaces (particularly relevant in Brazil) and an exaggerated concern with internal turmoil. Dissident groups were perceived as critical weak links or dangerous pollutants, capable of debilitating, contaminating, and potentially destroying the entire society.

The national security approach to the military's role, adopted by many Latin American militaries, perhaps can be seen best as an extension of geopolitical conceptualizations. The national security perspective takes a broad, integrated approach to the definition of the nation. Accordingly, defense against armed external attack is only a minimal component of a secure state. Economic development and various social and ideological factors are considered relevant to security, although the emphasis on particular aspects of the composite varies from case to case. For some militaries, development and self-sufficiency in certain goods may be considered primary; in other cases, factors such as ideology (especially Marxist tendencies) and education receive more attention.

In Argentina, the ideological components of the national security doctrine predominated. Argentina's national security doctrine clearly influenced the 1976-1983 military regime, although it was certainly not the sole reason for the regime's origination. To begin with, in Argentina, military interventionism pre-dated the maturation of the national security doctrine. The first military coup of major significance occurred in 1930, at least two decades before national security approaches came into vogue. Second, the coup of 1976 can not be attributed solely to military ideology. Rather, the extensive political violence of the mid-1970s from both the extreme Left and the extreme Right, and the atmosphere of generalized political and economic chaos that supported it, demanded a dramatic solution, especially given the Peronists' reluctance to impeach their own president.

Nonetheless, neither historic military interventionism nor the immediate chaos sufficed to explain the nature of the emerging regime. Like the military regime of 1966-1973, the 1976-1983 *Proceso* (Process of National Reorganization) differed considerably from military interventions of earlier eras. During both periods, the armed forces took power with the intention of governing and even reconfiguring Argentine society. Temporary replacement of undesirable leadership no longer was perceived as sufficient. This expanded perception of the military's role, described by Albert Stepan as the "new professionalism," conformed to the integrated perception of security incorporated in the national security doctrine.[2]

During Argentina's 1976-1983 military regime, some of the implications of this approach became clear. Militaries are trained in the use of force; they are prepared to discern threats and to combat them. Not surprisingly, when militaries subsume other less immediately defense-related tasks under the auspices of "security," they can succumb to the temptation to deal with these in an equally militaristic fashion.

Under the *Proceso*, military criteria defined both the government's goals and how they were pursued. The armed forces' concerns were by no means all imaginary: the pervasive violence and instability provoked by guerrilla groups during the 1970s did pose a very real threat, but socialist revolution in Argentina was highly improbable. Nevertheless, the military's treatment of the problem went far beyond merely battling organized guerrilla groups. These were only the most immediate target; the armed forces also sought to eliminate subversives, understood as anyone from community organizers to leftist academics who conceivably could contribute to the success of revolutionary movements or ideologies. Dissenting groups and individuals within the society were thus perceived and treated as enemies. In sum, the national security doctrine integrated various national concerns (economic, defense, social) but subordinated all of those concerns to a militaristic approach to security. The military government sought to achieve security, with the latter essentially defining well-being for the Argentine community. They succeeded in eliminating organized insurgencies (although they failed colossally with the economy) but concomitantly created a common perception within the society that it was the military itself that threatened the security of Argentine citizens.

Regional Relations

Relations between Argentina's military regime and the country's neighbors were little better, a problem that was hardly new within the region, despite repeated efforts at regional cooperation in South America.

Among the most notable such efforts was the 1947 Inter-American Treaty for Reciprocal Assistance, or Rio Pact, which pledged all Latin American states to support victims of aggression within the region. According to Augusto Varas, "This military alliance was refined through bilateral Military Assistance Programs (MAPs), signed by all Latin American governments and the United States between 1951 and 1958."[3] The Rio Treaty provided the basis for the U.S.-dominated Organization of American States (OAS).[4] On the more explicitly military side, the Conference of American Armies was established in 1960 in order to facilitate exchange and coordination in pursuit of shared goals, particularly with regard to internal security problems, often perceived as international in origin or potential.[5] Once again, U.S. influence shadowed the endeavor.

In spite of these regional efforts, tension characterized Argentina's relations with its neighbors during the 1960s and 1970s far more than peaceful cooperation. At least partially because of the influence of geopolitics, relations became increasingly precarious with Brazil, and Argentina came to the brink of war with Chile. The period culminated in a full-fledged conflict with Great Britain in the Falklands/Malvinas Islands off Argentina's Southern coast.

Brazil. Until the 1980s, Argentina's relations with the major power in the region had been infused with competition and distrust. During the 1960s and 1970s, relations deteriorated further. The primary tangible issue of contention concerned water rights in Rio de la Plata.[6] However, much of Argentina's concern emanated from geopolitical interpretations of the balance between the two countries. Brazil, already the larger and stronger country, achieved notable economic success during this period — dubbed by many as Brazil's economic miracle. From a geopolitical perspective, Brazil's growth could occur only at the expense of Argentina.[7] The Argentine version of geopolitics allowed no positive-sum solutions. Argentina's fear "was heightened by anxious readings of Brazil's supposed geopolitical intentions...."[8]

The Brazilian military's adhesion to geopolitical conceptualizations suggested that economic growth might not be Brazil's only form of expansion.

Chile. In contrast to Chile, however, Argentina's relations with Brazil were practically harmonious. In 1978, Argentina only narrowly avoided a war with Chile, in the culmination of a prolonged dispute over control of and access to the Beagle Channel. As the year came to a close, troops stood armed and ready, awaiting the order to attack. It was only the intervention and mediation of the Pope which, in these two very Catholic countries, preserved regional peace. Nonetheless, for years to come, Chile's finely tuned Prussian army continued to cause alarm among the Argentines.

Falkland/Malvinas Islands. Argentina's major conflict of the period occurred to the Southeast rather than in the West. By 1982, the islands had been British colonies for over 150 years. The few inhabitants, primarily sheep ranchers, considered themselves British subjects and demonstrated little identification with their Argentine neighbors. However, for Argentina, the Malvinas remained an important nationalist rallying point. Argentina's brief occupation of the islands in the early 1800s stimulated the devout conviction that the Falklands/Malvinas Islands, regardless of their relative lack of economic utility, rightfully belonged to Argentina. Rather than fading over time, this sentiment actually grew, fomented by Juan Domingo Perón in the 1940s. In 1982, Admiral Jorge Anaya and the de facto President, General Leopoldo Galtieri, took up the banner.

The war began with a bloodless occupation on April 2, 1982. The Argentines hoped that through the invasion, they could force Great Britain to the bargaining table and gain more permanent authority over the islands diplomatically. However, this rosy scenario was not destined to be. Argentina's military leadership drastically miscalculated both Britain's concern with its territory and U.S. loyalty to its European ally. Plans for the initial invasion may have been well conceived, but preparations to defend the island were virtually nil. The agony of Argentina's defeat rivaled only the delirium of the initial triumph.

Why did the military choose to invade the islands? According to the Argentine military leadership, the invasion was defensive, compelled by British demands for documentation from Argentine workers in the nearby South Georgia Islands.[9] However, more entrenched concerns undoubtedly underlay the Argentines' reaction. On the one hand, from a geopolitical perspective, expansion into bordering territorities would add to the country's security. Foreign occupation of these territories could be seen as a potential threat, a base for possible future aggression against Argentina. On the other hand, more symbolic motivations also encouraged the venture. By the early 1980s, the military government had begun to struggle. Early economic successes had turned to debacles, and both international and domestic critiques of the regime's horrendous human rights record had begun to take their toll. The military needed some means of gathering national support, to appear as heroes rather than villains. For the military leadership, military action was the most obvious way to achieve this political transformation. Again, the national security perspective apparently helped direct Argentina's leaders toward military solutions to political problems.

Relations with the United States

Beyond its multiple internal repercussions, Argentina's war with Great Britain also terminated one of the smoothest periods of Argentine-U.S. relations. Argentina's physical distance from the United States permitted it somewhat more autonomy from the modern Western power than that encountered by Latin America's northern states. Argentine nationalism contributed to that autonomy, creating a relationship "characterized by long periods of distrust and mutual hostility alternating with relatively brief intervals of rapprochement and collaboration."[10]

Argentina's ambivalence for the United States stood out particularly during the World War II period and the ensuing Peronist regime. Argentina exhibited no anxiety to join the Allied powers in their efforts, preferring to retain sufficient neutrality to continue trading with countries on either side of the conflict. After Argentina's 1943 coup, its official neutrality became infused with an added dose of nationalism, not without some European influence. German military advisors had played quite an important role in the Argentine army, arguably influencing not only military formation and tactics but ideology as well. For the United States, Colonel Juan Perón, an increasingly powerful member of the 1943-1946 military government, was particularly suspect. Perón made no pretense of sympathy for the United States. Nevertheless, as World War II neared its end, the Argentine government agreed to symbolic allegiance to the Allies, declaring war against Germany and Japan in March 1945.[11]

Yet Perón remained a power to be reckoned with, a source of irritation for the United States. The colonel had taken an apparently minor position in charge of the Ministry of Labor and used it to create a powerful independent support base among the Argentine working class. U.S. Ambassador Spruille Braden, appointed in April 1945, was determined to rid Argentina of Perón. He accused Perón of being a fascist and attempted to demonstrate ties between the Argentine junta (especially Perón) and the Nazis.[12] Braden's attacks destroyed U.S. relations with Argentina but only enhanced Perón's power. Given the choice "Braden or Perón," Argentines opted for Perón.

Despite the historic discord, during most of the 1976-1983 military regime, Argentine-U.S. relations enjoyed relative harmony. The positive relationship between Argentina and the United States during the *Proceso* stemmed largely from shared concerns with guerrilla movements in Latin America. Argentina's new military leadership was adamantly anti-Peronist and perhaps even more strongly anticommunist (although the two were perceived to be linked in Argentina). Although the Argentine repression of the mid-to-late 1970s did generate some disquiet in the United States, this was offset by the ideological accord between the two countries, particularly after the 1980 election of Ronald Reagan.

The Central American crisis provided the perfect mechanism for solidifying the new friendship. The Reagan administration was determined that the recently established Sandinista regime in Nicaragua not survive. Yet, scarred by Vietnam, the U.S. public had little tolerance for direct intervention. The Argentine military, well practiced at combatting leftists, assumed much of the task of training and organizing counterrevolutionary forces, saving the U.S. government from the political costs of overt involvement in the area. The Falklands/Malvinas War brought the era of Argentine-U.S. cooperation to a dramatic close. From the Argentine perspective, U.S. support for Great Britain constituted not only ingratitude but betrayal. Many Argentines ceased considering the United States a friend and ally, instead viewing the country as a power-hungry and fickle hegemon.

The Transformation of Argentine Security Doctrines

After 1982, Argentina began a series of changes that eventually transformed the country's approach to achieving national security. The defeat in the Falklands/Malvinas War led to crisis and reevaluation within the armed forces, as well as to the definitive collapse of the military regime. Democratization created new challenges for the military. The transition government, faced with the recent history of military repression and the not-so-new legacies of military interventionism, chose to face the armed forces head on, attempting to punish them for past actions and diminish their potential for future intervention. Finally, the end of the Cold War and the election of a second postauthoritarian Argentine president, free from the constraints and expectations of the immediate transition period, created a context in which military roles could be redefined in a more positive direction.

Alfonsín: Demilitarization and Diplomacy

The Argentine government began confronting the problem of redefining the military's role at the end of 1983 with the transition to democratic rule. For nearly eight years, the armed forces had governed the country, believing that a political role was essential to ensure national security. From the perspective of the new democratic government, however, that political role constituted a primary threat to national security. Responding in part to human rights organizations, the government exhibited much more concern with preventing a relapse of military intervention and repression than with creating a more positive defense role, either internal or external. The administration of Raúl Alfonsín was quite clear about what roles the military should not carry out but less clear on what future missions would be.

In some respects, the government was fighting an imaginary enemy — an enemy that only came into being after the battle had begun. At the time of the transition, the military was in the process of reassessing its role. On the one hand, the rationale for maintaining a political role had largely disintegrated. Argentina's situation in the early 1980s differed significantly from eight years earlier. Guerrilla warfare, at any significant level, had succumbed by the mid-1970s. By the 1980s, the possibility of leftist revolution had diminished to considerably less than a trickle (represented by a single, small, and disorganized attack on a military regiment in January 1989). Thus, despite the perseverance of the Cold War bipolar world, revolutionary communism was increasingly irrelevant in Argentina.

On the other hand, the last bout of military rule had produced considerable doubt within the armed forces themselves about both their capacity to govern successfully and the consequences that such a role might have for national defense. Military organization and efficiency certainly had not salvaged the Argentine economy; rather, the military left the economy in much worse condition than at the time of the 1976 coup. In addition, the Falklands/Malvinas War had revealed a number of weaknesses within the organization. The planning and organization of the war were disastrous. For example, the military leadership chose to leave the trained soldiers on the border with Chile, sending recently drafted, unprepared soldiers into the islands to fight Great Britain. Furthermore, while individual actions were frequently quite effective, coordination among the military services was weak. The years of military rule had left the army, navy, and air force more accustomed to dividing tasks than to sharing them. Many within the armed forces had begun to desire a much more apolitical and professionalized role than they had shouldered in the past, fearing that the expansion of their role had left them incapable of success in any area.

Alfonsín's Military Policies

In spite of these conditions, Alfonsín's mandate was to democratize Argentina and defend human rights. Confronting the armed forces directly appeared the only way of meeting this mandate.

Military Reductions. To begin with, the government reduced both the military budget (almost unavoidable, given the state of the economy) and the size of the military itself. To a large extent, budget cuts merely returned the military's portion of the gross national product to its pre-Malvinas level. However, with the help of inflation, salaries plunged far below levels to which the armed forces were accustomed, eventually compelling even officers to seek supplemental employment. In addition, the reduction in the size of the forces went beyond adjusting to some earlier norm. From 1983 to 1986, the number of soldiers drafted for the compulsory one year of military service shrank from 64,640 to slightly under 25,000.[13] This left many of the tasks previously assumed by privates to the noncommissioned officers, who, not surprisingly, became increasingly disgruntled with their lot.

Limiting the Military Role: The Defense Law. The government also sought to diminish the future role of the armed forces through juridical means. In 1988, the government passed a National Defense Law that attempted to delineate which areas the military services should consider their purview and, specifically, which areas they should ignore. According to the new law, the military should focus exclusively on matters of external defense. As Article 15 states, "Questions relative to the internal politics of the country shall under no circumstances constitute working hypotheses of the military intelligence organizations."[14] Issues of internal security were relegated to the police forces, the gendarmerie, and the coast guard.

In many respects, the law was irrelevant. In case of crisis, the national constitution (superior to any law) authorizes the president to utilize the armed forces however he sees fit. However, the Defense Law was extremely important as a symbol, demonstrating very clearly to the armed forces that contemporary political leaders would not condone future military repression.[15] At the same time, the law also communicated to the armed forces their highly marginal status within Alfonsín's government. The new law was unaccompanied by any positive mandate informing the armed forces what their function would be in postauthoritarian Argentina.

Human Rights Trials. For the armed forces, the most problematic facet of Alfonsín's policy involved not the troop reductions or the lack of positively defined roles but the trials of officers for human rights offenses. Almost immediately after taking office, Alfonsín ordered an investigation into the disappearances (estimated at 9,000 to more than three times that) and other human rights violations of the military regime, along with the prosecution of the military juntas. As the civilian courts sought to identify those responsible for ordering and carrying out the repression, the number of cases increased exponentially. In one respect or another, almost all the armed forces were affected. Some were charged with crimes; others were merely called in as witnesses. For many within the military, the trials amounted to condemnation for an essential and successful war. The government's efforts to divide the repressors from the innocent became meaningless in this context.

The results of the trials, at best, can be seen as mixed. Not surprisingly, no sector of the Argentine population was entirely satisfied. From the perspective of the human rights organizations, the trials did not go nearly far enough. Furthermore, subsequent backtracking, such as the "Due Obedience Law" (exempting lieutenant colonels and below) and Menem's later pardon, virtually nullified the early gestures. For the military, the trials demonstrated intense civilian hostility toward the organization and a lack of recognition of the military's sacrifices. The trials played a critical role in stimulating the military rebellions of 1987 to 1990.[16]

Regional Diplomacy

Alfonsín's most productive efforts in the area of defense had little to do with the armed forces. He began what would become the hallmark of the Menem regime — defense through diplomacy. In all the major areas of conflict, including Brazil, Chile, and the Falklands/ Malvinas Islands, Alfonsín made important advances toward resolving outstanding tensions diplomatically.

Brazil. Relations with Brazil actually had been improving since the late 1970s, largely due to the efforts of Argentine Ambassador Oscar Camilión (appointed Carlos Menem's Minister of Defense in 1993).[17] However, the friendship between the neighboring powers grew considerably after Alfonsín's election to the presidency. Alfonsín met with Brazilian President-elect Tancredo Neves in 1985,[18] and President Sarney in 1986, beginning the long path toward economic integration and wide-ranging cooperation. In 1986, the presidents of the two countries agreed on a plan for an Argentine-Brazilian Economic Integration Program (ABEIP):

> Economically, the ABEIP aimed at expanding and diversifying bilateral trade between Argentina and Brazil by adopting a sector-by-sector approach that emphasized capital goods, agribusiness, and the automotive sector. Politically, the integration was meant to help the consolidation of democracy in both countries.[19]

The economic crises suffered by the two countries delayed the expansion of Argentine-Brazilian trade; however, the spirit of cooperation fostered by the accord flourished.

Argentina and Brazil also began enhancing their relations on the military front, particularly with respect to nuclear power. During the authoritarian 1960s and 1970s, the two countries primarily shared their rejection of international nonproliferation agreements.[20] By the mid-1980s, President Alfonsín and President José Sarney of Brazil had "established a standing joint committee on nuclear policy" and had begun visiting each other's facilities.[21] Confidence-building became the newest buzzword for the region.

Chile. Relations with Chile also took a more positive turn during the Alfonsín government. Approximately a year after the transition to democracy, the two countries signed a Treaty of Peace and Friendship that finally put to rest the ongoing dispute regarding the Beagle Channel.[22] By the following May, Argentina and Chile had agreed on rights and powers within the area. The issue of the Laguna del Desierto remained to be solved. The decision over this disputed region was placed in the hands of international mediators who, in late 1994, awarded the territory to Argentina.

Falklands/Malvinas. Probably the most difficult issue to negotiate concerned the Falklands/Malvinas. However tense relations with Chile and Brazil might have been, at least in those cases, no blood was spilled. Many had died in the recent war against Great Britain. Nonetheless, Alfonsín was determined to use only diplomacy in pursuing a more favorable status in the islands. This did not mean relinquishing Argentina's claim to the Malvinas, but it did mean relinquishing force as a means of obtaining them.

Legacies of the Alfonsín Government

By the time Alfonsín left power, the euphoria surrounding his election had long faded. The economic crisis he had inherited, temporarily mitigated by the Austral Plan, had reemerged with a vengeance. With respect to the armed forces, the *carapintadas,* a nationalist rebel group that originated to protest Alfonsín's military policies, had become organized and entrenched. Important sectors of the armed forces thus had been repoliticized at the same time that the military's defensive capabilities were being destroyed.

Despite these apparent shortcomings, Alfonsín succeeded in creating a basis on which future administrations could build. The military was left incapacitated by Alfonsín's efforts to depoliticize them — too poor, divided, and disheartened to be of much use in providing security. However, that very weakness would permit the subsequent administration the freedom to remold them, actively to redefine the function of the armed forces in order to resume defending the country without threatening the democratic order. Even the country's severe economic difficulties held some notes of promise. Argentines had lost the fantasy that democracy would bring prosperity automatically. Furthermore, economic constraints helped justify tight budgetary controls to the military, once those measures were undertaken by a regime they did not perceive as hostile. In sum, the Alfonsín administration absorbed the majority of the traumas accompanying the transition, thereby facilitating the consolidation process for Carlos Menem's 1989 Peronist administration.

Menem: Redefining Security

Within a few short years, Carlos Menem virtually transformed Argentina's approach to security. Timing played an important role in making this possible. Menem inherited a post-Falklands and post-Alfonsín military. The intense animosity that had burgeoned between Alfonsín and the armed forces actually smoothed the way for Menem, leaving the military prepared to embrace almost any alternative. At the same time, the collapse of the Soviet Union brought the final defeat of Argentina's pre-1980s military doctrine.

Within this context, the Menem administration acted quickly to redefine Argentina's approach to security. As during the national security era, different national objectives became intertwined. Yet, with Menem, defense and security no longer dominated the picture. Instead, the government pursued economic and security goals simultaneously through internationalism. Within the region, developing economic ties helped improve political relations. Beyond the region, Argentina began to foster an extremely close alliance with the United States, at the same time becoming one of the United Nations' most active members. The military came to play an important role in this policy, contributing troops to several UN missions. Instead of independently defining national objectives, the armed forces became a tool in their pursuit.

End of the Cold War

The end of the Cold War dealt the final blow to the Argentine military's struggling definitions of its mission. Since the Cuban Revolution (1959), violent conflicts between the ideological Left and Right had pervaded the internal politics of countries throughout Latin America. The Right frequently found its model and key ally in the United States; just as frequently, leftist groups looked toward the Soviet Union or Cuba to guide or aid their efforts. Internal conflicts almost invariably acquired an international character. However, with the collapse of the Soviet Union (and the end of Soviet financial backing for Cuba), this aspect of Latin American politics declined. The threat of internationally provoked revolutionary movements ceased to be a reasonable possibility, granting a much different significance to potential or actual internal upheaval in the region.

The end of a bipolar world also implied that smaller powers could no longer count on the United States and the Soviet Union to keep conflicts in check. The international order appeared increasingly anarchical and conflict increasingly risky. Consequently, international organizations such as the United Nations assumed a much greater import. The UN forum and peacekeeping missions potentially could offer the security once tendered by the United States and the Soviet Union. The Argentine government quickly recognized this possibility.

The New Model of Security

Menem's new approach to pursuing national objectives had three major components: regional integration, expanded relations with the United States, and incorporation into UN missions. All three of these contributed to long-term Argentine security as well as aiding in the pursuit of economic objectives.

Regional Integration. Within the region, Menem continued and expanded Alfonsín's diplomatic efforts. Argentina's relations with its neighbors became better than at any time in recent history.

The growing friendship between Argentina and Brazil is particularly notable. In May 1993, Menem met with Brazil's president, Itamar Franco, to further the positive relationship begun around a dozen years earlier. Among other things, the two presidents agreed to "deepen political coordination between the governments, the armed forces, and business and labor sectors."[23] Earlier border disputes appeared to have been left far behind, while cooperation and confidence-building with respect to nuclear technology had intensified.

The heart of Menem's policies within the region concerned economic issues. Southern Cone leaders, beginning with the Argentines and Brazilians, have sought to replicate the efforts at regional integration just beginning in North America with the North American Free Trade Agreement and already maturing in Western Europe. In March 1991, Argentina, Brazil, Paraguay, and Uruguay initiated a project called MERCOSUR (Mercado Común del Sur), aimed at creating a regional common market.[24] Progress toward an integrated economy was somewhat slower than originally hoped; yet the leaders of these countries did succeed in placing MERCOSUR in effect on January 1, 1995.[25]

Efforts at boosting trade between Latin American countries were often successful. In 1980, the Montevideo Treaty created ALADI (Asociación Latinoamericana de Integración) to foster regional expansion of commerce. For Argentina, the Latin American region became particularly important in the early 1990s. Argentina's exports within the region rose 20 percent between 1990 and 1993, at the same time as exports to other parts of the world declined. In fact, ALADI trade in 1992 was "a full third of Argentina's worldwide trade."[26] Improved relations between the South American countries facilitiated this expansion.

Alliance with the United States. Argentina's closest relations during this period were with the United States. From the very beginning of his administration, Menem made clear his intentions to pursue an unlimited friendship. As Roberto Russell and Laura Zuvanic describe:

> [T]he Peronist administration prizes its relations with the United States, emphasizing the elimination of each and every possible area of conflict on their joint policy agenda, as well as increasing cooperation with the U.S. government on various global issues, such as the narcotraffic or problems of the government.[27]

To the horror of many nationalists, Menem opted to sacrifice considerable Argentine autonomy — an especially surprising policy for a Peronist government.

This posture was exemplified by the Condor question. Early in Menem's presidency, the United States discovered Argentina's development of the Condor II missile. Argentina agreed to end the missile project and transferred the Condor to civilian control in 1991 in order to avoid military interference.[28] Around one year later, it was found that important components of the missiles had been left intact. The government admitted that the motors had not been dismantled but claimed that they would be used only for other purposes.[29] After further pressure from the United States, the remaining components ostensibly were shipped to Spain. It was later revealed, however, that the visit to Spain was merely a ruse, intended to ameliorate nationalist complaints about Argentina's subservience to the United States. Not surprisingly, the missile components made their final landing on U.S. territory.[30]

Another area in which Argentina has demonstrated compliance with U.S. priorities concerns narcotics trafficking. In 1992, Argentina purchased several reconnaissance aircraft to aid in combatting the narcotics trade and began negotiating with Germany in early 1993 for additional equipment.[31] Given Argentina's rather remote location, the necessity of intensive and militarized counternarcotics efforts seems rather dubious.

Argentina's allegiance to the United States soon began to produce some benefits. For example, by the end of 1992, the United States had "lifted the freeze on the supply of military equipment which had been in place since the Falklands war of 1982."[32] By early 1994, the United States had authorized the sale of Skyhawk fighter planes to Argentina. In the economic arena, Argentina became a beneficiary of the Brady

Plan and in April 1993 was able to secure a 30-year refinancing of the debt.[33] Improved relations with the United States thus aided both Argentina's security and its economy.

United Nations. Argentina's embrace of the United Nations can, in part, be seen as a continuation of the friendship with the United States. Incorporation into UN peacekeeping missions supports U.S. policies abroad. Yet the extent of Argentina's involvement seems to go beyond this. Argentina sent nearly 1,000 troops to Croatia,[34] along with others to Angola, Haiti, and elsewhere. In almost every region where UN forces are active, Argentine troops can be found.[35] In January 1993, Argentina was even prepared to send several hundred troops to the Gulf, "as part of a 4,000-strong contingent they were expecting the UN Security Council to authorize."[36] While the troops never departed, Argentina did send two supply ships to provide logistical support.

Why has Argentina granted such extensive support to the United Nations? Part of the reason stems from Argentina's desire to please the United States. The increasing importance of the United Nations in world security certainly also contributes to the government's new policy, a policy which, in this respect, demonstrates considerable foresight.

However, a few more immediate, practical issues also come into play. As discussed above, democratization left the Argentine military without a mission. Given the state of the economy, the government also had very little to offer the armed forces in terms of material benefits (or, for that matter, even salaries). Participation in UN missions offered a partial — albeit, very partial — solution to both of those problems. UN missions provided a positive, useful role for at least some members of the military. Furthermore, the United Nations could help pay the bill. At the same time, Argentina could hope for UN (or, at least, U.S.) reciprocity in case of conflict. In sum, Argentina found in the United Nations a relatively low-cost aid to the nation's security problems, which smoothly complemented the government's other goals.

Conclusion

The 1982 war with Great Britain and the 1983 advent of democracy in Argentina inaugurated a dramatic period of change for the armed forces. Prior to this time, military decisionmaking had been influenced strongly by a national security approach. The national security conceptualization not only encouraged the armed forces to govern but also inspired them to place security concerns and military means above other national goals.

The failures of the 1976-1983 military regime and the Falklands/ Malvinas War began to break down the military's confidence in the national security approach. During Alfonsín's government, the crisis within the armed forces intensified, leaving the military without a positive role and with little capacity to defend the nation. Finally, the collapse of international communism destroyed any remaining justification for the national security orientation.

From this relative chaos, Carlos Menem began to reconstruct Argentina's security mechanisms, largely by inverting the national security orientation. Different national objectives were again integrated — however, without a dominant emphasis on defense. Instead, the military came to be utilized as an aid to the government's strategy of enhancing international alliances. Nation-state cooperation had replaced nation-state competition for Argentina.

Notes

1. Jack Child, 1990, "Geopolitical Thinking," in Louis Goodman, Johanna Mendelson, and Juan Rial, eds., *The Military and Democracy: The Future of Civil-Military Relations in Latin America* (Lexington, Mass.: Lexington Books), 145.

2. Alfred Stepan, 1973, "The New Professionalism of Internal Warfare and Military Role Expansion," in Alfred Stepan, ed., *Authoritarian Brazil: Origins, Policies, and Future* (New Haven, Conn.: Yale University Press), 47-68.

3. Augusto Varas, 1989, "Hemispheric Relations and Security Regimes in Latin America," in Augusto Varas, ed., *Hemispheric Security and U.S. Policy in Latin America* (Boulder, Colo.: Westview Press), 48.

4. Alain Rouquié, 1987, *The Military and the State in Latin America* (Berkeley: University of California Press), 131.

5. Carlos Moneta, 1988, "El papel de la cooperación intermilitar en la autonomía y la democratización de América Latina," *Defensa y Sociedad* 1, 3(December): 49.

6. Carlos Portales, 1989, "South American Regional Security and the United States," in Augusto Varas, ed., *Hemispheric Security and U.S. Policy in Latin America* (Boulder, Colo.: Westview Press), 157.

7. Child 1990, 154; and Wayne Selcher, 1985, "Brazilian-Argentine Relations in the 1980s: From Wary Rivalry to Friendly Competition," *Journal of Interamerican Studies and World Affairs* 27(2): 28.

8. Selcher 1985, 28.

9. Interview with Admiral Jorge Anaya, Buenos Aires, December 19, 1988.

10. Aldo Vacs, 1989, "A Delicate Balance: Confrontation and Cooperation between Argentina and the United States in the 1980s," *Journal of Interamerican Studies and World Affairs* 31, 4(Winter): 23.

11. Mario Rapoport, 1990, "Foreign and Domestic Policy in Argentina during the Second World War," in Guido di Tella and D. Cameron Watt, eds., *Argentina Between the Great Powers, 1939-46* (Pittsburgh: University of Pittsburgh Press), 86.

12. Callum MacDonald, 1990, "The Braden Campaign and Anglo-American Relations," in Guido di Tella and D. Cameron Watt, eds., *Argentina Between the Great Powers, 1939-46* (Pittsburgh: University of Pittsburgh Press), 149.

13. Rosendo Fraga, 1989, *La Cuestión Militar: 1987-1989* (Buenos Aires: Editorial Centro de Estudios Union para la Nueva Mayoría), 173.

14. Congreso Argentino, 1988, *Anales de Legislación Argentina* (Buenos Aires: Congreso Argentino), 1427.

15. The military's initial internal campaigns of 1975 were authorized by President María Estela Martínez de Perón.

16. See Deborah Norden, 1996, *Military Rebellion in Argentina: Between Coups and Consolidation* (Lincoln: University of Nebraska Press).

17. Félix Peña, 1988, "Argentina y la cooperación latinoamericana," in Rubén M. Perina and Roberto Russell, eds., *Argentina en el Mundo (1973-1987)* (Buenos Aires: Grupo Editor Latinoamericano), 211; and Selcher 1985, 29.

18. Tancredo Neves died before he was able to take office.

19. Luigi Manzetti, 1992, "Economic Integration in the Southern Cone," *North-South Focus* (December): 1.

20. John Redick, Julio Carasales, and Paulo Wrobel, 1995, "Nuclear Rapprochement: Argentina, Brazil, and the Nonproliferation Regime," *The Washington Quarterly* 18, 1(Winter).

21. Redick, Carasales, and Wrobel 1995.

22. Portales 1989, 157.

23. *Nación Internacional* (Buenos Aires), May 31, 1993, 5.

24. Manzetti 1992, 1.

25. *Clarín Internacional* (Buenos Aires), January 3, 1995.

26. *Latin American Weekly Report*, May 6, 1993, 196.

27. Roberto Russell and Laura Zuvanic, 1990, "Argentina: Deepening Alignment with the West," *Journal of Interamerican Studies and World Affairs* 33, 3(Fall): 121.

28. *Latin American Weekly Report*, March 25, 1993, 137.

29. *Informe Latinoamericano*, September 10, 1992.

30. *Latin American Weekly Report*, March 11, 1993, 115.

31. *Latin American Weekly Report*, February 18, 1993, 77; *FBIS-LAT*, February 4, 1993.

32. *Latin American Weekly Report*, February 18, 1993, 77.

33. *Nación Internacional* (Buenos Aires), April 12, 1993.

34. *The Washington Post*, January 29, 1993, A15.

35. Nonetheless, the Argentine military has been adamantly opposed to involvement in "peacemaking" missions, such as Somalia in 1993.

36. *Latin American Weekly Report*, February 18, 1993, 77.

XIII

Peru: The State Under Siege

Dirk Kruijt

P eru is in deep trouble. It has been in trouble for quite a number of years, and it will be in trouble for the next ten to 20 years. Peru is a country whose economy, society, and political system are slowly disintegrating. Since 1980, a civil war has been accountable for 20,000 deaths and $20 billion in property damage. Extreme poverty and extreme violence have resulted in an unprecedented process of informalization of economic and social relations and of political and moral consciousness.

The Peruvian economy is a mess. It is the logical consequence of an unnerving series of short-term contradictory experiments, rivaling policies, and dramatic changes in economic strategy, running from orthodox state capitalism in the 1970s, orthodox laissez faire in the early 1980s, heterodox state intervention in the late 1980s, and heterodox adjustment in the early 1990s.[1] Peruvian society is a jungle: of the estimated national population of 23 million (1992), one million are internally displaced, refugees in their own country. The misery in the capital is beyond proportion; of its estimated population of 8 million, 64 percent survive in the informal sector.[2] Informality affects the functioning of the legal institutions, the political parties, and the public sector.[3] Two guerrilla movements, the Shining Path (Sendero Luminoso) and Tupac Amaru, and a variety of organized drug traffickers and urban criminals permeate society with violence and account for most of the victims. "Counterterrorism" carried out by the police and the military explains the remainder of deaths among the peasant population and slum dwellers.

Peruvian politics is chaos. Traditional political parties ceased to represent significant segments of the national population in the late

1980s. The Left, until 1988 in charge of Lima's municipal governments, virtually disappeared. The Right and the Center suffered a spectacular loss in the presidential campaign of 1990. A complete unknown, Alberto Fujimori, whose most significant virtues seemed to be political virginity combined with intuitive insight into the day-to-day opinions of the unorganized masses, attained the presidency. Then, amid a nationwide political crisis and a civil war that reached the suburbs of Lima, the president realized an *autogolpe*, exercising a new brand of civil-military relationship of "armed democracy,"[4] an uneasy alliance between the presidency and the military, legitimized by a new *constituyente* of political novices.

Since 1990, the country has fought its war against misery, poverty, criminal violence, drug mafias, and the guerrillas alone. What a difference, compared with the situation 20 years ago! In 1975, Peru's reformist military government still thought[5] that it could complete the program of "structural reforms" elaborated and executed in order to alleviate some of the root causes of the guerrilla uprisings in the 1960s. It enjoyed international prestige as a Third World leader, having successfully concluded negotiations with the United States on expropriations and with the Soviet Union on sophisticated weaponry. Peru in 1993 was an international pariah, excluded from the international development community, criticized because of its chronic human rights violence, battered by the death and destruction caused by civil war, drug trafficking, and virtual national bankruptcy. To explain this sustained deterioration, one needs to undertake an analysis of civil-military relations and the style of governance of the military and the civilian presidents.

The Peruvian Army: Political Presence and Ideology

Military government is a constant in Peruvian politics. The country has an outspoken history of coups, military presidents, and dictatorships. Fujimori's autogolpe recalls the days of civilian dictators in the first decades of this century. Yet in the coup d'état business, the army holds the best cards. Statistically speaking, an officer's training is the safest way to the presidency of the country. Since the nation's independence on June 28, 1821, 71 presidents have come and gone. Three liberation armies in succession saw their commander invested with presidential authority. Twice, a president rose to power through a civilian revolt. No less than 26 times a member of the military managed to become president by staging a coup. Even in the occasional constitutional elections, the population preferred military leadership. Of the 71 presidents, 51 were officers, eight marshals, 34 generals, six colonels, and two commanders. The navy could boast only one presidential rear admiral.

With a few exceptions, until the turn of the century, Peruvian political history was, in fact, a stream of coups, palace revolutions, revolts, and wars waged by military caudillos and political adventurers. Productive in acquiring political power, the army was less effective when dealing with its principal tasks: the protection of national integrity. Peru's disastrous defeat by Chile in the Pacific War in the 1870s put its stamp on the military system for decades; the army and navy's humiliation is still vividly remembered.

The solution sought was professionalism and technical training. Chile was the first of all Latin American countries to call upon the services of foreign training officers. Chile, Uruguay, and Bolivia's armies were trained by German officers; Peru, and later Brazil, Ecuador, and Guatemala, engaged the French. The structure of the Peruvian army, of the officer corps, and the training schools bears a French stamp, and conceptual affinity with French military views and doctrines continues to this decade. The impact of the French military missions in Peru took place primarily via schools founded by French instructors,[6] including the Escuela Militar (1898), the Escuela Superior de Guerra (1904), and specialized schools such as the Escuela de Caballería, Escuela de Infantería, and Escuela de Artílleria. Before World War II, French officers even filled the post of inspector-general of the armed forces. High-ranking Peruvian officers were sent abroad, to France mostly, to attend special courses at the higher military academies. In a limited number of cases, the navy and the air force — established as part of the army in 1920 and made independent in 1943 — preferred training in the United States.

U.S. influence on the navy started in the 1920s, some years after the creation of the naval ministry in 1919. Initially, U.S. influence on naval training was less pronounced than the French stamp on the army. Naval training remained in Peruvian hands, although staff officers went to the United States for follow-up courses. Yet just before and during World War II, U.S. officers also held high-ranking naval posts, including those of inspector-general and chief-of-staff. After the war, both the army and air force turned to the United States as well, following the general trend in Latin America. U.S. army, navy, and air force missions arrived in Peru in 1947. Like other Latin American medium-sized military powers, Peru soon became very dependent on aid and armaments from the United States. This dependence on U.S. weaponry remained until the 1970s. Repeated Pentagon refusals to provide the Peruvian army and air force with the latest defensive weapons, however, led the Peruvian high command to shake off this dependency on U.S. military deliveries.

When the United States supplied Augusto Pinochet's Chile with modern weaponry and ceased delivery of spare parts and new equipment to Peru, Peru sought to diversify its military relationships. The Juan Velasco government (1968-1975) turned to the Warsaw Pact states and to the country's old ally France. Soviet tanks, Eastern bloc armored vehicles, Russian fighter bombers, and French guided missiles were obtained under favorable conditions. It was to be the last time a Peruvian president bought arms. During the Francisco Morales Bermúdez government (1975-1980), the first symptoms of a deepening economic crisis emerged. New purchases were postponed; maintenance was abandoned; equipment became obsolete.[7] Since 1980, the three consecutive civilian governments of Fernando Belaúnde Terry (1980-1985), Alan García (1985-1990), and Alberto Fujimori (1990-present), in spite of the aggressive appearance of the Shining Path, have not permitted the purchase of appropriate heavy equipment. The police and army, as well as guerrilla forces, are fighting with light arms.[8] The Peruvian army fights against an anachronistic, but very efficient, guerrilla movement with obsolete material; its heavy equipment (tanks, ships, airplanes) is inadequate for an offensive war.

The Peruvian armed forces — that is, the army and especially the intelligence services — maintain an interested watch over domestic political affairs. Military control over national politics has been a standing tradition since the nation's independence. Within the armed forces, especially the army, a new type of officer emerged in Latin America after World War II: the "military intellectual." Military intellectuals hold staff functions in the higher echelons, at training schools for colonels and one-star generals, and within the intelligence services. In Latin America, intelligence is preoccupied with internal rather than foreign enemies of the nation and with the strategy and tactics to combat these. Interpreting its objectives liberally, it provides analysis of the (desired) development of the nation and formulates recommendations about the role to be played by the armed forces. A derivative of this is the self-imposed task of producing a military ideology. Thereby, the prescription of the role of the armed forces in national development and national politics came to be included in the intrinsic tasks of the intelligence services and the training schools. The linkage of intelligence, planning institutes, and higher training schools renders conspicuous the reason that Latin America's military intellectuals came to formulate national security theses as doctrines of politico-military models.

As distant heirs of the former German geopolitical schools, the military establishments of Brazil, Argentina, Peru, and Guatemala emerged during the 1950s from the higher studies centers. In Brazil, between 1952 and 1956, the major national security theses were developed at the Escola Superior de Guerra (ESG). Between 1964 and 1985, the authors and alumni were given a chance to put their ideas into practice as advisers or ministers to the military governments.[9] Argentina's Escuela Nacional de Guerra (ENG) did not produce such precise theses, but the antisubversive ideas of the military theorists are reflected in the government programs of Generals Viola and Videla. Guatemala's Centro de Estudios para la Estabilidad Nacional (Centro ESTNA) was created recently, some years after the long period of military governments. Peru's Centro de Altos Estudios Militares (CAEM) elaborated a training program and a national security doctrine, most comparable with its Brazilian equivalent. Founded in 1950,[10] the CAEM reflects the personal influence of a progressive army reformer, General Marín, who in articulating the center's program, placed considerably greater emphasis on nationalism and less on anticommunism than did his Brazilian colleagues.

The Brazilian ESG as well as the Peruvian CAEM soon became training institutes in military and political security, in development theory and development policy, and opened their doors to military and police officers aspiring to be promoted to general, as well as to higher-ranking civil servants. The CAEM instructors turned rapidly to reformist development models: economic reform, state reform, and the creation of new line ministries (public health, public works, mining, and energy). In general, programs of poverty alleviation were emphasized by the first two CAEM directors and their advisers who were recruited from leftist middle-class intellectuals.[11] The radical tone of the CAEM economic and social reports, written by the center's alumni, resulted in a sort of censorship by the civilian government; the prime minister ordered CAEM management to limit its curriculum strictly to military matters.

CAEM's critical tone, however, did not diminish, and the spreading of its messages continued, even if they were no longer heard outside army circles. The newly created intelligence service was the next natural consumer. In 1956, another nationalistic General, Rodríguez Martínez, was called to reorganize the army and to create an intelligence service. His closest associates[12] were put in charge of the creation of military intelligence and the intelligence schools and became the virtual founders of army intelligence, national intelligence, and the training schools for intelligence officers. The literature pays little attention to the vital role of intelligence in the formation of nationalist cadres and geopolitical authors.[13] The Plan Inca of the military governments in the 1970s was formulated by a five-member team,[14] all of them former or future intelligence directors. Even during the 1980s — the years of civilian government — the intelligence services were considered to be "leftist," the object of Belaúnde's, and later García's, distrust. Yet even some of Fujimori's cabinet members and closest advisers have or have had ties to the intelligence services, presently associated with his trusted security adviser Vladimiro Montesinos.

The CAEM and the intelligence doctrines are nationalistic. The first CAEM security theses, formulated by Marín, reflected the influence of a Latin American tradition of thinking. Most of the economic and social topics are related to the ECLAC school (United Nations Commission for Latin America and the Caribbean) in Santiago de Chile, where Raúl Prebisch had launched new concepts of "underdevelopment" to explain Latin America's lag as compared with the United States. The direct relationship between national security and national development and poverty alleviation are stressed explicitly by Marín and later by Edgardo Mercado Jarrín and Sinesio Jarama, the three main authors of Peruvian security theses.[15] Given the affinity with French military tradition, French assistance was sought in the establishment of the intelligence schools and the drafting of the first intelligence tactics. If the ideas came from France, the United States provided the technology. A third partner was Argentina, geopolitical ally in the never-ending antagonism with Chile. The Argentines contributed to the organizational structure.

The military and intelligence ties with Argentina have remained strong until now. Junior intelligence officers visited Buenos Aires, and future or former intelligence directors[16] were posted as military attachés in the Argentine capital to strengthen the good relations between the services. The French-Peruvian-Argentine connection again became apparent during the Malvinas/Falklands War, when Peruvian armed forces delivered to Argentina "their" French naval missiles, successfully used against British cruisers. U.S. Central Intelligence Agency (CIA) influence remained limited primarily to naval and police intelligence. The Peruvian navy acquired, during the late 1970s and early 1980s, sophisticated intelligence hardware from the United States, and CIA instructors had trained the Peruvian antiguerrilla police units, the so-called "Sinchis," that would become the first units to fight against the Shining Path in Ayacucho.

Army intelligence became incorporated into the public sector during the last years of the military government. In the 1970s, army, navy, and air force intelligence merged with comparable police and civil services into the Sistema de Inteligencia Nacional (SIN).[17] In each ministry, in all branches of the public sector, an intelligence sector was created, headed by a colonel who reported directly to the office of the prime minister. In 1975, the Escuela de Inteligencia Estratégica was created, serving the whole national system of intelligence and security. During García's presidency, the three armed forces — each with its own organizational culture and its own minister — and the three (rival) police forces were unified in new ministries, Defense and Internal Affairs, commanded by army generals.[18] Armed forces and police now are considered to act as a coherent system of Fuerzas del Orden.

From the polar winter under Belaúnde, national intelligence entered a period of lukewarm government support under García. In 1982, an antiterrorist detective department, Dirección Contra el Terrorismo (DINCOTE), was created as a specialized task force within the police. The department started in a miserable atmosphere and with a virtually nonexistent infrastructure.[19] García provided better terms. Recently, under the Fujimori administration, especially since his autogolpe in April 1992, DINCOTE was provided with more authority, personnel, and money.

Roughly the same can be said about military intelligence. Rivalry between police and military services is strong, the Ministry of Internal Affairs also being the home base of intelligence gathering for the ruling political party. Police and military intelligence do cooperate, each of them governing its own realm and following its own rules. Military intelligence expanded slowly toward the entire public sector, the ministries, and the decentralized government bodies. However, the police, not military intelligence, were capable of infiltrating, at a high level, the Shining Path's political and combat organization.

CAEM security and development theses remained substantially the same since the 1950s; national development and national well-being were an integral part of national security conditions. General Jarama, the youngest of Peru's geopoliticians, became the CAEM director in 1985. He tried to open the way for a new national debate about civil-military relations, inviting leftist senators and human rights defendants to lecture at the CAEM, but the military establishment turned a deaf ear. Jarama's modification of national security theses was a combination of antiterrorist strategy and local development projects in regions occupied or disputed by the Shining Path. Even the national government did not listen, looking for the quick tactics of bullets instead of the long-term strategy of development. So gradually, the CAEM lost its public influence, and long-term security and development strategy was replaced by emphasis on tactical issues such as the composition of armed forces combat groups and the direct commanding authority in the "emergency zones." These new Peruvian intelligence theses are completely of national design, with few references to other Latin American or foreign intelligence communities.

The Military Government: National Security Put into Practice

After a short campaign against "conventional" guerrilla movements in the late 1960s, the Peruvian army took control of the national government to execute a revolution. The "Revolutionary Government of the Armed Forces" outlined a reform program and carried out most of it. The reforms, conceptualized as a coherent antipoverty strategy, were to prevent another guerrilla uprising in the future. The direct confrontation with the country's poverty and the peasants' misery left its mark on the commanding officers. Even though the guerrilla movement collapsed soon, the fighting changed the army officers, as illustrated by General Arturo Valdés Palacio:

> I maintain that the guerrillas in the 1960s greatly influenced the coup. At headquarters, we received the people who were sent against them and who came to report. I read reports written by the officers themselves. So, just as it nauseated me, it hit them too. Often I heard them say: 'This just is not possible.' I heard them talking: 'Yes, we are putting the guerrillas down, but we are forgetting what causes the guerrilla. And it is the cause that must be removed; otherwise, it will begin over and over again!' And so they began to think that we need reforms and that the reforms have to be structural.[20]

It is no exaggeration that those "structural reforms" were an operational translation of the military's security and intelligence theses. The reforms were elaborated by the military, executed in military style and under complete military guidance. In fact, a body of 12 colonels, a kind of political staff to the president — the armed forces and intelligence elite, the majority of whom later obtained cabinet posts — drafted all reform decrees and additional legislation. This military committee, Comité de Asesoramiento a la Presidencia (COAP),[21] acted as think tank, inner parliament, steering committee of the public sector, and designer of macro-policy from 1968 until 1980. It proposed junior and senior appointments of the military in virtually all state organs: ministries, enterprises, decentralized institutions, and advisory groups. It even worked as a clearinghouse in disputes within the armed forces: budgeting, promotions, and the composition of inter-institutional task groups. It designed and recruited the principal staff members of the reform apparatus: the new line ministries, the National Planning Institute (INP), the Popular Mass Mobilization System (SINAMOS), the state enterprises, and the regional administration. COAP was the armed forces elite, and it recruited the lower-echelon elite (*espadas de honor,* top students of the army schools) during the 12 years of military governments.

As a consequence, the marrow of the Peruvian armed forces was given on-the-job training in reforms and administration. The armed forces top brass today — and for the next five years if Fujimori does not carry out a purification in the upper rank — consider themselves the heirs of the "good military governments, without corruption, terrorism, and desolation." In private, they speak with pride about the *docenia militar*— when they were in charge of ministries or regional development bodies — and lament the absence of someone of the stature of *el general* (Velasco). It is, of course, nostalgia, but the nostalgic tone is mixed with grief about civil incompetence and indolence.

In describing the military government years, the strong points of the program of "structural reforms" are emphasized: nation building through development and guerrilla prevention through "good governance." The military assured themselves a maneuvering space by engaging in appropriate activities approved by the international community. Building up a strong "Peruvianized" economy through expropriations and nationalizations, they expected a confrontation with the United States in the long run and a strong effort to isolate them in the diplomatic and donor community. So it became constant in Peruvian foreign relations to look for alliances and multilateral agreements:

> Our geopolitical conception assumed a world split in two: the northern and the southern hemispheres. It stood to reason that we tried to make common cause with the other Third World countries. So we developed a strategy of three concentric circles. The first circle was to look for solidarity among neighboring countries to form a common front against the United States. The Andean Pact between Colombia, Ecuador, Peru, Bolivia, Chile, and later on Venezuela was a godsend. The second concentric ring was to look for solidarity among all Latin American countries. The third concentric circle was support of the Third World. We took on a prominent role of the 'group of 77' and the group of Non-Aligned Countries.[22]

It worked well. The relationship with the United States remained tense. However, that nation was exhausting itself in the Vietnam War, and — according to Peruvian military thinking — it would not react simultaneously and repressively to developments in Latin America, thinking twice before continuing its self-appointed role of policing the continent. Relations with all Latin American countries became cordial, as with most other Third World countries. Javier Pérez de Cuellar, one of Peru's brilliant diplomats and later elected as UN Secretary-General, signed the first trade agreement with the Soviet Union. Improvement in relations with the Warsaw Pact countries followed. Peru acted as Cuba's and China's intermediary to the United States.[23] Its Third World and multilateral prestige assured the military governments of a generous — perhaps, too generous — access to the international banking and donor community during the late 1970s' crisis years when Peru first experimented with a long series of austerity and adjustment programs.

The military governed through a strong public sector. It gave this sector the instruments for their "revolution from above," with authoritarian and paternalistic rule but with state presence in each provincial village as well. The public sector was a command structure for "development" and "people's participation." It meant security in the city and in the province, water and sewage in the slums, peace judges in the Indian communities, alphabetization campaigns, visiting nurses in the highland villages, and community workers in the jungle. It meant law and order for all, the rich and the formerly excluded and marginalized as well. It meant giving the benefit of the doubt to the unions, sympathy for the poor, admission of new popular organizations into the political game, and listening to the Quechua-speaking Indians. Moreover, it meant SINAMOS, that complex institution of civilian training officers and counterintelligence and security people, idealists and opportunists, as explained by General José Graham:

> It was obvious that we had to make a choice. To which political forces should we have recourse to support the process of transformation? The armed forces are no political institution, nor do they represent a political point of view. How to bring the structural reforms to the groups that make up society? You simply cannot treat society as if you are laundering old socks. To bring about social change, planning and caution are needed. Change evokes counterforces, opposition, resistance. You have to organize support. How do you do that without a political party? How can you get the masses in motion without a political party? So what we did was create a new organization to mobilize the masses and to organize them. Its activities would be political all the way, but without a party: SINAMOS.[24]

SINAMOS was created after a sudden increase in thousands of spontaneous popular actions and wildcat organizations, such as the defense committees of the revolution or of land reform. The cabinet was afraid of communism behind the mass support, and the only feasible alternative seemed to be a bureaucracy instead of a political party. SINAMOS was "to achieve conscious and active participation by education, orientation, and organization of the national population to contribute to improved performance in the public sector, including change in the attitude of the civil servants."[25] The SINAMOS think tank was composed of nationalistic and leftist intellectuals, including a former guerrilla leader. To counterbalance them, the cabinet decided that 12 military commanders would be appointed as regional directors. Gradually, other military personnel were stationed at the local level, including intelligence and security people, and the police provided some good detectives as "union advisers." Nevertheless, SINAMOS became a powerful organization, capable of large-scale deployment of personnel, vehicles, and auxiliary material in the regions. The regional directors could hire and fire as they saw fit and were able to act more quickly and efficiently than other bureaucrats could. A friend of SINAMOS' vice-minister describes the organization:

> . . . most of them were leftists; they made trips through the provinces, worked in the field. Carlin, the famous illustrator, the designer Carlos Tovar. They created the large billboards for the mass meetings. They made the pamphlets, the convocations. Frederico García, who made the motion pictures. Poets, painters, illustrators, writers, linguists. I recall vividly how they prepared a trip of Velasco to Pucallpa. First, a group would set out from Lima to scout the place. They would pick up the street slang and look at the women and the children in the market, to picture them on the posters later. They listened to the Indian stories, paid attention to their magic, their symbolism. They took Velasco up in a chopper to hover over a multitude. . . . There was plenty of money; whatever you needed you got. A twenty-yard screen? There you are. A film crew? Right. A plane? You can take off tonight.[26]

SINAMOS was also present at the regional and the local level. It assisted in the establishment of mass organizations for peasants, deeply influencing the formation of the national peasant federation (CNA), unifying in 1977 some 160 peasant leagues with 4,500 local unions and a total of 675,000 members. It helped set up workers' communities in industry, trade, mining, and fishery. It was empowered to recognize or dissolve cooperations. It started to organize "federations for landless peasants"; it organized and unified local squatter movements in the urban and metropolitan slums. It created "revolutionary youth organizations" in provincial universities, and it controlled, together with the national planning institute, the performance of the local bureaucracy. Possibly, it was the only decade of this century when the state was present in the most remote regions, the most forgotten villages.

Even in the aftermath of the revolutionary government and the relative degeneration and militarization, corruption and inevitable distrust of the mass organizations, the conservative junta members of the late 1970s tried to guarantee the presence of the state and local development efforts in the provinces, the Indian highlands, and the jungle regions. True, they dismantled the mass organizations, the peasant and slum associations, and put most of the reforms in semi-paralysis. SINAMOS was disbanded. However, much was mollified by the last reform of the military government: the creation of the ORDES, regional development organs with the rank of a ministry and with enormous local power (budget autonomy, fixed revenues from the public treasury, and complete transfer of regional line ministry dependencies to the new ORDES. Of course, the regional commander was appointed as the new regional minister. Nevertheless, the ORDES continued — until its premature dissolution by the civil government in 1980 — as an efficient instrument of regional autonomy and local development in terms of village infrastructure, public health, and primary schools.

Morales Bermúdez's government degenerated slowly. Shortly after his acclaimed "deepening of the revolution toward socialism," the army's hardliners let him choose between retirement or political change. So he shifted from the left to the center, and then to the conservative end of the political spectrum. The last two years of the military government were years of bitter confrontation between the government and the heirs of the revolution. The government started the first adjustment and austerity program, accompanied by a package of antipopular and repressive measures. Half-organized local protests, followed by regional and national strikes, paralyzed the country. The government called for elections of a *constttuyente* that would codify most of the reforms and prepare the way for civil democracy. The military had become tired, exhausted.

> I am sure, the armed forces themselves, and especially the army, felt exhausted after ten years of government and politics. And it was not in the benefit of the institution to continue confronting a substantive part of the civil society, the former supporters of the revolutionary process. We should transfer the government now or next year. It is sure that Morales Bermúdez grasped the hidden sentiments of the majority of the army officers.[27]

During the last months before the change of government, the three junta members decided to maintain the continuity of military command.[28] By mutual consent with President-elect Belaúnde, they nominated themselves the new commander generals of the army, the navy, and the air force, leaving the appointment of the three military ministers to the new civilian government. Thus, Belaúnde lived the first year of his presidency in peaceful coexistence with his former adversaries. Even worse, General Hoyos, one of the co-authors of Velasco's Plan Inca, the military's blueprint for national development, had been appointed as the army's chief-of-staff. After his death in 1981, another Velasquista, the prestigious General Miranda who had drafted the public edition of Plan Inca, took office as his successor. It became standard presidential policy to keep the military at a distance and to look to others for support.

Shining Path, the Guerrillas, and the Drug Lords

If Peru is the land of Job, Ayacucho is the place where his children died. Ayacucho and the surrounding departments are stigmatized with the wounds of poverty, illiteracy, exploitation, and underdevelopment. The Land Reform of Velasco was halted prematurely in these parts of the Andean highlands. For centuries the capital of a miserable region of medium-sized haciendas and forgotten Indian communities, the city of Ayacucho obtained a regional university in the 1950s. Soon, this university's graduates would compete for jobs with the students of 20 other provincial universities, most of them better connected with sources of income and employment. Most of the Indian students returned to their villages.

In the early 1960s, a parochial philosopher, Abimael Guzmán, went to Ayacucho to teach at the university and its related teachers' normal school. Guzmán became the undisputed leader of a Maoist splinter of the Peruvian Communist Party, the Shining Path.[29] While the pro-Moscow wing allied with the Velasco government and other neo-Marxist party leaders participated with success in the elections of the 1980s, the Shining Path's leadership chose the anonymity of a diligent cell structure, the cocoons to be matured for a final "People's War." Guzmán took his time to strengthen his organization and to acquire strong roots in the peasantry. The very moment of his first armed presence was a brilliant choice: May 1980, the election day of the first democratic president when the military felt weak and the future civilian leadership in Lima would be powerless.[30]

The Shining Path grew during the relatively prosperous years of the military governments. Their progressive educational reforms favored lower-class universities and similar institutions. A clash between the military and the university students in the early 1970s brought an uneasy distance between the government and the Ayacucho people. However, the emphasis on cell structure, ideological pureness, slow proselytism, absolute loyalty and devotion, and strict morality gave the Shining Path a protective ambience and contributed to the movement's impenetrability in the following years. The Shining Path had sought and acquired a strong popular base and started to fight in its home region.

Two other important reasons explain Shining Path's fabulous growth and consolidation in the short period between 1980 and 1982. First, the new civilian government did not trust the army and thought it better to keep them quiet. Velasquista generals commanded the army, and army intelligence was considered to be the heir of the Velasco team. Belaúnde downplayed Shining Path, depicting its members in cabinet sessions as "petty cattle rustlers." Thus, instead of the army, Lima police forces, untrained and unfit for guerrilla fighting, were mobilized against Shining Path.[31] The indolent president unwittingly transformed the metropolitan police into Shining Path's principal arms supplier! Second, the movement's tactics to destroy public sector infrastructure blindly and the continuous expulsion or execution of local magistrates, teachers, rural police officers, and public health personnel, aggravated by the withdrawal of funds and people by the central government and the lack of interest in sustainable local development in Lima, provided the guerrillas with a monopoly on pressure, power, and legality in the Ayacucho region and surrounding departments.

Apparently, the Shining Path's ideology reflects a variety of transplants from other continents. Peru's economy is "semi-feudal." The ethnic civil war is explained — in orthodox Stalinist concepts — in terms of class. Public messages refer to disputes by Jiang Quing, Lin Biao, and the Gang of Four. Dead dogs are found hanging with signs: "Deng Xiaoping, Son of a Bitch." The messages appear to be incongruent and anachronistic, imported from other times and other worlds. Yet the ideology explains all things or explains all things away. It is the simple abracadabra of the effective presence of a crude and poor movement in the desolate milieu of extremely poor peasants and slum dwellers. It symbolizes a violent justice, displayed by the selective assassination of "bad" people; a cruel morality that implies the public punishing of adulterers and drinkers; a merciless redistribution, emphasizing the necessity of small plots of land and a minimum of food and cattle for survival; and a haranguing pedagogy, indoctrinating very humble and acquiescent people, who have deep respect for teachers and apostles. The Shining Path uses a vocabulary that varies from region to region, from one population segment to another. It incorporates sympathizers and recruits new membership using inducement and coercion, gradually relying more on terror and violence:

The urban cell members receive political and military instructions. Focal point is *el pensamiento Gonzalo* or Guzmán's thinking[32] (his *nom de guerre* is Gonzalo): The linear succession of historic phases since the creation of the universe, the appearance of mankind, the social organizations and the necessary evolution toward communism following Marx, Lenin, and Mao, whose nucleus is the elimination of the existing society by the purifying action of the People's War. The new society will be basically agrarian, self-supporting, theocratic, dictatorial, and moralistic (the old Inca ethics). Emphasis is put on class struggle against concrete enemies, such as wholesalers and retailers (*bourgeois*), rich peasants (*kulaks*), and political enemies (members of the government parties and the revisionists and opportunists of the legal left). The military training concerns elements such as physical condition (extended marches and night exercises, surpassing the effects of hunger, thirst, and fatigue), technical instruction (knowledge of local attack and defense possibilities, inventory of suitable buildings and safe houses, practice in short- and medium-range arms and homemade bombs), psycho-sociological awareness (conviction of the truth of the doctrine and the justice of the actions, recruiting other brothers-in-arms and hidden *aides-de camp* to form the '1,000 eyes and 1,000 ears' of informers and watchdogs); and operational activities (pass on information, write down slogans, put up bombs, participate in armed assaults and special raids).

The rural bases are real military training camps *in situ*. Their members receive theory and practice as well, based upon *el pensamiento Gonzalo* and the characteristics of the local situation. They are trained in the identification of friends and foes. In the use of firearms, dynamite, and homemade bombs. In espionage and surveillance, proselytism, and intimidation. Finally, they participate in combat operations and urban terrorism. They are allowed to assault groups of six to eight persons, based on cell structure and fragmented command.

Rural control is stricter than urban rule. Landowners of medium-size properties are forced out. Independent leaders of the Indian communities were changed for more obedient officers. Smallholders pay regular tribute. Local market people do business under the Shining Path's regulations; otherwise, they risk losing their trade or their lives. Regional Offices of the Ministry of Agriculture, Education, and Public Health are threatened or paralyzed, their technical assistance reduced to zero. The clergy is under control. Church services and mass celebrations are permitted, but the sermon's global content should be previously authorized.

The basic objective is to establish political and military control over agricultural production and distribution and control over the deliverance to the regional centers to facilitate posterior overmastering and domination of the urban population. They proceed in the following order:

- Discovering conflicts between leaders and members of cooperatives, landlords and tenants, proprietors, and peasants without land, rich and poor community leaders;
- Installing military presence to influence the conflict favorably toward groups or persons upon whose sympathy one can count;
- Armed support for the chosen individuals and groups and progressive marginalization of the opposition, effectuated by local land reform, privatization, and distribution of land and animals and legitimized by a "popular assembly" of the Shining Path's representatives;
- Imposition of *mittimaes*, i.e., the migration of reliable peasants and military from older zones under control (*bases*), who receive the best lands and who act as leaders of the assault groups and as political supervisors in the new zones;
- Transformation of the new zones in regular bases, where they establish the type of production, the quantities for local consumption and regional commerce, the social and political life-style, as well as the morality in public and private affairs;
- Consolidation of the bases as self-supporting defensive zones.[33]

These are the procedures in provinces. With the extension of the Shining Path's realm to the metropolitan areas of Arequipa, Trujillo, and Lima, the ingredients of the persuasion and terror cocktail change. The first areas of infiltration are the urban slums and the industrial cordons. The first category of persons to be intimidated are the independent or leftist union leaders, slum leaders, local mayors and councilors, and the directorate of the local development organizations. Sometimes they are "persuaded" to retire; sometimes a "popular tribunal" has to be organized to condemn the obstinate representatives and blow them up with dynamite after trial. With the appointment of a more cooperative leadership, the Shining Path establishes training schools and selects supervisors. Public sector officials, NGO workers, lawyers, doctors, and journalists are paid a warning visit at home or in the office. Car bombs and bus bombs panic the inhabitants of the industrial zones and the middle-class areas. The "1,000 eyes and 1,000 ears" are rumored to be omnipresent, and to demonstrate their potential for public control, the Shining Path periodically organizes "armed strikes" in metropolitan areas, organizing selective punishing by killing disobedient taxi drivers and shopkeepers.

The Shining Path is[34] — or, at least until Guzmán's arrest, was — composed of a strong political Central Committee, with a personal cult surrounding the leader-as-saint, and a network of regional and provincial committees. In principle, military and operational planning are realized at the regional level. Although the overall strategy is — was — a matter of national concern, most of the movement's flexibility and perseverance can be attributed to regional and local decentralization. The Shining Path is strong where the government — the military, the police, the public sector — is weak, and that is mostly in the highland villages and the metropolitan poverty belts. During the 12 years of the "People's War," the Shining Path operated — in the strictly military sense — prudently, defensively against military formations, avoiding direct contact, allowing only ad hoc raids against isolated units and provincial police stations. Until the 1990s, the organization reflected basically an uncomplicated attack-defense strategy, operating through a loose structure of "military columns." There are a few ranks, without uniforms or complicated command hierarchy. A commander — women's representation in the higher ranks is surprisingly high — controls a small, versatile unit of ideologically immaculate and highly motivated loyalists. This nucleus — a wild estimate gives a hard core of 3,000 to 7,000 persons — is supported by local sympathizers and novices. They are mostly recruited — was it because of a vague sympathy, a deep resentment, or by coercion? — in the "liberated areas" in the highland departments or the pauperized metropolitan slums. A secondary support structure consists of a network of lawyers, medical personnel and paramedics, students and other sympathy organizations, including a sort of diplomatic representation in foreign countries. When the Shining Path tried[35] to expand its range of operations to Bolivia, Ecuador, and Chile in 1992, the first organizations and persons to be "touched" by sympathy and support were the local NGOs and the doctors.

Until recently, the Shining Path took and maintained the initiative. Favored by the central government's indolence in the early 1980s, the Ayacucho region was transformed easily into a guerrilla stronghold. When in December 1982 the regular army took the plaza of Ayacucho and a special military command for the emergency zone was created, the movement avoided open confrontations but continued exercising constant pressure by surprise attacks. At night, guerrilla columns controlled the departments in the South-Central highlands. When in September 1982, the Shining Path's 19-year-old commander Edith Lagos died by police fire, 30,000 persons attended the burial, and the conservative archbishop Frederico Richter Prada[36] celebrated the solemn funeral mass. The movement's popularity among the peasants lasted until the mid-1980s, when the Shining Path columns began to cruise the highland departments systematically from Ecuador to Bolivia. The local *comuneros* usually refused to prepare food for the pursuing army units.

The guerrillas suffered their first serious setback in the Alto Huallaga Valley, the most important coca-producing region in the world, while trying to establish control over the taxable regional economy. Their columns were resisted and initially driven out. However, after a second effort in the late 1980s, the better part of the valley was under control, and the urban middle class in the regional capital Tarapoto, from the local supermarket owner to the police inspector, paid their tax quota on a regular, sometimes daily basis. Since then, Shining Path has tried to surround and penetrate Lima, making its presence visible in the metropolitan slums and distributing land and animals in some of Lima's rural coastal valleys. The movement could not easily penetrate the labor unions and industrial organizations. A selective wave of terror against the legal left and the fabric of independent slum organizations, added to an armed strike that paralyzed Lima around Independence Day in 1992, contributed to a generalized sense of demoralization. This war of nerves was suddenly replaced by a wave of official euphoria after the capture of Guzmán and the Shining Path's Central Committee.

The Shining Path is by no means the only agent contributing to the Peruvian horror scenario. A second guerrilla movement, Tupac

Amaru (MRTA), began its operations in the early 1980s, partly as a competitor to the Shining Path. If there is officialdom in guerrilla warfare, Tupac Amaru belongs to the "formal sector" of uniforms, military-style command, and "normal" behavior, including the public appearances and the Romanesque bravado of its leadership.[37] Both the Shining Path and Tupac Amaru tried to acquire control of the Alto Huallaga, Shining Path being the major force of the two and the ultimate winner in the region.[38] The same can be said about its confrontations with the regular army.[39] Being the smaller, the weaker, the more predictable, and the more "civilized" of the two, the performance of Tupac Amaru is normally considered to be less significant than the more mysterious Shining Path.

"Normal" urban criminality is also to be taken seriously. Spectacular raids, kidnapping, and hijacking began to be chronic during the García presidency. Mass discharges of suspected criminal police officers, unemployed ex-conscripts of the armed forces, and former members of the private police organizations (a booming branch in the 1980s) mixed up with petty criminals in the metropolitan areas. The problem became so acute that the National Chamber of Industry and Commerce, in the 1986 collective negotiations with the government, formulated an "effective protection against kidnapping" as the most important priority on behalf of the private sector. Sometimes urban criminality dropped, then rose again. It never disappeared, its presence sometimes confounded with guerrilla terrorism or antisubversive police and military activities.

The drug economy is another factor that contributes to the process of informalization and violence. Originally mainly a Peruvian affair,[40] with its local drug aristocracy laundering money through the Banco Amazónico and establishing fragile ties with the regional military, it became a matter of Colombianization and a division of labor between foreign and Peruvian involvement in the early 1980s.[41] Ten years later, the coca production in the Alto Huallaga Valley alone provides a source of income for some 300,000 people. Nobody tried to analyze deeply the interactions among the drug lords, the drug traffickers, the Shining Path, Tupac Amaru, the police, the army, the navy, the air force, and the government.[42] The economic impact of coca is enormous; the coca share in the national violence statistics should be proportional.

The Civilian Government: The New Democracy

Opinion polls should reflect something of the nation's values and beliefs. The journal *Debate* publicized in August 1992, a month before Guzmán's capture, the result of its yearly survey of 1,000 Peruvian opinion leaders about the top ten people in the national power structure. Of course, President Fujimori obtained the number one position, and Finance Minister Carlos Boloña — the virtual prime minister — became the number two. However, Abimael Guzmán received the next position, against General Nicolás Hermoza, the army general commander, who obtained number seven in the national ranking.[43] Fujimori's presidential position was not only challenged by the two guerrilla movements, the drug lords, the mafia bosses, and the urban criminals, but it was also disputed in 1990 by the elected bicameral parliament and an unknown segment of the armed forces. A framed or real coup attempt that failed, the favorable electoral results in the new constituyente, and the fact that most members of the Shining Path Central Committee are behind bars opened the way for presidential initiatives. Yet the president shares his power with his adversaries: the guerrillas, the drug and criminal leaders, and a new element in the political arena, part of the army officer elite and the political losers of his autogolpe, the formal political party structure. Maybe the political structure prior to 1990 can disappear without damages; however, the army, the armed forces, and the police are the only defense instruments of a state that is under siege.

During the governments of Belaúnde, García, and Fujimori, civil-military relations were uneasy and tense. Belaúnde's distrust toward the military and his indolence toward the Shining Path caused a deep contempt in military circles against the president and most of his ministers. The higher echelons never acquired a respect for García's presidency because of his zig-zagging between the police and the military and his disastrous economic policy. Fujimori is considered to be a political sphinx, producing populist ideology instead of security and development. Army ideology did not change after the years of military government. As indicated in the first part of this chapter, the old Marín maxim that "security = development" is one of the major themes the CAEM students still discuss. The army still recruits the same ideal type of officers it attracted three and four decades ago. So it reproduces its ideology and its officer corps.

Apparently, the army also reproduced its geopolitical enemies: the northern border with Ecuador and the southern one with Chile are of traditional Peruvian concern. The three principal military regions are I, II, and III (Northern zone, Lima, Southern zone), with regions IV and V (highlands and jungle) the forgotten ones. Even in the late 1980s, only 20 percent of the military forces were dedicated directly to the containment of the guerrillas and other "sources of terrorism."[44] Only recently did the central government decide to create a new military region VI (Huallaga) in order to coordinate the antiguerrilla and antidrug war. During the 1980s and the years of Fujimori, the U.S. military diplomatic establishment defined the drug problem as the number-one priority.[45] New and more adequate antiguerrilla equipment was not obtained.

The economic crisis and hyperinflation in the late 1980s and early 1990s had a catastrophic impact on the military's maintenance and budget, on salaries as well as on officers' morale. When interviewed in December 1990 and 1991, the retired army elite admitted having to live on US$300 a month. Army captains in activity, who were commanders of antiterrorist units from the emergency zones on leave of absence in Lima, were working as free-lance taxi drivers to buy their children Christmas presents. In private, and sometimes in public, retired generals and officers in activity complain bitterly that the army has had to do the job fighting the guerrillas and drug trafficking alone but receives the blame for failure and human rights violence and that successive presidents — Belaúnde, García, and Fujimori — have been interested only in politics and money. Moreover, García's and Fujimori's social and economic policies earned Peru the status of international pariah.[46]

In addition to the "forces of public order," the military and the police, private equivalents (security services) proliferated from the mid-1980s on. In the urban and metropolitan areas, the private police companies constitute a booming industry. The generalized climate of tension and fear, violence, and terrorism created a necessity to assure protection and vigilance. The slum population invented homemade defense instruments like staves, sticks, and bicycle chains. In the mine encampments and the industrial cordons, workers employed self-defense, virtually transforming themselves into local private armies. The government thought about a rural militia and distributed firearms to organized peasants. These *rondas campesinas* became the semi-institutionalized fourth branch of the armed forces, in 1991 and 1992 marching with the regular army, the navy, and the air force at Independence Day. Of course, the *rondas urbanas* acquired popularity in the slums. Metropolitan middle classes in Lima bought police cars and uniforms and acted as a regular police force at night; their vigilante corps were recognized as *serenazgo* units and trained by the police.

Recently, the coca peasantry in the Huallaga Valley took up arms and formed a self-proclaimed militia. The legal Left and, during the García years, the governing APRA party as well created paramilitary units; the APRA-inspired Comando Rodrigo Franco earned a reputation as a "political death squad" among terrified adversaries. In this way, the informalization process of social institutions in Peru, running from the disintegration of the public sector to the rise of an entire "private public sector" of NGOs, advanced to the military sphere and the police forces. It requires, effectively, a sharp eye to distinguish among the actions of the regular armed forces, the police, the paramilitary units, and the death squads. Sometimes nobody knows who killed whom. Was it the Shining Path? Tupac Amaru? A frightened *serenazgo* member? Did the drug mafia give the order? Or was it a political settlement? Was a presidential advisor involved?

Fighting a guerrilla war and looking for antisubversive military answers is a policy of trench warfare. The central government chose, during the 12 years of the civil war, bullets instead of development, emphasizing the military and police operations without directing a coherent antipoverty policy. In one of the most impoverished and informalized countries of the world, the economic cabinet executes one of the most draconian adjustment programs ever heard of. There is no social development plan; there are no social compensation schemes.[47] With the public sector absent in one-half of the country, without civilian support action and with lukewarm government support, the army and the police represent the state in all departments of the Peruvian highlands and in the disputed zones of the jungle and the coastal valleys. "In Peru, the state is a foreigner in its own territory," says General Edwin Díaz, director of the Sistema Nacional de Inteligencia from 1986 to 1991, describing the climate of contained frustration and demoralization in the officers' corps.[48]

In the last year of García's government, army intelligence prepared a plan for a coup against the disgraced president. The execution of this Plan Omega was postponed after a tense discussion with the army's general commander, but most of the scenario was integrated in the final draft that was used during Fujimori's *autogolpe*.[49]

The armed forces joined the coup, but it is known publicly that there is disagreement between the army's top echelon — the part affiliated with the president and his advisors — and the army's intelligentsia — the part affiliated with the army's tradition. At best, Fujimori's civil-military co-government was interpreted in army circles as providing a tactical advantage and as the elimination of political obstacles of the antisubversive warfare. The capture of the Shining Path's Central Committee in September and October 1992 seemed to confirm the beneficence of an alliance, but again, the unhappy feelings remain. When army and intelligence people, politicians, and Fujimori's cabinet members were interviewed the week before Guzmán's sudden arrest, the general feeling was "we are losing the war." Peruvian society in the early 1990s is a crater landscape with porous tunnels, dugouts, and flamethrower corridors. In Peru, the rich devour the lower classes, and the poor eat the pauperized. The growth of the informal sector in economy and society is so spectacular that a sensitive reporter, looking for an explanation of the Shining Path's following, concluded in a study about the slums of Tacna at the Chilean border:

> There are people in Tacna who do not know their own names. . . .The most basic task was getting people legally registered with names and birth dates. The problem was that few of the women knew these facts about themselves. Their employers chose names for them when they came to Tacna.
>
> The word "rights" is a popular word in Peru. In 1979, a new constitution had been written. A document that is now published in every phone directory in the country, it provides for freedom of speech and assembly, decent wages, access to justice, and guarantees of good working conditions and equality for women, children, and Indians. It is an excellent constitution and at times bears some resemblance to reality. Progressive, educated people. . .are very proud of it. They talk a lot about the rights of the poor in Peru. But the poor in Peru do not talk about rights. They recognize the constitution for the bit of poetry it is. If they have heard the word, they think that it does not apply to them. Rights exist only for the powerful, meaning, of course, that they do not exist at all.[50]

Thus, the conflict seems never-ending. The level of violence may decline. Shining Path may lose initiative and suffer a long-term leadership crisis. The military may advance in some of the emergency zones.

The government may feel confident that the war can now be won. But which war, against whom or what? The country's misery? The extreme poverty of the peasants, of the *informales,* as the urban paupers call themselves? In a country where the state is being demolished, the society is transformed slowly into a ruin.

Notes

1. For a detailed discussion, see Paul Glewwe and Dennis de Tray, 1989, *The Poor in Latin America during Adjustment: A Case Study of Peru*, LSMS Working Paper 56 (Washington, D.C.: The World Bank); David F. Ruccio, 1991, "When Failure Becomes Success: Class and Debate over Stabilization and Adjustment," *World Development* XIX, 10: 1315-1334; Rosemary Thorp, 1991, *Economic Management and Economic Development in Peru and Colombia* (Pittsburgh: University of Pittsburgh Press), 67-143; and Manuel Pastor, Jr., and Carol Wise, 1992, "Peruvian Economic Policy in the 1980s: From Orthodoxy to Heterodoxy and Back," *Latin American Research Review* XXVII, 2: 83-117.

2. Data obtained in an interview with Minister of Labor Augusto Antonelli on September 10, 1992.

3. See Luis Pasara, et al., 1991, *La Otra Cara de la Luna; Nuevos Actores Sociales en el Perú* (Buenos Aires: CEDYS).

4. Expression coined by Colonel Roberto Letona, chief-of-staff of the minister of National Defense of Guatemala. For a general discussion, see Kees Koonings, "La Sociología de la intervención military en la política latinoamericana," in Dirk Kruijt and Edelberto Torres-Rivas, eds., 1991, *América Latina: Militares y Sociedad*, Tomo II (San José: FLACSO), 29-142.

5. See Dirk Kruijt, 1991a, *Entre Sendero y Militares* (Lima: Editorial Robles), 231.

6. Efraim Cobas (1982) presents an historical review of the presence of foreign missions in Peru in *Fuerza Armada, Misiones Militares y Dependencia en el Perú* (Lima: Editorial Horizonte).

7. Kruijt 1991a, 107.

8. Recently, the Fujimori government acquired some second-hand Soviet helicopters, leftovers of the Sandinista air force. Nicaraguan maintenance service is not considered the best in the world.

9. See Alfred Stepan, 1986, *Os Militares: Da Abertura a Nova República* (Rio de Janeiro: Paz e Terra), 26-39, 57-66; and Stepan, 1988, *Rethinking Military Politics; Brazil and the Southern Cone* (Princeton, N.J.: Princeton University Press); and Maria Elena Moreira Alves, 1987, *1985; Estado e Oposiçao no Brasil (1964-1984)* (Petropolis: Vozes), 19 ff.

10. Victor Villanueva, 1972, *El CAEM y la Revolución de la Fuerza Armada* (Lima: IEP/Capodónico Ediciones), 54 ff.

11. Jorge Rodriguez Beruff, 1983, *Los Militares y el Poder; Un Ensayo sobre la Doctrina Militar en el Perú, 1948-1968* (Lima: Mosca Azul), 106 ff.

12. General Carlos Bossio Collas, a minister in the junta of 1962, dismissed a year later because of his attempts to nationalize foreign enterprises, Colonel Edgardo

Mercado Jarrín, and Lieutenant-Colonel Jorge Fernandez Maldonado. During the Velasco years, General Bossio was the Peruvian ambassador to Spain.

13. Data obtained from extensive interviews with Generals Jorge Fernandez Maldonado and Edgardo Mercado Jarrín in 1986 in Dirk Kruijt, 1991b, *La Revolución por Decreto; Perú durante el Gobierno Militar* (San José: FLACSO/Mosca Azul), 85-87, 102-106, and 111-114. In December 1990, I interviewed General Fernandez Maldonado again.

14. General Edgardo Mercado Jarrín and Colonels Jorge Fernandez Maldonado, Leonidas Rodriguez Figueroa, Enrique Gallegos, and Rafael Hoyos. Hoyos would be the director of national intelligence during a substantive part of the Velasco years.

15. Reported in Kruijt 1991b, 89-94 and Kruijt 1991a, 85-86, 101 ff, and 113 ff. I interviewed General Sinesio Jarama in February 1991.

16. Such as Lieutenant-Colonel Jorge Fernandez Maldonado in 1960 and General Edwin Díaz in 1991.

17. Most of the following arguments come from an interview on September 11, 1992, with General Edwin Díaz, former chief of the SIN during the García and early Fujimori years (1986-1991).

18. Analyzed in Dirk Kruijt, "Perú: Relaciones entre civiles y militares, 1950-1990," in Kruijt and Torres Rivas 1991, 124-126. Also see David Scott Palmer, "National Security," in the manuscript by Rex Hudson, ed., n.d., *Peru: A Country Study* (Washington, D.C.: GPO).

19. Gustavo Gorriti Ellenbogen, 1990, *Sendero Luminoso: Historia de la Guerra Milenaria en el Perú*, Tomo I (Lima: Editorial Apoyo), 223 ff.

20. General Arturo Valdés Palacio in Kruijt 1991b, 112-113. Valdés was an army lawyer, adviser to the Ministers of War from 1958 to 1968, presidential adviser and secretary of the cabinet from 1968 to 1976.

21. Advisory Committee to the Presidency.

22. General Edgardo Mercado Jarrín in Kruijt 1991a, 48-49. Mercado was the first Minister of Foreign Affairs in Velasco's cabinet.

23. Peruvian former cabinet ministers were, as retired generals, received in Beijing with full military honors. China never supported the Peruvian "Maoist" parties, including the Shining Path.

24. General José Graham, Minister of State and President of COAP from 1969 to 1976 in Kruijt and Torres Rivas 1991, 68-69.

25. Kruijt 1991b, 209.

26. Wilma Delprich, a personal friend of SINAMOS' Vice-Minister Carlos Delgado in Kruijt 1991b, 212-213.

27. General Ramón Miranda, Minister of Education from 1975 to 1977 and the army's chief-of-staff in 1981 and 1982, in Kruijt and Torres Rivas 1991, 83.

28. Interview with General Carlos Quevedo, president of COAP from 1976 to 1980 in Kruijt 1991a, 74.

29. Officially called the Communist Party of Peru after the Shining Path of José Carlos Mariátegui, in honor of Perú's most original Marxist theorist. The best analytical publications about the Shining Path are those of Gustavo Gorriti Ellenbogen (see note 19); María del Pilar Tello, 1989, *Sobre el Volcán: Diálogo frente a la Subversión* (Lima: CELA) and Tello 1991, *Perú: El Precio de la Paz* (Lima: Ediciones PETROPERU); Carlos

Iván Degregori, 1990a, *Ayacucho 1969-1979; El Surgimiento de Sendero Luminoso* (Lima: IEPE); and David Scott Palmer, 1992, *The Shining Path of Peru* (New York: St. Martin's Press).

30. The military high command in Lima consulted with the Presidential Palace and obtained a "Do not worry!" The army commander, however, sent troops by helicopter to restore law and order and let the populations vote again. Interview with an, at his request, anonymous commanding general in Kruijt 1991a, 105.

31. Without exception, all general commanders between 1980 and 1992 — I interviewed most of them personally — blame Belaúnde for his negligence and complete lack of interest.

32. All hagiographic pictures of Guzmán are of a kind of prophet wearing glasses and carrying a book. See Carlos Iván Degregori 1990b, *Qué Difícil es ser Dios; Ideología y Violencia Política en Sendero Luminoso* (Lima: IEP/Zorro de Abajo Ediciones), 19.

33. Quoted from "Sendero en el Norte del País," an extensive unpublished document written by United Nations officials in May 1991, a team of sociologists with family ties in the departments dominated by Shining Path.

34. Gabriela Tarrazona-Sevillano gives a coherent insight in her "The Organization of the Shining Path," in Palmer 1992, 171-190. I used her data, publications of the well-informed *Si* (1991, 1992) and the update, published in the special number of *La República* (September 14, 1992) two days after Guzmán's arrest.

35. I used the reporting in *Si* and interviewed related diplomatic and development representatives in September and October 1992.

36. Partly responsible for the discontinuation of the Land Reform in Ayacucho.

37. Tello 1991, 109-110.

38. See David Scott Palmer, "The Shining Path in Peru: Insurgency and the Drug Problem" in Edwin G. Corr and Stephen Sloan, eds., 1992, *Low Intensity Conflicts; Old Threats in a New World* (Boulder, Colo.: Westview Press), 151-170; and Raúl González, 1987a, "Sendero versus MRTA," *Quéhacer* 46 (April-May): 47-53; González 1987b, "Coca y Subversión en el Huallaga," *Quéhacer* 48 (September-October): 59-72; González 1988, "MRTA: La Historia Desconocida," *Quéhacer* 51 (April-May): 32-44.

39. Kruijt 1991a, 76-86.

40. For a description of the Peruvian drug economy in the 1960s and 1970s, see Rita Haring, 1985, "La Región Amazónica Peruana, 1880-1980," *Estudios Sociales* I, 3: 5-19.

41. For a discussion, see David Scott Palmer, 1992, "Peru, the Drug Business and Shining Path: Between Scylla and Charybdis?" *Journal of Interamerican Studies and World Affairs* 34 (3): 68.

42. The weekly magazine *Caretas* sometimes published a special report. The October 6, 1986, number related the names of five high-ranking police officers (four generals and one colonel) and a retired army general with mafia boss Reynaldo Rodriguez Lopez. His legal adviser was to become the new presidential adviser, Vladimiro Montesinos.

43. Vladimiro Montesinos got the fourth position.

44. Corr and Sloan 1992, 165.

45. Palmer 1992, 73-76.

46. For a detailed statement, see Kruijt and Torres Rivas 1991, 129-134; and Rainer Hukle, 1992, "Der 'Kaiser' setz aufs Militar," *ILA* (May): 46-48.

47. Interviews with Jorge Lau and Manuel Vara, Minister and Vice-Minister of the Presidency, September 10, 1992. The Ministry of the Presidency assumed the functions of the dissolved National Planning Institute (INP), the elite bureaucracy during the military years.

48. Interview with General Edwin Díaz, ex-director of the SIN, September 11, 1992.

49. Interview with *ingeniero* Máximo San Román, first vice-president of Peru until April 5, 1992, and later nominated as constitutional president by the dissolved parliament. The interview took place on September 11, 1992, the day of the capture of Guzmán.

50. Tina Rosenberg, 1990, *Children of Cain: Violence and the Violent in Latin America* (New York: Penguin), 167-168.

XIV

The Future of Latin America's Armed Forces

Richard L. Millett

When academic analysis of Latin America's armed forces began at the end of the 1950s, the military was widely perceived as a static, conservative institution, generally supportive of U.S. positions in world affairs and aligned with the traditional elites in domestic politics. Today, traditional assumptions concerning the makeup, ideology, political role, and future missions of the armed forces no longer hold true in many, if not most, of the nations of Latin America. In some, the very future of the armed forces seems in doubt. In recent years, both Panama and Haiti have seen their traditional military establishments essentially destroyed and their functions taken over by civilian-controlled police forces. Even traditional views of sovereignty, something that most Latin American militaries felt was a clear, solid, and basic concept on which they constructed much of their national security doctrine, show signs of breaking down. In an era of international economic integration, multilateral peacekeeping, and globalized communications, it is even difficult to define just what it is that the military defends and what it defends against.

As the essays in this volume make clear, Latin America's military institutions are entering a period of difficult and potentially traumatic change. Missions, threats, relations with other actors, both foreign and domestic, even the traditional immunities and privileges of the officer corps are all open to constant re-examination. For institutions as conservative and traditional as the armed forces, this calls into question assumptions that have endured for decades. The ability (let alone the desirability) of the armed forces to act as an institution separate from civil society and with the power — indeed, the obligation — to judge that society seems to be disappearing. Even the military's internal autonomy, its traditional control over assignments, promotions, and finances, is being questioned. Moreover, while old models of the military's role in society are breaking down, no clear new consensus is emerging, leaving many officers frustrated and apprehensive about the future.

In Latin America, unsettling change is by no means confined to the military. The political class, the private sector, intellectuals, indigenous groups and other minorities, women, labor, the judiciary, and even the churches are facing unprecedented challenges as they strive to adapt to a radically altered world. Issues of globalization, problems of modernization and urbanization, and declining state powers and resources challenge traditional norms and concepts of the national state and require radical readjustments by all major institutions, military and civilian. Issues of globalization include the creation of a world economy and the accelerating trend toward economic integration, the development of international communication and information networks, the tendency to seek multilateral solutions to security issues, the rise of global environmental movements, and the problems posed by increasing international linkages among criminal organizations. Problems of modernization include the inadequacy of existing governmental structures (notably, the administration of justice), the escalating costs of modern technology for both civil and military institutions, the challenge of providing services and maintaining order in rapidly expanding urban areas, and the need to decentralize government in order to compete economically.

All of this is taking place in a rapidly changing political context. Transitions to more or less democratic governments have been the rule in Latin America for the past decade. With the restoration of President Jean-Bertrand Aristide in Haiti, only Cuba maintains an openly authoritarian system. This has brought to power civilians who frequently have had very negative experiences in past dealings with the military, who lack governmental experience — especially in security issues — and who often are besieged themselves by hostile legislative bodies, declining levels of popular support, and massive financial problems. Add to this the emerging issues mentioned above, and the potential for confusion, tension, and conflict is obvious.

Environmental issues provide an excellent example of how changing political and economic realities impact on the military. In the 1960s, the mission for many Latin American militaries was not defending the environment but enhancing the ability to exploit it. Opening up areas such as the Amazon Basin involved the armed forces in a variety of more or less traditional roles. Military missions and elite interests were generally compatible, as both sought to maximize the exploitation of available resources. This provided both the military institution and individual officers with opportunities for lucrative profits. Indigenous rights were generally ignored, and the wider world took little notice of the methods utilized or of the effects of such policies.

Today environmental and indigenous rights groups are found throughout the world and have become significant actors in the international political arena. In addition, most Latin American nations have developed their own environmental groups. Defending the environment and protecting indigenous peoples from outside exploitation now are often part of the military mission. At the same time, given past history, there are serious questions about using the armed forces in such missions. For many, having the military defend indigenous peoples or the environment is a classic case of setting the fox to guard the chicken coop. However, given the paucity of state resources, there are few if any alternatives available.

All of this poses special challenges for the armed forces, placing them in roles for which they are ill prepared. Defending the environment in response to international pressures often runs directly contrary to their traditional views of sovereignty. The potential for corruption presents the twin dangers of further dividing and discrediting the military institution. Yet, for forces whose traditional missions are diminishing and who face the prospect of significant reductions in both budget and personnel, the needs of institutional self-justification can make undertaking such missions surprisingly attractive.

Similar issues arise in confronting rising levels of criminal activity. Counternarcotics operations are especially difficult and potentially disruptive. Latin American officers are understandably reluctant to risk their lives and expand their resources combating a problem they perceive as caused by consumption in the United States and other developed nations. The corruption associated with narcotics peddling can undermine institutional loyalty and coherence. Subordinates can be influenced without the necessity of going through their superiors; operational capacity can be severely disrupted with just the suspicion that someone might be on the cartel's payroll. Counternarcotics operations, such as crop burning, can pit a military against its own population, and ultimately, narcotics dealings can undermine the armed forces' prestige, disrupt their international linkages, and, as demonstrated in Panama in 1989, even lead to the destruction of the entire institution. However, with traditional sources of external assistance vanishing, budgetary resources dwindling, and narcotics and other criminal activity often linked with insurgencies and other threats to effective sovereignty, participating in such operations may be the only way in which armed forces can secure the equipment and technology they need.

All of this relates to wider issues of using the military in police roles. Professional officers often despise such duty, yet, at the same time, are unwilling to give up all control over police forces. In addition, as happened in Venezuela, the military may find itself pushed into the role of anti-riot forces, defending an unpopular and corrupt civilian regime against popular rage. Resentment over this was a major factor in the two unsuccessful coup attempts in Venezuela in 1992. Yet, various forms of policing may be the most available and current mission for the armed forces. Existing police forces are overwhelmed by the rising tide of crime. The weapons, technology, and other resources available to globalized crime dwarf those to which existing police forces have access. Countering such activities demands effective intelligence, and in many nations, the only functioning intelligence services are under military control. Air and naval capabilities are overwhelmingly, if not exclusively, under military control. While combating international criminal activity may fall outside the military's traditional and desired missions, it all too often appears to be a threat to which only the military has even a remote chance of effectively responding.

As several chapters in this study make clear, governments often face a series of cruel choices in determining how to involve the military in such situations. To utilize the military in the fight against crime runs major risks. It adds both to human rights abuses by and corruption within the military. It fuels tensions between military and civilian authorities while at the same time contributing to discontent within the military institution. It diverts resources from the regular administration of justice and creates vested interests in maintaining military involvement in such operations. With extremely limited resources and rising public pressures to do something about rampant criminality, governments are tempted to involve the military, overwhelming longer-range concerns. This was the case in the 1994 decision of Brazil's government to send the army into the slums of Rio. In nation after nation, the line between police and military functions is increasingly blurred, usually to the detriment of both the military and the administration of justice. There are no simple answers, no pat formulas for dealing with such cases. Uncertainty, improvisation, and the search for the lesser evil will increasingly be dominant themes.

Traditional coups are no longer in fashion, but this does not mean that the military no longer believes it has the right to judge civilians. Verbal commitments to democracy are not seen as incompatible with such attitudes. In most nations, officers still perceive themselves as serving *el estado* or *la patria* rather than the government or the population. If the government fails in its mission to serve *el estado*, then the military has the obligation to judge and correct this situation. These attitudes were formed in the nineteenth century and are likely to survive for some time to come. What has changed is the method by which such missions are carried out. Increasingly, the armed forces are reluctant to move without significant civilian support. In Peru, it was support by the president against the Congress; in Haiti, it was Congress and business elites against the president. In Guatemala, pressures from a wide range of civil society groups and individuals caused the military to end its support for President Jorge Serrano's attempt to suspend the constitution and, instead, compel Serrano to resign.

Even if a coup takes place, few in the armed forces envision the creation of any long-lasting military government. The experiences of the 1970s and 1980s with such governments were generally more negative than positive. They divided the armed forces, damaged their prestige, and made them responsible for areas, such as the economy, that they could not manage effectively. This is even truer today. A growing majority understands that military coups damage the economy, in effect, undermining national security. Coups cause countries to risk international sanctions, disrupt vital economic relations with neighboring states, and both discourage external investment and contribute to domestic capital flight. The extreme reluctance of both civilian and military leaders to risk such a situation has been demonstrated amply in the tense negotiations over the fate of two high-ranking Chilean officers convicted of involvement in the 1976 murder in Washington of former Foreign Minister Orlando Letelier.

Even when some elements of the armed forces are still willing to attempt a coup, they are much less likely to use it to establish a prolonged period of direct military rule. The Venezuelan coup plotters knew they would have to install a largely civilian government and move quickly to new elections. At most, coups are seen increasingly as a form of emergency surgery by which a malfunctioning part of the body politic may be removed, allowing something more functional eventually to take its place. Like surgery, this is an extreme procedure, only utilized when other alternatives fail.

The threat of such "surgery" can prod civilian institutions to deal with problems. Traditionally, legislative bodies in Latin America have had only a very limited role in curbing abuses by the executive. Yet in 1993, in both Venezuela and Brazil, they were able to oust unpopular and corrupt regimes while acting within the limits of constitutional procedure. While it might be debated whether pressures from outraged civil society or the potential threat of military action provided the strongest incentive for such action, it seems clear that both were involved.

The military's role on the international as well as the domestic scene is also changing. As Jack Child makes clear, peacekeeping, both within and outside of the region, is gaining strength as a mission of Latin America's armed forces. Recent joint maneuvers conducted by the U.S. Southern Command with troops from several Latin American nations have emphasized such missions. Of greater complexity is the issue of international cooperation against criminal activity, but here, too, there are signs of increased recognition that such cooperation is vital to any chance of success in this area. Intelligence sharing, however, remains a peculiarly sensitive area.

At the same time, relations with the United States and other external powers, such as Russia, are also changing. Both officers and civilians seem to be learning not to place fundamental reliance for national security on other nations. The problems the Cubans are facing as they try to adjust to the end of Soviet support are being replicated, on a somewhat reduced scale, by traditional U.S. allies in Central America and elsewhere. At its most extreme, this has given rise to wild rumors of a secret U.S. plot to destroy the region's armed forces. On a more rational level, it produces both a deepening cynicism as to U.S.

reliability as an ally and a growing sense that national realities and resources — not international ties — must determine national security policies.

In this context, domestic civil-military relations assume ever-growing importance as the twentieth century draws to a close. Obstacles to fundamental improvements are profound. The heritage of the past 30 years has produced high levels of distrust, even hatred. Communications between civil society and the military, never very good, became increasingly difficult and dominated by negative stereotypes. The resurgence of civilian rule has not cured any of these problems. Divided and frequently corrupt governments, often lacking public support and unable to deal with increasing criminal violence, do little to change the armed forces' negative images of civilian leadership. In such circumstances, efforts by governments to reduce budgets, establish civilian defense ministries, and hold officers accountable for abuses of power frequently are seen as part of a plot to destroy the military institution. What is worth noting is not that such paranoid attitudes exist, but that most officers do not share them.

In an era characterized by such rapid change and high levels of uncertainty, attempting prognostications is extremely risky business. While projecting the analyses of this volume into the next century is far from certain, there are several trends that most likely will continue to develop for years to come. Latin America's armed forces will do whatever they can to maintain their autonomy, privileges, and power. Their size likely will decline, their budgets shrink, but they will remain a potentially potent political force. They will proclaim (and, in their own terms, increasingly believe) that they support democratic political systems and civilian supremacy. However, supremacy will not equal subordination. For the majority of officers, belief in civilian supremacy is not seen as incompatible with the conviction that watching over politicians and, when they deem it necessary, defending *la patria* from their abuses and failures are basic duties of the military institution. What is most likely to emerge is a complex pattern of negotiation between civil authorities and the military over everything from missions to budgets to the designations of commanders. Civilian authority will increase in most nations, but the process will be neither smooth nor steady. The nature of military leadership slowly will evolve as the officer corps discovers that its interests are served best by someone who can negotiate effectively with, rather than confront and attempt to bully, civilian authorities. The rotation of the high command

will become more regularized, and the capacity of any individual —
or, in the larger nations, any service — to dominate the armed forces
will decline.

While border clashes may occur, a major conflict between nations
in the hemisphere is unlikely. The recent conflict between Ecuador and
Peru demonstrated the strong constraints operating on military establishments to limit such conflicts and the determination of nations
throughout the region to end fighting and promote peaceful settlement
of disputes. Existing insurgencies also are likely to wind down slowly
or end altogether following formal peace agreements. New national
insurgent movements are unlikely, but ethnic-based violence, as
exemplified currently in Chiapas, is a real possibility. In dealing with
such threats, the Mexican model of emphasizing negotiations over but
not to the exclusion of force as the official response will prevail.

There may be occasional coup attempts, especially in smaller
nations, and one or two actually may succeed in the coming decade.
However, these will be rare exceptions, and pressures for the military
to return power to civilians will be overwhelming. Prolonged periods
of military rule are highly unlikely. When coup attempts do occur, two
conditions generally will be present. First, there will be a failure of
effective civilian rule, and second, there will be strong support from
significant civilian sectors for a change in government. Except in the
more backward nations, simply challenging existing military prerogatives will not be sufficient cause for a major coup attempt, and even
in the least politically developed nations, such efforts will be opposed
by major segments of the military as well as by the bulk of civil society.

The military's relation to the administration of justice will be a
dominant theme in the coming decade. Part of this will involve
ongoing efforts to reduce levels of military immunity and to extend
the jurisdiction of civilian courts in dealing with matters involving the
armed forces. Conflicts in this area will persist well into the next
century and will be further complicated by the related problems of
using of the military in police roles and military control over police
forces. Formal links between military and police forces will decline,
but the tendency to utilize the military in police roles will continue
and, in the short run, may well increase. The police will remain
underfunded and poorly prepared to deal with the increasing
challenges of domestic and global criminality, urban disorders, and
environmental destruction. Governments, however reluctantly, will
find themselves repeatedly calling on the armed forces to act in these

areas, a trend that will strengthen the military's hand in dealings with civil authorities over a host of other matters. One of the greatest obstacles to progress will be continued weakness and corruption in the judicial system. Indeed, corruption in all branches of government, including the military, will be a major obstacle to efforts to consolidate the democratic process.

An emerging issue in the next decade will be control over the intelligence apparatus. Pressures to reduce military involvement in this area will grow but will encounter strong resistance. At the same time, the growing internationalization of both criminal activities and threats to the environment insures that the need for reliable intelligence probably will increase. This issue will prove divisive for both civilian and military leadership. Here, too, is an area where efforts to promote greater transparency within military institutions will encounter the strongest resistance.

Civilian capacity to deal with security issues and even to manage military affairs will grow, but the process will be slow. As both officers and civilians struggle to adapt to a rapidly changing world, redefining military missions; reordering and often reducing budgets; reacting to a variety of nontraditional threats, miscommunications, tensions, and even efforts at intimidation — all will be common. Progress will be greatest in those nations where a civilian framework for dealing with such issues exists, such as Colombia and Argentina, and most difficult where that framework remains very weak or nonexistent, such as Paraguay and Honduras. However, the trend toward more effective interaction between civilians and officers will be generalized. Security issues will never again be the exclusive preserve of a military caste.

Cooperation between military establishments in security matters will increase. This will reflect both the growing realization of the non-utility of force as a means of resolving international disputes and the growing perception that problems of crime, environmental destruction, and migration cannot be confronted effectively solely on the national level. Programs of joint training and education will expand and increasingly involve civilians as well as military personnel. There may even be some more formal hemispheric security structure, but for this to happen, the profound suspicions of nations such as Mexico must be overcome, and this will prove no simple task. In this regard, Ambassador Hernán Patiño Mayer's observations on both the need for and the obstacles to the creation of a new framework for hemispheric security are highly instructive.

Regional nations will continue to play a role in peacekeeping, although whether this role will continue to expand will be determined largely by events beyond this hemisphere. Within the Americas, it is unlikely that any formal OAS peacekeeping structure will emerge. Instead, the United Nations probably will remain as the preferred vehicle for regional peacekeeping efforts. At times, the urgency of individual situations or what the United States perceives as its overriding national interest could lead to unilateral or ad hoc international arrangements. Evolving situations in Haiti and Cuba will have the greatest influence on this particular area.

While links between national militaries will grow, so too will the differences. It will be increasingly difficult to talk about "the Latin American military" as trends diverge. Officers in one nation will be less inclined to offer unquestioning support or even sympathize with their counterparts in another nation when they enter into a confrontation with civilian authority. Some nations will attempt to maintain a configuration for traditional military roles, emphasizing combat arms units, fighter aircraft, submarine and anti-submarine naval units, and so on, while others will emphasize mobility, communications, and logistics to enable them to undertake a wide variety of less conventional missions. These different approaches will be reflected in differing approaches to leadership, civil-military relations, and regional security issues.

In a few smaller nations, the military may find itself actually struggling to survive. The appeal of the Haitian, Panamanian, and Costa Rican examples will continue in nations such as Nicaragua, where resources are most scarce and the heritage of civil-military relations most divisive. Former Costa Rican President and Nobel Peace Prize winner Oscar Arias will remain a leading advocate of making radical reductions and perhaps even eliminating military establishments, but similar efforts are very unlikely to succeed in the coming decade.

In summation, hemispheric security issues and civil-military relations will continue to provide ample material for research and analysis for decades to come. The more or less stable patterns of the past will not return, and no generalized new pattern is likely to emerge. Uncertainty will continue to be the order of the day; change, the only constant. Latin America's armed forces clearly are moving beyond praetorianism, but exactly where this journey will take them remains to be seen.

Contributors

Gary Brana-Shute teaches anthropology at The Catholic University of America and The George Washington University, both in Washington, D.C.

Jack Child is Professor of Spanish and Latin American Studies in the Department of Languages and Foreign Studies at The American University in Washington, D.C. Dr. Child served in the U.S. Army and retired with the rank of Lieutenant Colonel. He has written extensively on peacekeeping, geopolitics in Latin America, inter-American relations, and translation. He is the author of *The Central American Peace Process, 1983-1991: Sheathing Swords, Building Confidence* (Lynne Rienner Publishers, 1992).

Michael Gold-Biss is Assistant Professor of political science and Assistant Director of Latin American Studies at St. Cloud State University in Minnesota. He has taught at the University of Minnesota, Twin Cities, and at The American University, where he also received his doctorate. He has published articles and reviews on civilian-military relations, democratic change, and political and social development in Latin America. He is the author of *The Discourse on Terrorism: Political Violence and the Subcommittee on Security and Terrorism, 1980-1986.* Dr. Gold-Biss was formerly Associate Director of the Democracy Projects, The American University, which conducts scholarly research on democratic transitions in Latin America and political party development in Central America.

Luis Humberto Guzmán was President of the National Assembly, Nicaragua, until 1995 and is currently a member of Congress. He has been involved closely with the reform efforts of post-Sandinista Nicaragua. Educated at the Free University of Berlin, he is author of *Políticos en Uniforme/ Politicians in Uniform.*

Tricia Juhn worked with the Latin American and Caribbean Center of Florida International University in Miami and received her doctorate in international studies from the Graduate School of International Studies, University of Miami. She has also worked with the Democracy Projects at the American University and at the Inter-American Foundation in Washington, D.C.

Dirk Kruijt holds the Chair in Anthropology at the Anthropological Institute and is professor at the Centre for Latin American and Caribbean Studies, Utrecht University, Holland. He has worked extensively with civilian-military relations and development issues (urban poverty, the informal sector, and the social-productive sector) in Central and South America. His publications include *Perú: Entre Sendero y los Militares, seguridad interior y relaciones cívico militares 1950-1990/Peru: Between The Path and the Military, Internal Security and Civilian-Military Relations 1950-1990* and *La Revolución por decreto: Perú durante el gobierno militar/Revolution by Decree: Peru during the Military Government.*

Max G. Manwaring is an Associate with Booz-Allen & Hamilton, Inc. He has over thirty years' experience in political-military affairs, having retired from the U.S. Army with the rank of Colonel, and has served in various academic and military positions, including the U.S. Army War College, the United States Defense Intelligence Agency, and the U.S. Southern Command's Small Wars Operations Research Directorate. Dr. Manwaring was a Fulbright Fellow in Brazil and received his doctorate from the University of Illinois at Urbana-Champaign. His published works include *El Salvador at War: An Oral History* and *Uncomfortable Wars: Toward a Paradigm of Low Intensity Conflict.*

Richard L. Millett, an Adjunct Senior Research Associate at the North-South Center of the University of Miami, is Professor of history and Chair of the Latin American Studies Committee at Southern Illinois University, Edwardsville. Dr. Millett frequently testifies before congressional committees on Central American politics and society. He is author of *Guardians of the Dynasty* and co-editor of *The Restless Caribbean: Changing Patterns of International Relations.*

Deborah L. Norden, who received her doctorate from the University of California, Berkeley, is Assistant Professor of government at Colby College, in Waterville, Maine. She has conducted extensive research on the military and politics in Argentina. She was recipient of an Organization of American States dissertation award and a fellowship from the Ford Foundation for a workshop on civilian-military relations and transitions to democratic rule in Chile (1992).

Ambassador Hernán Patiño Mayer is Argentina's Ambassador to Uruguay. He was Permanent Representative of the Argentine Republic to the Organization of American States. He has served as President of the Working Group and Special Commission on Cooperation for Hemispheric Security (1991-1993) and has represented Argentina in Geneva before the International Disarmament and International Human Rights Conferences in 1990. Ambassador Patiño Mayer received his law degree from the Catholic University of Argentina.

Carina Perelli is Director of PEITHO, Sociedad de Análisis Político, and has written on ideology, the military, and society. She was trained at the University of Grenoble, France, and is finishing a doctorate at the University of Notre Dame. She contributed "Youth, Politics, and Dictatorship in Uruguay," to *Fear at the Edge: State Terror and Resistance in Latin America*, Juan E. Corradi, Patricia Weiss Fagen, and Manuel Antonio Garretón, eds.

Juan Rial is Senior Researcher at PEITHO, Sociedad de Análisis Político, and Professor of political science at the School of Law and Social Sciences, University of Uruguay. Dr. Rial has written widely on the military and politics in the Southern Cone. He contributed "Makers and Guardians of Fear: Controlled Terror in Uruguay," to *Fear at the Edge: State Terror and Resistance in Latin America*, Juan E. Corradi, Patricia Weiss Fagen, and Manuel Antonio Garretón, eds.

Bonnie Tenneriello was Senior Associate for Central America at the Washington Office on Latin America (WOLA) and is now pursuing a law degree at the University of Michigan, Ann Arbor. While at WOLA, Ms. Tenneriello worked with scholars, practitioners, and activists to enhance the understanding of Central American human rights and civilian-military relations in the United States.

Stephen J. Wager, Lieutenant Colonel, recently retired from the U.S. Army and from the U.S. Military Academy at West Point, where he was Associate Professor of history. He received his doctorate from Stanford University and is the author of many articles, including "Mexico's Uncertain Quest for a Strategy to Secure its Southern Border," *Journal of Borderlands Studies*, Spring 1992, Vol. VII, No. 1.

Index